ARMS CONTROL AND INSPECTION IN AMERICAN LAW

by LOUIS HENKIN

with a Foreword by PHILIP C. JESSUP

1958

COLUMBIA UNIVERSITY PRESS *New York*

COPYRIGHT © 1958 COLUMBIA UNIVERSITY PRESS, NEW YORK

PUBLISHED IN GREAT BRITAIN, CANADA, INDIA, AND PAKISTAN
BY THE OXFORD UNIVERSITY PRESS
LONDON, TORONTO, BOMBAY, AND KARACHI

LIBRARY OF CONGRESS CATALOG CARD NUMBER: 58-13767
MANUFACTURED IN THE UNITED STATES OF AMERICA

ARMS CONTROL AND INSPECTION IN AMERICAN LAW

CONTENTS

	FOREWORD *by Philip C. Jessup*	vii
	PREFACE *by John M. Kernochan*	xi
I.	INTRODUCTION	1
II.	ARMS CONTROL PROVISIONS	17
III.	ARMS CONTROL AND THE CONSTITUTION	25
IV.	INVESTIGATION OF COMPLIANCE WITH ARMS CONTROL	47
V.	CONGRESSIONAL IMPLEMENTATION OF ARMS CONTROL	84
VI.	STATE LAWS AND LOCAL COOPERATION	97
VII.	INTERNATIONAL ADMINISTRATIVE REGULATION	104
VIII.	INTERNATIONAL TRIBUNALS	122
IX.	CONCLUSION	153
	NOTES	159
	CASES CITED	249
	CONSTITUTIONAL PROVISIONS	263
	SELECTED STATUTES	264
	TREATIES AND OTHER INTERNATIONAL AGREEMENTS	266
	BOOKS AND ARTICLES	270
	INDEX	279

FOREWORD

Disarmament has been advocated by many persons and sporadically sought by many governments throughout this century. It was Russia under Czar Nicholas II which took the lead in advocating it at the First Hague Peace Conference of 1899; it is Russia under Premier Khruschev whose agreement is vital to even the first steps toward disarmament today. But the agreement of the United States is just as essential. The perfection of thermonuclear weapons leads some to believe that there is reason for hope in a "balance of terror"—in the mutual capacity for annihilation. No government takes the position that we may rest assured that this is true. Even if the insistent fears of nuclear holocaust were quieted, there would still be the demand that the vast sums swallowed up annually in armaments be devoted to needs of man other than mere survival.

Of the obstacles to an accord upon disarmament, or the limitation of armaments, distrust occupies a primary place. If our future safety and very survival are to rest on trustworthy agreement that nuclear weapons will not be used, rather than on the deterrent effect of the possibility of retaliation, we must have more than a bare promise. We assume that the Soviets are equally unwilling to entrust their future to our good faith. Analysis of their slogan, "banning the bomb," leads quickly to the realization that the disarmament problem encompasses all weapons and all the armed forces available to use them.

The elimination of distrust in the relations of the Soviet Union and the United States cannot be achieved by a formula, no matter how ingenious. But in specific relation to disarmament, there is an identified counter to distrust; this counter is inspection. Inspection is the means whereby we tell whether governments, Russian or American, are actually doing or not doing what they have agreed to do or not to do. Much of the recent disarmament discussion has concentrated on the effort to reach agreement upon inspection. The latest impasse (as this is written) involved the United States proposal for international aerial inspection in the Arctic to quiet the fears of both the Soviet Union and the United

States. The United States has been more insistent upon the need for prior agreement on an inspection system, but the Soviets have not denied its importance and have advanced their counterproposals.

Of the other obstacles to disarmament agreement, some are technical. Given the best will in the world on both sides, the problems of technical detail which must be mastered are staggering. Even the perfection of a formula for limiting the number of persons in the armed forces of all the countries of the world presents enormous difficulties, but these difficulties are exceeded as one begins to deal with the vast complex of interrelationships of business and industry required for the manufacture of items which go into arsenals for war.

Curiously enough, despite the vast number of published discussions —both official and nonofficial—of inspection, no one seems to have heretofore studied the problem from the point of view of the legal and administrative problems involved in enforcing an inspection system in the United States. Perhaps the failure to look at these and other implications of disarmament for the United States is one of the reasons why the whole subject has seemed so far removed from the individual, from the community. Control of sputniks and other earth satellites and arctic patrols are remote governmental business. The right of an international inspection team to enter the factory and even the home, on the other hand, concerns every citizen. Is this what we demand as assurance that a disarmament agreement is being kept by those against whom we are on our guard? Is it worth the price? What is the price in terms of the impact on our traditional processes and institutions?

This study by Professor Louis Henkin does not try to outline the technical procedures of an international inspection plan—what can be detected by aerial photography under an "open skies" proposal, what seemingly harmless industrial or mining processes may actually represent preparation for war and how one ascertains this fact. A report just published deals with such matters: *Inspection for Disarmament,* a technical study, edited by Professor Seymour Melman for Columbia University's Institute of War and Peace Studies, with the support of Earl D. Osborn and the Institute for International Order. Professor Henkin explores, rather, legal and practical paths even less traveled, indeed hitherto largely unsurveyed. To what extent is the treaty power under the Federal Constitution adequate to transmuting an international agreement on disarmament and inspection into effective local law? What further legislation by Congress would be needed? What legislative action

Foreword

by the States of the Union? Is our whole system of law enforcement from local policemen through courts and sheriffs and marshals and state police and federal forces, created for such different ends, available to guarantee, not only to ourselves but to distrustful foreign nations, that an international inspection system will accomplish its purpose? Until we see clearly the answers to such questions as these, we cannot safely negotiate the final terms of an agreement which must function successfully here as in other countries.

This study should be of interest to every citizen. It will be of particular interest to lawyers. It has special meaning also for all those who are interested in the development of international institutions. Since the Second World War particularly, the number of such institutions has multiplied. There has, however, been no previous study of the impact of international institutions upon those of the United States. The place of international law under the Constitution, the relation of international bodies exercising a form of administrative or judicial power to federal and state institutions, the rights of American citizens when they come into contact with such international bodies, are explored here in the context of arms control but they have significance, too, in other contexts in which international organizations operate. It is high time for such a study. It is time also for this further demonstration of the necessary link between the American lawyer interested primarily in domestic law and affairs and his often distant colleague concerned with matters international. It is time that each be made to see where he meets the other. It is time also—as the American Law Institute has realized in launching its current study of the Foreign Relations Law of the United States—that someone put effort and intelligence trained in American constitutional law to work at the problems of our relations with other nations.

This study required an author with the combination of experiences and skills which Professor Henkin possesses. His years of service in the State Department's Bureau of United Nations Affairs and Office of European Regional Affairs gave him the close acquaintanceship with the practicalities of foreign policy, with the working of the United Nations and NATO, and, from 1950 to 1954 when he was assigned to problems arising from the aggression in Korea, with the trials of patience required in seeking to reach an agreement with a Communist power. To his understanding of the realities of foreign policy, Professor Henkin joins rare skills in his appreciation of the whole body of constitutional doctrine, an appreciation developed in contact with two of the keenest American legal minds, those of Judge Learned Hand and Mr. Justice Felix Frankfurter, both of whom he served as Law Clerk. He is now Professor of Law at the University of Pennsylvania Law School. Even the layman will find the felicity of the author's English style leading him through those sections of the book which of necessity deal with legal complexities.

There may be those zealous to advance the cause of disarmament who will be apprehensive because this study calls attention to still more and largely neglected dangers and difficulties. I do not share this apprehension. The disarmament issue demands with imperative urgency that we seek a solution. No one of the possible obstacles or difficulties should be overlooked. Man has not yet found his way into all of the intricate recesses of this issue and into them should be thrown now the light not only of political wisdom, science, and technology, but also of legal knowledge and insight. This Foreword affords me a most welcome opportunity to express to a friend and former colleague in the Department of State and at Columbia University my own appreciation of a contribution courageously undertaken and masterfully rendered.

PHILIP C. JESSUP, *Co-Chairman*
Columbia University Council for
Atomic Age Studies

Columbia University
July 1, 1958

PREFACE

Professor Louis Henkin's study of *Arms Control and Inspection in American Law* presented here by the Legislative Drafting Research Fund of Columbia University has been a welcome undertaking for the Fund. It has offered a fresh opportunity to pursue a traditional Fund objective: the conduct of basic research at what is expected—at least hoped—to be a "growing point" of the law, a focus of significant future legislation. The subject partakes too, as noted in Professor Philip C. Jessup's illuminating Foreword, of the urgency that now attends all arms control matters. That urgency has of course resulted from the accelerating scientific and technological development of our time. Arms control problems thus represent also one aspect of the vast impact of science on society to which the Fund severally, and jointly with Columbia's Council for Atomic Age Studies, has assigned high priorities of exploration.

The study was originally proposed by Earl D. Osborn, President of the Institute for International Order, and executed with his support. In accordance with the terms set for the study, it is, in the author's phrase, a "memorandum of law." It is detailed and specialized, not a popularization. It is wide-ranging, not a selective text on how best to secure arms control by law, or on the legal obstacles thereto, though both avenues and obstacles are inevitably identified. To some extent, the task assigned has called for, and the author has provided, a clear, precise re-examination of relatively familiar areas of law. Mostly, it has covered new ground or explored new approaches. This has occasionally called for speculation or for hypothetical argument—uncongenial to lawyers —but Professor Henkin has dared also the "unpath'd waters, undream'd shores." In sum, he has performed with imagination, fullness, and care much of the legal "spadework" which must precede the establishment of international arms control in this country. The Fund considers itself to have been fortunate indeed to secure Professor Henkin's services as Associate Director in charge of this study. His unusual qualifications for the task are described in Professor Jessup's Foreword. They are, in our view, demonstrated conclusively by the report.

The publication of this study has been determined upon by the Fund, and aided by a grant from the Institute for International Order, in the belief that the insights, analyses, and research materials here developed cannot fail to be valuable to all who plan, build, or work for arms control and to all others who may be seriously concerned to explore its implications for our society.

Many acknowledgments are due. First, and chiefly, to Earl D. Osborn, whose foresight and generous support have made this study possible, and also to George A. Beebe, John F. B. Mitchell, Esq., and other members of the board and staff of the Institute for International Order, for creative assistance graciously given.

On behalf of both Professor Henkin and the Fund, warmest thanks are also extended here to many other persons, whether named or unnamed, for their aid. For example: to Dean William C. Warren of the Columbia University School of Law, for encouragement and courtesies, personal and institutional, extended to the study and its executants; to Professor Jessup (Co-Chairman, Columbia University Council for Atomic Age Studies) of Columbia's School of Law, for his guidance and for his Foreword to the study; to Professors Noel T. Dowling, Harry W. Jones and Herbert Wechsler of Columbia's School of Law, and to Professor William T. R. Fox (member, Columbia University Council for Atomic Age Studies) of Columbia's Department of Public Law and Government, for their critical suggestions and comment; to Grenville Clark, Esq., and to Associate Dean David F. Cavers and Professor Louis B. Sohn of the Harvard University School of Law, for advice in the early stages of the study; to Shirley S. Abrahamson, Herbert Adelman, Peter Ehrenhaft, George Kaufmann, Michael P. Rosenthal, and Richard S. Salzman of the staff of the Legislative Drafting Research Fund, for research assistance; and to Mariana Smith, Patricia Atwater, and Elizabeth S. Albro for secretarial assistance. Barbara Melissa Voorhis of Columbia University Press contributed helpful editorial counsel. None of course bears responsibility—that is Professor Henkin's alone—for the views and conclusions expressed in this study.

> JOHN M. KERNOCHAN, *Director*
> *Legislative Drafting Research Fund*
> *of Columbia University*

Columbia University
July 1, 1958

ARMS CONTROL AND INSPECTION IN AMERICAN LAW

Chapter I. INTRODUCTION

John Donne prayed God to deliver men "From needing danger." Others have in other words deplored the inability of men and societies to do what was necessary for their own salvation before war or disaster had nearly overwhelmed them. And so in wars alone men have died in numberless numbers. But man has survived, as have societies—in our time at least. The United States in fact has emerged more powerful after each war.

Now war is changed. Once, at least, it was preferable by far to be victor; following a future war, we are told, Rome will be one with Carthage. New and awful weapons making possible the elimination of man raise doubts whether the United States or any nation can thrive after a next world war, or even survive it. The weapons exist, more nations may soon have them, and there is neither assurance nor confidence that they will not come into use. Yet, perhaps because it is ever present, the danger, total and terrible as it may be, does not disturb and bestir us. Like the villagers on the side of Vesuvius returning and abiding over the centuries in the shadow of eventual destruction, most of us lead our lives with only spasmodic twinges of awareness and desperation.

Always, of course, there are responsible exceptions to whom the rest of us leave the complex problems of peace. Individuals cry out and warn. Leaders ponder and plan. Governments confer. The United Nations resolves. Committees meet and meet again. All make their bow to danger. And virtually all have professed agreement that only eliminating arms and armies can eliminate the danger. We are perhaps now in "the last days," it is said, and can no longer defer beating bombs into tractors, diverting all energy to the uses of peace. But if, as many believe, certain lasting peace is not a utopian quest; if, as they believe, such peace can be achieved only when armaments are abolished or controlled; although indeed there has been much effort toward that goal, there has yet been no important progress. Since the Second World War disarmament has frequently been called the crucial issue of these times;

the need for controlling weapons appears more urgent than ever before; yet failure has been stark.

Why, if disarmament is desirable and necessary, has it not been achieved? To what extent is the United States responsible for this failure? What can the American citizen do to enhance the likelihood of achieving arms control? These questions have no easy answers. The United States has been in the forefront of efforts and negotiations to bring about disarmament, or—more accurately—the limitation and control of armaments. Its power and leadership, its sole possession, in the early years, of the atomic bomb and of much of the information and "know-how" surrounding the new weapons, its apparently earnest efforts to attain arms control, made it inevitable that other nations would follow where the United States led. In disarmament negotiations the proposals put forth for the West were principally United States proposals. And the objections to Soviet plans, particularly the insistence on strict verification and inspection to assure compliance, were also interposed primarily by the United States. It is, of course, true that the agreement of the Soviet Union is essential to bringing about the control of armaments, and that has not been forthcoming; it is equally true that the agreement of the United States is and will remain essential to this end.

In general, the policies and positions of the United States on arms control have not been without support from the United States Congress and the citizen. But it is hardly support based on wide knowledge or deep understanding. Dependent as the United States position is in part on scientific and technological expertness of rare and high degree, in part on information still largely classified, the citizen is helpless before it. And so, governmental activities of greatest moment are isolated from him. The American people cannot intelligently scrutinize or criticize, nor can they intelligently support or encourage, because they do not know and understand. Even their representatives in Congress must act largely in ignorance. They must reach decisions and approve or disapprove policies vital to the nation on the word of a few individuals, although underlying these may be sharp differences among experts all able and trustworthy.

There has long been a need for some who can to penetrate the secrecy, and the confusion of change or contradiction; to uncover, articulate, and examine premises; to ask and to seek answers for fundamental, even unpopular, questions; and to introduce others into the mysteries of armament and disarmament and of their place in foreign and de-

Introduction

fense policies. The proper study of arms control should include an analysis of the foreign and defense policies of the United States, of the Soviet Union, and of other countries. It would investigate war and the technology of weapons, their production, storage, maintenance, transportation, and use. It would examine methods for concealment and methods for detecting what others were trying to hide—in military planning, in the manufacture and piling up of arms, in preparation for launching of war. And there should be consideration of the rules and the machinery whereby control might be exercised in and among the nations of the earth.

What follows is not such an undertaking. It is a modest single strand of the total effort. But it is not the less important or necessary. Those who conceived it recognized that behind dramatic and momentous governmental decisions lie also issues and considerations which, though they appear humble and unglamorous, may yet prove crucial. To concentrate intellectual effort on such questions while larger ones seem far from resolution may appear quixotic. Call it, perhaps, a labor of hope.

This report is essentially a memorandum of law, an examination of problems which arms control and inspection may raise under the Constitution and laws of the United States. Starting with what appear to be the likely provisions in a plan for the international control of armaments, we shall consider the legal implications of the limitations and prohibitions anticipated and the implications of various means of enforcing these controls. Do they present in particular significant constitutional obstacles? If so, how can such constitutional obstacles be eliminated or mitigated? What legislation will be necessary to implement the plan? What protections against abuse of the plan or against avoidable loss or damage can be afforded to American citizens? How can state and local cooperation be achieved?

Such an examination would appear essential to a formulation of United States policy and to its appraisal. It has not, apparently, been made. The first United States proposal, in 1946, for controlling atomic energy bore far-reaching implications for political and legal institutions, yet so far as is known these did not receive serious attention in or out of the government. Other, more current suggestions relating to arms control might also have significant impact on United States constitutional patterns and on the way in which Americans have been living under their laws. Surely this impact must be considered in determining whether a particular proposal will be acceptable to the people of the United States and whether it should be proposed or accepted by the government of the United States. And, if legal and constitutional issues are relevant to the kind of control agreement which the United States can accept, they are relevant also to what the United States can ask of other nations. Some elements in arms control proposals, on the other hand, may be exaggerated and distorted, and painted, with little warrant, as threatening deep and novel intrusions into American law and American life. This study, it is hoped, will help quiet undue concerns as well as alert attention to those which are due.

These are the conception and the purposes of this study. The other issues, the researches and analyses of political, military, and technological questions which underlie United States policy toward the control of armaments, must be left to others.[1] Inevitably, however, the range of this report, its assumptions and limitations, reflect the recent history of disarmament efforts, of United States policy toward arms control and related issues, and the positions of this government in regard particularly to the importance of inspection in the control of arms. These constitute the background and context for the study to follow; they suggest the probable character of any control plan which might be realized and hence the provisions whose legal implications most warrant examination. It appears worth while, therefore, before laying out the plan of this study, to sketch in briefest summary the story of disarmament efforts and United States policy since the Second World War.

DISARMAMENT AND UNITED STATES POLICY IN THE POSTWAR WORLD

THE COURSE OF NEGOTIATIONS AND EAST-WEST RELATIONS

One can, of course, adequately tell the story of disarmament efforts only in the context of the history of relations between nations. Since the Second World War, American disarmament policy reflects in particular relations between Russia and the United States, between East and West. Only headlines and highlights can be touched on here.

Efforts to achieve the voluntary disarmament of nations are not new.[2] They received new impetus and acquired new urgency when the atomic bomb ended the Second World War and altered fundamentally the character of the disarmament problem. Earlier attempts had been partial; they reflected also the traditional approach of sovereign nations—that

Introduction

the control of arms would be voluntary and self-policed.[3] Each nation undertook to comply with given limitations, and although treaty violations were hardly unknown, other nations were expected to assume that the parties to a treaty would comply with its provisions until there was denunciation of the treaty or clear evidence that it was not being observed. By 1946, sobered by another world war and terrified by the implications of the atomic bomb, nations appeared willing to break from established ways and do whatever seemed necessary to preserve civilization. The first comprehensive plan put forward after the Second World War, dealing with atomic control without regard to other armaments, entailed radical inroads into previously sacrosanct areas of "sovereignty" of states and privacy of peoples.[4]

The United States was the chief proponent of this plan. The Second World War had destroyed its isolation and left the United States out in front. This country now seemed prepared to consider organized international action, to accept burdens and limitations in common with other nations, and to subject common problems to joint judgment and joint measures.[5] The United States helped organize the United Nations and strove to establish it and make it effective. And this government, then sole possessor of the atomic bomb, took the lead in efforts through the United Nations to control the bomb —in the Acheson-Lilienthal Report, the important, seminal document, and in the Baruch Plan, based on that report and forming the basis of the first proposal approved by the United Nations Atomic Energy Commission. These sought to control atomic weapons by controlling all atomic energy. They contemplated a virtual monopoly in the hands of an international development authority with safeguards to assure against diversion for military purposes. Peaceful use would be permitted to nations only pursuant to license from the international agency. The United States led the fight for this program and most people believed that it did so with sincerity and the intention to make the plan effective. In retrospect, the goals professed, the means pursued, even the words spoken, in 1946–47, have an air of unreality.[6] It is difficult to imagine that a plan for international monopoly of atomic energy, viewed by many as a serious step toward supranational government, was consistent with political realities, American and international, even at a time when the Second World War was a fresh memory. Perhaps it was fantasy to imagine and to expect that the Soviet Union could agree to such a plan; perhaps it was even fantasy to expect that in the end the United States itself would agree to live by the implications of its own plan.

The Soviet Union rejected the United Nations proposal, and gradually hopes for the control of atomic energy and of other armaments froze in the developing cold war. And, after Soviet incursion into Azerbaijan, a Communist coup in Czechoslovakia, Communist rebellion in Greece, the cold war sent United States foreign policy in other directions. United States policy toward the United Nations and United States attitudes toward disarmament changed perceptibly. By a perhaps inevitable lag, United States representatives continued to speak of the United Nations as *"the* cornerstone" of United States foreign policy. American representatives also continued for some time to speak for the first United Nations plan for controlling atomic energy. But United States policy was moving from the Marshall Plan toward the North Atlantic Treaty. The United Nations became only *"a* cornerstone," and the quest for disarmament began to lose some of its force. Then, the Communist invasion of the Republic of Korea seemed to render ludicrous even the holding of meetings to discuss disarmament. The North Atlantic Treaty Organization and especially Korea also signaled a sharp reversal of the trend toward unilateral reduction of armaments by the United States and the Western countries, and even the Korean armistice did not reverse this trend or relax the hostile tensions between East and West, although disarmament efforts revived during the long armistice negotiations.

The story is told elsewhere: [7] the shifts of position by East and West; Soviet promises to the ear broken to the hope; the explosion by Russia of its first bomb; the growing despair that the Soviet Union would ever agree to effective inspection so that arms control could be achieved, and the relaxation of search for agreement on disarmament; the rearmament of the West; the policy of security through strength and peace through deterrence. Then, the death of Stalin, the alternating warm and cold winds of the "spirit of Geneva," controversy over the cessation of bomb tests, more changes in the Kremlin. Sputnik and its fellow earth satellites took man out into space, gave new prestige and confidence to the Soviet Union, brought dismay to the United States.[8] And still the efforts to control armaments move in and out of the limelight on the diplomatic stage.

Introduction 7

CHANGING ISSUES IN DISARMAMENT NEGOTIATIONS

Even before Sputnik there had been important changes in political attitudes toward disarmament from those of 1946–47. People began to wonder whether disarmament was feasible, or, in the shadow of the Soviet, even desirable. Doubts were expressed whether agreement of any kind was possible, whether the Soviet Union would agree, whether the United States would agree, whether other nations developing new armaments would agree. The positions taken by governments negotiating about disarmament also changed radically. In and around the United Nations Disarmament Commission representatives of governments no longer talked of prompt and total control of armaments. They sought agreement on smaller steps first, on control by stages, beginning with disclosure of the arms which nations had and verification of these disclosures before substantial limitation could come into effect at a subsequent stage. Later, in 1955, the Eisenhower proposal for the exchange of blueprints and aerial inspection was not basically a plan for the control or limitation of armaments but only a proposal toward assuring "early warning" of their use.⁹ Of course, it was said, if no nation could launch a major attack without warning to a prospective victim also armed, there would be less likelihood that the aggressive act would take place. And disclosure on both sides might tend to stabilize the level of armament and help discourage further development of even greater destructive power; it would also give assurance, which is itself a deterrent to launching war. The emphasis in disarmament policy shifted from the prevention of war by elimination of armaments to deterrence by mutual disclosure and verification.

Inevitably, then, changes in the thinking of governments about disarmament reflected the struggle between East and West and the radical readjustments in foreign policy as a result of that continuing struggle. But disarmament policy had to take account also of other change. "Progress," technological advances had been effective. The hydrogen bomb followed and dwarfed the atomic bomb, and intercontinental ballistic missiles advanced into the military planning of big nations. Nuclear knowledge and technology spread, the cost of an atomic bomb decreased, and chemical and biological weapons which were devastating and inexpensive were developed. Disarmament efforts, concentrated on controlling the giants who might be presumed to be aware of the implications of war between them, had to begin to take account of smaller nations which might now be able to start nuclear, biological, chemical wars which could hardly remain as local as the bitter differences between them. Even between the Big Powers themselves, reliable inspection to assure compliance had been—and still is—the crux of any plan acceptable to the West. But soon one began to read that methods of concealment had outpaced methods of detection, and that enforceable disarmament through effective inspection might soon be an obsolete concept.[10]

To those who must accept the views of the few who know, political and scientific changes did not afford encouragement that thorough control of armaments was a likely and early prospect. With the advent of the Soviet space satellite, the prospects for arms control became even more uncertain. Would Russian confidence and strength eventually lead to a greater willingness to negotiate? Or would the Soviet seek, rather, to maintain and enhance its apparent superiority in important weapons? Would the United States, in turn, relax its demands and seek early agreement? Or must the West accelerate its armaments, develop and test new weapons, to restore balance if not superiority, before there could be negotiation for a moratorium or a reduction in arms?

UNITED STATES DISARMAMENT POLICY IN THE YEARS AHEAD

Few would venture to guess whether substantial control of armaments will come about. What seems clear, however, is that for the next years as in the past years, only a limited agreement will be the primary target of governments, only a limited agreement can be achieved. This conclusion is inherent in the policy of the United States in the context of the cold war. There is no indication that Soviet scientific advances, or varying Soviet proposals, have changed this policy.

This prognostication, if accurate, has important consequences for the world, for the United States, and for the American citizen. It will be reflected in the scope and content of the legal study to follow. It may, then, be desirable to set this conclusion in context, by attempting a summary of the place of disarmament in American foreign policy for the foreseeable future. Gathered from diverse sources, it may be sketched as follows:

—United States foreign policy must preserve this nation's security as well as help maintain international peace. It must also take into account

Introduction

United States responsibilities in its affairs with other nations. United States positions on disarmament are but one aspect of this policy. In the present state of international tension this country must remain strong. Weakness invites aggression. Only the fear of retaliation deters would-be enemies from attack. It the United States remains strong, there will be no major war. No enemy would attack unless it had sufficient power to eliminate also American capacity for reprisal. So long as our "enemies" are developing new weapons, we too must continue to seek new weapons and new defenses against a possible breakthrough which would neutralize or eliminate United States retaliatory power and terminate its deterrent effect.

—The United States earnestly seeks disarmament. Immediate agreement on general disarmament, however, is not possible. An agreement must provide adequate assurances that it is not being violated. An unsound agreement is worse than none: it would lull this nation and its allies into a false security, causing them to reduce their strength and weakening its deterrent effect. An unsound agreement may also lead to violations, or suspicions of violation, with resulting recriminations which might lead to war. A complete agreement, moreover, may not be possible until methods are found for detecting accumulations of weapons. Agreement on general disarmament also must come after or together with settlement of political questions, for armaments are both a cause and a result of international tension. Again, major agreement would have to take into account other countries who are now or may soon be developing the power to conduct atomic war; in this connection, the expanding peaceful-uses program, while otherwise desirable, creates dangers of diversion of those materials to military use by many nations.

—The United States is prepared to enter into agreement on small steps, including limitations on the number of men under arms, and a moratorium on the testing of new weapons and on the production of nuclear materials for additional weapons. Observance of such agreement must be subject to inspection, including aerial inspection. These steps would be a good beginning; they would leave the world in a far better situation than it finds itself in today. These steps can be taken without danger to the United States or to the Soviet Union. Such partial steps, if observed by both sides, will breed confidence, as well as give experience in the operation and enforcement of controls on armaments. In the light of this experience further steps might be taken."[11]

ISSUES BEHIND UNITED STATES POLICY

To the layman, to those not in the secret councils, accepting the merits of the policy outlined must be generally a matter of faith. The details of the efforts of the United States Government and of other governments in regard to disarmament are frequently shrouded in high classifications. It is not known what positions and which alternatives are being considered and why some are rejected.

In general, the citizen accepts the assumptions underlying the policy of the United States. He accepts that the Soviet Union, if it had decisive military superiority, would destroy the United States and the Western democracies, or otherwise impose its imperialistic will upon them. From that conclusion it is a small step to the next, that the Soviet Union is striving constantly to achieve such superiority, that it will stop at nothing to achieve it, including the circumvention and exploitation of any arms control agreement. There can then be no unilateral relaxation by the United States, and an acceptable disarmament scheme must include effective methods for inspecting and verifying whether the agreement is being observed by others, particularly the Soviet Union. Mistrust of the Soviet Union, moreover, as well as the habit of reliance on and confidence in America's own armaments, have led, as the price for agreement to limit armaments, to demands of certainty: detailed inspection by armies of inspectors to give theoretically perfect security against violation or attack, security far greater indeed—if this can be measured in degrees—than the United States now enjoys through deterrence. New fears engendered by proof of Soviet prowess have inspired new efforts to arm the United States, rather than new efforts to obtain disarmament of the Soviet Union. Apparent Soviet superiority in the development of missiles may have shaken American confidence; it has not increased American trust in the Soviet Union. Indeed, Soviet scientific skill becomes an argument against arms control, for even if there appear to be means for inspecting and detecting violations, the Soviet Union, it is feared, is skilled enough to develop means to circumvent them.

In fact, the hopes deferred and the distrust of the Soviet Union, aggravated by repeated official accusations, may have rendered it difficult to obtain the support of Congress and of American citizens for even limited agreement, should the Executive prepare to enter into such an agreement. The result of cold war and frustration has been weakening of confidence, of interest in arms control, and even of the desire to

Introduction

achieve it. In the United States, too, new, undreamed-of weapons become common, "conventional." Although it is unthinkable that man should use them, men think about and plan their use. Even in the consternation caused by the missile race, leaders in Congress and in government, with few exceptions, appear to exclude arms control from serious consideration in the development of national policy. And the citizen must leave it to "Washington." He too accepts, however reluctantly, that major efforts to control armaments will for the present remain a footnote to a national policy of deterrence through strength. He accepts as well an unquestioned corollary that if strength fails to deter there will be "massive retaliation." Some might suggest that this implies a national policy whereby if an enemy is not in fact deterred and destroys half the world, the United States must retaliate and destroy the rest.[12] "Let me die with the Philistines," said blind Samson, and pulled the whole edifice down.[13] To the questions implied there may be answers, practical as well as moral; but even the questions have hardly been voiced.

Those who concern themselves with affairs of war and peace may not be content to accept United States policy relating to foreign affairs and disarmament without question. The assumptions that support the policy might be examined. And answers might be sought to questions going to the root of United States policy in time of violent fear and distrust between nations armed with the capability to destroy the earth: Why, if arms control is in the interest of all, has there been no agreement? And is arms control, in fact, necessary, desirable, feasible? Is it in the United States' interest at this time? Are the proposals which the United States has been pursuing the right kinds of proposals, containing the right kinds of limitations, the needed kinds of disclosure, the most appropriate kinds of inspection or verification? Is partial, gradual control of arms and arms development better than none? Must the United States continue the quest for military superiority beyond the levels of destructive power already achieved? What political acts and agreements might relax tension and lead to some measures of arms control? And, on a different tack, does the United States today seek or desire disarmament? Or are its negotiations designed to achieve more limited or different purposes? And have American negotiators been setting forth propositions which the United States itself would be willing to put into effect?

Here we would mention specially two or three issues on which views different from those underlying United States policy have been expressed, and which bear on the study of legal implications of arms control. A fundamental question is whether in a world sharply divided there is any sense to negotiating about disarmament. Even to put the question may be startling, for it has not frequently been asked, in public. Yet some may venture the opinion that negotiations are futile. And there is a sense, not frequently voiced, that they are even undesirable.[14] Negotiations, it might be said, compel the United States to take positions publicly on issues vital to its security. Allied and world opinion, particularly since the new rise of Soviet scientific and military prestige, tends to press the United States into postures which are not in the nation's interest. Disarmament negotiations in times of tension raise vain hopes and have adverse effect on the policies of this country and of its allies to maintain maximum deterrent strength. In any event, negotiation is undesirable now because arms control is undesirable; it is not in the interest of the United States to give up its freedom to catch up in the missile race so as to maintain its retaliatory power. In support of this conclusion may be cited also those who, while strong supporters of disarmament, stress that national disarmament must be accompanied by the effective organization of the world to maintain peace.[15] Even the suggestion, in another context, that war has been rendered as unlikely as it is unthinkable[16] can support an argument that disarmament is not needed and is perhaps undesirable.

The argument to the contrary is obvious. The effort to control arms cannot be abandoned. War is bad and can be in the interest of none; peace is good and fundamentally is in the interest of all. Nations like men should be mature enough to rule their relations by reason rather than by force. Armaments are at best a necessary evil and their control is obviously desirable. The elimination or control of armaments would render war, as terrible as man can now make it, less likely; it would reduce fear, relax tension, contribute to the solution of difficulties between nations; it would release for peaceful pursuits the tremendous resources and energies of great and small nations, so that they may leave the sloping road which may lead irresistibly from fear to armament, to poverty, to instability, to political upheaval, and perhaps to war and destruction. With so much at stake the efforts to achieve a more lasting peace cannot be laid aside. The new weapons and new scientific vistas make arms control urgent and essential, lest insane design, or accident, or chain reaction in international affairs lead to the annihilation of man.

Whether there should be negotiation for disarmament is not unre-

Introduction

lated to a more general question—the relation between disarmament and the solution of other international issues of the time. The United States has assumed and stated that other political issues must be resolved before major, meaningful arms control can be considered.[17] But, it may be argued, there will be no settlement between camps heavily armed. Competition in arms is not merely a reflection of political tensions between nations but is itself an integral element in and cause of such tensions.[18] Arms must be controlled before other issues can be solved.

There is also disagreement about limited arms control. Spokesmen for the United States as for other Western countries, we have seen, call only for small steps, for measures which will build confidence and accustom nations to small controls and intrusions.[19] They wish to assure compliance with small limitations before agreeing to big ones, to experiment with small inspections before agreeing to some that reach further. They stress that it is necessary to take account of military realities, of the needs of national security, if the nation is to be safe and if the people are to be persuaded to give up, even in part, reliance on total armament. There are suggestions, indeed, that in the present state of the art of armament, security can be found only in a blend of partial control of arms and arms development with continued deterrence through a good measure of armament retained.

From these views, too, there may be dissent. Perhaps partial disarmament is worse than none. It may cause nations to relax vigilance in the face of the Soviet threat and to weaken the efforts necessary to assure the security of the West. Partial disarmament tends to involve reducing ground forces and the less powerful arms and resting United States policy exclusively on retaliation by the largest weapons. This would leave the United States and its allies unprepared to meet local situations with local means; it would leave the United States in a position in which it must turn every small outbreak into total war, or, since it could probably not do that, find that it is without the means to deter or meet the use of limited force in a local crisis.[20]

INSPECTION

The questions most relevant to this study, those which most need examination, relate to inspection. This, we have said, has been the heart issue. The United States has frequently and bluntly told the Soviets that it did not trust them to comply with an agreement and that there must be full verification to insure that the agreement was being carried out. And the Russians have in large measure resisted thorough inspection as unnecessary intrusion. Apart from Soviet resistance, we have seen, there has also been growing belief that known methods of inspection cannot be relied on and that there is no assurance that the Russians could not find means for circumventing controls.

Is effective inspection possible? To some extent at least, judgments on the efficacy and practicability of various forms of inspection depend on classified scientific and military factors. Except that it is known that the United States has laid great faith in aerial inspection, the official United States views are not public. But views on the issues in regard to inspection have appeared in the public print. Already, we are told, some weapons, and atomic materials in being, easily convertible into weapons, can be hidden beyond the reach of known detection methods.[21] Even the processes of production can be ingeniously concealed. And intercontinental ballistic missiles, once manufactured, can be scattered and kept in readiness, their sites camouflaged, without the possibility of detection except, in theory, by combing the earth with larger armies of inspectors than could possibly be mustered or tolerated. Complete, verified disarmament in the sense once considered, it is said, is therefore no longer possible. All that could be hoped for now would be to establish a system which would carry early warning to intended victims. This itself would tend to deter any would-be attacker. In time, if the habit of peace takes hold, countries will themselves cut down on arms not used or likely to be used.

This pessimistic view is not universally shared. It has been suggested that, in general, there will be agreement on arms control only if it is in the interest of both the United States and the Soviet Union; that such agreement on elimination or limitation of arms is indeed in the interest of both; that it will also be in the interest of both that the agreement, once achieved, be maintained; that each side will wish therefore to have the other satisfied that there is no breach so that there will be no abrogation; and that each side might therefore encourage rather than resist opportunities for inspection and verification, to assure that the agreement is being maintained.[22]

As to methods of inspection, it has been stressed that, depending on what one wishes to learn, there is probably a way of learning it. The questions which must be asked, then, are: What degree of inspection, of "knowledge" must one have? How much would nations have to "pay"

Introduction

for that particular degree of knowledge—what cost, how many people with what skills, what intrusions, what sacrifices would it entail? Are nations able, and willing, to pay this price? And the price must not be exaggerated. If there are advances in the techniques of concealment, there surely are advances also in the techniques of detection. Further, it is not the lone "mad bomber" who threatens the peace of the world, nor the petty thief diverting small amounts of nuclear materials. The broader the scope of prohibition, the easier to detect violations, since there are more areas of activity which would constitute infringements that might be discovered. In any view, if arms and materials already in being are difficult to locate, agreement on a standstill, a moratorium on further increases in armies and further production of armaments, can still be made effective through inspection within practical limits.[23] And surely, intelligent inspection could detect preparations for global war. Even in the day of the new weapons, organization and planning for major war is a mass undertaking. Such a war cannot be launched without extensive and complex organization involving thousands of people creating a pattern of activity detectable at numerous points. Detection of such a large effort need not and should not concentrate on the overt acts of war themselves. "It is not important to know everything; it is important only to know important things." And it is more important by far to know well the few things that must be known than to diffuse energies in gathering mountains of ambiguous unprobative information about many things. Substantial deviation from agreed levels of armament, one suggestion has it, would be reflected in a number of critical indices in the integrated life of a large industrial nation.[24] To control these would not take unlimited inspection. What should be sought is not hypothetically perfect certainty that there is hypothetically perfect elimination of all possible weapons; such certain security is not for human affairs and is hardly what is had in the present unhappy alternative of peace through armed deterrence. What should be sought, what is still possible and practicable, is strong and reasonable assurance that no nation is making substantial preparations for war, or can launch such a war without adequate warning to others in time to take defensive measures. And this must be achieved before weapons are developed which might render even such control impossible, weapons which would hang over the world by a thread that can be easily and suddenly severed.

These differences as to inspection also cannot be resolved here. One may note, however, that an unclassified study recently completed at

Columbia University, with the aid of scientists from other institutions, affords the first public comprehensive examination of the technological feasibility of "Inspection for Disarmament." In the light of analysis by experts examining the feasibility and effectiveness of inspection by different methods at various "critical points," it is concluded that "workable systems of inspection can be designed to ensure compliance with international disarmament agreements." [25]

It seems appropriate to conclude on this note an outline of the efforts to achieve arms control and of the obstacles which beset these efforts. These efforts will undoubtedly continue with more or less earnestness, with more or less energy. Some of the issues mentioned may become less important, and new ones may arise. The policy of the United States, in its details at least, may change. And some limitation on uncontrolled armament, whether unilateral or by agreement—if only the cessation of nuclear tests—is not beyond a reasonable hope. One may yet venture to conclude that, despite coming satellites, space platforms, weather control, and undreamed-of weapons, the events, the considerations, and the issues indicated in this chapter will govern the kinds and degrees of arms control and inspection which, for the immediate future, are within the realm of the likely—if any are achieved at all. They thus afford the basis for the assumptions and hypotheses—set forth in the following chapter—on which this study builds.

Chapter II. ARMS CONTROL PROVISIONS

The impact on American law of an agreement for arms control and inspection will vary, it is obvious, with the character of the agreed provisions. Since no agreement exists and no agreement can be anticipated exactly, we must postulate the provisions to be examined, in greater or lesser particularity. These premises will frame the study and concentrate it on matters whose examination appears most fruitful. They will afford the concreteness and focus essential to significant legal analysis. They will serve also to make specific and actual what is meant by "arms control" and to compel realization of what it will entail.

In this chapter, then, we shall set down the provisions of a control plan whose legal implications will be considered in pages to come. These provisions are not to be found in any proposal hitherto made. Generalized, they suggest the kinds of provisions which may be expected in one or more control agreements, if control is achieved. They are suggested by the history of disarmament efforts and of United States policies sketched in the previous chapter and by the issues there identified. *Inter alia,* Columbia's researches have afforded guidance on forms of inspection which might appear in an agreement.

Inevitably, in selecting the control provisions—as in deciding which of possible legal implications deserve consideration—assumptions are made and limitations self-imposed. We shall seek to indicate these also, in this chapter, and to give reasons for them. Finally, we single out for articulation and emphasis some basic factors which, it would appear, must strongly influence the nature of the provisions included in any foreseeable arms control agreement, and which will necessarily affect, too, their legal implications.

THE CONTROL PROVISIONS IN THE UNITED STATES

We postulate:

(*a*) An international agreement would be ratified by the United States as a treaty and supported by a Congress ready to adopt necessary legislation to implement the treaty

(b) The treaty would include an undertaking by the United States to control (either eliminating entirely or beyond agreed limits) the possession of certain arms, munitions, and materials by the government or by its citizens; the manufacture by the Government of the United States or by anyone in the United States of certain arms, munitions, and materials; the conduct of activities, researches, and tests related to armament; the existence and character of military forces and their disposition within the country

(c) The treaty would provide for inspection to assure compliance with the control system and the limitations imposed, *i.e.,* various forms of verification to disclose production and related activities, and the existence, state, and disposition of arms and armies [1]

(d) Inspection may be by foreign nationals responsible to an international body (or to a foreign government) or perhaps by United States officials accompanied by such foreign nationals

(e) Inspectors must have freedom of access to military, industrial, and other installations, governmental or private, as necessary for the exercise of their functions

(f) Inspection might be by any known method, *e.g.,* aerial observation and photography, acoustic, seismic, and other devices, physical entry to various areas and installations

(g) Inspectors might require from government officials, corporations, or individuals, reports, returns, and other information, and have the right to examine books, records, and relevant documents and data

LIMITATIONS AND OMISSIONS

The control and inspection provisions in the above outline will become more particular, definite, and meaningful, when their legal implications are examined in later chapters. But some matters of approach, of inclusion or omission, may call for explanation here, and, perhaps, justification.

For example: We have posited a treaty and congressional implementation. It does not appear worth while to consider at length what kind of control and inspection the President could properly accept in the United States without a treaty.[2] Rather, it is realistic to forecast that if there is to be any substantial control of arms it will be achieved by international agreement which the President will sign and the Senate will

Arms Control Provisions

approve as a treaty. For like reasons it does not appear desirable to concentrate on the problems which would be created if Congress refused to implement such a treaty; this situation is not inconceivable, but neither does it present the problems to which this memorandum of law can be most usefully directed.

As to the substantive provisions there are also inclusions and omissions which may not be obviously justified. The outline reflects the view that not all aspects of a control plan call for equal attention here. A comprehensive arms control scheme would provide for (*a*) the prohibitions or limitations imposed; (*b*) inspection or other verification to assure compliance and detect violations; and (*c*) the consequences of any violation. Inspection, it will appear, raises the problems most needing examination. But if inspection cannot be separated in fact from that for which one is inspecting, neither are the legal problems of the two independent of one another. We have therefore postulated, not only inspection provisions, but also prohibitions and limitations on the activities of the United States Government, and of its citizens, and shall consider the constitutional and legal principles which they involve. This exposition, primarily of the fundamentals of treaty law, will also form a useful foundation for the subsequent discussion of more difficult issues.

The principal consequences of violation, on the other hand, are not mentioned above; they are hardly considered in this study. Primarily these are international and governmental in character and present few problems in domestic law. The emphasis on a control system as a source of early warning of a major violation, rather than a system designed to prevent or punish such violations, suggests that the chief consequence of a serious breach of the agreement will be that the other parties may feel freed from the limitations of the control treaty, take steps provided in the treaty for this contingency, bring the matter before appropriate United Nations organs, or adopt various measures of self-help. Of course, if an arms control agreement were incorporated into American law, it would presumably be made enforceable by criminal sanctions. The constitutional law involved in federal criminal enforcement in the United States is voluminous, and the issues presented by prosecutions for violations of arms control should not differ from those raised by other federal criminal law and procedure. This report need hardly concern itself with them.

STUDY OF THE IMPROBABLE

The plan outlined, we have said, includes the elements which might, with some probability, appear in an international agreement. And the bulk of this report concerns itself with the legal implications of these provisions. Proposals not likely to materialize or be given serious international consideration do not appear in the provisions assumed; they are less deserving of attention in a study of limited scope. Nevertheless, it has appeared desirable to deal later—in the final sections of chapter IV and in two special added chapters (chapters VII and VIII)—with several areas of the hardly probable. These discussions might be justified, perhaps, by a desire for completeness, or by an interest in constitutional questions which, if hypothetical as concerns arms control, have been raised but hardly considered in other contexts. In fact, there are more pertinent reasons for considering certain improbable features of arms control which have been urged, or feared. The suggestion is frequently heard—and is stressed by the Columbia Inspection Study—for example, that international or foreign inspectors must be allowed to go anywhere at will. In the United States this raises specters of foreign intrusion into private homes at all times without warning or warrant. As will be seen this evokes serious constitutional difficulties, and were it essential to effective control of arms, it might require amendment of the Constitution. But it seems a fanciful notion, and we do not interpret the Inspection Study as implying, that the right to descend upon private dwellings at any time without a warrant is indispensable to adequate supervision of limitations on the new weapons. If we consider such a provision, it is to emphasize its implications. This may lead those who truly seek arms control to weigh carefully whether this provision is indeed necessary. Similarly, we believe that the original United States plan calling for international monopoly over all atomic energy will not be presented again. We consider it briefly toward the end of this study, only because it is a plan once actually submitted by the United States, and because, perhaps, some of its features might yet be proposed. Again, the notion that criminal trials for Americans by international tribunals should be a principal feature of arms control enforcement seems extreme as well as unnecessary. Examination of the constitutional character of such tribunals will reveal how far such a suggestion would reach; it may also suggest the roles for international tribunals which might contribute to arms control without evoking sharp constitutional issues.

"REALITIES" OF CONTROL IN THE UNITED STATES

The character of the control provisions we have postulated and the discussion to come are largely influenced by certain "realities" of international life. Two considerations in particular, which permeate the study to follow, deserve prefatory emphasis.

The first of these, inherent in any system of arms control and inspection, is that such a system is primarily and fundamentally a scheme for the regulation not of private citizens or corporations but of the United States Government itself. If, at the outset, the suggestion that the Government of the United States should be subject to controls by outside agencies is disturbing, this idea, on careful consideration, may render arms control more rather than less acceptable; and it will reduce and mitigate rather than proliferate and aggravate legal problems.

The United States has laws, precedents and experience for regulating occupations, business and other activities in the United States, such as liquor, firearms, narcotics. In some of these, for example narcotics, the United States regulation supports and implements international agreements for cooperative control. In these cases the United States Government desires to maintain control over certain operations by private persons and corporations; there is, so to say, an adversary relation between the government and persons involved in these activities, and United States officials (or state officials in comparable local situations) may be generally counted upon to enforce these laws.

The control of armaments by international agreement differs fundamentally. One can conceive that certain private persons or industries may seek to manufacture or traffic in armaments for profit, in violation of a United States treaty and laws and contrary to the wishes of United States officials. One may conceive, also, though it appears far less likely, that some person or group in or outside the United States Government may say: "Our government has stupidly sacrificed our security by agreeing to disarm. We shall, however, hide some bombs or missiles and some day our country will need them and be grateful to us." These situations, however, are eccentric, and they can be controlled, by a government eager to do so, by laws and methods not different from those used to control narcotics or firearms. International personnel need do no more than observe United States enforcement and be satisfied that it is bona fide and effective. The crucial problem is of a different character. It is how to afford other nations "control" vis-à-vis the United States Government, its civil and military authorities; how to prevent collusion—and to assure suspicious, hostile foreign governments that there is no collusion—between the United States Government and industry and private persons to circumvent controls which the government does not truly wish to observe. That is what the United States would seek to assure in the Soviet Union; that is what others will seek to control here. It is this element which injects into any arms control scheme prohibitions on activities by the United States Government, and probably inspection by non–United States agencies of activities of the United States Government as well as private industries or persons. But while the idea is perhaps novel, analysis may show that the Constitution is less resistant to control and regulation of activities of the United States Government than of those of the citizen. And it may appear that international controls which so far as possible operate in relation to the United States, rather than directly to private citizens, more effectively meet both the necessities of arms control and the requirements of the Constitution.

The second "reality," related though different, is inherent in any system applied to sovereign and equal nations, and becomes particularly important in time of cold war. This is the element of reciprocity, already suggested. Whether an arms control scheme is universal and complete, or—like the Eisenhower air inspection proposal of 1955—merely preliminary and mainly bilateral, it is clear that both the United States and the USSR at least must be parties to it. Inevitably the control plan will have to operate equally in the United States and in the Soviet Union. And this factor lies at the heart of the problems to be studied. A system of inspection should be as minimal as is consistent with assurance that violations would be detected.[3] Obviously, fewer limitations on the United States and less inspection and intrusion by foreign officials within the United States would make a control scheme less onerous to the United States and more acceptable to American authorities, the Congress, and the people; and it would create fewer constitutional and legal problems. But these same American authorities, Congress, and people will wish maximum control and non-Russian inspection in the USSR, and inevitably, if there is to be agreement, the United States will have to accept reciprocal limitations and inspection. The Russians, in turn,

Arms Control Provisions

will face the same negotiating dilemma. Any plan the United States agrees upon, it may therefore be assumed, will be a compromise between how much control and how many rights and powers we wish to get for international or foreign inspectors in Russia and how few we would like to grant such inspectors in the United States.

In the United States, as will be seen, there are established patterns for inspection by federal officials under old and accepted systems of congressional regulation of various industries. Even arms and armaments are already subject to domestic regulation in varying degrees in war and peace.[4] It would be simplest from the point of view of the law and the Constitution, as well as for acceptability to both Congress and the public, to leave implementation of an arms control treaty to American officials and American inspectors. The American government could then be responsible to an international or foreign supervisory body for carrying out inspection and enforcement in the United States. The Russians, however, may not be content with such indirect inspection and control of American activities. And the American people would probably have no confidence in a system of inspection and control in the Soviet Union under which Soviet officials might have substantial opportunity to deceive international supervisors. If the United States insists on direct inspection in Russia, it will have to agree to direct inspection by international or foreign officials here.

Similarly, we may believe that foreign inspectors in the United States should in given circumstances be required to have a search warrant; such a warrant, we may believe, could be obtained from a United States court without fear that the court would refuse to cooperate and would seek to frustrate the inspectors in their legitimate search. The Russians, on the other hand, might not have such confidence in our courts. Again, we would probably have no such confidence in the Soviet courts and might therefore insist that inspection in Russia must be without warrant. But that could hardly be obtained without agreement, reciprocally, to search without warrant in the United States. In some situations that proposal might raise constitutional problems for the United States. That the United States would find it difficult to agree to such proposals for this country should encourage its representatives to seek alternative forms of inspection and detection which may be equally effective without reaching unnecessarily into the lives of a country and its people.

Negotiation in the circumstances, then, involves, in marked degree, the interplay of "realities." The facts of political life in the United States suggest a deep reluctance to accept intrusion here, particularly by a body which may include Soviet or satellite inspectors, and at the same time an eagerness to reach deep into Soviet life and activities. The realities of international life, on the other hand, require reciprocity. Or, one may, instead, describe the difficulty in terms of "unrealities." It appears unrealistic to expect that the United States would agree to arms control without thorough inspection in Russia. It appears equally unrealistic to expect that the United States would permit in this country the very same controls and inspections on which it would insist in Russia. The result may be an impasse—no or little inspection, no or few controls. But the result may lead instead to mutual understanding and agreed-upon compromise. Perhaps further examination, and the recognition that the same practices might not be acceptable here, would lead the United States to moderate demands not in fact necessary for adequate detection. Further examination may also increase the willingness of both the United States and the Soviet Union to accept some novelties, inconveniences, and perhaps sacrifices. For this country, if it indeed becomes possible to safeguard the security of the United States through disarming would-be enemies, instead of by constant striving to match or surpass them in armaments, it may be necessary to try some new methods, to disturb the inertia inherent in established ways and the eternal human preference for not doing. First steps may have to be taken, experiments essayed, if there is to be any hope for bringing forth a peace that is more than nonwar or cold war.

We shall proceed now to examine whether, if the political institutions of the United States are prepared to meet the challenge of arms control and inspection, its legal institutions will also be sufficient to the need.

Chapter III. ARMS CONTROL AND THE CONSTITUTION

A memorandum of law on the implications of arms control for the United States is essentially a memorandum of constitutional law. A number of constitutional issues suggested by the control plan which we have postulated will be considered in this chapter. While we shall not attempt to treat all the issues, flimsy or remote, which might be conjured up, we shall consider those which appear important, those which appear substantial, and some that are so manifest as to beg mention. And we shall begin at the beginning. Can the United States agree to control arms? If so, within what limits and subject to what limitations?

NATIONAL POWER TO CONTROL ARMS

The federal government has power under the Constitution to agree with other nations to control arms. While this may appear obvious, it is useful here to trace the obvious to its roots in the Constitution. We shall consider briefly, as foundation for the discussion to follow, the powers of the United States under the Constitution to act as a nation in relation to other nations.[1]

The Constitution intended that the United States would take an equal and sovereign place in the international community. While "foreign affairs" are assumed rather than expressed, there are explicit provisions in the Constitution establishing the power to make treaties; granting to the President authority to appoint and receive ambassadors; conferring upon Congress power to regulate commerce with foreign nations and to declare war. Congress is also given the power "to define and punish . . . Offences against the Law of Nations." There are, in addition, express limitations upon the powers of the states to enter into treaties or other arrangements or agreements with foreign countries.

The Constitution contemplated and provided for the conduct of foreign affairs for an indefinite future. But no doubt, the most farsighted and imaginative of the fathers of the Constitution did not envisage the scope and complexity of United States foreign affairs today. They could not have foreseen the participation in international organizations of our time—in the International Labor Organization, for example, or the United Nations. The agency contemplated in the first United States proposal, in 1946, for the international development of atomic energy was beyond their most fanciful dreams. The control plan assumed for purposes of this study, less far-reaching in important respects than the 1946 proposals, was equally beyond imagination when the Constitution was drafted.

It is not new to say that the world has changed since 1789. In domestic areas of national activity also, the facts of the nation's life have outstripped imaginings even more recent than those of the authors of the Constitution. And Congresses, under oath to support the Constitution, have adopted novel laws to meet the day's new facts. Presidents, also sworn to uphold the Constitution, have requested such acts of legislation and signed them into law. The Supreme Court, final arbiter on the limits of the Constitution, has upheld many of these laws. The Atomic Energy Acts,[2] for example, go perhaps as far as any laws in our history —certainly so in the absence of actual war—to assert broad powers in the national government, exclude the states, and limit the rights of persons. And if these acts have not yet been passed upon by the courts, others have—legislation enacted during comparative calm as well as during wars and depressions—and the Supreme Court has generally found the power of Congress and of the President sufficient to the nation's needs. The development has been long, not always clear-forward. But, in general, the authority of Congress to experiment, even to err, has been liberated from restraints based on the social and economic theories of an earlier day, which some would have found and fixed in the Constitution.

If there have been doubts, advances, and retreats, in regard to the "police" powers of Congress in domestic affairs, there have been few in regard to the powers of the nation in its foreign relations. That the Articles of Confederation did not enable the new states effectively to carry on relations with other nations was an important reason for the Constitutional Convention. At the convention the concern of the states for their own rights and their reluctance to give of their power to the federal government hardly applied to the establishment of the pattern for conducting the international affairs of the new nation. In the nation's

Arms Control and the Constitution

history since then, no Justice of the Supreme Court interpreting the Constitution has found there any insistence on "states' rights" in United States foreign affairs.[3] While the formulation now generally cited came in 1935, it was accepted from the beginning that the United States is a nation among nations with all the powers of other nations in its relations with them.[4] In 1935, in *United States v. Curtiss-Wright Export Corp.*,[5] Mr. Justice Sutherland expounded the powers of the national government in international affairs—that the Congress and the President are virtually plenipotentiary to do together for the United States what other nations can do in their mutual relations.

This is not to say that there are no constitutional limitations on the conduct of foreign affairs.[6] But it is fair to say that, in general, those who wrote the Constitution sought to guide, not to rein, future generations of the nation driving to meet international situations that could not have been foretold. Perhaps the fathers were wiser than we can imagine; perhaps they built better than they knew. For here, as in another context,

when we are dealing with words that also are a constituent act, like the Constitution of the United States, we must realize that they have called into life a being the development of which could not have been foreseen completely by the most gifted of its begetters. It was enough for them to realize or to hope that they had created an organism; it has taken a century and has cost their successors much sweat and blood to prove that they created a nation. . . . We must consider what this country has become.[7]

THE TREATY POWER AND CONTROL OF ARMAMENTS

A principal means by which the United States acts in concert with other nations is the treaty. Article II, Section 2, of the Constitution provides that the President "shall have Power, by and with the Advice and Consent of the Senate, to make Treaties, provided two-thirds of the Senators present concur." Article VI, Clause 2, of the Constitution is the Supremacy Clause: "This Constitution, and the Laws of the United States which shall be made in pursuance thereof; and all Treaties made, or which shall be made, under the Authority of the United States, shall be the supreme Law of the Land."

What a "treaty" is the Constitution did not deem necessary to define. Treaties were familiar to the Founders, and they did not see any issues concerning their content or scope. A treaty connotes an international agreement dealing with a subject of international concern. In *Geofroy v. Riggs*, Mr. Justice Field wrote:

That the treaty power of the United States extends to all proper subjects of negotiation between our government and the governments of other nations, is clear.[8]

Charles Evans Hughes, in a published statement, said:

What is the power to make a treaty? What is the object of the power? The normal scope of the power can be found in the appropriate object of the power. The power is to deal with foreign nations with regard to matters of international concern. It is not a power intended to be exercised, it may be assumed, with respect to matters that have no relation to international concerns.[9]

As much, perhaps, as any other federal power, the treaty power reflects the scope of the Constitution, the play, the elbow-room, the elasticity in that document enabling the United States to carry out its responsibilities. From the beginning, the United States, by treaties, has waged war, sought peace, maintained neutrality, acquired and ceded territory. As nations groped for cooperation, this nation entered into arbitration agreements, cooperated to control narcotics, adhered to the statutes of international courts, agreed to limit the size of its navy, joined international organizations to deal with postal systems and labor. Finally, the United States became a member of the United Nations, with hardly a question that under the Constitution it had the power to do so.

There can be little doubt, then, that the United States under the Constitution may as a nation agree with other nations about controlling armaments. Mutual limitations on the size of armies, on the possession and manufacture, use or disposition of armaments, are proper subjects for international agreement. The size of our armies, the character and extent of our armaments, whether we are or are not manufacturing weapons, are questions of deep interest to other nations on which they may wish to bargain. Actually, such questions have been the subject of numerous agreements between nations. Were this a new departure in foreign affairs for the United States, the Constitution, through the treaty power in particular, could accommodate new means for meeting the new needs, as it has shown itself able to do in the past. In fact, however, arms control would be a link in a chain of analogous United States actions in foreign affairs culminating in the United Nations Charter—and already including limitations on armaments, as early as 1817, as recently as 1936.[10] Although there has not been adjudication in the courts of the validity of any disarmament agreement of the United States, this nation has made agreements in the past to limit the size of its navy and

Arms Control and the Constitution

to disarm all vessels on the Great Lakes;[11] it has also agreed in the United Nations Charter that the appropriate organ of the United Nations shall consider and recommend to members proposals for disarmament;[12] and it has negotiated on disarmament on numerous occasions with a view to concluding a treaty. An arms control treaty brought into effect in accordance with the procedures prescribed in the Constitution, therefore, would be clearly a proper exercise of the treaty power.

CONSTITUTIONAL LIMITATIONS ON TREATIES

An arms control treaty made by the United States is an exercise of federal power. Like other acts of the federal government, it is subject to constitutional limitations. This principle has not always been clear. No treaty of the United States has ever been declared unconstitutional by any United States court.[13] And there grew a legend, supported by citation to Mr. Justice Holmes in *Missouri v. Holland,* that a treaty is not subject to the constitutional limitations which control acts of Congress.[14]

Except for the tentative and ambiguous suggestion by Mr. Justice Holmes, however, the dicta of Justices of the United States Supreme Court are uniform in asserting that treaties are subject to constitutional limitations.[15] And even the Holmes "suggestion" was otherwise explained, again very recently by Mr. Justice Black, writing for four members of the Court in *Reid v. Covert.*[16] Justice Black also declared there that "no agreement with a foreign nation can confer power on the Congress, or on any other branch of government, which is free from the restraints of the Constitution. . . . The prohibitions of the Constitution were designed to apply to all branches of the National Government and they cannot be nullified by the Executive or by the Executive and the Senate combined."[17]

IMPACT ON EXECUTIVE AND LEGISLATIVE POWERS

The dicta of the Supreme Court and the statements of authorities suggest that a treaty may be invalid if it conflicts with the basic pattern of separated, independent branches of government.[18] There might be argument that any treaty which eliminates or limits the armed forces of the United States, or places restriction on their use or disposition, deprives the President of the full and free exercise of his powers under the Constitution, particularly in his role as "Commander in Chief of the Army and Navy of the United States." It might also be charged that such a treaty curtails powers conferred upon Congress to "raise and support armies," to "provide and maintain a navy." Indirectly, the power "to declare war" is affected.

These objections are not substantial. The provisions cited confer power upon the federal government and indicate where among the separate branches of the governmnt the power is lodged. Of course, it was contemplated that the United States would have an army and navy. The Constitution can hardly be interpreted, however, as insisting that the United States *must* have an army and navy.

Basically, moreover, these arguments misconceive the nature of the treaty power and its relation to the other powers conferred by the Constitution. Every provision in a treaty promising another nation that the United States will take or not take certain action is by its nature an agreement which "bargains away" the earlier right of the United States —through the Congress or the President or both—to do or not to do the contrary. If the United States agrees by treaty not to impose certain tariffs or duties, the treaty has, so to say, "bargained away" the right of the Congress to impose such a tariff or duty. If the United States agrees by treaty to treat Chinese nationals like other aliens for purposes of admission to the United States, it has "bargained away" the right of Congress to exclude Chinese on a discriminatory basis.

In fact, however, it is also established that, at least as concerns its domestic consequences, no treaty "bargains away" powers conferred by the Constitution. For despite the treaty Congress can adopt legislation which is inconsistent with the obligation of the treaty. The character of a treaty as law of the United States and the relation of such law to laws adopted by Congress was settled early in the history of the country. A treaty when ratified becomes law in the United States without any action by Congress, unless by its terms, by the nature of its provisions, or by special reservation of the Senate, it is made clear that it shall not be self-executing. The relation of the legislative powers of Congress to treaties may be best described by two quotations from the Supreme Court. In a leading case [19] Chief Justice Marshall said:

> A treaty is in its nature a contract between two nations, not a legislative act. It does not generally effect, of itself, the object to be accomplished, especially so far as its operation is infra-territorial; but is carried into execution by the sovereign power of the respective parties to the instrument.
>
> In the United States a different principle is established. Our constitution declares a treaty to be the law of the land. It is, consequently, to be regarded

in courts of justice as equivalent to an act of the legislature, whenever it operates of itself without the aid of any legislative provision. But when the terms of the stipulation import a contract, when either of the parties engages to perform a particular act, the treaty addresses itself to the political, not the judicial department; and the legislature must execute the contract, before it can become a rule for the Court.

In *Whitney v. Robertson* [20] Mr. Justice Field observed:

By the Constitution a treaty is placed on the same footing, and made of like obligation, with an act of legislation. Both are declared by that instrument to be the supreme law of the land, and no superior efficacy is given to either over the other. When the two relate to the same subject, the courts will always endeavor to construe them so as to give effect to both, if that can be done without violating the language of either; but if the two are inconsistent, the one last in date will control the other.

A treaty is valid and binding as law in the United States although inconsistent with a previous act of Congress; and, for domestic purposes, a congressional enactment can repeal a treaty provision.[21]

Regardless, then, of any undertakings in a treaty to control arms, Congress is free to adopt legislation inconsistent with these treaty obligations. Domestically this subsequent legislation is valid and will prevail. Put differently, whatever the international consequences of a breach of a treaty, the Constitution does not deny to the appropriate political branch of the United States Government the power to break treaties. Congress has in fact adopted legislation inconsistent with United States treaties, as in the tariff and Chinese immigration cases cited, and the courts have upheld the legislation.[22] Similarly, Congress could constitutionally adopt legislation which disregards a treaty eliminating or limiting the United States Army and Navy and prohibiting or limiting United States armaments.[23]

THE POSSIBILITY OF IRREVOCABLE AGREEMENT

The power of Congress to disregard the obligations of a treaty, and the desire, in turn, to insure that other nations—the Soviet Union, for example—could not violate their treaty obligations, might give rise to a suggestion that a provision be inserted into an arms control treaty eliminating the power of all parties to denounce or breach the treaty. For the United States such a provision would presumably rule out the power of Congress, as well as that of other branches of the government, to adopt measures or perform acts inconsistent with the treaty provisions. Would such a provision be effective?

Every treaty provision, of course, implies an international obligation to abide by it. It may be denounced or terminated only in the circumstances provided in the treaty or in others recognized by international law. Yet, any nation has the power, though not a right under international law, to break any treaty and suffer the consequences. An additional provision that the United States will not break its treaty would have no greater legal effect than any other treaty provision. The international consequence of the breach of this provision would not be different from those following breach of the basic substantive provisions of the treaty. And if Congress has the power under the Constitution to legislate domestically in disregard of substantive treaty provisions, it would seem equally to have that power even in the face of a specific provision in the treaty that Congress will not so legislate.[24]

In fact, of course, what is suggested is an effort to compel sovereign nations to carry out the provisions of their treaties when they do not wish to do so. However reprehensible it may be, the power to break treaties exists in a society of sovereign nations, and is inherent in the character of treaties among them. Only some form of supranational government, and a supranational law requiring the specific performance of treaties and backed by police power capable of enforcing it, could bring about actual compliance by reluctant nations.

The United States could perhaps amend its Constitution to deprive the various branches of the government of authority to break a treaty or to perform acts inconsistent with a treaty. This would mean that while the United States, like other nations, might theoretically have the power to disregard its constitutional obligations, there would be no branch of the government which would have constitutional authority to act in this way on behalf of the United States. There may be serious question whether the United States should tie the hands of the branches of its government in this way; there is no way, by treaty, of compelling other nations to disable their governments from breaking treaties. Even amendments to the constitutions of other states, like the one here suggested for the United States, would not avail if persons in authority refused to abide by these constitutional limitations. Also, constitutional amendments, both in the United States and elsewhere, can themselves be amended or eliminated.

Yet the fact that all nations in today's world have the power to break treaties should not be an obstacle to the negotiation of an agreement. In fact, the ability to terminate an arms control agreement, by breach if necessary, might allay the fears of nations and overcome their reluctance to enter into arms control arrangements even tentatively. Indeed, there may be argument for a provision in the treaty permitting denunciation by any party upon a period of notice. The knowledge that they can retreat will encourage nations to enter. The knowledge that they can retreat legally and openly may help discourage them from clandestine violation. In course, although nations had gone in tentatively with an eye on the exit, experience might breed confidence and the power to abandon the agreement might never be exercised.

THE RIGHTS OF STATES

An arms control treaty might be challenged as violating specific provisions of the Constitution reserving rights to the states or to citizens.

TREATIES AND THE RESERVED POWERS

Since an arms control agreement is a valid exercise of the treaty power, it is, by virtue of the Supremacy Clause, the law of the land, superseding any inconsistent provisions in the laws or constitution of any state. Congress could enact legislation necessary and proper to implement this treaty, even in respects as to which in the absence of a treaty such legislation would be beyond the power of Congress under the Constitution. The treaty and the legislation would nullify any inconsistent state law and remove from state control the manufacture, use, or possession of armaments or materials, to the extent preempted by the treaty and implementing acts of Congress.

This has not been always and uniformly understood. At different periods in the history of the international relations of the United States there were some who said that treaties could not deal with matters not otherwise in the federal domain. Usually cited was the Tenth Amendment which reserves to the states (or to the people) powers not delegated by the Constitution to the United States or prohibited to the states.[25] In the debates over the "Bricker Amendment" some proponents of the amendment appeared to believe that the right asserted by the federal government to deal by treaty with matters otherwise in the domain of the states was a novel, usurping extension springing full-blown from the mind of Mr. Justice Holmes in 1920. This is not so. The authority normally cited is indeed Mr. Justice Holmes's opinion in *Missouri v. Holland*,[26] which upheld both a treaty and implementing legislation regulating the hunting of migratory birds, although it was assumed, for purposes of the argument, that in the absence of the treaty this was not a proper subject for congressional regulation. In fact, the power of the United States to deal by treaty with matters otherwise local in character has been recognized from the beginning. In 1796, in *Ware v. Hylton*,[27] the Supreme Court held that a treaty with Great Britain superseded a Virginia statute canceling debts owed by its citizens to British subjects if they paid the sums into the state treasury. Standard commerce, friendship, and navigation treaties through our history have dealt with matters as local as the right to inherit land, frequently disregarding state laws.[28] *Ware v. Hylton* was decided after the adoption of the Tenth Amendment to the Constitution and the result was not affected by that amendment. Since the treaty power is delegated to the United States Government, and implies the power to deal by treaty with matters of legitimate concern and agreement between nations, the Tenth Amendment cannot be read as a limitation on that power. Neither that amendment nor any "invisible radiations" from it can be read to mean that treaties may not deal with matters which would be reserved to the states in the absence of treaty.[29]

It is not intended to stir here the "Bricker Amendment" controversy. But speaking of arms control alone, it would seem obvious that this involves national policy of the highest importance which cannot be subject to veto or interference by the states. In today's race for supremacy in destructive weapons, the policies adopted by the United States vis-à-vis other nations affect the very life of the nation. Congress has, even without a treaty, exerted strict and far-reaching controls of atomic energy in the interest of national defense and security. If the United States decides that the peace, the security, and the survival of the people will be served by agreement with other nations to control, prohibit, limit, or regulate arms and materials, it could hardly be suggested that a state should have the power to frustrate that policy and have the right to keep a few atomic bombs of its own. The events and developments of the atomic age, yet again, confirm the judgment and foresight of the constitutional fathers in lodging the treaty power exclusively and supremely in the federal government.

THE STATE MILITIA

Apart from the "reserved powers" of the states, the Constitution includes a number of specific guarantees to them which presumably could not be violated by treaty.[30] Possibly relevant to arms control are the

Arms Control and the Constitution

provisions dealing with the state militia. These provisions, together with related prohibitions on the maintenance of troops by the states, will be considered briefly even though it is unlikely that they would be affected by foreseeable plans to control arms.

The Constitution provides that "no State shall, without the Consent of Congress . . . keep Troops, or Ships of War in time of Peace, enter into any Agreement . . . with a foreign Power, or engage in War, unless actually invaded, or in such imminent Danger as will not admit of delay."[31] Since the states may not keep troops without congressional consent, an arms control treaty would not be depriving the states of any right to keep troops, unless Congress had earlier given them such a right. In that event, the treaty would supersede the earlier congressional legislation, but there would seem to be no basis for constitutional complaint by the states. The last quoted phrase may imply that the states have a right to engage in war if actually invaded or in imminent danger of invasion. The prohibition on the keeping of troops by the states in the earlier part of the same section, however, would seem to make it clear that the states are not guaranteed the right to keep troops and arms in anticipation of such invasion.

The status of the state militia, on the other hand, may raise some minor questions if—as seems unlikely—an arms control agreement should go so far as to require the elimination of even such bodies. The Constitution empowers Congress "to provide for organizing, arming and disciplining, the Militia, and for governing such Part of them as may be employed in the Service of the United States, reserving to the States, respectively, the Appointment of the Officers and the Authority of training the Militia according to the discipline prescribed by Congress."[32] The Second Amendment to the Constitution provides: "A well-regulated Militia, being necessary to the security of a free State, the right of the people to keep and bear Arms shall not be infringed." In the following section we shall deal with the Second Amendment as it relates to the rights of private citizens. Its relevance for the present discussion lies in the possible implication that in the portions quoted, particularly in the phrase "a well-regulated Militia, being necessary to the security of a free State," the Constitution guarantees to the states the right to maintain a militia even though Congress has been granted considerable control over such militia.

The Constitution distinguishes between troops, forbidden to the states without the consent of Congress, and the militia.[33] The right of the states to keep a militia was clearly contemplated—was it guaranteed? The history of the development of the Constitution suggests that some considered the militia in part a bulwark for the states against a tyrannical central government,[34] although, for the common defense and for the sake of uniformity, it was finally agreed that Congress would organize and arm the various state militia and call them into the national service as needed. The states retained the power to appoint the officers and to train the militia, according to the discipline prescribed by Congress. In practice, on the other hand, Congress has exercised fairly full control over the militia and occasionally seems to have forgotten its distinction from troops under the Constitution.[35] The organized militia is now the National Guard, treated in many respects identically with United States troops, even in time of peace. Indeed, it has been suggested that the power of Congress to "organize" the militia included the power not to organize it and to abolish or prohibit the militia entirely.[36]

That is the problem for our purposes. If Congress has the power to abolish the militia, there is no reason why this could not be done by a disarmament treaty. If, however, the Constitution is interpreted as specifically reserving to the states the right to maintain a militia, there may be doubt whether the states could be deprived entirely of this right without their consent.

In the absence of an authoritative judicial ruling, and with commentators divided,[37] there is little basis for a certain opinion on this question. In any event, as we have said, this is not likely to be a serious obstacle to the achievement and implementation of an arms control plan. Under its authority to provide for organizing and arming militia Congress could certainly limit these bodies to small arms. With such a limitation the militia becomes more akin to a police force necessary for internal order rather than an army with which an international agreement is likely to concern itself. In the extreme situation, if an international agreement should cut across the right to maintain state militia even with small arms, it may have to be decided whether the consent of the states through legislation or resolution or an amendment to the United States Constitution would be necessary.

STATE ENTERPRISES

What of other activities by the states which might run afoul of an arms control agreement? Suppose, for instance, that a state owns nuclear materials, or builds an atomic reactor, or engages in other manufacturing, mining, or related activities which are subject to international arms control. Does the fact that these activities are carried on by the state itself

Arms Control and the Constitution

render them immune to international control? The answer would seem to be that it does not. The United States might tax such activities by the state under a general tax applicable to all engaged in such operations.[38] A railroad run by a state is subject to regulation by Congress under the interstate commerce power.[39] A state university must pay customs duties imposed by Congress under its power over foreign commerce.[40] The federal government may take state property by eminent domain, paying just compensation.[41] Federal price regulation under the war power may be applied to timber owned and sold by the state.[42] While, as we shall see in a later chapter,[43] there are aspects of "sovereignty" of the state and its governmental functions which raise more difficult questions, activities of the kind we are here discussing are subject to the supremacy of the national government acting under the treaty power and other federal powers.

PRIVATE RIGHTS

Does a treaty which prohibits, limits, or otherwise regulates the right to possess arms, or to manufacture or traffic in arms and other war materials, violate any constitutional right of persons or corporations?

Treaties, we have accepted, are subject to the limitations on the federal government expressed in the Constitution or in the amendments to it. Particularly, we assume that the Bill of Rights is a bulwark against infringement by treaty. It may be noted that most of the amendments are written in the passive voice, thus asserting, one would say, that the rights described shall not be infringed by any action of any branch of the national government. The First Amendment, it is true, provides only that *"Congress* shall make no law . . . ," but the rights protected by that amendment have been deemed immune to infringement by the Executive as well,[44] and the same limitation would presumably be applied to the treaty power—also an Executive power, with legislative aspects.

Does our treaty run afoul of any of the protections of the Bill of Rights?

THE RIGHT TO BEAR ARMS AND THE SECOND AMENDMENT

On its face the provision of the Second Amendment that "the right of the people to keep and bear Arms, shall not be infringed" might appear a substantial obstacle to total disarmament. In fact, it is a small obstacle indeed.

In *United States v. Miller*[45] the Supreme Court upheld the conviction of the defendant Miller under the National Firearms Act. Miller had been convicted of transporting in interstate commerce a 12-gauge shotgun with a barrel less than 18 inches long, without having registered it and without having in his possession a written order for it with stamp affixed, as required by the statute. Justice McReynolds, for a unanimous Court, held, relying on the precedent of federal regulation of narcotics, that the National Firearms Act was not an unconstitutional invasion of the reserved powers of the states. Neither was it a violation of the Second Amendment. He said: "With obvious purpose to assure the continuation and render possible the effectiveness of such forces [the militia], the declaration and guarantee of the Second Amendment were made. It must be interpreted and applied with that end in view." At another point:

> In the absence of any evidence tending to show that possession or use of a "shotgun having a barrel of less than eighteen inches in length" at this time has some reasonable relationship to the preservation or efficiency of a well regulated militia, we cannot say that the Second Amendment guarantees the right to keep and bear such an instrument. Certainly it is not within judicial notice that this weapon is any part of the ordinary military equipment or that its use could contribute to the common defense.

The Second Amendment therefore confers no absolute right to bear arms. Still, if the Second Amendment, as interpreted by the *Miller* case, means that only weapons which could not be useful for a militia may be taken away by the federal government, the amendment might become a more serious obstacle, since—whether in commando tactics or otherwise—a large variety of weapons might be useful to a militia. In fact, however, it is hardly likely that the courts would interpret the amendment as protecting weapons merely because they *might* be used by militia. Rather, in order to gain the protection of the amendment, a person would have to show that his weapon is not merely capable of being used in the militia but is required and intended for such use in accordance with the commands of the state and subject to the prescriptions of Congress pursuant to Article I, Section 8, of the Constitution.[46]

The right reserved by the Second Amendment therefore is only to keep arms which may be required for the militia. It is not a constitutional right of a citizen to keep arms otherwise. If, as has been suggested, Congress can abolish the militia, the right to keep arms reserved by the Second Amendment would also disappear. If, on the other hand, the states have a constitutional right to maintain a militia, the right of the

Arms Control and the Constitution

people to keep arms needed by this militia would also be protected by the Second Amendment. This right, however, would seem to be one subject to control by the state and regulation by Congress under Article I, Section 8; it is the state which may have the right guaranteed by the Constitution to maintain a militia and to insist on a minimum of arms for it. If the states consent to the total abolition or disarming of their militia, there is no constitutional right which can be asserted by a private person.

LIBERTY AND PROPERTY UNDER THE FIFTH AMENDMENT

The Fifth Amendment includes the provision that "no person shall . . . be deprived of . . . liberty or property, without due process of law; nor shall private property be taken for public use, without just compensation." Would an arms control treaty implemented by federal legislation violate these provisions insofar as it required individuals or corporations to divest themselves of forbidden arms or materials, or forbade their possession or manufacture, or traffic in such arms and materials for the future? Is there any requirement of just compensation?

DUE PROCESS. Hundreds of cases and volumes of comment have been devoted to "substantive due process." "Due process of law," required of the states in the Fourteenth Amendment and of the national government in the Fifth, was long ago held to include far more than fair hearings and adequate procedures. It was established that the phrase imposes a standard, however vague and variable with reference to time and circumstance, requiring that the exercise of various governmental powers by state or nation should be fair and reasonable. In *Nebbia v. New York*[47] the Court said of this standard as applied to action of the states:

And the guaranty of due process, as has often been held, demands only that the law shall not be unreasonable, arbitrary or capricious, and that the means selected shall have a real and substantial relation to the object sought to be attained.

Despite this pronouncement, one cannot say with confidence whether substantive due process continues to be an important obstacle to state or federal regulation of economic activity. In more than twenty years no legislative enactment, state or federal, has been held by the Supreme Court to be an invalid deprivation of property, of "economic rights." And in 1955 a unanimous Court said:

The day is gone when this Court uses the Due Process Clause of the Fourteenth Amendment to strike down state laws regulatory of business and industrial conditions, because they may be unwise, improvident, or out of harmony with a particular school of thought.[48]

Earlier the Court said:

Our recent decisions make plain that we do not sit as a superlegislature to weigh the wisdom of legislation nor to decide whether the policy which it expresses offends the public welfare. The legislative power has limits. . . . But the state legislatures . . . may within extremely broad limits control practices in the business-labor field, so long as specific constitutional prohibitions are not violated and so long as conflicts with valid and controlling federal laws are avoided.[49]

It may be, then, that substantive due process, whatever heed the legislature or the treaty makers may give it, no longer represents a substantial judicial limitation on federal or state "infringement" of economic rights. Most of the limitations on private activity and property which arms control may entail would not, then, be in danger of invalidation by the courts. Still, something is undoubtedly left of the constitutional limitation, and obvious discrimination or confiscation would probably be struck down. In any event, for the purpose of this study let us assume that substantive due process may still deserve serious attention.

On that assumption, we note that the "liberty" protected by the Constitution is not limited to physical liberty from arrest, restraint, or imprisonment. It includes the freedom to carry on all activities unless forbidden by proper and reasonable exercise of governmental power which meets the standards of "due process" as etched out by the courts. The "liberty" of an individual to manufacture arms, to possess or use them is thus protected; and the property interest in the conduct of arms trade, in the ownership and possession of arms and materials in being, and in patents in the arms field may also be "deprived" only if the government's action, under a recognized federal power, keeps within "due process." The "person" who cannot be deprived of property without due process includes a corporation.[50]

No treaty of the United States has thus far been held to deprive any citizen or corporation of property without due process of law. *Ware v. Hylton,* cited earlier, might suggest that—at least on the facts of that case—due process considerations are not relevant to the validity of a treaty, but perhaps courts had not yet begun to think of substantive due process then. In that case, it will be recalled, the Court upheld and applied the provision in the peace treaty with Great Britain which required American citizens to pay their debts to British citizens, although a Virginia statute had earlier declared that its citizens should pay their British debts into the state treasury and that they would thereby be discharged from their obligation. In affirming that a citizen who had paid once into the Virginia treasury was required to pay again to his British creditors, the debtor was being made to pay twice, a requirement which would appear to raise serious questions under the due process clause. The Supreme Court, however, did not consider that this affected the validity of the treaty; it did assume that the debtor would somehow be relieved of the dual burden.[51]

It would seem, then, that a treaty which deals with a subject of international concern and which, we assume, pursues the national benefit is not invalid for lack of substantive due process because some private property interests may be sacrificed. And the courts would probably not examine whether it was reasonable for the treaty makers to sacrifice the rights of one citizen or one group of citizens to achieve the national interests involved.[52] Probably, too, a case like *Ware v. Hylton* would be decided the same way today.[53] And certainly, in the case of an arms control agreement, the courts will have little trouble finding that there is no serious question under the due process clause. A valid treaty, properly implemented, dealing with a subject of legitimate international concern and reasonably related to goals of national security which the federal government is charged with furthering, would not appear open to serious question on the grounds of "substantive due process" even if the private interests of some should suffer incidentally. And the courts will not question the wisdom of the treaty makers in entering into a disarmament agreement or of the Congress in implementing it. Since such an agreement is within the power of the federal government, there is no greater problem under the due process clause than was presented —even in the heyday of that clause—by incidental private loss or deprivation resulting from the neutrality acts, the embargo of munitions of war under the foreign commerce and other powers, federal prohibitions on the transportation of narcotics or firearms under the interstate commerce power, the banning of gambling devices in the territories, or, similarly, by various acts in the exercise by the states of their police power in the face of the due process clause of the Fourteenth Amendment.

Nation and state within their respective domains can regulate varieties of industries; prohibit some occupations entirely, even as to persons already engaged in them; confiscate property or cause it to be destroyed—if there are considerations which make these actions reasonable. A state can require the destruction of food in cold storage not fit for human consumption [54] or of cedar trees which might infect near-by apple orchards with cedar rust.[55] A state can render useless a man's brickyard,[56] his livery stable,[57] his oleomargarine factory,[58] his brewery.[59] The United States in the exercise of its proper powers may similarly forbid the importation and retention of inferior tea,[60] the cultivation of narcotics poppies,[61] the interstate transportation of inferior or deceptive food products,[62] or of firearms; [63] or it may make paper money legal tender, regardless of incidental damage or loss.[64] It can subject property to rent control in time of war, even affecting rights previously acquired.[65] Any limitation on freedom of activity or any deprivation of property, such as are involved when citizens are denied the right to engage in the arms industry, are also safely within the permissible area of substantive due process.

The limitations on the rights and activities of private persons which an arms control plan would entail are, therefore, no more extensive than those resulting from established and accepted forms of federal regulation. We have mentioned narcotics, liquor, and others. A word should be said about atomic energy. Without the sturdy support of an underlying treaty, without explicit limitation to interstate and foreign commerce, the Atomic Energy Act of 1946, even as revised in 1954,[66] established a virtual monopoly on all products, activities, and information relating to atomic energy. Private persons and industry are excluded, and admitted only by grace of the Atomic Energy Commission. While the constitutionality of various features of the Atomic Energy Act has not been adjudicated, it may be expected that the key provisions of the act will survive any attack on constitutional grounds. In addition to aspects which are or can be related to commerce, interstate or foreign, the entire act in its conception would probably be upheld as an exercise of the powers of Congress and the President loosely known as the "war powers," extended to include provisions necessary in the national defense, even when the United States is not at war.

An arms control treaty, including effective regulation of nuclear weapons, would probably require for its implementation legislative provisions prohibiting and limiting private rights and activities which

Arms Control and the Constitution

are similar to some of those already adopted—in another context—in the Atomic Energy Act. And—even apart from the power to implement a treaty—the power to legislate in the national defense would seem broad enough to cover legislation which seeks the defense of the nation through disarmament rather than through armament.[67]

In some instances, it may be suggested, whether there is due process may depend on whether the person suffering a loss as a result of governmental action is compensated.[68] If he is paid, he is being afforded due process of law; or—it may perhaps be put differently—he is not being deprived of any property. In the instances of federal and state regulation cited, there was no requirement that the person be compensated in order to make the governmental action valid. Similarly, that there is a financial loss to those who are engaged or wish to be engaged in the arms business or who own patents in armaments which would be rendered worthless does not deprive them of property without due process of law. Where the federal government has constitutional authority to forbid or regulate activities, incidental loss to individuals or industry does not vitiate the regulation or create any obligation for the federal government to compensate for such regulation. Police power aspects of valid federal activity, like similar action by the states within their spheres, frequently cannot avoid financial loss to some segments of the community, and the Constitution does not require that such loss be avoided or compensated.

PUBLIC TAKING. A related but distinct question is raised under the final clause of the Fifth Amendment, which requires that private property shall not be taken for public use without just compensation. In concept, at least, there is a distinction between the requirement of compensation for property taken for public use and the above suggestion that in certain cases compensation may be necessary in order to render "due process of law" to someone being deprived of a property right by government regulation. This distinction is frequently obliterated. In regard to state action, indeed, both conceptions are deemed to be included in the same phrase "due process of law." As regards the national government, the explicit provision for compensation in the final clause of the Fifth Amendment requires that there be a "taking" of "property" and that it be for a "public use." A taking of property for a use which is not public does not fall within this requirement of compensation but would presumably be forbidden as depriving the owner of the property without due process of law.[69] If there is no "taking" of "property" there is no constitutional obligation to compensate,[70] and there will be no recovery against the United States under the legislation which confers jurisdiction on the Court of Claims to render judgment against the United States upon a claim "founded upon the Constitution." [71]

In regard to the treaty power, it may be suggested that in situations like *Ware v. Hylton,* while the treaty may be valid and binding internationally, it constitutes a taking of the property of the individual for a public use—the national interest furthered by the treaty—and that such a taking requires compensation.[72] In a case of that sort a court might entertain suit against the United States as being based on a "claim founded upon the Constitution." In regard to the arms control plan, however, this suggestion would probably remain largely irrelevant. Of course, if the control agreement required requisition of atomic materials, or metals and ores, there would be a taking requiring compensation.[73] But any financial loss to persons engaged in the manufacture of or commerce in armaments, or to those owning patents rendered valueless, is an incident of proper federal regulation. It is not, we have said, a deprivation of property without due process; it would not seem a "taking" for a "public use" either. This would hardly seem to be an instance where "regulation" goes so far as to become a "taking." If, in implementation of an arms control plan, Congress should require existing stocks of arms or materials to be destroyed or confiscated by the federal authorities, there might still be no taking of property for a public use; it might resemble, rather, the destruction or confiscation of other forbidden products or contraband. If a state does not have to compensate for cedar trees cut down, for confiscating liquor legally distilled, now illegal to possess; if the United States need not compensate for food products confiscated because their shipment is in violation of law, or for property destroyed by the United States Army to keep the enemy from using it,[74] one might say that there need be no compensation for arms rendered illegal and confiscated under treaty and legislation. Perhaps as to stocks of arms and materials legally manufactured or possessed prior to the treaty or legislation, it might be argued that such property is being taken in the public interest of achieving disarmament and is therefore being taken for a "public use"; and that it should therefore be paid for, thus spreading the financial burden of the introduction of the disarmament plan to the community as a whole. In practice, of course, the question may be academic since an arms control scheme is likely to be introduced gradually and in stages so that existing stocks would probably not be affected. And it is unlikely that many of the armaments covered will be owned by private persons. In any event, if there should be some small

Arms Control and the Constitution

group entitled to claim compensation, that will not affect the validity of the arms plan. The compensation will be minimal; whatever it is, it will only be a small financial element for the United States in the arms control plan—a light burden indeed for the nation now bearing the heavy weight of the costs of weapons.

PATENT RIGHTS

The Constitution confers upon Congress the power "to promote the Progress of Science and useful Arts, by securing for limited Times to Authors and Inventors, the exclusive Right to their respective Writings and Discoveries." Under this provision Congress has promulgated the patent laws.[75] Nothing in this provision, however, entitles an inventor to a patent for an invention which has been rendered unlawful under a valid act of Congress or a valid treaty.[76] And the patent system has been largely superseded in the atomic energy field by a special system, the Atomic Energy Act providing a different kind of financial protection for inventors in that area.[77]

RESEARCH AND ACADEMIC FREEDOM

It is not inconceivable that a control agreement may prohibit or regulate specified scientific research—*e.g.,* the development of, or experimentation in, biological or chemical warfare, or nuclear or missile studies relating to war. No serious issues are raised if these are forbidden to the United States Government. To bar them to private scientists suggests issues under the due process clause and perhaps under the First Amendment.

Academic and intellectual freedom received, in 1957, emphatic recognition in the Supreme Court, as liberties protected by the due process clause of the Fourteenth Amendment against state infringement.[78] Undoubtedly, then, it would be held to be one of the liberties protected also against infringement by the federal government. Nevertheless, like other freedoms to act, there can be little doubt that the research in question can be barred "for reasons that are exigent and obviously compelling," [79] by proper treaty or act of Congress to eliminate or regulate the study of war. Precedent already exists in the Atomic Energy Acts for the regulation of research, for requiring disclosure of the fruits of research, and for permitting their appropriation by the federal government.[80]

Above are constitutional issues suggested by arms control. Most of them are small, and their importance may indeed be exaggerated by treatment even as brief as that given to them. None of the issues is a serious obstacle to foreseeable plans for the control of arms. It would appear, in fact, that such control is less novel in concept, more familiar in practice, than might have been believed.

Other specific elements in an arms control plan may raise more unusual and more troublesome constitutional questions. In the next chapter we shall deal with the constitutional problems raised by international inspection and other forms of verification to assure that this nation—like Russia in return—is complying with the limitations of the control agreement.

Chapter IV. INVESTIGATION OF COMPLIANCE WITH ARMS CONTROL

The key to the future control of armaments may lie in inspection: there must be investigation and "verification"; there must be ways to satisfy nations that other nations are living up to agreed limitations. This was not a serious problem in earlier efforts to disarm. Before the First World War, and even after, the "politesse" of relations between nations seemed to require at least the pretence that they, like gentlemen, could of course be trusted to keep their agreements. Perhaps there were other reasons: perhaps animosities and fears between principal nations were less acute; perhaps wars were still an extension of international politics not an unspeakable threat of world destruction; perhaps an illegal battleship or weapon was less terrifying, or more difficult to keep secret. Or, perhaps nations were naive, trusting.

Since the Second World War all that has changed. Today we have new, awesome weapons; new methods of concealment; and a distrust of the Soviet Union in a degree also new in contemporary international relations, at least in its avowedness. The United States, if not others, will not agree to disarm unless it can be satisfied that violations by the Soviet Union will be quickly detected. No verification, no disarmament. In fact, recent efforts have been directed to verification without disarmament, or with very little. Agreement, for example, to stop nuclear tests, with inspection to insure compliance, may be desirable but will not itself disarm anyone. The Eisenhower plan for exchange of military blueprints and aerial inspection, for another example, as well as the 1958 proposal for international inspections in the Arctic, involved no limitations on arms; they provided for inspection, but only to give each nation some knowledge as to what the other was doing with its armies and its arms.

The changes in relations, in the character of war and the character of armaments, have stimulated also the search for new methods of detection. Science and technology have provided new weapons, new methods for creating those weapons, and new methods for concealing them as well as their manufacture; science and technology can perhaps, in return, develop methods for penetrating these wraps, for probing recesses, for detecting what would be carefully hidden. Perhaps new devices will revolutionize the art of detection. Perhaps methods have already been suggested which would reveal what one needs to know in supervising an arms control system with only limited direct inspection, as it is normally conceived, by a corps of persons visiting installations to make on-the-spot investigation.[1]

On the basis of what is known of the plans and proposals of negotiating nations, however, this study has assumed a control plan that includes provisions for investigation by various means, among them direct inspection, probably by international or foreign officials. Columbia's Inspection Study and others suggest that verification might include: air reconnaissance to locate large installations, transportation systems, and the concentration or movement of troops; the establishment of monitoring stations with acoustic or seismic instruments to detect tests and other explosions; control of critical "bottleneck" components and check points, by requiring, for example, reports on the manufacture of precision instruments and on rare metals of use in missile production, and ground inspection to check on the veracity of these reports; registration and reporting by, and interrogation of, scientists; checks on hospitals and doctors to uncover injuries, *e.g.*, from radiation, due to clandestine illegal activity. Constitutional issues may be suggested by the method of inspection or verification; in some instances, perhaps, the foreign character of the inspecting personnel may also raise some question.

Let us consider some of the proposed forms of verification and examine them in turn. We begin with those that raise fewer questions under the law.

INDIRECT METHODS OF INVESTIGATION

VOLUNTARY REPORTS BY GOVERNMENTS. Some measure of verification may be obtained by a provision requiring governments to report voluntarily on their compliance.[2] The reports may be required to provide details and specifications: for example, how many men are under arms, where they are stationed, the size of the defense budget and its breakdown, details on industrial activity—including the production or use of

Investigation of Compliance

rare metals, precision instruments, and strategic items—the activities of key scientific personnel, hospital cases of radiation injuries.

To the extent that a nation's word can be trusted, these reports will indicate whether the nation is complying. If the proper questions are asked, indeed, the answers themselves may reveal to experts whether they are truthful; they may disclose other information as well, far more than the reporting country may mean to divulge. Such reports, together with statistical information which nations prepare for their own use and which cannot be easily falsified, may give examining experts at the headquarters of an international body strong evidence as to whether a nation is or is not complying with the limitations of the agreement.[3]

So long as we speak only of reports by governments, such submissions, and the requirement in a treaty that they be submitted, present no serious constitutional problems for the United States. Nothing in the Constitution requires secrecy on any aspect of governmental activity; nothing in the Constitution prevents the Executive from collecting and collating data of the kind in question and making it public or reporting it to anyone, including a foreign government or an international body. Of course, such reporting may be inconsistent with requirements of secrecy in the laws; these laws, however, can be repealed and would be willingly repealed, we have assumed, by the provisions in the treaty or any implementing legislation which Congress will adopt.[4]

Neither are there major difficulties when, in order for the United States to make the necessary reports to an international or foreign body, the Government of the United States requires reports in turn from its own citizens. As we shall see, the right to require returns and reports from those participating in industries regulated by the federal government has, in general, been upheld in the face of challenge that such requirements constitute deprivations of property or liberty without due process of law; or that they violate the constitutional privilege against self-incrimination; or that they infringe "the right of the people to be secure in their . . . papers, and effects, against unreasonable searches and seizures."[5] There would seem, therefore, no difficulty in having the United States require reports and returns from persons engaged in activities related to the production of armaments which Congress regulates in implementation of a disarmament treaty. The obligations of the United States under such a treaty confer upon Congress the duty as well as the power to pass necessary legislation to implement it. Such implementation may validly require from owners of uranium mines, for example, reports on the production of their mines; from owners of steel mills, information on their production, their customers, and the amounts sold to them; from manufacturers of designated armaments, reports on the amounts of arms produced and on their disposition. Probably, the United States could require scientists to disclose any research relevant to an arms control agreement, and doctors and hospitals to report any cases which might indicate radiation or unlawful contact with regulated materials.[6] And the United States Government can transmit such information required from its citizens to an international body.

EXTERNAL VERIFICATION. We then approach forms of active verification by inspectors, independent of or in implementation of submissions by authorities of the host government. Again, there are some inspection arrangements—unfortunately, probably the less effective ones—which do not suggest difficulties under the Constitution and our laws. Thus, what we may call external verification. To the extent that inspectors placed in other countries or on the high seas or in the air (not over United States territory) can by radar, seismic, or acoustic instruments, or other existing or to-be-developed devices detect the flying of planes, the explosion of bombs, the presence of other activities or conditions which violate the limitations in an arms control agreement, these are outside the orbit of the United States and outside the control of the Constitution. Such activities can be carried on by international inspectors, and the United States can agree that they should be carried on without being troubled constitutionally.

Similarly, the United States can permit inspectors in this country, or in areas under United States jurisdiction, to engage in such detection of activities going on here or in other countries. The admission of inspectors to United States territory, their privileges and immunities, and the terms of their stay will be discussed later as provisions which would have to be made under United States law. They do not, however, raise important problems under the Constitution.

AERIAL INSPECTION. Some other forms of inspection, though taking place in or over United States territory, will also raise no constitutional problems and may be quickly dismissed here. Thus, for example, the proposal of President Eisenhower in 1955—already mentioned—that the United States and Russia exchange blueprints of military installations and facilities and permit aerial inspection by the other side.[7] The Inspection Study also suggests aerial reconnaissance as effective for

Investigation of Compliance 51

limited purposes. There is nothing in the Constitution, we have said, which would bar the United States from agreeing to give, and actually giving, to a foreign power information including maps, sketches, and statistics about its armies and armaments. Neither is there any constitutional obstacle to agreement on the part of the United States that Soviet planes may fly over American territory and take photographs of our installations. Again, amendment of existing laws may be involved.

Neither the states nor private persons could interpose substantial constitutional objection to aerial inspection. States have asserted "sovereignty" in the air space over their territories, but this "sovereignty" is surely no greater than that which they assert over the land within the state; both are subject to the paramount "sovereignty" and powers of the national government.[8] The United States asserts its superior national interests in the air in many forms, in defense measures, in military uses, in the regulation of commercial aviation; there can be no serious claim that the United States cannot permit international air inspection over state territory as part of an armaments control plan agreed to by treaty.

The private person over whose territory inspectors may fly also, generally, has no basis for asserting that he is being deprived of his property without due process of law. Despite ancient maxims, a person owning property does not "own" it to the sky.[9] His rights are in no way violated, his property is not taken, by commercial or military flights authorized by the United States, and they would not be by flights for aerial inspection under an arms control agreement either. In a rare case, perhaps a question of "public taking" may arise. Inspectors may require the right to fly frequently and quite low over particular property. If damage is done to the property by such overflight, or if the use of the property is seriously limited thereby, there may be a taking of property for a public use for which the owner would be entitled to compensation.[10]

WIRE TAPPING. An arms control proposal might contemplate that inspectors would employ various mechanical devices, including "wire tapping," for detecting from the outside activities and conversations taking place inside a building or room. Domestically, in the past, these methods have suggested issues of "search and seizure" under the Fourth Amendment. But since, both in practice and in law, these intrusions are considered different from physical entry onto premises, it appears convenient to deal with this suggestion here.

Wire tapping has been called a "dirty business."[11] That practice, and the divulgence to anyone of material garnered from wire tapping, are at present forbidden by federal statute, and—with some exceptions—by state statutes.[12] The Supreme Court, however, has held that tapping wires is not a search or seizure within the Fourth Amendment,[13] and so long as that remains the law, the United States could provide by treaty or statute that international inspectors may tap wires. It is a different question whether this is necessary or desirable, even to obtain similar rights for international inspectors in other countries.

REGISTRATION OF SCIENTISTS. It may be proposed, as one element in a thorough control plan, to require all persons with a certain level of scientific achievement or training to register and to report their whereabouts and their "whatabouts" at regular intervals. Does it violate the liberty of the scientist to require him to report on his activities, especially when other Americans are not so required?

We are without clear precedent or authority. Some areas of the problem may be carved out for answer with greater certainty. The United States, for example, could agree to report on the activities of all the scientists which it employs. Similarly, regulated industries could probably be required to report on personnel engaged by them in research. The United States might also require all persons who make scientific discoveries related to arms or arms control to report and make them available to the United States, although if these discoveries were to be used it might have to pay for them as a "taking" of property by eminent domain.[14]

The core of the question—whether it is possible to require individual citizens, merely because of their past education, activities, and skills, to inform the United States, or through the United States an international body, where they are and what they are doing—is subject to argument. On the one hand, it may be said that it is a valid provision in a treaty for a legitimate national and international end, particularly since it violates no explicit provision of the Constitution. That scientists only would be required to register might well be a reasonable classification, since their activities are pertinent to the control of armaments, which is a legitimate concern under the treaty power. The United States has in at least one instance required the registration of persons merely on the basis of their qualifications and training—those who had had training in espionage by a foreign government.[15] On the other hand, it may be argued that the registration of scientists would run counter to the "liberty" of the scientist and that substantive due process of law, and the concept of the equal protection of the laws which it may contain, are

Investigation of Compliance

not satisfied.[16] Those trained in espionage might be distinguished as a special group, with a special, potentially hostile skill not having a legitimate use. The registration of aliens [17] and foreign agents and propagandists [18] could also be distinguished, and registration for Selective Service, applicable to citizens generally, presents different issues.[19] On balance, one might guess that a provision for such registration, in a treaty, or in legislation implementing a treaty, would probably be upheld. But persons engaged in scientific activity which had been rendered illegal could probably not be compelled to report that fact in view of the privilege against self-incrimination.[20] We shall discuss that privilege conferred by the Fifth Amendment in greater detail later.

DIRECT INSPECTION AND INTERROGATION

The previous section dealt with some methods of verifying whether a nation is complying with its arms control undertakings. They were, for the most part, indirect methods impinging little on the activities of governments and private individuals and raising few difficult legal problems. Direct inspection and personal interrogation, which we shall now consider, have figured prominently in government proposals as essential to any system of substantial arms control.[21] Presumably, they will continue to do so, unless other effective indirect methods are developed and made known. But they suggest a number of important issues under the Constitution.

A special situation is created by the fact that the inspectors might be foreign personnel. Of course, some problems could be eliminated if the direct policing, the inspections, and the interrogations could be left to United States officials. International or foreign officials might learn enough to satisfy themselves from general forms of investigation not involving the exercise of authority over private places and persons. Or they might be present to observe while national officials inspect or interrogate—a plan of cooperative inspection like that contemplated for the EURATOM power program to assure the United States that the nuclear materials it supplies are not being diverted to military use. Documents, records, books, and papers might be obtained for international officials by officers of the United States through established procedures. If the international officials were not content with the action of national officials, and their complaints went unheeded, they might assume that something was being hidden and act accordingly.

The use of established national channels would avoid problems, political as well as legal, in the United States; it might not, however, be feasible internationally. Negotiations have been in terms of direct inspection and interrogation by foreign officials, or by representatives of an international body, which seems more likely and more acceptable. This is what the United States apparently contemplates for assuring Soviet compliance; it is what the United States, then, would have to accept in turn. The questions raised by the foreign character of the inspectorate should thus be examined.

We shall consider the constitutional problems raised by an inspection system which, as it applies in the United States, might have the following features:

(*a*) A corps of international personnel is admitted to the United States to carry out inspection to assure that the United States is complying with the prohibitions established in the arms control treaty.

(*b*) These inspectors may freely enter government installations, perhaps including offices engaged in military and foreign affairs, examine relevant documents, and count and account for equipment and materials.

(*c*) The inspectors may interrogate government officials (civilian or military) and request that they produce relevant documents and records.

(*d*) They may subpoena and interrogate persons engaged in activities related to armaments, or other persons suspected of activity unlawful under the control plan, and require them to answer appropriate questions.

(*e*) They may require reports and returns from private citizens and corporations engaged in activities related to the manufacture of armaments.

(*f*) They may require such persons or corporations to keep books, records and accounts in prescribed form.

(*g*) They may come to factories, industrial or commercial establishments dealing in equipment or materials covered by or relevant to the control agreement and inspect in any detail necessary the processes and fruits of production.

(*h*) Inspectors may come to such place of business or manufacture and examine the books, records and accounts required to be kept at all reasonable times (or at any time). Inspectors may also be permanently stationed in some establishments.

(*i*) They may inspect at any time other industrial or business establishments not ostensibly dealing in arms or regulated materials but

Investigation of Compliance 55

suspected of manufacturing or other activities forbidden by the control agreement.

(*j*) They may inspect all planes [vessels, trains, or other means of transport], military or civilian, national or foreign, entering or leaving the country or traveling within the United States, as well as receive and examine flight plans for all such planes.

(*k*) They may require reports from hospitals and doctors, inspect hospitals and hospital records, and interrogate doctors for evidence of radiation or similar cases which might indicate activity violating arms control.

(*l*) They may interrogate scientists and inspect laboratories.

What problems do these elements create? Can the difficulties they raise be mitigated?

THE INTERNATIONAL CHARACTER OF THE INSPECTORATE

Inspection and interrogation suggest a number of constitutional issues, if they are carried out by federal officials under authority of federal law; do these apply as well to foreign or international officials? While the Bill of Rights and other constitutional provisions regulate the actions of federal officials—not of private persons—it would seem that the constitutional limitations apply to all who act pursuant to federal authority. If foreign or international officials inspect in the United States pursuant to authorization and consent by the United States, these activities are presumably subject to the same constitutional limitations as if they were executed by federal officials. The United States cannot confer on foreign officials authority to do what the United States could not do through its own officers.[22]

On the other hand, that the activities under discussion would be executed by non–United States personnel suggests possible additional issues under the Constitution. The seriousness of the difficulty might differ with the function exercised, but we shall first consider, in general, grounds on which the non–United States character of the inspectorate might make a difference. Can the United States, under the Constitution, agree to confer the functions we are discussing on foreign officials? Assuming that the authorization of the particular interrogation or investigation is a valid exercise of the treaty power and does not violate any specific provisions in the Bill of Rights, can international or foreign officials perhaps be considered as agents of the United States? They would be acting pursuant to federal authorization under the treaty power, just as federal officials act under authorization by Congress pursuant to statute. Does it matter that international officials are not in fact United States officials, that they are not employed and paid and controlled by the Executive Branch pursuant to legislative authority, that they do not take an oath to support the Constitution? In regard to the functions we are considering, these would not seem to make a constitutional difference. In contexts other than arms control, whatever may be true for officials of a character for which the Constitution requires presidential appointment and Senate confirmation, inspectors and police officials acting under authority of the United States, and others authorized to issue subpoenas or administer oaths, probably need not be regularly constituted officials of the United States and need not meet the constitutional requirements for officers of the United States.[23] There would, therefore, seem to be no special problems of "delegation," and one could view these persons as *ad hoc* federal personnel. There would seem to be no strong basis for doubt, for example, that international officials may be authorized to require testimony. Since by law or by treaty the testimony of Americans, official or private, can be compelled, in appropriate situations, there would seem no fundamental "due process" objection to requiring that such testimony be given in the presence of international officials or even in their exclusive presence where this would be necessary to implement the effective operation of an arms control treaty. And there would seem to be no objection to allowing the international inspecting body to issue subpoenas enforceable by criminal penalties in United States courts. True, it would be the international inspectors who decided, in the first instance at least, who should be interrogated and on what subjects relevant to the arms control plan; and if a witness refused to answer or answered falsely, he would be subject to contempt proceedings or criminal conviction in the federal courts. Nevertheless, whatever "delegation" to the international officials this involves would appear to be minor, and does not do violence to accepted principles and standards.

There seems to have been little question in the past about conferring on admittedly foreign or international personnel at least some of the functions with which we are here concerned. Although precedents are few, the United States has had some experience with international and foreign officials acting within this country, using American courts and processes to enable them to perform their tasks effectively. Thus, the United States–Canadian International Joint Commission, under a treaty

Investigation of Compliance 57

with Canada as implemented by Congress, is authorized to administer oaths and take evidence in the United States in proceedings within the commission's jurisdiction.[24] Further, by application to the United States court in the district within which the commission is sitting, the commission may compel the attendance of witnesses and the production of evidence, and the courts are directed to make all necessary and proper orders to insure compliance. Failure to comply is deemed contempt of court for which penalties may be imposed.[25]

Later Congress passed legislation giving even broader authority to administer oaths to any international tribunal or commission considering a claim in which the United States or any of its nationals is interested, and making perjury under such oaths punishable in the same manner as perjury before American courts.[26] The act permits such tribunals and commissions also to require the attendance of witnesses and the production of evidence by direct subpoena, without invoking the aid of a United States court. Such subpoenas may be signed by any member of the tribunal and served by a United States marshal. Failure to comply with the subpoena is rendered contempt of the tribunal, punishable in the courts of the United States in the same manner as contempt of these courts.

There is also precedent for lending the aid of the courts of the United States not merely to international bodies of which the United States is a member but to officials of foreign governments. For many years foreign consuls have enjoyed the right to call upon the courts and officials of the United States for assistance in arresting, interrogating, and imprisoning persons subject to their jurisdiction under the laws of their country and consistent with treaties and international law.[27] In order to enable the Allies of the United States to maintain discipline over their forces in this country, the Service Courts of Friendly Foreign Forces Act of 1944[28] authorized federal district courts to issue orders for the subpoena of witnesses—presumably even American citizens—to appear in trials before these foreign service courts. The act also makes persons subject to United States jurisdiction liable to fine and imprisonment if convicted by a United States court for contempt of, or perjury before, the foreign service court.

There is authority, therefore, for provisions which would allow an international inspecting body to subpoena witnesses or to have them subpoenaed by a United States agent or tribunal and to administer oaths to witnesses and interrogate them. There is precedent also for contempt or perjury penalties in United States courts for refusal by witnesses to testify or present evidence before the international inspection body, or for testifying falsely before such body. So long as the United States is intent on carrying out its commitments under an arms control plan, and the judges of the United States comply with their oath to uphold the laws of the United States, which include this plan, these procedures should be effective to give the inspectors the information they require.

In the system we assume, as in the precedents cited, enforcement of the interrogation and inspection functions would be lodged in the federal courts. Whether the United States could agree to the establishment of international tribunals giving them direct contempt and perjury jurisdiction over recalcitrant American citizens refusing to cooperate with the inspecting body is not dealt with here. Such a proposal seems unnecessary; it is hardly likely to be adopted. We shall, however, treat some of the questions it raises in a later chapter dealing with proposals to establish international tribunals for various purposes related to arms control.

DIRECT INVESTIGATION OF GOVERNMENTAL ACTIVITIES

The problems of direct inspection may be divided for purposes of analysis into two general categories: those which pertain to inspection of activities of the United States Government, its departments and officials, and those which deal with inspection of corporations and individuals in private activity in the United States. We deal first with inspection of government installations; inspection of private establishments requires and will receive extended consideration later in the chapter. The activities of states suggest special difficulties which will be briefly noted.

INSPECTION OF FEDERAL INSTALLATIONS AND DOCUMENTS. If governments should some day arrive at such agreement as we are assuming, the right of international inspectors to come to government offices and inspect documents which now are generally classified, to enter military and other federal establishments and examine equipment and papers will raise numerous practical difficulties. If not handled intelligently, the process of inspection could irritate and exacerbate relations and threaten the effectiveness of the inspection system. Indeed, it may be difficult to imagine the climate in which such practices would be acceptable; it would in fact require major adjustments to shed habits and attitudes based on the need for secrecy. So far as the law is concerned, however, direct inspection of this sort would create no problem which could not be disposed of by legislation and executive order. We repeat: nothing in the Constitution requires the United States to maintain secrecy against anybody, including foreign governments and international bodies. The constitutional separateness and independence of the President permits him to maintain the privacy of the Executive Branch vis-à-vis Congress,[29] but the Constitution does not require the secrecy of executive departments if the President agrees to bargain it away by treaty. The privacy of congressional premises and documents can also be abolished if Congress agrees.[30] Secrecy concerning governmental installations whose inspection will be necessary and significant—the depots and arsenals, atomic energy plants, perhaps power and related facilities like those of the Tennessee Valley Authority and other authorities—would raise fewer political difficulties and no legal ones. The Constitution does not stand in the way.

INTERROGATION OF UNITED STATES OFFICIALS. Suppose the inspectors are authorized by the treaty to interrogate military or civilian officials of the United States engaged in activities related to armaments. Could these officials be required to testify?

Clearly the United States could require federal officers or former officers to testify about their official activities. Again, the privacy of the Executive Branch is not in issue when the President has agreed to such interrogations pursuant to an arms control treaty. Similarly, if by statute pursuant to treaty the Congress has given consent, there is no constitutional immunity from subpoena available to members of Congress or employees of the Congress. Members of both Executive and Legislative Branches could then be compelled to appear and produce official documents before an international body. As to his nonofficial activities, the officer, executive or legislative, is like any other citizen, whose rights are discussed later in this chapter.

Of course, like the citizen, the official also enjoys the constitutional privilege not to testify against himself. That a federal officer is being asked about his official activities, present or past, does not deprive him of the privilege against self-incrimination, if his replies might incriminate him under federal law.[31] His private papers also may be withheld on this ground, as in the case of any other citizen. But official documents in the possession of a United States officer are not his, and he may not refuse to give them up even if they should contain matter which would incriminate him.[32]

In the case of the official, it may be particularly important to surmount this privilege in the Fifth Amendment, so as not to frustrate international inspection of governmental activities. One approach, that of the immunity statute, is discussed in relation to the privilege of citizens generally.[33]

STATE ENTERPRISES AND ACTIVITIES. Issues of a different order are raised if it be desired that international officials also scrutinize the activities of the states and state officials. In an earlier chapter we concluded that arms control by the United States would preclude inconsistent activities by the states themselves: *e.g.*, a state could not engage in the manufacture of arms or possess materials in violation of a treaty.[34] If such activities may be forbidden or regulated, there would seem to be no constitutional objection to subjecting them to inspection. The states do not have the same right as persons to protection against search and seizure or "self-incrimination," which we shall consider as to private persons and corporations; the basis for state objection would be intrusion on its sovereignty, and this objection falls before the Supremacy Clause, as to activities which may be subjected to federal regulation.

Suppose the international agreement, however, should provide further for inspection trenching on the "governmental activities" of the states. May the United States agree by treaty that international inspectors can penetrate freely into state governmental establishments, examine their activities and their documents, demand reports, and interrogate state officials about their official functions? Is the supremacy of the United States in all matters relating to international affairs and the conduct of war and peace paramount to the sovereignty and the privacy of state governments?

The issue may appear largely imaginative. And yet, if only federal governmental processes, premises, and documents were included in an inspection scheme, it might be argued by those who mistrust the United States that if this country wished to violate the scheme, it could hide behind the governmental machinery of the states. Certainly, the United States would not accept it lightly if, in the Soviet Union, while international inspectors could scrutinize activities in the Kremlin, activities in Kiev or Ashkabad or Petrazovodsk were immunized from scrutiny by an assertion of the sovereign independence and inviolability of governmental activities of the republics constituting the USSR.

To the constitutional question, no authoritative answer can be given. The powers of the national government, supreme to those of the states,

Investigation of Compliance

have not in the past been exercised so as to intrude into the workings of the state governments.[35] If this issue should become importantly relevant to arms control it might be necessary to obtain the consent of key states or to consider a constitutional amendment.

DIRECT INVESTIGATION OF PRIVATE ACTIVITIES

Effective international scrutiny of arms control compliance must take into account also activities in installations and establishments not belonging to the government, of individuals who are private citizens rather than government officials. While, as we have suggested, private violations would be unlikely and would not be important, it would be important to assure that private persons and corporations were not acting in collusion with the government to circumvent the control agreement. And private persons might have information of violations by governments which international inspectors should be able to obtain. Direct investigation of private activities, then, is a key feature of arms inspection. It also raises the most difficult constitutional issues.

INTERROGATION OF PRIVATE PERSONS. The international inspectorate might wish to interrogate not only officials of government, but also persons in key industries, or other possible witnesses. Mill owners and scientists, doctors and mine foremen might all have information concerning arms or armament materials in which the inspectors might have proper interest under the control agreement. The authority of the United States to require private persons to give testimony in an appropriate inquiry is not subject to doubt. And, we have concluded, Congress, pursuant to treaty, could agree that the inspecting body, even if international in character, may issue or obtain subpoenas for testimony and documents, administer oaths, and request American citizens and residents to testify or produce papers before it.

The Privilege Against Self-Incrimination. The issues raised by interrogation are principally those of the privilege against self-incrimination. The Fifth Amendment provides, *inter alia,* that no person "shall be compelled in any criminal case to be a witness against himself." It is now established that the right to refuse to give evidence which might incriminate him is not limited to "any criminal case," but applies to any official interrogation under federal auspices.[36] It is a privilege available not only to one who believes he has actually been guilty of a crime, but even to the innocent who may wish to avoid possible prosecution for a crime.[37]

If by treaty and statute certain activities in regard to armaments are forbidden, answers to interrogations by inspectors might in given circumstances be testimony "incriminating" under United States law. And the privilege against self-incrimination in the Fifth Amendment limits compulsion of such testimony by the federal government.[38] In our context, while it would not be a federal body which issues the subpoena, or which receives the testimony, the international officials requiring it would, we have assumed, have behind them the compulsion of federal contempt or criminal process. As the treaty power and the implementing legislation are subject to the limitations of the Fifth Amendment, testimony before international inspectors, if compelled by federal law and federal authority, would be subject to the limitation of the self-incrimination clause.

If, then, the testimony of a witness might reveal evidence of a crime —whether the crime of violating the arms control agreement or another federal offense—he may refuse to testify. Particularly in the case of the government official, a refusal to testify might frustrate the legitimate inquiry of the inspectors. They may conclude that the witness is hiding something, though, since the privilege is available to innocent persons as well, the conclusion may not necessarily be warranted. In any event, international interrogation would be more effective if the witness could be compelled to testify. This could be achieved by an immunity statute. The Supreme Court has held, recently again, that the privilege against self-incrimination is not a privilege to refuse to give testimony required by law but only an exemption from prosecution for crimes which such compelled testimony reveals. Congress can therefore require the testimony to be given if it provides by law that the witness shall be exempt from prosecution for crimes revealed.[39] This would not be a new departure, for in numerous instances in the past Congress has determined that eliciting information may be of greater value than prosecuting malfeasance, and has conferred authority to grant an immunity from prosecution to obtain this information.[40] The Supreme Court has held such statutes valid so long as the immunity granted effectively protects the witness from prosecution.[41]

In our situation, prosecution of individuals for violation of the arms control agreement is hardly the primary purpose of inspection. On the other hand, obtaining information regarding violations is very much the purpose of the interrogation. An immunity statute would seem particularly well suited for an arms control plan. If the Fifth Amendment is neutralized through such a statute, the individual who violates the arms control law may be immune to prosecution, but the information will be available to the inspectors, and the world will know.

It is hardly necessary to add here that international inspectors could not use physical force to coerce testimony. This would, in the crudest form, compel an individual "to be a witness against himself"; even if the testimony sought were not "against himself" it would deny him due process of law.[42] If a person whom the international inspectors interrogated remained recalcitrant, he would be subject to contempt proceedings or criminal penalties. The inspectors and the rest of the world might deduce what they wished from the silence of a witness; they might also try to find out from other sources what the witness might be hiding; but there could be no physical coercion to compel the witness to talk.

Procedural Due Process. Interrogation by international officials, whether of United States officers or private persons, would have to conform to the principles of fairness implied in procedural due process. It is difficult to define what constitutes "fairness." And wherever there are lines of degree to be drawn in the application of a standard difficult to make definite, men may differ on where the line must fall in particular circumstances; "recognition of differences of degree is inherent in due regard for due process."[43] There may be nice questions—*e.g.,* whether interrogation may be in secret—but the general limits of "fairness" are plain enough, and in the majority of instances there would be agreement on cases of unfairness even short of physical force.

One possible claim of due process deserves mention. A witness may wish to be accompanied by counsel at an interrogation by international officials. He would probably get little help from the Sixth Amendment, which requires that "in all criminal prosecutions, the accused shall enjoy the right . . . to have the Assistance of Counsel for his defense." This guaranteed right to counsel, it has been held to date, applies only in criminal proceedings, and there it does not arise until after indictment or arraignment; it cannot be demanded, for instance, in preliminary investigations or before a grand jury.[44] But whether in other circumstances a person can insist on counsel as a matter of fairness and due process cannot be answered with any confidence.[45] Even if, as we assume, in this context the international interrogator must afford whatever rights could be demanded of federal officials, there appears to be no precedent requiring counsel under the Fifth Amendment where the Sixth Amendment does not demand it.

In *In re Groban*,[46] involving state government, the Supreme Court held that the due process requirement in the Fourteenth Amendment does not entitle a person under interrogation by a local fire commissioner to the right to insist on counsel. Four justices dissented. Of the majority of five, Mr. Justice Frankfurter, in a concurring opinion joined by Mr. Justice Harlan, stressed the "non-prosecutorial" character of the inquiry in the case. He said:

What has been said disposes of the suggestion that, because this statute relating to a general administrative, non-prosecutorial inquiry into the causes of fire is sustained, it would follow that secret inquisitorial powers given to a District Attorney would also have to be sustained. The Due Process Clause does not disregard vital differences.[47]

The international proceedings we are considering have some of the characteristics of police proceedings, if not a "prosecutorial" character; the privilege against self-incrimination is involved, and the guidance of counsel as to its intricacies may be more important where the investigators are international officials rather than American.[48] Would these add up to "vital differences" leading to an opposite result? There is no confident answer.

INSPECTION OF PRIVATE PROPERTY AND RECORDS. Under our hypothetical inspection system, major efforts of arms inspectors may be concentrated not only on public but also on private installations in the United States. If they were supervising "ceilings" only, they might wish to inspect factories where arms and other materials were made or stored. If there were absolute prohibitions, on the other hand, they might wish to investigate any installation where they suspected that a prohibited activity or article might be discovered. Objections to inspection of factories and depots, and of required books and records, may be anticipated on the grounds, possibly of due process, principally of the Fourth Amendment. As to records, there may also be questions involving the privilege against self-incrimination.

The Fourth Amendment provides:

The right of the people to be secure in their persons, houses, papers, and effects, against unreasonable searches and seizures, shall not be violated, and no Warrants shall issue, but upon probable cause, supported by Oath or affirmation, and particularly describing the place to be searched, and the persons or things to be seized.

This amendment has been frequently invoked and in many instances the rights claimed under it were vindicated in the courts. Its scope and sig-

Investigation of Compliance 65

nificance have been etched by the Supreme Court of the United States, but not always in a clear and unwavering pattern, and frequently over sharp and continuing dissent.[49] Two propositions, general and preliminary, may be derived from the cases:

1. The amendment guarantees the people security against searches and seizures which are "unreasonable." What is unreasonable may differ with circumstances.[50] It is not necessarily and in all cases unreasonable to provide for search without a warrant.

2. The amendment protects rights of corporations as well as of individuals, business establishments as well as residences. But what may be reasonable in regard to a business establishment may not be in regard to a residence; "corporations can claim no equality with individuals in the enjoyment of a right to privacy." [51]

It may aid analysis to note briefly here the relevance also of "due process." If there were no Fourth Amendment, most of its protections might have been discovered in the due process clause, as indeed they have been, in regard to the states, in the same clause in the Fourteenth Amendment.[52] While the explicit protection of the Fourth Amendment looms as a stronger safeguard, it appears that in addition to any rights against unreasonable search which the citizen would have under the Fourth Amendment, he also enjoys the right not to be deprived of his liberty or property without due process of law, by inspection as by any other means. This suggests that the due process clause also requires that inspection be "reasonable" or at least not clearly "unreasonable." [53]

If this be so, whether or not inspection can be challenged as "unreasonable" search and seizure, it is subject to challenge as "unreasonable" process of law. The standard may not necessarily be the same, in the term as used explicitly in the Constitution to describe forbidden search, and as suggested by the courts as an approximate, general description of the standard of fairness implied in "due process." It may be, for instance, that for the Fourth Amendment a search must be reasonable as to the individual case, just as the amendment requires that a warrant must describe "particularly . . . the place to be searched." The due process clause, on the other hand, may not be violated by inspection or search if the system of regulation is reasonable as a whole. Still, we may assume that, in general, inspection which qualifies as "search and seizure" subject to the Fourth Amendment, and which, as a result of a warrant or otherwise, is not "unreasonable" search and seizure is also not "unreasonable" deprivation of the owner of his rights without due process of law. The importance of the due process claim here suggested is that due process would apply even where the Fourth Amendment may not, even, for example, if, as is argued below, certain inspections are not "search and seizure," or are for other reasons outside the protection of the Fourth Amendment.[54] That the owner of an establishment, for instance, is deemed to have waived his rights under the Fourth Amendment and consented to search would not prevent him from claiming that as effected the search went so far as to deny him due process.[55] So a factory owner may claim that he is being unnecessarily harassed by inspectors to the extent that it seriously interferes with his business. Perhaps, in an extreme case, the owner can also claim that his property is being "taken for public use" and that he is entitled to compensation.[56]

For the basic constitutional questions we may concentrate our discussion of inspection on issues under the Fourth Amendment. One thinks of the Fourth Amendment as a protection against search by police officials. It is generally raised by persons charged with crime who seek the exclusion of evidence introduced against them on the ground that it was obtained by illegal search and seizure.[57] But may not arms control inspection also constitute "search and seizure" which must not be "unreasonable"? And if calling it inspection rather than search hardly closes the constitutional issue, are all "inspections" of equal constitutional significance?

Industrial and Commercial Establishments. Government installations apart, the important objects of international inspection would be the factories, the depots, the laboratories in private hands which are engaged in activities covered by the control agreement. There may be installations openly carrying on affairs which are subject to international supervision under the agreement. There may be others clandestinely doing what they are not supposed to be doing at all.

Armaments as "Regulated Industry." In so far as the control plan imposes limitation and regulation, rather than complete prohibition, on private activity, the major part of our problem may be separated and examined, and conclusions reached with confidence based on an abundance of precedent. To this extent, the arms control plan would mean that by treaty and legislation the United States has regulated the manufacture of armaments and related activities in the same manner as, under other powers, Congress has regulated the transportation of firearms, the manufacture and handling of narcotics, alcohol and food and drug products, the development of atomic energy, and other activities. So far

Investigation of Compliance

as concerns such regulated industries, in the present state of the law the following propositions may be asserted with considerable citation of authority:

(*a*) When Congress regulates a business or occupation under any of its powers, it can require that private persons or corporations engaged in this activity shall keep records and books in a prescribed form. It can require reports and returns about these activities. These books, records, reports are not excluded from search or seizure by the Fourth Amendment.[58] They are not protected from disclosure by the Fifth Amendment, although they may contain materials incriminating those who keep the records, the owners of the business in question, and the corporation or its officers.[59] The Fourth and Fifth Amendments also will not protect from seizure and disclosure books other than those specifically prescribed which contain information relevant to a proper inquiry.[60]

(*b*) Congress can require those engaged in these regulated occupations to permit inspectors to come to the premises to examine the papers, books, records, etc., required to be kept.[61]

(*c*) And Congress can provide for inspection of the operations of regulated industrial establishments, requiring that inspectors be admitted and permitted to make such examination as is necessary to assure that the activities carried on are not in violation of law.[62] While, as suggested, extreme, harassing inspections may be unreasonable under the Fourth Amendment, or a denial of due process of law under the Fifth Amendment, there is precedent for inspection "at all times," [63] and even for the permanent stationing of inspectors in industrial installations.[64]

(*d*) Congress can impose criminal penalties for failure to keep books and records required, and for interfering with inspection of such books or records, or with inspection of industrial premises.[65] Congress can also authorize inspectors to use force necessary to overcome any resistance to inspection authorized by law.[66]

These propositions derive from the various federal acts providing for regulation of alcohol products, narcotics, adulterated foods, and others. Some of these have been approved by the courts; others have not yet been passed upon by the Supreme Court, but have the sanction of long standing and long use.

We assume that the provisions in the Fourth and Fifth Amendments we are discussing have the same scope in regard to a system established pursuant to a treaty as they have for regulation of industry pursuant to the interstate commerce or taxing power of Congress. The above principles would apply, *mutatis mutandis,* to our inspection plan, whether the inspection were carried out by national or international inspectors.

There would seem little difficulty, therefore, in providing for inspection of the arms industry subjected to regulation by treaty. As far as the Constitution is concerned, the United States could agree and Congress could require, that reports be made and books be kept by those engaged in arms and related industries; that these reports be made available for international inspection at all times; that international inspectors be permitted to come at any time, without warrant, to any industrial establishment within the framework of the arms control regulation scheme, including mines, factories, and depots, to inspect such reports and records, as well as to check operations and inventory. The inspectors might make spot-checks, or inspectors might be stationed permanently in a factory or other installation. Congress could make it a crime punishable in the courts of the United States to falsify the records or reports required to be kept or to interfere with inspection. And the inspectors could be authorized to use force to carry out inspection were it resisted.

As a form of "regulated industry" one may include those who transport arms. It may be important to inspect not only depots but also centers and means of transportation which might be employed in clandestine carriage of forbidden weapons or materials. So far as these transportation centers or transportation media are government-owned or operated, inspecting them, as has been said, raises no special difficulties. An inspection system, however, would be concerned not only with assuring that the United States were not violating the agreement; it would be concerned also with assuring that other countries were not bringing forbidden weapons and materials into the United States, whether for or against the United States. It might become necessary, therefore, to inspect commercial planes to assure that no one was carrying forbidden weapons or materials. And trains and trucks might also require inspection.[67]

The inspection of commercial methods of transportation would raise the same kind of questions as the inspection of other regulated enterprises. The aviation industry, the railroads, and interstate trucks are subject to federal regulation in other respects, and there would seem no reason why they could not be subject to inspection in implementation of a national arms control system to the same extent as an arms factory.

The "Button Factory." In the course of disarmament negotiations in the United Nations, the Soviet representative once asked rhetorically

Investigation of Compliance

whether the contemplated inspectors should have the right to enter and inspect a button factory. The reply to this question was that they should be able to enter a factory representing itself as a button factory to make certain that it was.

This presents the difficult issues of inspection. In the main, inspection provisions in a control plan which limits and regulates, rather than prohibits, would, we have seen, cause little difficulty. Certainly this is so when the activity concerned is open and admitted. Avowed armaments enterprises and related businesses may then be carefully circumscribed and scrutinized. International inspection, if provided, would fit into such regulation in the same way as national inspection in other regulated industries in the United States. Where, however, an activity is prohibited, there is of course no permitted industry to regulate; there is no registration of such activities with the authorities; there is no consent to inspection which might be implied from such registration. And even activities which are permitted within limits or under supervision may be carried on clandestinely instead to avoid such regulation. To the extent, then, that activities are prohibited, rather than merely regulated—and even under regulation as regards those not registered and accepting regulation—all industrial installations are "button factories." It is necessary to consider therefore whether there can be inspection of factories ostensibly doing a permitted thing to assure that they are not doing something prohibited.

We are discussing, of course, inspection without warrant, perhaps without warning. Constitutional questions could be eliminated if the inspectors were required to obtain a warrant. But obtaining a warrant from a United States court involves satisfying substantial constitutional requirements of "probable cause, supported by Oath or affirmation, and particularly describing the place to be searched, and the persons or things to be seized." [68] Inspectors with less than probable cause, or desiring perhaps to "spot-check," could not meet this standard. And if the United States objected in the case of Russia to the requirement of a warrant, others might object to requiring international inspectors to obtain a warrant from a United States court.[69]

At this point it may be desirable to re-examine the concept of "regulated industry" to determine how the button factory might relate to it. While the phrase is lightly used and is convenient, it may, like other shorthand appellations, mislead rather than clarify constitutional analysis. When we speak, for example, of the alcohol industry as a regulated industry, there is nothing about alcohol, in this context, which differentiates it from buttons for constitutional purposes. To call the alcohol industry "regulated" is merely to say that under one of its powers Congress decided to legislate in regard to alcohol, and, for our purposes, that the legislation provided also for a system of inspection in order to give effect to the substantive provisions which Congress desired. Thus, as to some of the industries we have called "regulated," Congress, under its taxing power, has imposed taxes on the operations and products involved and has provided for inspection to assure the revenue. Again, Congress under its power to regulate interstate commerce has acted, for instance, to prevent fraud or injury to health as a result of interstate shipment of deleterious food products. This proper statutory purpose too is implemented by provisions for inspection appropriate to the system of regulation. And so, in this study, we have concluded that if Congress, pursuant to treaty, or under its power to define offenses against the law of nations, or other powers, imposes control and limitations over the arms industry, it may assure compliance with these regulations by appropriate inspections. We concluded also that inspection could probably be reasonably required at all times; and the fact that it might be done directly and exclusively by international officials would not invalidate it.

What we are now considering is legislation authorizing the inspection of commercial or industrial establishments which themselves are not otherwise regulated by Congress. We suggest for examination the proposition that the treaty makers and Congress could, in order to implement United States obligations under an arms control treaty, provide for inspection without warrant of any commercial or industrial installations to satisfy the international inspectors that no treaty violation is taking place.

One may perhaps approach this issue, under the Fourth Amendment, by asking first the question suggested earlier. Is this inspection within the concept of "search and seizure" so that it must not be "unreasonable"? On this question of concept the regulated industry cases themselves do not afford firm guidance. No inspection of a regulated industry has been held to be an unreasonable search and seizure violating that amendment.[70] And it has not always been clear whether, when Congress provides for inspection of a regulated industry without a warrant, it is justified because those who engage in such industries in effect consent to "search and seizure," to the pattern of inspection imposed by Congress; or because such inspection for these industries is not "unreason-

Investigation of Compliance

able" as that standard is laid down in the Fourth Amendment; or because such inspections of the industries are not at all within the concept of search and seizure and the Fourth Amendment is irrelevant. Which of these is the proper explanation of these cases may be critical for deciding the case of the "button factory." Those who admit and register their activity in a regulated industry submit to regulation and inspection; those who enter or continue in the arms industry, like those who deal with alcohol or narcotics, or certain foods and drugs, know they are regularly subject to inspection, and may be deemed to consent to it. But to presume consent or waiver in the case of all industry and commerce in a commercial country where many have little choice but to be in commerce is fiction. And to indulge such fiction to imply consent to inspection, even if it is extremely unlikely to occur and then only by international arms inspectors, is to carve a big exception out of the protection of the Fourth Amendment—if the amendment is relevant.

One may, however, seek some guidance elsewhere, for inspection also exists in the United States in another context. Perhaps the most common "inspections" are municipal—by the health inspector, or the building inspector, or the fire inspector. Their activities are a common phenomenon of American living. No State of the Union appears to require a warrant for inspections by such officials to satisfy either the "search and seizure" requirements of state constitutions or similar concepts inhering in the due process clause of the Fourteenth Amendment.[71] Where federal authority prevails and the Fourth Amendment applies—as in the District of Columbia—such municipal inspections are a routine matter, and there is no provision for a warrant. And such inspection without warrant is made not only of commercial buildings but of dwelling houses, whose privacy is the principal concern of the Fourth Amendment. It might be said that these are searches deemed "reasonable"; more likely the inspections are not deemed searches at all. Though this pattern of municipal function is probably older than the Fourteenth Amendment, and perhaps as old as the Fourth, the Supreme Court of the United States has not yet dealt with the relation of these inspections to either of these amendments.

Once, in 1950, the Court had a case in hand. In *District of Columbia v. Little*,[72] a health inspector, informed that unsanitary conditions existed in a dwelling house, sought admittance to inspect the dwelling. He had no warrant. None was required by the statutes and regulations of the District of Columbia governing his activities. The occupant of the house refused to admit the inspector. She was tried and convicted for violating a regulation of the District of Columbia making it a misdemeanor to prevent the inspection of any building reported to be in an unsanitary condition. The Court of Appeals for the District of Columbia, one judge dissenting, reversed the conviction on the ground that the Fourth Amendment was relevant and was violated.[73] On review, the United States Supreme Court affirmed. The Court, however, avoided the constitutional question which concerns us. Instead, the majority interpreted the District regulation as not intending to make criminal the defendant's refusal to permit the inspectors to enter.

These municipal inspections, therefore, may perhaps not be within the scope of the Fourth Amendment. If municipal inspections are made without warrant even as to dwelling houses, the "button factory" would certainly be a less troublesome case. But is the arms control inspector like the health inspector? The health inspector or the fire inspector is an official concerned with assuring by routine, occasional check that conditions are not allowed to prevail which would endanger the citizen or the community. For such spot-check, not necessarily based on any information or suspicion of a violation, the traditional warrant is not appropriate; the official could not obtain a warrant since he would not be able to satisfy the requirement of "probable cause." Even in situations like that in the *Little* case where there is information of a health violation, it may be argued that to require warrants would overwhelm the courts as well as the inspectors and break down the system, that although technically the inspector is examining a situation to see whether a law is being violated, his purpose is not to seize evidence or even to obtain evidence for conviction. He does not rummage. Generally, there will be a warning and a requirement to abate the unlawful situation. That is the primary purpose of the law, and of the inspection; that is the common expectation and attitude of the occupant. The purpose and the consequences are akin to the discovery and abatement of a public nuisance, which states have done and do, without—it has been assumed—entering the domain of police search and seizure and the need for warrants.[74]

Without purporting to decide the question which the Supreme Court avoided in the *Little* case, we may suggest that in any event the *Little* case is not our case. The international arms inspector when he came to the "button factory" would generally come on the basis of information or suspicion. He could not dissipate limited energies on spot-checks of a myriad of installations at random. The situation he would be seeking to

Investigation of Compliance 73

monitor would not be a routine one, or one he would be concerned to have a careless or willful occupant eliminate or remedy. Even if it were not necessarily his purpose to seize evidence for presentation in a criminal proceeding against the violator before an American tribunal, he would be seeking evidence of a serious, intentional violation of law, perhaps representing a sinister conspiracy in which the most powerful forces of government are involved. He would look hard and carefully, including hidden places and things. The inspector might not be a police official in the usual sense; he would be one in a real sense for this unusual context. In analogy, as in "flavor," the arms inspector would seem to fall with the police officials, and the occupant of the building subject to inspection would be likely to consider him as such. That a guilty person actually engaged in a conspiracy to violate an arms control agreement in collusion with officials of the United States Government might not fear the international inspector or the consequences of his inspection might make less material the reasons underlying the Fourth Amendment but would not render them inapplicable.

If then the analogy of the municipal health inspector offers no basis for deciding that the arms inspector is not within the Fourth Amendment, if the regulated industry cases do not give a clear answer, one should proceed on the assumption that the Fourth Amendment may apply. But to conclude that the Fourth Amendment governs is not to conclude that a warrant is essential. While a warrant meeting the amendment's stringent requirements would, one may assume, render a search "reasonable" (apart from any excesses in its execution), a search, we have said, may not be "unreasonable" although there is no warrant.[75] It may be necessary to ask also whether, even as to industry, the Fourth Amendment—perhaps unlike due process—requires that search without warrant be "reasonable" as to the particular inspection or search. Or is it sufficient that the inspection arrangement viewed generally be "reasonable"? Is it sufficient that in the circumstances of international arms control it is not "unreasonable" search if inspectors are authorized to enter all industrial establishments so that they can be sure that there is no unlawful "regulated" activity? Or, in another direction, is it not "reasonable" to dispense with a warrant because in the mind of other parties to the treaty an American court might be disposed to refuse a warrant to protect an operation in which American officials might be circumventing an international obligation?

There is little direct guidance to answers. Perhaps—because of lack of close precedent; because of continuing doubt as to whether inspection of industry, where there is some basis for regulation, is within the Fourth Amendment; because of the uncertainty of all that may go into the scope of "unreasonable" in the circumstances, for purposes of the amendment or of the due process clause—perhaps for these reasons the question may reduce to whether such agreement providing for inspection is reasonably required, is "necessary and proper," to carry out a purpose within the power of Congress and the treaty makers; or whether, on the other hand, the intrusion on those engaged in industry and commerce is too great to be justified by the aim.

We are here, as in many areas of the law—especially where concepts like "reasonable" are determinative—engaged in judging, weighing, drawing lines. One may assume, perhaps, that as regards industry and commerce, the courts will not lightly strike down any regulation, particularly one in implementation of a treaty expressing vital national policy. And one may cite precedents for deeper, more extensive regulation with inspection of virtually all industry. While inspection is normally viewed as an adjunct to congressional regulation of a particular industry under the taxing or commerce power, there is no reason why inspection could not be a proper adjunct in support of a congressional regulation which applies to industry generally. Thus, for example, even apart from special taxation of industries like alcohol or narcotics, general taxation leaves few areas of commercial activity beyond federal scrutiny. The investigating power of Congress too, akin perhaps to inspection, can reach deep into any industry or commerce. Inspection itself has in fact been provided in support of congressional legislation applicable to all industry. During the Second World War, Congress did in effect turn virtually all commercial enterprise into "regulated industry." Under the Emergency Price Control Act, the ordinary business entries of every small businessman became "required records" subject to inspection.[76] And if that could be done to implement price control legislated in the national defense, could not commercial activity be subjected to inspection pursuant to arms control agreed to in the national defense? Indeed, the price regulations were continuous, burdensome, intrusive into every establishment; by comparison, the possibility of arms inspection for any factory would be minimal.

As another approach, Congress can go very far in regulating interstate commerce;[77] it can regulate matters strictly intrastate, not otherwise subject to regulation, if it is "necessary and proper" to make ef-

Investigation of Compliance

fective a regulation of interstate commerce.[78] Similarly, Congress may impose inspection—a limited regulation—on all industry as "necessary and proper" to make effective the regulation of armaments under the treaty power.

Finally, it may be suggested that although the Fourth Amendment affords some protection to corporations, its basic purpose was to protect the dwelling against invasion under a general warrant.[79] Whatever the theory of the regulated industry cases, they reflect that the right of industry and commerce to be free from scrutiny is limited. Industry and commerce are entitled to freedom from abuse and harassment—whether under the Fourth Amendment or the due process clause—but not to privacy or secrecy.[80] And a regulation by Congress pursuant to treaty, subjecting industry to the possibility of arms control inspection which inevitably would—for almost all—remain only a theoretical possibility, is hardly a harassment and, in the circumstances, is not "unreasonable."

These are arguments, not answers. But one should add that the "reasonableness" of such inspection would surely be enhanced by limitations and qualifications upon it: for example, if such inspection were permitted only in certain defined installations, perhaps based on size, or location, so that the possibility of their being a "cover" is not absurd; if limitations were admitted as to the time or frequency of inspection; if warning were required; perhaps if United States or local officials were also present. And the entire arrangement would seem still more "reasonable" if congressional implementation of arms control included provisions to protect or compensate American industry for damage due to abuse of the inspection.[81]

INSPECTION OF HOSPITALS AND MEDICAL RECORDS. The physical dangers entailed in handling nuclear materials, explosives, and other weapons suggest another possible auxiliary aid to detection. The implementation of an arms control plan might include provisions to enable inspectors to discover atomic and similar accidents by investigation of the hospitals and doctors who would treat the victims of such accidents. Congress might provide that all hospitals and all doctors in the United States must report to the inspection body, or to a federal agency for transmission to the inspectors, any cases indicating radiation accidents, injury due to explosives, and contact with other weapons or materials which are prohibited or subject to control. Provision might also be made for inspecting hospitals and hospital records, as well as for interrogating, pursuant to subpoena, hospital officials, attendants, and others.

Private doctors and their records might also be subjected to interrogation and inspection.

In regard to hospitals of the United States Government, their officials and doctors employed by the United States, the issues are the same as those discussed above in regard to interrogations and inspections of other United States officials. There are no serious constitutional obstacles here, except that the privilege against self-incrimination might require an "immunity statute" if testimony were to be assured.

State hospitals and state officials, and the medical practitioner generally, are normally subject only to state regulation. Yet, we have seen, matters normally subject to state control are subject to regulation by the treaty power; in this category the conduct of state hospitals and state officials also is not immune from control by treaty.[82] Reasonable regulation in regard to the practice of medicine, normally within the police power of the states, is within the treaty power if it is a legitimate subject for international agreement.[83] So long as the regulation of hospitals and doctors which we are discussing related to the implementation of a treaty, it would not violate the Constitution any more than do the other forms of regulation of activities normally under state jurisdiction, like local manufacture or the possession of strategic materials. Such regulation would not violate any explicit protections accorded by the Constitution to the doctors or to their patients; the privilege still recognized in some jurisdictions excusing a doctor from testifying as to matter divulged to him by his patient is certainly not of constitutional rank and can be abolished by a proper treaty.[84] The inspection, reporting, and testifying aspects of this suggestion in regard to medical data would of course be subject to the same limitations in regard to the Fourth and Fifth Amendments which were discussed earlier in this chapter.

INSPECTION OF LABORATORIES. The control agreement, we suggested, might authorize inspection of research laboratories to assure against prohibited activities, *e.g.,* forbidden nuclear research, or the development or preparation of materials for biological or chemical warfare. The inspection of government laboratories, like inspection of other government installations, raises no special difficulties. State laboratories also could be subjected to inspection, as indicated in the previous discussion of state hospitals. The laboratories of commercial enterprises would be subject to inspection on the same basis as other activities of these enterprises, in the light of the discussion earlier in this chapter.

Investigation of Compliance

Question remains in regard to inspection of laboratories run by private educational or research institutions or by individual scientists.

In an earlier chapter we concluded that neither the First Amendment nor the Fifth Amendment would invalidate a treaty which forbids research and development in relation to arms by scientific institutions or scientists.[85] We have also said that scientists could perhaps be required to register and report their activities. In a proper inquiry scientists, among others, might be questioned as to activities which might violate an arms control agreement. The issue now is whether the right to inspect without warrant may be provided as necessary and proper to implement treaty prohibitions or regulations, or whether, as in regard to other criminal violations by individuals, there can only be search on the basis of a warrant issued where there is "probable cause."

As to the educational or research institutions, it may be argued that inspection necessary to implement the arms control prohibition is a reasonable requirement and that there is no countervailing serious intrusion on privacy. As to the individual scientist, on the other hand, even though he might be forbidden various activities and research and might even be required to register and report his activities, it is something else to permit intrusion into his private laboratories without warrant, in the guise of "inspection." Such laboratories, we have seen, may be subject to inspection by municipal health inspectors; it does not follow, however, in the light of the discussion earlier in this chapter that they would also be subject to inspection by international arms control inspectors. The case may be close. Particularly if the laboratory is in the scientist's dwelling, inspecting it might well be treated like other attempts to inspect a dwelling house discussed in the following sections of this chapter.

THE DWELLING HOUSE

One has occasionally heard that to assure that no violation of arms control is going on, international inspectors must be able to go anywhere at any time. As a suggestion that governments should not be able to cut off areas from scrutiny, the proposal of course has sense. In its broadest form, however, it would seem to imply also the right of inspectors to descend upon any private dwelling in the land at any time of day or night without a warrant and rummage for evidence of possible arms control violations. If this is what the suggestion means, it makes little sense. Serious violations in a day of hydrogen bombs and intercontinental missiles will hardly be taking place in private dwellings. If some forms of biological and chemical warfare might be prepared or secreted in small areas, perhaps even a private house, their detection could hardly be effected simply by giving a blanket right to inspect all dwellings without a warrant. If there were a basis for suspicion, a warrant could be obtained, directly by international officials, or through national officers, and refusal of national officers to cooperate would no doubt be some indication that something was being hidden.

It may be that large estates could lodge industrial or military operations, and a government eager to conceal something might concentrate it in some such location. But this suggests a small and special situation, for which special remedies might be necessary. It hardly requires that all private dwellings in the land be rendered open to inspection without warrant.

Since the suggestion has been deemed implied in proposals actually under consideration, we will underline the constitutional difficulties which such arrangements would entail. For the most part, they have been covered in the discussions of the "button factory." We there concluded that, whatever is the case with municipal fire and health inspection, the international arms control inspector probably comes within the requirements of the Fourth Amendment. Certainly in regard to a dwelling house, he is more like the police inspector trying to enforce a criminal law than like the health inspector seeking immediately to protect the health and welfare of the occupant and his neighbors. The arms inspector then would generally need a warrant based on "probable cause" as required by that amendment. To justify his inspection without such warrant would require a finding that his search, in all the circumstances, would not be "unreasonable." The argument for that may find some support in a broad treaty power; in the necessities of national defense as reflected in an arms control agreement; in the need to agree in principle to the inspection of an occasional dwelling in order to make it possible for similar inspection in other countries, thereby to achieve greater security for the United States; in the inability to rely on warrants from national courts; in the extreme unlikelihood that a particular dwelling, or any dwelling, would in fact be inspected; and in the fact that it is only an extraordinary power in a special group for a very limited purpose, most unlikely to materialize, not a general warrant in the hands of police.[86]

Investigation of Compliance

The arguments are difficult to weigh. If no feasible way were found for meeting the special problem of the estate, there would be a possibility that the "dwelling" here or in other countries might appear to be a loophole of significance in preventing security against violation. A constitutional amendment, then, would probably be necessary here to circumvent the problem. Certainly the American people should have explained to them the implications of such a proposal, and an opportunity given to them to indicate their willingness to make the sacrifice involved.

IMMUNITY STATUTE UNDER THE FOURTH AMENDMENT

There is another possibility, not involving constitutional amendment, which deserves some consideration. It may be proposed that the problem posed by the dwelling house, or other inspections which raise serious questions under the Fourth Amendment, be handled in the same way as analogous difficulties under the Fifth Amendment. As regards the privilege against self-incrimination, we have seen, a person may be compelled to be a witness against himself, provided Congress confers upon him immunity from prosecution for the crimes revealed by his testimony. Could Congress similarly provide for search without warrant, in circumstances where it would otherwise be "unreasonable" to do so, if it confers an immunity from prosecution for crimes revealed by such search? In the case of arms control such a solution might commend itself as especially felicitous, since, we have said, criminal prosecution of the individual arms control violator is not the primary goal of inspection.

The suggestion is interesting but highly questionable. Its validity depends on how broad or narrow a view one takes of the Fourth Amendment. Does the Fourth Amendment guarantee only that a person will not be convicted of crime on the basis of an unreasonable search or seizure? Or is there a broader right, akin to a right of privacy, quite apart from the use to which evidence obtained in a search or seizure is put?

The Fourth Amendment, it is true, is usually invoked to exclude evidence in a criminal case, and the Fourth Amendment is usually coupled with the Fifth, so that unreasonable search and seizure has frequently been viewed as an aspect of self-incrimination.[87] In its origins, also, the principal purpose of the amendment was to bar unreasonable police search for materials which might form the basis of a criminal prosecution. Nevertheless, the view that the protection of the Fourth Amendment is exhausted if there is no incrimination as a result of an unlawful search is subject to serious doubt. The language of the amendment says nothing of criminal proceedings or of self-incrimination.[88] What is assured against violation is "the right of the people to be secure." While the Fourth and Fifth Amendments are often joined, the relationship between them would seem to be that stated by Mr. Justice Brandeis (although the particular formulation comes from a dissenting opinion): [89]

They conferred, as against the Government, the right to be let alone—the most comprehensive of rights and the right most valued by civilized men. To protect that right, every unjustifiable instrusion by the Government upon the privacy of the individual, whatever the means employed, must be deemed a violation of the Fourth Amendment. And the use, as evidence in a criminal proceeding, of facts ascertained by such intrusion must be deemed a violation of the Fifth.

The limitations of the Fourth Amendment would seem to have independent validity, quite apart from the fact that the use of materials found is barred by the Fifth Amendment.

In *Wolf v. Colorado*,[90] the Supreme Court considered whether it is a violation of due process of law under the Fourteenth Amendment for a state to allow the admission in evidence of materials obtained by search and seizure without a proper warrant. The Court, though it went on to hold that the exclusion of the evidence was not required by the due process clause, said:

The security of one's privacy against arbitrary intrusion by the police—which is at the core of the Fourth Amendment—is basic to a free society. It is therefore implicit in "the concept of ordered liberty" and as such enforceable against the States through the Due Process Clause.

As to the states, then, under the Fourteenth Amendment, police intrusion is barred, without regard to the use of the evidence to incriminate.

The language of Mr. Justice Brandeis is broad and suggests a right to privacy not to be disturbed except in established circumstances usually pursuant to warrant. On its face, indeed, the quoted language may be considered determinative of the issue left open in the *Little* case. It is not necessary, however, for our purpose to decide, or to assume, that the Supreme Court would bar municipal inspections which it might consider basically not of a police character. A court might find historical and practical reasons for upholding those established practices of American municipal life, generally accepted by the citizenry. But, again, our case is not the *Little* case. If the Fourth Amendment applies to the arms inspector, certainly in regard to a dwelling house it would seem that the protection is against intrusion except in the unusual circumstances where a warrant can be obtained, or in the still more unusual circumstances where search may be reasonable without a warrant. The right is not limited to nonincrimination; it is a right to nonintrusion, and an immunity statute would not substitute for the protection.

This must be our conclusion, at least if we think of an immunity statute analogous to that used for the Fifth Amendment. Another possibility may be worth mention. It is interesting to speculate whether, assuming that the protection of the Fourth Amendment is as broad as we supposed, an immunity statute could be devised which is as broad as the protection and might be a constitutional substitute for it. Assume the following: that the exigencies of international negotiation in the context of existing international mistrust produced an agreement under which international inspectors could move about and inspect at will; that in the United States this would mean that they could approach and enter any industry or, for purposes of this discussion, any dwelling house, without a warrant, and regardless of any "probable cause" for suspicion. Could Congress, earnestly endeavoring to implement such an international agreement, eliminate Fourth Amendment objections by supplying or compensating for the constitutional protections which the agreement would violate? Would it be deemed sufficient, in a situation which requires extraordinary measures to achieve a national policy of extraordinary import, to offer a citizen (*a*) immunity from prosecution for crimes discovered by the international inspectors; (*b*) minimization of the intrusion and its effects by limitations as to the time of search, provision for adequate identification of the inspectors, warning and notice if only of a minimum time, and inspection in the presence of the occupants and perhaps American officials; (*c*) assurances against or compensation for destruction or damage by the inspectors, and against revelation by them of private matters discovered in the course of inspection? Do these afford the citizen the equivalent of his constitutional protection? If not, can others be conceived which might measure up to the full protections of the amendment? Or is there no equivalent substitute for the privacy of the citizen even if national considerations of great moment are at stake? One can only speculate.

ASSERTING CONSTITUTIONAL RIGHTS

Before concluding the subject of inspection, a word needs to be said about the protection of American citizens against possible abuses. In so far as some of the activities involved in inspection may impinge on rights under the Fourth or Fifth Amendment, international inspection presents a situation different in a critical, practical respect from inspection or search in a national context. The constitutional problem generally is raised when inspectors have entered upon premises and seized evidence of violation of a law and the defendant in a criminal trial for such violation asserts his constitutional rights in an effort to have the evidence excluded. In our inspection system this is not the way such questions would be likely to arise. Inspectors would not be looking primarily for evidence to present in a criminal court in the United States. They would be seeking evidence of violation of a treaty by the United States for transmission to other countries or to an international body. There would therefore be little question of admissibility of evidence, and the fact that evidence seized might not be admissible in a court of the United States would not serve as a deterrent to any inspection which might be illegal or unconstitutional.

The validity of an inspection could of course be challenged in other ways.[91] A manufacturer might seek to enjoin inspectors from coming into his factory on the ground that the inspection, or some aspects of it, violated his rights under the Fourth Amendment. Or the manufacturer might physically resist the inspectors and prevent them from entering. Of course, if his resistance were overcome, the inspection would in fact take place. Later he might be subject to trial for resisting the inspection contrary to law forbidding such interference, and he might set up the unconstitutionality of the inspection in his defense. Alternatively, he might bring a civil action of trespass against the inspectors and assert that the entry was not pursuant to law because the law under which the inspectors were operating is unconstitutional. Of course, if, as suggested below,[92] the international inspectors were to enjoy an immunity from such action, the constitutional issues would not be reached in such a case or in a suit to enjoin the inspectors. A citizen might argue that such immunity, where it deprives the citizen of an opportunity to question an unconstitutional exercise of authority pursuant to a federal treaty, is itself unconstitutional. But every grant of immunity to suit in effect deprives a would-be plaintiff of a remedy, and thereby, it might be urged, of "property" without due process of law. Yet the grant of immunity has never been successfully challenged. It is unlikely that United States courts would refuse to recognize an immunity to suit for international officials granted by treaty or law even if

Investigation of Compliance

the opportunity to assert a constitutional right were thereby denied.[93]

At this point, it may be useful to emphasize that the courts are not the primary or the exclusive guardians of the constitutional rights of citizens. Those who make laws for the United States and those who enter into treaties in its behalf should assure the protection of the rights of Americans even if—especially if—United States courts might not be available in the present context to vindicate these rights. If the proposed arms control plan should entail far-reaching modification of accepted institutions and practices, a constitutional amendment might be necessary, or at least desirable.

In this chapter we have concentrated on how far inspection can go in imposing on the rights of Americans before the Constitution calls a halt. A plan for arms control and its implementation should include also the assurance that the rights of the citizen will be protected against unnecessary infringement. In addition to prohibitions and injunctions in the control agreement against abuse by the international inspectorate,[94] United States legislation might afford other safeguards and compensations to its citizens. We have suggested possible compensation for "public taking" under the Fifth Amendment in a previous chapter. Special provisions for compensating a property owner for damage resulting from abuses of the inspection process are considered as an aspect of the legislation for implementing arms control in the next chapter.

Chapter V. CONGRESSIONAL IMPLEMENTATION OF ARMS CONTROL

Congress, we have assumed, will be prepared to adopt legislation necessary to make an arms control treaty effective. The validity of such legislation, in general, has been considered. Here we shall indicate briefly the substance of some of the domestic legislation which might be adopted to implement various provisions for control, verification, and inspection. This will include basic legislation to establish the controls and make them effective. Specific provisions will be enacted for inspecting government installations, offices, and military bases, as well as industrial and commercial establishments, hospitals and laboratories, to assure compliance with the prohibitions or limitations of the plan. There will be provision for interrogating government personnel and for relaxing—as called for by the plan—security and classification rules. Power will be given to the inspectors to interrogate private citizens and to subpoena relevant documents in their possession. Immunity statutes may be necessary to offset the privilege against self-incrimination and to assure the inspectorate access to information. Necessary privileges, immunities, and facilities for the inspecting body will need definition. Also indicated will be some important respects in which other existing federal laws either will be modified automatically or might be amended explicitly. We shall consider as well possible stand-by legislation which Congress might wish to enact. For this and other legislation suggested, there is precedent in existing federal regulatory enactments, including some regarding arms and munitions.[1]

BASIC REGULATORY LEGISLATION

Even if an arms control treaty is to be self-executing, it will presumably require further implementation by Congress. There should probably be legislation setting out the system for control, defining its prohibitions and limitations, authorizing the inspectors to carry out their agreed

Congressional Implementation 85

functions, providing the machinery to enforce their orders, requiring United States officials or private persons to cooperate, and making it criminal for them to interfere or fail to cooperate with the inspection. Here we suggest in some detail the character of such legislation and the probable range of its application.

ACTIVITIES OF THE GOVERNMENT AND GOVERNMENT OFFICIALS

The arms control treaty would operate, *sua sponte,* to limit the activities of the United States itself. Without congressional legislation, the Executive would be required to implement these limitations, since the treaty is a law of the land which must be executed like other laws.

Nevertheless, it might be useful to have the limitations repeated in legislation, and legislation would be necessary if these limitations are to be backed by criminal sanction. Relevant laws dealing with men under arms, with defense producton, with size of armies should be modified expressly.[2] In addition, Congress would require all officials of the Executive Branch to comply with these limitations; to permit inspection of governmental installations as required by the treaty; to answer interrogations and give testimony to the inspectors; and to cooperate with the inspectors in all ways necessary to the conduct of their functions. Willful violation of these requirements by officials would be punishable as a federal crime.

The control plan would have major impact on legislation dealing with classified security information and its protection. If the plan and inspection system are comprehensive, they will involve a radical change in the concept of secrecy and classification of materials and entail modification of a number of laws relating to the control of information by the United States Government.[3] The inspectors would be entitled to know information which now bears the highest classifications and which is controlled by strict laws and regulations subject to extreme penalties. It is conceivable that such information might remain classified, that inspectors might be entitled to know but only under injunction of secrecy, unless a violation were found. More likely, what is subject to inspection will be rendered open, unclassified. The practice of classification of defense material might be virtually abolished. The concept of espionage and the laws enforcing it may then be virtually superseded. Laws which forbid the disclosure of defense information would be replaced by laws which require officials and citizens of the United States to disclose such information and, indeed, perhaps by laws which make it criminal not to disclose such information.⁴ Even under a less comprehensive system, information might be disclosed which today is protected by criminal penalties; these would be abolished.

INTERROGATION AND SUBPOENA OF PRIVATE PERSONS

The inspecting body would be authorized by legislation to subpoena, either directly or through a United States court, private persons and documents in their custody and to interrogate such persons under oath. Legislation would enforce this power to obtain testimony either through the contempt power of United States courts or by criminal sanctions.⁵

In order to enable inspectors to obtain information by interrogation of officials or private persons in the United States, legislation should provide for immunity from prosecution in exchange for testimony before the inspection body. The immunity presumably would be made as broad as the privilege accorded by the Fifth Amendment.

Immunity statutes in other contexts raise nice questions: the scope of the constitutional privilege; the extent of immunity granted; whether the immunity protects from state prosecution as well as federal; who shall determine whether the interrogation should be pressed and the immunity conferred or whether the public interest might be better served by not according the immunity and seeking other evidence to convict the witness of the crime involved.⁶ Under our assumption that in the present context it is disclosure, not prosecution, which is paramount, these questions may receive special answers.

ARMAMENTS, ATOMIC ENERGY, AND RELATED INDUSTRIES

Among the principal provisions of any foreseeable, comprehensive arms control treaty would be those specifying the controls and the necessary inspections for those industries connected with the production of weapons, their storage and transportation. Implementation of this regulatory scheme might run as follows:

(*a*) Congress would declare the arms industry, including essential related strategic materials covered by the treaty, to be an area whose regulation is required in the national interest. To the extent required by the treaty, Congress would prohibit or limit the manufacture, use, possession, or transportation of indicated arms and materials.⁷

(*b*) Persons continuing to engage in the manufacture of arms or strategic materials, or to possess, use, or transport them, within the

Congressional Implementation

restrictions of the treaty would be required to obtain a license from a designated federal body.[8]

(c) Corporations and other persons (official or private) carrying on activities forbidden under the treaty and implementing legislation, or carrying on any activity without the indicated license, or beyond the scope of this license, would be guilty of a felony and punished by imprisonment or fine.[9]

(d) All persons engaged in the regulated activity pursuant to license would be required to keep books and records, to make reports and returns on their activities, in the form prescribed and at indicated times; the required records would be subject to inspection.[10] The legislation might itself prescribe the requirements or declare that the prescriptions are to be made by the designated inspecting body or by a United States body acting on behalf of the inspectors.

(e) All enterprises carried on pursuant to license would be subject to inspection by the international inspectors in their discretion, at any time and without the requirement of a warrant.[11] Or the inspection body might decide to post inspectors permanently at important installations.[12]

(f) Willful failure to file the required reports or returns or to keep the required books and records would be a felony. It would be a felony to falsify them. It would also be a felony to refuse entry to the inspectors or to interfere with their operations in any way.[13]

(g) The legislation would require federal, and perhaps state and local, officials to assist the inspectors, if called upon, to make their inspection effective.[14] The inspectors might be authorized to use force to overcome resistance or interference with inspection.[15] They would be authorized to seize materials unlawfully possessed.[16] There might also be provision for rewards to those who inform the inspectors of any violations.[17]

(h) In addition to criminal sanctions to punish violators of the control and inspection systems, Congress might also make the equity power of United States courts available to the inspection body. Inspectors could then use the courts not only to obtain warrants, enforce subpoenas, and seek contempt citations; they might also be authorized to go into a court for an injunction, mandamus, or other appropriate writ.[18]

The above might constitute the principal provisions in the basic legislation. There would also be indirect effect on other laws, which might be modified by implication or might require express amendment. The principal impact of arms control would be on existing provisions of law which relate to armaments and strategic materials. Legislation controlling production, transportation, and the import and export of armaments might be modified or superseded by the principal implementing legislation under the arms control treaty.[19] And the Atomic Energy Act, with its comprehensive and far-reaching system of regulation of all matters relating to atomic energy, might have to be sharply revised, the degree and character of the revision depending, of course, on the arms control plan. That the impact on this act would be extensive and intensive is obvious from examination of its provisions. These include: provision for government ownership of nuclear materials; strict regulation and control by the federal government of research, production, possession, and distribution of source materials and by-products of nuclear production; a system of licensing of designated research and production activities by the Atomic Energy Commission; a radical departure from the patent system as applied to the atomic energy field; and a host of related miscellaneous provisions relating to control and enforcement.[20]

There are other, auxiliary provisions, to some of which we have alluded in earlier chapters, which would aid in the implementation and enforcement of arms control. Thus, for example, the arms control system, if it forbade manufacture of arms and strategic materials, would also suggest modification *pro tanto* of the patent system. Presumably the patent laws would bar the granting of patents for inventions which fall within the treaty prohibition. Special legislation would be needed if patents in the arms field were placed under special controls, perhaps provisions patterned after those of the Atomic Energy Act.[21]

PRIVILEGES AND FACILITIES FOR THE INSPECTORATE

We have assumed an international inspecting body, created by an international agreement taking the form of a treaty of the United States. The composition of this body, its functions and authority, would be spelled out in the treaty. The treaty would undoubtedly contain at least a general provision requiring nations to accord the inspecting body and its personnel the privileges, immunities, and facilities necessary for carrying out their functions under the treaty.[22] Or the treaty might provide such status in explicit detail, leaving little to legislative discretion.[23]

Congressional Implementation

What the treaty provided would determine whether and what implementing legislation would be needed.

STATUS OF THE INSPECTING BODY

Presumably the treaty would establish an inspecting body enjoying the character of a separate entity by whom the inspectors would be employed. The inspecting body itself would probably require a juridical personality and status, and immunities including inviolability of its premises, equipment, and documents and immunity from judicial process. Its status and immunities might well depend, in their specific implementation, on the relationship of the inspecting body to the United Nations.[24] It might be accorded powers of eminent domain, but for this it would presumably be required to act through United States authorities.[25]

STATUS OF THE INSPECTORS

Perhaps even more important, however, would be the status, privileges, and immunities of the inspecting personnel and the facilities accorded to them for the execution of their functions.

It may be that the treaty itself will provide for full diplomatic privileges and immunities for members of the inspecting body. Such diplomatic status, including complete immunity from arrest and detention, from civil and criminal jurisdiction and process for any purpose whatever, can be justified as necessary to insure the inspectors against interference in the full and free execution of their functions. Nations, among them the United States, have traditionally accorded such immunities to diplomatic personnel, but many have recently extended them to selected international officials.[26] While there is sentiment against extension of such diplomatic status, especially to persons who are not diplomats in the traditional sense,[27] the United States would probably be willing to accord such status to international inspectors, if only to assure that such inspectors would enjoy similar status in other countries, *e.g.,* the Soviet Union.

If the treaty provided for full diplomatic privileges, this provision would need no implementing legislation in the United States. Such a provision by its character can be self-executing; its scope and content, while far from certain, have traditional outlines and substance, and it might not be desirable to attempt to spell out in advance all the privileges and immunities included in the concept "diplomatic immunities." On the other hand, it might be desirable, without attempting an exhaustive list, to specify elements vital for purposes of arms control, *e.g.,* freedom of movement, freedom from arrest and judicial process.

To the extent that the treaty itself was not specific on the status and privileges of the inspectors, federal legislation would be necessary. Such legislation, like the treaty itself, would of course be binding on all federal, state, and local officials.

If the nations did not agree on full diplomatic privileges, the inspectors would require, as a minimum, freedom from arrest and judicial process in regard to matters arising out of the conduct of their functions and other privileges presently enjoyed by international officials in this country under the International Organizations Immunities Act.[28] The provisions of that act could be applied or adapted for this purpose.

SPECIFIC PRIVILEGES AND IMMUNITIES NEEDED

FREEDOM OF EGRESS AND INGRESS. Inspectors would have to be able to enter the country without regard to immigration restrictions. This should present no serious problem since diplomatic personnel and international officials already enjoy freedom from these restrictions and from onerous immigration procedures, including fingerprinting.[29] At the time of taking up their duties here, the complete absence of formalities delaying their entry might not be essential and the normal procedures applicable to diplomats would probably suffice.[30] If additional inspectors were necessary in an emergency, or to replace inspectors already here, it might be more important to assure no delay and to allow inspectors to fly in to their posts without regard to visas and immigration procedures and formalities. It would be simplest and would not present serious problems to the United States to waive the normal requirements for all inspectors bearing the proper identifying document, perhaps the United Nations *laissez-passer*.[31] It might indeed prove desirable to agree that in all countries inspectors might fly in at will and in their own planes, with safety precautions and radio identificaton as the only prerequisites.

The freedom of exit must also be guaranteed, both to assure the safety of the inspectors and their freedom from coercion, and to enable them to report on any violations they might have found. Today there are in the United States few exit restrictions on foreigners and none on diplomats.[32] There are, however, delays and it might be necessary to assure that inspectors could leave at will. Any American citizens or resi-

Congressional Implementation

dents employed as international inspectors might have to be accorded freedom from exit restrictions which apply to other American citizens or residents.[33] An appropriate international document (like the *laissez-passer*) requiring no visas or exit permits offers a simple solution. American law and regulations would have to be modified to permit freedom of entry and exit for holders of this document. And it might be desirable to have full freedom for the inspectors to fly out at will in their own planes.

FREEDOM OF TRAVEL AND TRANSPORTATION FACILITIES. The inspectors would require freedom to move about as essential to their functions. So far as the law is concerned, what would be necessary is freedom from restrictions, arrest, or detention, and from interference by various officials or private citizens. Legislation to make it a crime to interfere with inspection has been suggested. In addition, the inspectors might be accorded personal protection applicable everywhere and at all times. Thus, the law at present makes it a crime to assault or molest ambassadors and diplomatic personnel,[34] and this law could be extended or adapted to assure to inspectors full immunity from harassment by anyone at all times. Generally, these needs could be satisfied by giving the inspectors diplomatic status. Problems, if any, would be primarily practical rather than legal, *i.e.,* providing the proper identification of inspectors, and education of officials and citizens.

It would also be necessary to assure the inspectors of the necessary facilities to travel at all times. In the United States, normally, this presents no difficulties; in time of rationing of transportation or fuels it might be necessary to assure inspectors of priorities. Local transportation should also be made available to the inspectors without interference. More likely, however, to assure their effectiveness it would be necessary for inspectors to have their own facilities—automobiles and perhaps private planes or helicopters. Diplomatic status and special privileges accorded should give them immunity in regard to such vehicles from regulation other than, perhaps, safety regulations by the Civil Aeronautics Board and local motor and flight regulations.[35] National and international air traffic control would have to provide for free access to all air space for aerial inspection purposes and for the right to use all public landing areas.

For the most part, assimilating the inspectors to full diplomatic status for all purposes would meet their transportation requirements also. Alternatively, it might be necessary to permit the inspectors to import, without limitation, control, tax, or duty, the means and materials necessary for their transportation; this might involve amendments to revenue laws and to customs regulations.[36]

EXEMPTION FROM CUSTOMS LAWS. Inspectors coming in and out of the country would have to be accorded freedom from customs limitations on materials brought in and out.[37] This goes without saying for official equipment necessary for the performance of their functions, *e.g.,* means of communication, detection devices, documents, etc. In order to prevent delays and to avoid affording a government a pretext for detaining and holding up an inspector, the immunity from customs regulations would have to apply as well to personal effects, as in the case of diplomats. Again, this may be implicit in diplomatic status, if that is accorded, and no further legislation would be necessary. By administrative regulation, any minor procedural delays involved in diplomatic customs could also be eliminated. Any abuse of these privileges or immunities would have to be taken care of in the same manner as with diplomats, by seeking a waiver of the privileges and immunities from the international body controlling the inspectors or by seeking an inspector's removal.

INVIOLABILITY OF PERSON AND PROPERTY. The inspectors would be immune from service of legal process, civil or criminal arrest. They would have to be exempted from the provisions of the Foreign Agents Registration Act and the Alien Registration Act as are diplomats.[38]

Similarly, it might be necessary to exempt inspectors from various forms of taxation and from service requirements such as military service, jury service, etc., to the extent that they might otherwise apply.

Equipment, documents, and the like in the possession of inspectors should be immune from any seizure, detention, or examination.[39] Again, this is true of diplomatic personnel generally, but legislation implementing the treaty could make this immunity explicit.

FREEDOM FROM ARBITRARY EXPULSION. In the case of diplomats accredited to the United States, the United States can, at will and without cause, declare a member of the diplomatic corps *persona non grata* and request his removal. Inspection personnel would have to be accorded an even better status in this respect.[40] Certainly the host country should not be able to have an inspector removed without cause, else this would give the government a way of pressuring inspectors which might interfere with the inspection. It might also enable a nation designing violation to remove key personnel at opportune times and make it possible by de-

Congressional Implementation

feating the inspection to carry on clandestine violations. Protection against abuse by the inspectors, *e.g.,* by serious violations of the United States law in matters unrelated to the arms control plan, would take the form of request by the United States to the authority controlling the inspectors for a waiver of immunity or for the person's removal.

FREEDOM OF COMMUNICATION. Inspectors must have freedom and facilities to communicate with the parent international body, whether in the United States or elsewhere, without delay or interference. This might involve setting aside for them cable, telephone, and radio facilities. The Federal Communications Commission would be expected to respect and carry out such provisions.[41] The Communications Act might also have to be amended if it is desired to permit wire tapping by the inspectors.[42]

PROTECTION OF CITIZENS AGAINST ABUSE OF INSPECTION

To this point in the study we have considered principally how far a treaty and Congress can go, and may have to go, in giving rights and powers to international inspectors to implement the control plan. But what of the rights of the citizen against abuse of this plan? Some of the most important rights were, of course, those considered as constitutional obstacles to undue control or inspection. We suggested also how control could be carried out while respecting these rights: interrogation and inspection consistent with the safeguards of the Constitution; the possibility of requiring warrants, with their inherent protections, before some kinds of inspection could take place; perhaps provision for payment, as "just compensation" and due process, for persons engaged in arms activities or for those who own patents for arms, or those who possess existing stocks of arms at the time these are rendered illegal. Are there also additional rights which might be granted by Congress to afford further protection against unnecessary loss due to the inspection system or to possible abuse of that system?

DESTRUCTION OF PROPERTY

If inspectors broke into a factory because the owner unlawfully resisted or interfered with the inspection, the latter, of course, could not pretend to compensation.[43] Suppose, however, that maliciously, negligently, or accidentally, inspectors caused physical damage to property of an establishment not engaged in unlawful activity. We have said that the inspectors would be, and probably should be, personally immune from suit, and there would therefore be no successful tort action against them, even if the injury were due to negligence or willfulness. And it might not be feasible to establish, by international agreement, a system of compensation against the international inspecting body. On the other hand, Congress might provide compensation for damage incident to such inspection, covering at least situations of malicious destruction or negligence. And perhaps agreement might be reached that part of the amounts awarded on such claims be contributed by an international fund.[44] The United States might have no financial recourse over against the inspector or the international parent body, but in serious cases could ask to have the inspector's immunity waived or to have him removed.

Such compensation could be provided in special legislation, or perhaps by amendment and extension of the Federal Tort Claims Act.[45] Damage inflicted by a United States inspector under United States regulatory legislation, where the act causing damage is within the scope of his employment, may be covered by the Federal Tort Claims Act.[46] International inspectors, of course, we have assumed are not United States employees, and would not be treated as such for purposes of this act unless Congress so provided.[47] On the other hand, if under an alternative suggested, the control scheme should contemplate inspection by United States inspectors accompanied by international inspectors, perhaps even by one United States official spreading the cloak of federal authority over the acts of international inspectors, an argument might be made that damage by the international inspectors would be attributable to the United States under the Federal Tort Claims Act, even in its present form. It is not, however, desirable to leave these questions open to doubt and conjecture, and explicit legislation authorizing a claim against the United States in these cases should be considered.

Alternatively, special claims procedures before an administrative body might afford effective machinery. The establishment of such a claims "commission" would not raise serious legal problems, since, as we have seen, the person injured could probably not assert a constitutional claim to be compensated.[48]

DISCLOSURE OF TRADE SECRETS

What of damage other than physical damage? If the control and inspection system might under a comprehensive scheme virtually abolish

Congressional Implementation

the concept of secrecy from government activity in this area, must it necessarily abolish elements of secrecy in private manufacture? Today, quite apart from United States requirements of classification, business enterprises jealously guard "trade secrets,"[49] including formulae, ingredients, methods of production, etc., which are or may be claimed to be of tremendous financial importance to them. Federal legislation under existing inspection laws in regard to a number of industries includes provisions forbidding or limiting disclosure by United States officials of information contained in the returns or reports filed with them, or obtained from inspection pursuant to law; criminal penalties are provided for violation of these provisions.[50] Some statutes, indeed, expressly exempt trade secrets from the report required or the inspection authorized;[51] others require the information but also enjoin on the officials who receive it confidential treatment of it unless the national security demands disclosure.[52] There are, in addition, provisions for compensation to the owner for damage due to disclosure by federal officials.[53]

It is probably justice to the manufacturers, and certainly would help to gain their support for arms control inspection, to make provision to compensate them for proved damage due to disclosure of their trade secrets. Although the international regulations under which inspectors would operate would undoubtedly enjoin them from unnecessarily disclosing or in other ways abusing information they obtain in the course of inspection as to activities not unlawful,[54] there might be cases of such disclosure or abuse. Proof of damage in such cases to a particular manufacturer might be difficult, but he should not be deprived of compensation if he can prove his case. Suit against the inspectors, as in the case of the torts discussed above, would presumably be barred by their diplomatic immunity and would probably be rendered ineffectual by their lack of financial responsibility. If there were to be compensation, therefore, it would have to be provided either by a parent international body, following an appropriate proceeding before a claims body or other tribunal, or negotiation on diplomatic levels; or, more likely, compensation might be provided by the United States. It should not prove a substantial expense for this country, and can be justified as a distribution of the cost of disarmament and inspection among the entire population. The United States might perhaps arrange, in turn, for an international fund out of which it and other countries similarly situated could be made whole, and, of course, the inspectors who abuse their position in this respect could probably be removed.

Today, the Federal Tort Claims Act probably does not cover any claims against the United States for trade secret damages, even if caused by United States officials.[55] It is uncertain also whether disclosures by government inspectors of trade secrets obtained in the course of the inspecting process are actionable under general principles of tort law.[56] It might therefore be desirable to provide by statute a comprehensive plan for identifying those injured by abuse of the arms inspection process, including damage due to disclosure of trade secrets, with an adequate opportunity to the complainant to prove his claim. Recovery over by the United States against the international body raises the same questions discussed in connection with other abuses by the inspectors.

STAND-BY LEGISLATION

When Congress enacts legislation to implement an arms control plan, there is an additional and very different kind of legislation it might wish to consider. It might prepare contingent, stand-by legislation for the eventuality that breach of agreement by other parties might compel the United States to consider itself free of the agreement and proceed to take steps in self-defense. The character of such legislation would, of course, depend in large part on the nature of the limitations in the control agreement, the extent to which the United States will have agreed to disorganize its armed forces, disarm, dismantle weapons production, and terminate existing security procedures. Congress might adopt such stand-by legislation to take effect in a described contingency; it might authorize the President to determine when that contingency has taken place and to bring the legislation into effect. Or, it might merely have the legislation prepared for enactment at a future time. Some models for such stand-by legislation might be found in statutes adopted in recent years to go into effect when there is war or a national emergency.[57]

Some may question whether it would be desirable, at the time this country is prepared to undertake arms control, to indicate by such legislation its abiding skepticism as to whether other countries will observe the control agreement. Others may say that one cannot be too careful. Certainly, the adoption of such legislation might make the Congress and the people more secure and alleviate hesitations and doubts about undertaking arms control. Whether that is necessary, and how this would weigh against the possible undesirable international consequences of adopting such legislation, can be considered only when the time comes.

Chapter VI. STATE LAWS AND LOCAL COOPERATION

Arms control, it is here assumed, will be the nation's policy. The President and Senate as treaty makers, the Congress as legislators, the President as Executive, will pursue this policy, implement it, and make it effective. When these branches of the government bring arms control into effect, it will be with the approval, consent, or—at the least—acquiescence of the American people. Public support and urging will have led to the treaty and the legislation; the process of treaty making and legislation, in turn, will educate the citizen and enhance understanding and approval.

This pattern, reflected in all accepted legislation, should not fail in regard to arms control. The process may be gradual and not always forward or without opposition. Arms control and arms inspection may, in degrees differing with the details of the plan, introduce concepts and practices which may evoke suspicion and attack. Opponents of arms control, not necessarily from bad motives, may emphasize the new, may even exaggerate the elements of intrusion into private activity, of "foreign" impingement on United States institutions. Still the process of education for legislation, and education by legislation, should assure that when the Government of the United States has joined an arms control agreement, the people of the United States will not be far behind.

This we must assume. Without this assumption arms control could hardly be effective. The unhappy experience with Prohibition will long recall the futility of attempts at law enforcement without a minimum acceptance of the law by those whom the law would affect.[1] Fortunately, arms control and liquor are very different in their impact on the citizen. Few are they who will be directly affected by arms control, and not many more may even be aware that arms are being controlled. Control and inspection will reach no farther into the lives and awareness of private persons than regulation and control of atomic energy today. Unlike Prohibition, there will be few temptations to violate or circumvent the law, no comparable resentment that the law is invading sacred privacies. Instead, arms control will promise termination or limitation of compulsory military service and radical reductions in national expenditures and therefore in taxes. Arms control should, then, be appealing and popular, regardless of any novel inconveniences to which a few may be subject.

Nonetheless, experience with Prohibition, and with other attempts at federal control and regulation, underlines the need for popular acceptance; it emphasizes also how far effective control demands the aid of state and local authorities.[2] Some eccentric elements in a control scheme, we have suggested, might even require formal state consent by legislation or constitutional amendment. In other respects, state action, legislative, executive, or judicial, might be important or helpful. Beyond that, cooperation and compliance from local officials and citizens could be crucial. Inspectors appearing in various areas of the country must, of course, as a minimum, be assured personal protection; the privileges and immunities granted them by treaty and by act of Congress must be respected everywhere, the needed facilities ungrudgingly accorded. It would also be necessary to have the assistance and support of state and local officials in smoothing the inspection process, in gaining its acceptance, in assuring cooperation from those engaged in the industries subject to inspection. The appointed rounds of an arms inspectorate might be more swiftly and ably completed if these officials took an active part. Routine inspections, the collection and transmittal of data, the procurement of warrants from American courts, the apprehension of violators—these might be delegated to state or local officials to do or to help the international inspectors to do. The energies available to an international inspectorate operating with limited personnel would thereby be much increased. Local authorities would not be superseded, a new, foreign police power would not be imposed on and over them; theirs would be instead a crucial role in making effective new national policies of the highest import. And working through or with the officials and agencies known to the people should make more acceptable international inspection and international inspectors.

Direct local cooperation with foreign and international agencies in the furtherance of international commitments of the United States has some but limited precedent. In several respects the Headquarters Agreement between the United States and the United Nations provides that "appropriate American Authorities" shall take action; some provisions contain prohibitions applicable explicitly to "federal, state or local" officials

State Laws and Local Cooperation

or authorities.[3] But there has never been need or occasion to decide whether state and local officials could be compelled to take affirmative acts under these provisions. The State of New York, host to the United Nations Headquarters, has in fact adopted limited legislation to implement its hospitality.[4] Informally, local officials, in New York as in the District of Columbia, supply services and information directly to foreign or international officials. In the absence of persuasive precedent in treaties or legislation, or in the history of United States relations with foreign or international bodies, the precedents and analogies which suggest themselves are those which have developed since the republic began between the Government of the United States and state and local officials. We shall examine some of this history and the extent to which cooperation was voluntary on the part of the states, or could be required through the supremacy of the federal government. For we assume that the international inspection body, operating in this country pursuant to treaty and laws of the United States, would stand in a position similar to that of a federal agency vis-à-vis state and municipal institutions.

We shall consider state action which would be necessary or desirable: legislation called for by the arms control plan generally, or by special provisions in it; a possible role for state courts; and forms of cooperation by state and local officials and institutions.

STATE LAWS AND ARMS CONTROL

Earlier in this study it was established that inconsistent state laws would present no obstacle to arms control; nor is state legislation or consent necessary, in general, to bring control into effect. It is legal, proper, and indeed wise that in the American federal system the problems of arms control, like other problems of war and peace and the relations between nations, be dealt with by the federal government by treaty and congressional and executive action. No state need give its consent, no state can withhold consent, or otherwise frustrate the national effort to achieve peace and security by agreement with other nations to control arms.

Under the Supremacy Clause of the Constitution, as we have seen, the treaty and implementing legislation would be superior to the constitutions and the laws of all the states. The treaty and federal laws would be written into state law and override any state provisions which might be inconsistent. State legislatures need not take action to repeal or modify such inconsistent laws. The treaty and the acts of Congress would do that of their own force, although it might avoid confusion and uncertainty, and contribute to efficient operation, if the states acted to repeal or modify provisions in their laws which were superseded or limited by the treaty and federal statutes.

A treaty and laws of Congress do not of course merely repeal local laws. They write into the framework of the law provisions forbidding or requiring action by citizens and aliens, individuals and corporations. This too is achieved without need for "implementing" state legislation. Nor will state legislation be necessary in order to subject to international control and inspection state activities or facilities relating to armaments. If, for example, a state should engage in the manufacture of arms, or own uranium mines, those, we have seen, would be subject to federal regulation in the same manner as if they were activities of private persons.

There might be instances, however, where an affirmative act of a state legislature or executive was necessary to make the treaty or federal act effective. Obviously, this is so in the rare cases where a state's consent is expressly required by the Constitution—say, to the purchase of property in the state by the federal government to create a federal enclave for the purposes of the inspection agency.[5] We have suggested also that state consent might be necessary if arms control should involve total abolition of the state militia; or if strictly "governmental activities" of the state were to fall within the control of the arms treaty.[6] Thus, for example, the control agreement might require that the premises and documents of the executive and legislative branches of state governments be subject to inspection, or that state officials be available for interrogation about their official acts. For this, the consent of the states might be necessary. There is no way under the Constitution to compel a state to consent or to adopt any state legislation needed.

USE OF STATE COURTS

In a previous chapter we discussed the extent to which the courts of the United States would be available to the international inspectorate for implementation of its responsibilities under the treaty. Can state courts be made available for similar purposes? Can Congress so provide without the consent and agreement of the state?

Inevitably, a purpose and function deriving from a treaty implemented by Congress are, in our federal system, national in character. To invoke the aid of state courts to further such purpose and function is to use the

State Laws and Local Cooperation 101

local judiciary to a federal purpose. When the Constitution was being created there was indeed a view that the state courts should serve as the lower courts of the country for federal purposes as well, and that it was not necessary to establish a federal judiciary other than the Supreme Court.[7] In fact, however, an independent federal judiciary was established in the early days of the nation.[8] But Congress also provided for the use of state courts to enforce federal regulatory acts.[9] In the days when states and nation were developing their respective positions in the federal system, there were, however, expressions of extreme independence for states and state tribunals. Borrowing concepts from the law of nations, it was said, for example, that a state being an independent sovereignty did not have to enforce penal statutes of the United States, another sovereignty.[10] In 1947, in *Testa v. Katt,* the Supreme Court redefined the relationship of state courts to federal penal law.[11] The Court held that a state court can be required by Congress to entertain a suit under federal law for triple damages. As a result, it may now be said with some confidence that in areas which are within the federal domain national supremacy includes the power to compel the states to enforce federal laws, even in proceedings of a penal quality.[12] Whether, as the broad language of *Testa v. Katt* intimates, states may be required to enforce federal law of a truly criminal character is less clear.

In other respects, state courts have from the beginning consistently availed federal officials. Thus, for a relevant instance, federal officials seeking evidence of a violation of a federal crime have been able to go to a state court for their warrant of search or arrest.[13]

In the implementation of an arms control treaty, therefore, Congress could probably require that state courts also make their existing procedures available to international inspectors or to federal officials on behalf of the international inspectorate. The state courts might be required to subpoena witnesses and administer oaths, issue warrants and relevant writs. They might even, if *Testa v. Katt* is extended that far, be required to bring to trial those who interfere with inspection and those who violate the arms control agreement, if Congress deemed it preferable to have such violations tried in state rather than—or as well as—in federal courts.

COOPERATION OF STATE OFFICERS

State courts to buttress the implementation of arms control would then be available; whether this is of practical importance is less clear.

Cooperation of executive and police officials of states and municipalities appears more clearly desirable and helpful. Can such cooperation be made mandatory by Congress?

Here the independence of the states looms as a great obstacle. State officials cannot, of course, violate valid federal laws or treaties. It is constitutionally another matter, however, to require them to carry out official functions imposed by the federal government rather than by state legislatures. With the exception of narrow areas specified in the Constitution,[14] there would seem to be no precedent to support coerced official cooperation by municipal and state officials.[15]

On the other hand, the history of the country abounds with examples of voluntary cooperation between state and national authorities—by formal state legislation or informal acts of officers. Perhaps the most fertile area is interstate commerce, where the national power is supreme but the necessities of a complicated civilization have resulted in patterns of cooperation between nation and states. The adjustments are still in process: where two authorities have jurisdiction, it is impossible to avoid all conflict; and occasionally areas will be allowed to fall unattended between the two jurisdictions.[16] For the most part, however, voluntary state and federal cooperation has been growing in scope and efficiency. It has also taken varied forms. In regard to enforcement of federal laws, which is our interest here, the federal government has deputized state inspectors, for example, to act also under the federal law.[17] And the states have implemented federal regulation—for example, economic controls during the Second World War—by enacting state penalties for its violation.[18] The result, of course, in that instance, was that state officials were seeking to prevent, discover, and prosecute acts which would also violate federal law.

There are certainly no obstacles under the law of the United States to voluntary cooperation between states and municipalities and an international arms inspectorate, whether through federal mediation or directly.[19] In some instances local officials might be limited by restrictions in state constitutions or laws, but most of the relevant forms of voluntary cooperation by local officials are not likely to be curtailed, and hopefully, state legislation or amendment of state constitutions would remove any limitations to, or even affirmatively command, cooperation. Whether a major role for local authorities in the implementation of arms inspection would be acceptable to other parties to the treaty and to the international body implementing it is more difficult to determine.

State Laws and Local Cooperation

Whether active participation by local officials would be essential to make arms control effective in the United States may depend on the details of the control and the specific purposes and goals of the inspection. Certainly it would be important for inspectors to maintain good relations with local officials. Local police, it has been mentioned, might still be necessary to protect the persons and property of the inspector and to assure that he enjoyed in fact the facilities, privileges, and immunities accorded by treaty and federal law. Habits of cooperation might also serve to make available on a voluntary basis records and documents maintained by the state in implementation of the manifold functions of government, which might provide an international inspectorate with clues to possible control violations.

Perhaps the most important cooperation which local groups could afford the inspectorate would be educational. Before arms inspection began and after it was launched, local authorities might be the ones best able to render arms control and arms inspection intelligible and acceptable to the local community, even those elements in it which might be the object of inspection. Education for cooperation would probably require federal support and federal funds, but local officials and local communal leaders may have to be its effective agents.

Chapter VII. INTERNATIONAL ADMINISTRATIVE REGULATION

To this point we have dealt with an arms control scheme of the kind which the United States has been seeking and which might come about. In this as in the next chapter we shall examine proposals which are not to be found in the deliberations of governments. Here we deal with suggestions once made which might have entailed far-reaching consequences for American law and institutions. They may be examined against the day when they might be made again. It is indeed possible that future proposals may contain some elements once found in plans now discarded; such elements may already be developing in areas other than arms control. Examination may define how far, in fact, they reach, and may suggest alternative methods of achieving desired results which avoid or reduce difficulties.

Once it was contemplated that the control of armaments, so far as applied to the then most important weapons, *i.e.*, atomic weapons, would be effected by an international agreement providing for complete international control and development of all atomic energy.[1] Under that system an international development authority was to have a monopoly of atomic materials and nations would be required to obtain a license from such agency for peaceful uses. Individual nations, under this plan, could be denied the right to prospect, mine, and refine uranium and thorium, to enrich the isotope U-235, to operate various types of reactors and separation plants, to carry on research or develop atomic explosives. International inspectors would scrutinize national activities to assure compliance.

At the time the nations of the world were considering United States proposals along these lines, apparently little public attention was given in the United States to constitutional problems which might be raised by United States participation in such an international scheme. Perhaps it was believed that there was no serious prospect that the plan would be adopted or that the United States would ratify it.[2] Perhaps it was

International Administrative Regulation 105

believed that so novel a plan would in any event be adopted by the United States by constitutional amendment to eliminate doubts as to its validity and to assure public awareness and support.

In recent years the international control of atomic energy has not even been suggested. The scheme of foreseeable arms control treated to this point in this study does not entail international regulatory activity. The treaty, it was contemplated, would set forth prohibitions and limitations. There would be international inspectors to observe whether a nation was complying with the agreement. Beyond that, if in order to comply with these restrictions a nation considered it necessary to regulate by administrative process the armaments industry or related industries, that was entirely a national matter. It would be carried out through national administrative officials and enforced in national courts.

It may be that some different, unforeseen plan will contain elements definitely requiring a system of regulation, a system which would involve making rules, issuing orders, and granting licenses. And the scheme might lodge these functions in an international body. The United Nations proposal for international atomic development may have contemplated such a system, although since negotiation did not achieve progress on the main principles, proposed details for their implementation were not given careful attention. It appears to have been contemplated in general that an international development authority would have such functions, but perhaps only in relation to nations, that it was not to exercise administrative authority over private citizens and groups in any country.

In regard to any plan containing these or similar regulatory elements it is of course desirable that administrative intrusion be kept at a minimum consistent with achieving the desired results. This cardinal principle of democratic administration requires even stricter observance where there is to be administration by an international body over important national activities. Maximum respect for national sensibilities would obviously render a proposal more acceptable, less onerous in operation, easier to administer, and more effective. And in the United States it would reduce the constitutional problems—themselves an indication that proposals are being considered which are untried or disruptive, which might evoke resistance from the citizen.

In the United States, then, any system of international administrative regulation should minimize the exercise of authority or control by the international agency directly over American industry and the citizen. The agency should deal with the United States Government and its officials. And the United States would stand between the international body and its citizens. The international administration would promulgate regulations, setting limits to what might be done in the United States. The regulations and requirements of the agency would be directed to the United States; licenses would be issued to the United States Government; the United States would assure compliance with the requirements of the agency. In turn, of course, the United States would, through legislation and national regulation, control activities of persons in this country, in conformity with the limitations imposed by the treaty and the international agency.

Such a system would raise few special problems under American law. We shall mention briefly those arising from "control" by such an international administration over the United States Government and its activities. There would, of course, also be numerous legal problems involved in the administration by the United States of the activities of its citizens, but these will be only incidentally indicated. They are the problems raised by existing national administrative agencies, the Atomic Energy Commission, or the Federal Communications Commission, or the Civil Aeronautics Board.

Of course, the system suggested would mean that, as applied in Russia, the Soviet Government, in turn, would stand between the international agency and its citizens. But in the Soviet Union, as in the United States, the international body through its inspectors should be able to uncover whether the government is perpetrating or permitting violations, whether in fact it is carrying out its obligation to assure compliance with the requirements established by the treaty and the international agency.

Most of the problems with which this chapter will deal should, therefore, not arise in relation to arms control. Still, it may be that because of fear and mistrust, or an inadequate understanding of the operations of government and administrative bodies, there would be a desire to regulate more closely activities in the Soviet Union or Communist China, or other countries not beyond our suspicions. There may then be proponents for a plan, or elements in a plan, which would involve international administration and scrutiny not only of governmental activities, but also directly of private undertakings, the issuance of international regulations and orders to private persons, and the granting of licenses to them. Whatever the consequences of differences between Soviet socialism and American private enterprise, such a suggestion would involve

International Administrative Regulation 107

reciprocal operation in the United States as well. This chapter will consider whether, to what extent, and on what basis the United States could constitutionally accept such direct international administrative regulation in this country.

PRECEDENTS FOR INTERNATIONAL REGULATION

The questions suggested may be described as those raised by international administration and international administrative law. For the United States, perhaps, these have not in the past had practical significance in any sense comparable to similar categories and concepts in domestic law and government. For other countries concepts we know as those of administrative law have, on the contrary, been acquiring an international dimension. The European Coal and Steel Community, for example, is in the process of offering a proving ground for practices and theories of administrative law on an international basis, not unlike those which are familiar within the United States. The European Atomic Energy Community (EURATOM) and the European Economic Community (Common Market) should also contribute to the development of "international administrative law." [3]

Of course, "administrative" action in the United States includes matters as different as the rummaging through a tourist's valise by the customs inspector, and the regulation of the entire communications industry by the Federal Communications Commission or the aviation industry by the Civil Aeronautics Board. And there are some international activities to which the United States is already party with elements and characteristics which in a domestic context may be viewed as part of the body of administrative practices and problems. Action of the United States Government, for example, may be subject in given respects to decisions and conclusions of international bodies which may be characterized as administrative or regulatory. The activities of the principal organs of the United Nations may in some respects be deemed regulatory.[4] Among specialized agencies of the United Nations, the International Bank for Reconstruction and Development and the International Monetary Fund, for example, also possess authority to make rules for member nations and to settle disputes among them.[5] The World Health Organization recommends practices to member states, some of which the United States has adopted and implemented.[6] The long-established Universal Postal Union has developed common international practices by which the United States abides, and must abide if it is to maintain the advantages of participating in an international postal system.[7] Other fields of international regulation include the control of narcotics, where international officials have propounded, and the United States has applied, cooperative practices for making more effective the international control of drugs.[8] International marketing agreements in various commodities—*e.g.,* wheat, sugar—establish international councils with power to set export and import quotas.[9] The International Atomic Energy Agency has some supervisory functions as concerns recipients of nuclear materials.

There are also numerous examples of international regulation on a bilateral or regional basis, particularly in the fishing industry. We mention only some arrangements to which the United States is party. A treaty with Canada in 1930 established a mixed commission to make rules limiting or prohibiting the taking of certain salmon and allowing the commission to fix net mesh size; fishing areas and seasons were made subject to approval of the commission. Halibut fishing has also been regulated under comparable arrangements with Canada.[10] And an international convention for the Northwest Atlantic Fisheries, which came into effect in 1950, established an international panel to deal with fishing in that area.[11] A wider, multilateral Convention for the Regulation of Whaling established a commission with extensive power to recommend rules.[12] The activities of the United States-Canadian International Joint Commission may also be considered of the character of international administrative action.[13]

The international experience in which the United States is already partaking, however, differs fundamentally from, say, the actions of the Federal Communications Commission, or from the powers once anticipated for a proposed international atomic development agency. The regulatory powers of existing international bodies are, as we have seen, limited in scope. More significantly, whether for legal or political reasons, these bodies cannot, in general, bind the United States without its consent. Some of these bodies have only the power to recommend, *e.g.,* the United Nations General Assembly and comparable bodies in the Specialized Agencies. In the Security Council the United States has a veto. In other international bodies, like the commodity groups, there are "weighted-voting" arrangements, and blocs of countries with similar interests can align themselves to prevent violence to these interests.[14] In some bodies the protection of the United States against the imposition of decisions of which it disapproves lies in its leading political and economic situation and, in the background, its power to withdraw from the arrangements. Even in regional agreements like the Convention for the Northwest Atlantic Fisheries, the presence of United States members on key panels and the agreed method for reaching decisions make it unlikely that regulations could be established which do not have the concurrence of the United States Government. The halibut and salmon conventions with Canada now require approval by the United States for regulations of the international commissions.

For constitutional purposes, there is a more important, critical distinction between past and present arrangements of the United States and those which international administration and regulation would entail. The regulations of existing international bodies do not control or directly affect the rights and interests of individuals in the United States. In some instances, as suggested, this is so because the United States Government stands between the international body and the American citizen and itself determines whether it will make a regulation proposed by the international body applicable in the United States.[15] Or, in other instances, the character of the regulation is such that it applies to the action of the Government of the United States, not to the actions of private persons.[16] And even, for example, when a treaty with Canada permits its officers to seize an American vessel violating the Sockeye Salmon Treaty, the Canadian officials seizing such vessel must immediately turn it over to United States officials for disposition and any criminal proceedings.[17]

The disposition of claims of American citizens by an international claims commission should perhaps be mentioned here. While the disposition may seem judicial or quasi-judicial in character, rather than regulatory, it appears to be an exercise of authority by international or foreign personnel over the rights of Americans. By treaty the United States has at different times agreed that claims of American nationals against another nation or its nationals shall be determined by an international commission, whose findings shall be binding.[18] Disposition of international claims by machinery of this kind has deep historical roots. The United States has treated the claims of its citizens in this way since the Revolution, and there has been no successful challenge to it under the Constitution.[19] Any unfairness to a private citizen might be compensated by voluntary act of Congress, but the citizen could only recover what Congress afforded.[20] The accepted rationale of this practice has been that when a nation asserts through diplomatic channels a claim of one of its citizens, it is deemed to be pressing a claim of the nation. It is the United States which is the party to the international agreement and the United States which is the claimant before an international commission determining claims. The award is made to the United States and turned in to the United States Treasury. Only as Congress sees fit to recognize the merit of a citizen's claim and to appropriate funds is payment made to an individual American claimant.[21] In general, the courts will not interfere in order to scrutinize the original agreement, the merits of the determinations by the international claims commission, the procedures before it, or the action of Congress pursuant to the award.[22] Control of activities in the United States by an international regulatory body would be quite different: there would be continuous supervision and regulation, not merely a quasi-judicial rendering of a money judgment; there would be regulation of activities of private citizens, and not just a determination of rights of the United States; there would be regulation of activities which take place within the United States, and not only those of American citizens which take place in other lands, on the high seas, in far space.

International administrative law involving intensive regulation of American industry—like the armaments industry—would therefore be new for this country. But if the familiar is not to be confused with the necessary, so the novel is not to be assumed to be the undesirable, the unnecessary, the illegal, or the unconstitutional. Although rooted in practices as old as the republic, United States administrative law itself has had its major growth quickly and recently in response to urgent requirement.[23] This growth was not without pain, and was greeted with alarm and forebodings.[24] The international community may be and may long remain a wishful concept. But necessity engendered by the scientific revolution may yet mother international machinery, not only of kinds already known, but others yet to be invented. Such international machinery, of a character resembling what has been called "administrative," will then seek acceptance in United States law and institutions.

INTERNATIONAL ADMINISTRATION AND CONSTITUTIONAL LIMITATIONS

Elements in direct international control which might be proposed for a future arms control plan might include the following:

(*a*) An international agency is to assume title to and control of certain products and materials.

(*b*) The United States and its officers, as well as its citizens and residents, may not mine, process, or possess such materials or manufacture weapons from them without approval, license, and supervision by the international agency.

(c) The agency may make rules, administer a licensing system, and enforce its decisions by appropriate remedies—*e.g.,* cease and desist orders, closing down plants, confiscation of illegal materials, or cancellation or nonrenewal of licenses—enforceable perhaps through national tribunals.

One may assume that any treaty to which the United States will be party will seek maximum protection for the rights of Americans which might be affected by the action of an international agency. The personnel selected to administer the agency, the standards established to guide and control the administrator, the procedures he is required to follow in reaching decisions—these would certainly be provided in the plan so as to assure in some measure competence, fairness, and reasonableness. At the same time one must anticipate, keeping in mind that such an administrative agency also has to operate in other countries and "live" with their systems, that an international administrative agency would be independent of American political bodies and American courts. In its method of operation, it would develop its own procedures and its own precedents. If there is to be any review of the decisions of this body, appeal would lie, not—probably—to an American tribunal, but to an international tribunal, whether of a judicial or of a political character. Safeguards against administrative caprice, like those which have developed in the United States, might be available; but these would not, we may assume, include recourse to United States courts.

What constitutional problems are presented by such a system? At the outset we are met again by the suggestion that perhaps constitutional limitations do not apply. In a previous chapter, we considered whether actions of the United States Government under the treaty power are subject to the same limitations which apply to other acts of the federal government, principally to legislation by Congress. We decided that the treaty power is subject to these constitutional limitations. But there may be invoked a different suggestion, that the United States may by treaty establish a system of international law, under international sovereignty, which is not United States law and to which constitutional limitations on United States law are irrelevant. Several nations would by treaty be establishing a new administrative authority with quasi-legislative power. This would not be a United States body; it would be an international body. Its officials would be international officials chosen by international machinery and responsible to an international parent created by international agreement. In entering into such an arrangement the United States would not be attempting to give new powers to its own officials by exercise of the treaty power; it would be joining with others to establish a new legislative authority in the international field, which, in that limited area, would be acting under an international "sovereignty," in the same way that United States administrative bodies act under the sovereignty of the United States pursuant to legislation by Congress.

In support of this view it would be argued that if nations feel the need to deal with international problems by such international machinery, the treaty power is sufficient to meet this need of the United States to join other nations in this enterprise. The United States has all the sovereignty that other nations enjoy in international affairs,[25] and the treaty power is the principal mechanism for exercising it. This treaty law of nations is outside the pattern which the Constitution prescribes for actions by the United States, and the basis for such distinction is inherent in the treaty power. On this view, the authority conferred upon the international body, the law which it will administer, the procedures which it will provide are all outside the framework—and not subject to the limitations—of the Constitution. The Constitution applies to United States action. It does not apply to international action, even international action in which the United States has voluntarily joined.[26] American citizens would be subject to the new administrative law of nations established by treaty, as they would be if this law antedated the Constitution and were deemed incorporated into it. On that basis an arms control treaty dealing with matters of international concern and put into effect in accordance with procedures established by the Constitution could create its own pattern of regulation different from administrative programs established—for an instance—by congressional regulation of interstate commerce. Specifically, the international administration of an arms regulation program would not have to meet issues of "delegation" or of judicial review, or satisfy other requirements of due process, substantive or procedural.

One need not conclude that this argument goes too far, to suggest that it goes quite far. The argument against this position may be simply stated. The United States cannot, by treaty or otherwise, set up a new "sovereignty" in the United States over citizens and residents. Any effort to do so is a delegation of the authority of government and is subject to stringent constitutional limitations. The legislative power is lodged by the Constitution in Congress; no other body can be given legislative power. The executive power is in the President; no other can be given executive power in this country. Congress and the President may delegate their authority to administrative bodies, but these delegations are sharply limited and authority exercised by the delegates remains inevitably federal action subject to all the limitations on the federal government. The treaty power is only another federal power, subject to the Constitution. It cannot circumvent constitutional limitations and the Constitution's careful balance of separated powers by purporting to create an independent sovereignty in the United States outside the framework of the Constitution. The present proposal would mean an administrative process not subject to control or limitation, to check or balance by other branches of the government.

There is no precedent or extended discussion to cite for one or the other of these views. There is also no theory or principle which is conclusive. The argument for the broader view is the unlimited, equal sovereignty of the United States vis-à-vis other nations; against it is the traditional view that the Constitution established limited federal authority of enumerated powers carefully circumscribed. One can state the arguments on both sides; beyond that, although the consequences for the character of American government may be extensive, there is no basis for a clear choice. The broader view would imply virtually no constitutional limitations on the international administrative process, and requires little further consideration. For purposes of this study, it is useful to proceed from the narrower view, and examine what could be done within its limitations. We shall consider, then, that when the United States joins other nations to confer power upon an international body in regard to activities of its citizens within the United States, the international body, for constitutional purposes, is deemed to be exercising federal power and is subject to the limitations which apply to such exercise of federal power.

Since constitutional limitations are deemed to apply, we shall consider problems raised by several aspects of the plan for international development and regulation. Two of these present few difficulties. The prohibition on activities of the United States has been considered, and we concluded that the right of the treaty makers under the Constitution to agree that the United States Government would not manufacture defined weapons, or process materials related to such weapons, is hardly open to doubt. A second aspect of the regulation might be the assumption of ownership and control by the international agency of nuclear sources and materials. In so far as mines, minerals, or other materials belonging to private persons are taken and transferred to an international body, this would constitute a taking by the United States for a public use, for which the Fifth Amendment requires compensation. The federal government, in effect, would be taking these properties from private persons and then transferring them to the international body. That the federal government did not retain these materials itself would not render the taking any the less a taking for a public purpose. That United States resources are, for example, transferred to allies does not render such transfer unconstitutional; nor does it render the exercise of the federal power of eminent domain or taxation for these purposes an abuse of constitutional power.[27] The treaty makers and the Congress may decide that such transfers are in the national interest. Similarly, they might decide that a transfer of strategic materials to an international agency so that other nations would do likewise was also in the national interest.

INTERNATIONAL ADMINISTRATION AS A DELEGATION OF FEDERAL POWER

The major objections on constitutional grounds to international administration would be addressed to the regulation of activities of American citizens.[28] The first basis for challenge to international regulatory provisions might be on the ground that the federal government was delegating its authority and control to an international body.

What is the nature of the "delegation" in our hypothetical situation? The treaty makers and Congress would agree that the United States Government and American citizens would not manufacture, possess, or use certain weapons or materials. The policy, therefore, would be established by the federal government and would involve no delegation. The treaty and legislation might go further, however, and require giving possession of products and materials to the international agency; this, too, would seem to involve no serious question of delegation. Finally, there is provision for license and approval by the international agency of certain activities "delegated back," as it were, to the United States and to its citizens. So far as the activities of the United States Government are concerned, there appears to be nothing in the Constitution which deprives the United States of authority to agree by treaty not to

International Administrative Regulation 115

carry on such activities, or to carry them on only subject to approval of an international body.

Serious questions are raised by delegation of control of the activities of private citizens, however. In the past difficult problems in American constitutional law have revolved around the transfer of authority by Congress: the delegation of legislative power to the Executive, to administrative bodies, to the courts, or to private groups; and the assignment of judicial power to administrative agencies.[29] At different times such delegations have been upheld; a very few delegations by Congress have been struck down.[30] In foreign affairs and in the exercise of the war power, the merged powers of the President and the Congress have never been unraveled and no such delegation by Congress to the President has been struck down.[31] Today a delegation to an American agency of the powers here envisaged would almost surely be sustained. Would the international character of the administrators affect the validity of the delegation?

The Constitution says: "All legislative Powers herein granted shall be vested in a Congress of the United States," and "The Executive Power shall be vested in a President of the United States of America." Reading these with other pertinent provisions of the Constitution might suggest, therefore, that United States executive and legislative power could only be entrusted to United States officials, appointed by the President, confirmed by the Senate, and taking an oath to support the United States Constitution. Yet as regards some activities on behalf of the United States, these may not be constitutionally essential. Many acts are done on behalf of the United States by persons not officers of the United States. We have seen in an earlier chapter that inspection might be delegated to international officials not meeting the formal requirements noted. Whether regulatory functions can also be delegated to such non–United States officials may well turn on the nature of the system of regulation and the functions reserved to the international administrator. The international character of the agency would loom smaller as a possible constitutional obstacle if it were authorized only to fill the interstices of a policy determined in the treaty, rather than to make broad determinations of policy itself.[32] No definite conclusion is possible. Perhaps some support for the exercise of some regulatory functions by international officials might be derived from decisions upholding delegation to private groups in the United States, *e.g.,* tobacco marketing committees, although delegation in those cases left to private persons only a veto power or, at most, limited "interstitial" determinations.[33] It might also be argued that since by treaty or act of Congress the activities in question could have been forbidden entirely, it is not improper to make them permissible only upon the consent of an international group.[34] And this international body, while not immediately subject to congressional control, would be governed by standards established in or pursuant to the treaty, and ultimately subject to control through diplomatic action; and finally the treaty establishing it would be subject to termination and repeal. Again, one can only suggest the questions, and some arguments. There are no confident answers.

There would be no problem of delegation in regard to enforcement. This, we here assume, would be in the hands of the United States. Congress presumably would make it a crime to carry on activities in violation of the agreement and contrary to the regulations issued by the international body. Such legislation would be authorized by the Constitution as an implementation of the treaty; or it might be considered a definition of a new offense against the law of nations.[35]

"DUE PROCESS" BY INTERNATIONAL TRIBUNALS

There are other difficulties. United States administrative law has grown up within limits, not always clearly defined or determined, allowed it by the Constitution. In addition to problems of "delegation," the administrative process has had to meet assertions that administrative regulations deprived persons of constitutional rights, principally the due process of law. Since, we have here assumed, the establishment of an international administration in the United States is an exercise of federal power subject to constitutional limitations, must an international administrative agency meet the same constitutional standards, afford the same constitutional guarantees, be treated for all constitutional purposes as though it were a federal administrative agency for the development of atomic energy? If in the international context it is not possible to fulfill these requirements in the same way, are there international substitutes which might meet the requirements of the United States Constitution?

Even the questions cannot be fully explored here. Possible answers can only be suggested, and with considerable hesitation. Without attempting to distill and restate in a word or paragraph the complex learning of United States constitutional law as it relates to the adminis-

International Administrative Regulation

trative process, some propositions may be stated for American administrative law which may at least suggest answers for our international problems.

The difficulties are aggravated by considerable uncertainty in regard to what the Constitution demands of the United States administrative process. There have been statutes and cases setting forth standards which the federal administrator must meet, but which of these are required by the Constitution, which freely accorded by Congress, is not always clear.[36] Also, administrative action in the United States includes quite different kinds of acts affecting quite different kinds of rights; only the most general kind of generalizations can be made which would apply to all of them.

Still, in regard to the kind of administrative regulation of industry approximating most closely the concern of this chapter, some rules are fairly well established. When a federal regulatory agency acts—*e.g.,* when it grants or withholds, renews or fails to renew, or cancels a license—it must go through proper motions to reach its decisions, that is, it must accord procedural due process appropriate to the particular action or decision.[37] This would generally include notice and an opportunity to be heard, and a requirement that the administrator receive relevant evidence and give it due consideration.[38] An applicant will be heard in a United States court to claim that he was not accorded his due procedures, and the court will enjoin the administrative action if it finds that these were not granted.[39] The right to procedural due process, and the right to assure it by appeal to the courts, appear to be not matters of congressional grace but of constitutional guarantee.[40]

Administrative action must also, the courts tell us, be reasonable; administrators must accord "substantive due process."[41] And the right to challenge the constitutionality of the administrative action in the courts, on the ground that it deprives the petitioner of property without due process of law, or that it violates other substantive provisions of the Constitution, is also, it would seem, guaranteed by the Constitution.[42] United States courts have also heard objections, apparently on a constitutional basis, that the administrator exceeded his authority under the statute and was therefore acting outside the law.[43] And the courts have considered claims that administrative action requiring support in evidence was not, in fact, supported by evidence.[44]

Must our international licensing system meet similar standards of substantive and procedural due process? Must there be an opportunity in the courts to present a claim that these standards were not met? That the action of the administrative body exceeded its authority under the treaty? That there was no evidence to support its finding? If, for example, an American manufacturer sought a license from the international administrator to carry on regulated operations under an arms control or atomic development agreement, must the international licensing body give notice and hold hearings on his application? Must the applicant be afforded an opportunity to challenge the decision denying him a license or canceling a license on the ground that there was no hearing, or that the action was arbitrary or discriminatory? If the opportunity to raise these questions in some tribunal is required by the Constitution, would it be satisfied by review by an international body?

In the first instance, of course, whatever the Constitution requires of the administrative process itself could be accorded by an international administrative agency. Apart from any need to satisfy United States constitutional requirements in order to make United States participation possible, the international community, and its members, concerned for their national rights and the rights of their citizens, would in any event wish to provide fair procedures and reasonable results. All that could be asked in the name of the Constitution, it would seem, is that the procedures satisfy standards of fairness acceptable generally in our civilization. The standard of substantive due process, too, would probably be met if the proposed action did not clearly violate accepted notions of reasonableness. The higher those standards, the less basis would there be, of course, for objection that the international arrangements left something constitutional to be desired. A system of review by international machinery would be an important element in these safeguards. If the standards were high, if some kind of international review were available, there would be less disposition also to hold that those standards could be tested in the courts of the United States.

It is this element in United States administrative-constitutional law —judicial review—which raises what may be the most serious difficulties. In the United States, appeal is generally provided from a final administrative ruling of a regulatory agency to a court. It would seem to be a constitutional right to go to a court to challenge such final administrative action at least on grounds of due process.[45] In our situation, there could hardly be appeal from the action of the inter-

International Administrative Regulation 119

national agency to an American court,[46] if only because the nations would not agree—just as the United States might not agree to review of the international administration by courts of some other country. Nor could this need be fully met by an international court. An international body, judicial in character, could perhaps afford some review of the propriety of administrative action; it might conceivably be required to apply standards comparable to those of the United States Constitution. But if there is a constitutional right to have a court consider constitutional objection to administrative regulations affecting the rights of an American citizen, it might need to be provided by a United States court.

One answer to the problem of judicial review of international administrative decisions might be that United States courts would not undertake it. The field of international relations is perhaps the leading example of situations in which, even if private rights are asserted, the courts have declined to scrutinize the activities of the political branches of the government.[47] The constitutional rights of persons involved in the exercise of foreign relations are in many cases left entirely to the political branches to vindicate; the courts will not interfere. It may be, therefore, that if the political branches of the government, the treaty makers and the law makers, have agreed to the establishment in the United States of an international regulatory body, the decision of the government to enter into this arrangement, as well as all the actions of the international body, might be declared by the courts to constitute "political questions" about which the citizen must go to his Congress or President with any petitions or complaints.

Even if the courts did not treat the entire arrangement and all the actions of the international body as "political questions," it might be that this right to have constitutional claims considered by a United States court would be indirectly avoided. In the United States a principal method for pressing a claim that an administrative ruling does not pass constitutional muster is for the aggrieved to seek an injunction against the administrator. In our case, it may be that the status of the international agency and its personnel would protect it against suit in United States courts, so that an American citizen objecting to a ruling of the agency could not in fact get the opportunity to assert his constitutional claim. In regard to action by the United States Government, the doctrine generally described as the sovereign immunity of the United States to suit in its courts without its consent has been held not to bar a suit to enjoin action by a federal official under authority of a law, the constitutionality of which is being challenged.[48] For doctrinal purposes, the suit is deemed to be not one against the United States. But an American official has no personal immunity. If as proposed in an earlier chapter the international administrative body and its officials should enjoy diplomatic or quasi-diplomatic immunity, they could not be brought into court, even to challenge the constitutionality of their official action under the treaty. No suit to enjoin the international body or its officers could lie and the constitutional questions could not be raised. Even an indirect attack, by suit against a United States official whose action might also be involved, might fail if the immune international official was an indispensable party to the suit.[49] As said in another connection, such grant of immunity would probably not be invalidated even if its effect were to deprive the citizen of an opportunity to assert a constitutional claim.[50]

On the other hand, that the suit to enjoin might not be available does not preclude all forms of judicial protection. If the claimant were willing to risk the test, he could violate the regulation of the international administrator. This would, as we have assumed, be a violation of federal law. In his trial for such crime he could challenge the validity of the administrative regulation, alleging violation of either procedural or substantive due process; if the allegation were sustained, he would go free.[51] Or, the citizen could refuse to comply with the international ruling, necessitating the use of force to compel him. If the international agency used federal machinery and officials to enforce its orders, the citizen might seek to enjoin the federal marshal. Unless the immune international official were deemed an indispensable party, the action would be entertained. Whether in such an action, or possibly even in a criminal proceeding, the court would look behind the order of the international body and check it for due process might depend on whether it would consider this a "political question."

In sum, it would seem that national administration under international supervision affords in general the best system of regulation and would involve few constitutional difficulties. If direct international administrative regulation were called for, the United States and other nations creating an international agency would have to take measures appropriate in the international context to insure that the actions of the agency were fair procedurally and reasonable in substance. International machinery should be available to consider challenges to the action of the international administration, including claims that the administrator had exceeded his authority under the treaty, had acted unreasonably, or had failed to meet the standards established in the international agreement or in regulations approved under it. If some opportunities for challenge and review were afforded, if the international arrangement as a whole were reasonable and fair, courts of the United States might be more disposed to refuse to consider challenges to either the arrangement as a whole or to actions under it. In any event, the doctrine that courts will not interfere in political questions may be a protection to an international agency against interference by United States courts, and the immunity to suit of the agency and its officials would be another. On the other hand, if criminal prosecution of Americans in United States courts were an element in the program, the courts would be reluctant to convict an American without giving him an opportunity to challenge the fairness and reasonableness of the international order which he is accused of violating.

One may mention again that regardless of what courts may do or refuse to do later, the treaty makers and the law makers have also sworn to uphold the Constitution; theirs is a duty to act consistently with the Constitution and to protect the rights of citizens thereunder, whether the courts will or will not.

Chapter VIII. INTERNATIONAL TRIBUNALS

In this chapter we shall consider the impact on American law of international tribunals. While, in general, disarmament proposals and negotiations have not included any significant role for such tribunals, earlier sections of this study may suggest uses for such a body which deserve examination in the light of American law. We shall examine first what functions in support of an arms control agreement might usefully be conferred upon such tribunals—perhaps the settlement of differences, whether between the United States and other parties, or between the United States and an international inspecting body. We shall consider as well possible uses such a tribunal might have in the implementation of the activities of international inspectors in the United States.

Much of what follows is devoted to the possibility of conferring upon international tribunals criminal jurisdiction over individuals performing acts in violation of a control agreement. Even to suggest such inquiry requires explanation.

Arms control, we have said, will consist primarily, if not entirely, of a number of limitations on the activities of nations. Whether there is a ceiling on the number of troops under arms, or a nearly total abolition of armies; whether weapons are reduced in number, or eliminated; whether production of new weapons is stopped or curtailed—it is primarily the government and its policies which are being controlled, regulated. And in a society of sovereign nations the enforcement of such controls and limitations can take few forms: if there is a breach by one party, other parties to the treaty make diplomatic representations, or bring the matter before the United Nations or perhaps the International Court of Justice. They may themselves feel and act free of the treaty's limitations; or take measures—perhaps even go to war.

It seems most unlikely that any foreseeable arms control plan would include, as a principal feature, international enforcement against individual violators. While serious arms control violations might be declared "war crimes" and heads of state and political leaders brought to trial, that—as at Nuremberg—could hardly occur except following victory in war. Even as to the kind of "war crime" dealt with there, while the "Nuremberg principles" have been approved by resolutions of the United Nations General Assembly,[1] no nation has bound itself for the future to hand over its leaders for international trial.

International trials for lesser officials or private persons for arms control violations also seem most improbable. The individual violating arms control for private purposes contrary to the wishes of his government would be tried by his government in its own courts. The violations of arms control which would be of most serious international concern—governmental circumvention or violation of treaty obligations—would also involve individuals, official or private. These individuals, of course, would not be tried and punished by their government. But there would also be little purpose in reaching through to punish an individual for acts desired by his government and done on its behalf. Besides, in the present world order there is no way of doing it.

In the United States, too, we must assume that the individual who violates arms control will be treated by American authorities as a violator of American law. He will be dealt with in accordance with the due process of the same laws applicable to violators of national controls on atomic materials, or narcotics, or a host of other subjects and areas whose regulation is enforced by criminal trial and penalty in American courts. If, on the other hand—and some may consider the suggestion insulting or ludicrous—he were acting in collusion with the nation's authorities, he would hardly be prosecuted, even though arms control might still remain officially part of the nation's criminal law. The purposes of the criminal law—whether prevention, or deterrence, or rehabilitation, or even a measure of retribution—are not relevant in those circumstances, and would not be served by punishment of the individual. And this nation, like other nations, would not agree to his punishment by others for such "violations" reflecting the highest national policy. If, in different circumstances, the nations of the world should recognize the need for a system of international criminal law which might apply even to such national violations, the time will be one of supranational needs and tendencies. For the United States, the Constitution, in such a hypothetical contingency, will have been adjusted to those needs, and the adjustments can take account also of the need for international criminal tribunals.

For the effective control of arms, then, this study has considered that it is the United States Government which will be responsible to other parties, to any international investigating body created, and to the international community. The United States will undertake to abide by the controls and to enforce them in the United States against all who would violate them. Interference with inspection or infringements of substantive limitations of the control plan will be violations of the law of the United States punished in American courts. Even contempt and perjury proceedings in support of the inspectors would be left to United States courts. This system of enforcement would be effective, easy to accept, and would raise fewest constitutional questions.

Consideration of criminal jurisdiction for international tribunals in this study, then, has different purposes. First, fear and mistrust of the Soviet Union might lead some Americans to the suggestion that arms control be enforced against Russian leaders and citizens by a criminal law which is supranational, in international courts. Then, one must repeat, the same controls would have to be accepted for the United States. And the examination which follows will help put the implications of such a proposal in the context of United States constitutional and legal institutions.

There is another reason for this chapter. At one time there were serious proposals for the establishment of international criminal courts to exercise an agreed jurisdiction. Those courts were intended to deal with offenses by individuals—perhaps piracy, or slave trade, or forms of genocide—which nations might agree would be better handled by international tribunals under an international law. International criminal courts might in the future also be suggested for some purposes related to the control of armaments—not for important breaches on behalf of the nation, but for violations by individuals or groups for their private gain—for example, international "rings" running arms on the high seas or across national borders. In such cases, where arms violations reflect private purposes rather than national policy, nations might more seriously consider cooperative action for their suppression, and in those circumstances, a common system of enforcement through a common system of tribunals in all participating countries might commend itself. Such proposals in the past have not been adequately examined from the point of view of the Constitution;[2] it appears desirable to suggest, in the context of arms control, some of the major issues involved.

We shall, then, later in the chapter, deal with such criminal courts, principally as they might apply in the United States to Americans. We shall also suggest special cases and situations where such international criminal courts might raise fewer constitutional difficulties and offer greater likelihood of acceptance.

INTERNATIONAL TRIBUNALS AND THE TREATY POWER

One might begin with basic questions, the answers to which have been assumed, usually without examination. Can the United States agree by treaty to establish international tribunals? To call a body a "tribunal" or even a "court" does not, of course, necessarily determine its status for either international or constitutional purposes. We are concerned here primarily, as will appear, with a body which might exercise functions of "judicial" character; if that phrase is not beyond ambiguity, it has a recognized content in the law of the United States.[3]

The question we have put, if put that generally, is not difficult to answer. It is not beyond the power of the United States to join by treaty in the establishment of an international body which would exercise judicial functions. The treaty power, we have seen, is broad enough to support any international agreement on matters of legitimate international concern. It is surely a legitimate subject for a treaty for the United States to join with other nations to establish international tribunals to implement international law, or treaty provisions, or the law of nations as developed in treaties. An international arms control agreement is solid basis for the establishment by treaty of a tribunal to make it effective.

If the establishment of a judicial body by treaty suggests questions, it is because of Article III of the Constitution. That article provides that

the judicial Power of the United States, shall be vested in one supreme Court, and in such inferior Courts as the Congress may from time to time ordain and establish. The Judges, both of the supreme and inferior Courts, shall hold their Offices during good Behaviour, and shall, at stated Times, receive for their Services, a Compensation, which shall not be diminished during their Continuance in Office.

Article III provides further that the judicial power shall extend to certain cases and controversies, including—what most matters here—"all cases, in Law and Equity, arising under this Constitution, The Laws of the United States, and Treaties made, or which shall be made, under their Authority"; "Controversies to which the United States shall be a Party"; and controversies between citizens and "foreign States, Citizens or Subjects." One might perhaps object that the power of the United States to establish courts, especially courts dealing with controversies of the categories indicated, is limited to such "constitutional courts" established by Congress under Article III, and that the United States cannot agree to establish different courts, even by treaty.

TRIBUNALS NOT EXERCISING UNITED STATES JUDICIAL POWER

The scope of the objection may be immediately reduced, on grounds which are narrow but adequate. Article III prescribes "the judicial Power of the United States." This suggests judicial power exercised on behalf of the United States Government, or in places and circumstances where the exercise of judicial power belongs to the United States as a function of its sovereign, governmental authority. As we shall see, if certain functions are accorded to an international tribunal in the United States, particularly if it is to exercise criminal jurisdiction here, the tribunal may indeed be exercising United States judicial power. In general, however, the fact that an international tribunal has judicial functions, that these judicial functions were conferred upon it by a treaty to which the United States is party, and that the United States or its citizens may in some contexts be the object of these judicial functions would not, *per se,* render the power exercised by this tribunal "judicial Power of the United States"; there is then no question raised under Article III. In this regard, the judicial power is no different from the other powers conferred by the Constitution. That other international bodies which the United States has joined by treaty may have a kind of legislative or executive power—*e.g.,* the Security Council of the United Nations—does not mean that those bodies are exercising the legislative power or the executive power of the United States in any sense material to constitutional law.

Consider the following accepted United States actions, some of which have already been mentioned in this study:

—The United States has in a number of treaties agreed that claims

International Tribunals

of United States citizens against a foreign government be submitted to an international commission.[4] It might be argued that such treaties establish a tribunal other than one under Article III of the Constitution to consider a case between a citizen and a foreign state, one of the categories of jurisdiction conferred by that article.

—The United States has accepted and submitted to the jurisdiction of international tribunals, *e.g.*, the International Court of Justice.[5] It might be argued that since the judicial power of the United States extends to "Controversies to which the United States shall be a Party," other tribunals for considering such controversies are forbidden.

—By treaty and implementing legislation the United States has given to foreign consular officers exclusive judicial power over matters involving their nation's seamen,[6] although these might otherwise be within the admiralty and maritime jurisdiction of the United States courts.

—And the North Atlantic Treaty Organization Status of Forces Treaty, like federal legislation during the Second World War,[7] has recognized the right of military forces of allied nations to try their personnel in this country by their own Service Courts, even for acts which also violate United States law and would otherwise be subject to trial in American courts.

While there may be argument as to whether some of these foreign or international tribunals are judicial in character, others clearly are. These instances support the view that the United States may agree that other tribunals shall exercise judicial power, where such a tribunal would not be exercising "the judicial Power of the United States"; even if it is a judicial body, it is not one representing the governmental power of the United States. Nor is it material that some of the cases before an international tribunal might, in some other form, have also appeared before a United States court. Claims by an American citizen against a foreign government, for example, might—if that government waived immunity—be the basis for a suit in an American court. When taken up with the foreign government by the United States, however, such a claim, as we have seen, becomes a diplomatic claim of the United States.[8] It may be settled by diplomatic negotiation, by arbitration, perhaps by an international court in a judicial proceeding. In that context, however, even the judicial proceeding is not an exercise of the judicial power of the United States. So also, controversies between the United States and other countries might conceivably come up in a domestic court of the United States as one of the "Controversies to which the United States shall be a Party" under Article III; fundamentally, however, they are international and diplomatic in character rather than judicial, and even if subjected to a judicial proceeding before an international judicial tribunal, the latter would be exercising judicial power not of the United States but perhaps of some international community. Again, when the United States allows a foreign sovereign to try its own nationals in the United States for a violation of its own laws, or when the United States extradites a person to a country where he is charged with crime, the foreign tribunal is exercising governmental authority of its own sovereign; the judicial power of the United States is not involved.

ARMS CONTROL JURISDICTION IN RELATION TO THE
UNITED STATES GOVERNMENT

The discussion and the precedents cited suggest a number of functions related to arms control which might be conferred upon an international tribunal. Basically, it appears, there are few constitutional problems if it is the Government of the United States, not its citizens, which is subject to the jurisdiction of the tribunal. Thus an international tribunal might usefully serve such purposes as these:

(*a*) It might settle disputes between the United States and other parties to the arms treaty as to the interpretation, implementation, or application of the control agreement. The nations might agree to compulsory jurisdiction of such a court, and bind themselves to abide by its judgments, decisions, or awards.

(*b*) A tribunal might hear cases between the United States and the international inspecting body. These might include charges by the inspecting body that the United States had violated the control provisions; that it had failed to cooperate with the inspecting body; or that it had interfered with or frustrated its efforts. Or, the United States might bring charges against the inspectors, *e.g.,* that there had been abuse of the inspection process, or that inspectors had otherwise misused their presence in the country.

(*c*) The tribunal might even serve in the nature of a claims commission to hear and determine claims by United States citizens—perhaps for damage due to inspection; or on account of wrongful disclosure of trade secrets;[9] or, if the control plan contemplated it, for seizures of goods which the inspectors claimed to be unlawful. In exercising such functions, the tribunal might, in fact, be determining the rights of United States citizens. But if it did so pursuant to an international agreement

International Tribunals

by the United States, this would seem analogous to standard United States treaties settling, or arranging machinery for settling, the claims of American citizens against a foreign state or its citizens which we have considered previously. That in this case the arrangement would deal with future claims should not make a critical difference. And it is the United States which may be regarded as the party to these international proceedings, the United States which would have responsibility to assure that the tribunal was acting in accordance with the treaty which established it.

ARMS CONTROL JURISDICTION IN RELATION TO
UNITED STATES RESIDENTS

The uses of the tribunal described in the previous section relate primarily to the United States Government, not to its citizens. We now leave the traditional role of international tribunals as determining rights of governments and consider possible functions which would directly impinge on the citizen and resident of the United States. Here we shall consider functions, suggested by earlier chapters of this study, whereby the tribunals might implement the investigating duties of the international inspectors. The activities we consider—particularly the issuance of subpoenas and the administration of oaths—may be an appropriate adjunct also in the operations suggested for the tribunal in the previous section.

SUBPOENAS AND OATHS. While it might be done as well through United States officials and courts, there would seem to be little problem connected with conferring on the international tribunal itself the power to subpoena witnesses or evidence and to administer oaths in relation to arms control. These are not necessarily judicial functions, not necessarily part of the judicial power of the United States; these are auxiliary functions, available to various authorized bodies, including, for example, legislative [10] and administrative agencies.[11] Congress, as we have seen, has in implementation of international treaties conferred the power to administer oaths on foreign service courts and on international commissions.[12] And the latter have been authorized to issue subpoenas, not merely to request their issuance by a federal district court.[13] There is no prohibition or limitation in the Constitution which is violated by granting such powers to an international body by treaty and implementing legislation.

Again, a strong case can be made that such international tribunals, sitting in the United States, although not United States courts, or exercising United States judicial power, must observe the Fourth and Fifth Amendments. They may not tolerate "unreasonable search and seizure," they must respect the privilege against self-incrimination. The Bill of Rights affords protection against federal authorities.[14] But where the federal government confers upon an international tribunal in the United States authority to obtain testimony or evidence, it is doubtful whether it could do so without including the limitations of the Fourth and Fifth Amendments.

WARRANTS. To the extent that previous discussion has indicated that no warrant is necessary for a particular search or inspection, to provide that inspectors should obtain a warrant from an international tribunal is unobjectionable. Such a warrant is certainly no worse than none at all. Where the Fourth Amendment is deemed to require a warrant, it would be desirable that a warrant be obtained from a United States court or officer by a United States official who would accompany the international inspector on his search, or by the international official himself. But would the requirements of the Fourth Amendment be satisfied by a warrant—otherwise meeting all the constitutional requirements—from an international tribunal established by treaty?

Again we are on uncharted waters. The Fourth Amendment does not say who may issue warrants. And to issue warrants is not necessarily a judicial function, part of the judicial power of the United States. Present legislation and the rules of criminal procedure do not limit the issuance of warrants to United States courts; they provide for warrants not only by federal judges but by other federal officials, or by state courts.[15] On the other hand, no precedent has been found for the issue of warrants by others. And the fact that authority to issue warrants may be conferred on federal officials who are not judges does not necessarily mean that such authority may be given to private persons—or international officials. But if the control and inspection plans are established by treaty, it may be argued that warrants to make them effective are auxiliary powers also within the treaty power, and that international machinery to issue a warrant meets the requirements of the Fourth Amendment. The purpose of the protection would appear to be met by a warrant from such a tribunal, if the warrant meets the constitutional standards of "probable cause, supported by Oath or affirmation, and particularly describing the place to be searched, and the . . . things to be seized." While international officials are not under oath or obligation to support

International Tribunals

the Constitution of the United States, there is some control over their activity, initially through the standards set up and the international machinery established by treaty, then through diplomatic means and, in the last resort, by denunciation of the treaty and termination of the arrangements.

Of course, unlike the subpoena which is normally enforced through contempt proceedings for failure to obey it, a warrant is not subject to enforcement in the same way. A person might resist search pursuant to a warrant on the ground that it is an unlawful warrant;[16] more often, the search will be made and when the evidence seized is introduced in the criminal proceeding, the accused will claim that the search was unlawful because not based on a valid warrant and seek to have the evidence quashed. In regard to arms control, we have assumed that criminal prosecution is not the primary purpose of the search or inspection, but rather obtaining the information that there has been a violation. If there is no criminal prosecution, the normal occasion for testing the validity of the warrant would not arise.[17] If there should be a criminal prosecution in a United States court, the accused would have the opportunity to challenge the validity of the search and the seizure of the evidence in question, and thereby the validity of the warrant.

CONTEMPT PROCEEDINGS. Again, orders of international inspectors should be enforced by United States courts, by citation for contempt where appropriate. But could the United States confer on international tribunals the power to punish for contempt? The power to punish for contempt is not necessarily a judicial function; legislative bodies may themselves cite and punish for contempt.[18] Perhaps, if international tribunals may be established and given power to issue warrants and to subpoena witnesses, the power to protect and give effect to this jurisdiction of the tribunal by contempt proceedings may also be implied. On that basis, the international tribunal could enforce its valid orders by contempt proceedings under its own authority, without invoking the aid of United States courts. Criminal contempt proceedings, on the other hand, have been assimilated in many respects to criminal prosecutions and may involve many of the considerations involved in such prosecutions.[19] Certainly a perjury trial before the international tribunal, in support of its power to administer oaths and subpoena witnesses, would be a "criminal prosecution,"[20] considered in the following sections of this chapter.

INTERNATIONAL CRIMINAL COURTS

We now approach the second part of the inquiry of this chapter. We shall seek to determine whether, to what extent, and on what basis the United States can agree by treaty that international tribunals exercise criminal jurisdiction.

PRECEDENTS FOR INTERNATIONAL CRIMINAL JURISDICTION

Some instances of what may be called international criminal law, and some international tribunals to apply such law, have existed, but these differ in fundamental respects from the kind of law and tribunals to which we are accustomed in the United States, and from those which are here considered. The traditional law of nations includes laws which may be deemed criminal. Most of the principles of international law, however, apply only to the acts of nations, not of individuals, and nations or the heads of nations which violate these rules are not brought for criminal action before any judicial tribunal. Some of the laws of nations do apply to individuals, *e.g.,* the laws against piracy. These, however, are enforced in effect as the law of the nation which captures the accused pirate, by its own criminal procedures, in its own courts.[21]

As noted, the Nuremberg trials and their less renowned counterparts both in Germany and in Japan represent a substantial step toward the application of rules of criminal law to individuals in an international tribunal. This is not the place to examine, from the point of view of international law, the significance of this development and the criticisms directed against it.[22] For purposes of the present, we have noted that the principles were promulgated by the nations victorious in war, and the tribunals were established to try officials of vanquished countries after the war. Most relevant here, these trials did not involve the enactment of international criminal law by the exercise of United States treaty power and its enforcement against American citizens through international tribunals sitting in the United States.

In other contexts and for other purposes, it has been noted that the individual—not merely the state—is becoming the concern and the subject of international law.[23] So far as the United States is concerned, moreover, the rights of individuals, including Americans, have been the subject of treaties since this country began, and some of the provisions in these treaties bear some relation to criminal law. An obvious, if not a proximate example, is the extradition provision in many treaties by which

International Tribunals

persons—even American citizens—who are charged with having committed crimes in foreign countries may be extradited to those countries for trial in their courts.[24] The NATO Status of Forces Agreement, for a different instance, deals with rights and obligations of a host country, as well as of a sending state, in regard to crimes by visiting members of an allied force; these provisions are applicable in the United States to foreign servicemen and in other countries to American servicemen.[25]

What concerns us here goes far beyond these precedents. We are considering the creation by treaty of new international crimes and the establishment by treaty of international tribunals to bring individuals, including Americans, to trial for violation of these laws. The issues to be examined may be reflected in a number of questions: so far as the United States Constitution is concerned, in what circumstances can criminal jurisdiction be exercised by international courts applying international law? Can such international courts be enlisted to enforce arms control as part of United States criminal law? Can difficulties raised by the international character of the tribunals be alleviated by considering them as special courts of the United States? And whatever the character of these tribunals, must they accord all or any of the safeguards which the Constitution affords to persons accused of crime in the United States? The questions take us into unprobed reaches of the treaty power, into the mysteries of its relation to the legislative and judicial powers of the United States, into the intricacies of federal jurisdiction and the federal courts.

INTERNATIONAL CRIMINAL COURTS UNDER THE TREATY POWER

The States of the Union apart, there can be little doubt that bringing American citizens to trial for acts committed in the United States is a function of government of the United States. And the courts before which such trials are held are exercising judicial power of the United States. Can such functions be vested by treaty in international tribunals?[26]

It is not the purpose of this study to debate the desirability of such proposals. We seek only to show whether they would fit into the context of the Constitution and the United States legal institutions which have been established under it. Arguments in favor of their validity will be stated, as well as those against.

One may begin with the most sweeping bases for the view that such tribunals may exercise criminal jurisdiction over American citizens and residents for acts in the United States. Perhaps the broadest is analogous to that discussed in the previous chapter;[27] that in its relations to other nations the United States is equally "sovereign" and of equal power; with other countries it can join to establish a system of international law for the community of nations, including a criminal law applicable to individuals everywhere, even in the United States, which is outside the framework of United States national law. And international judicial tribunals to apply this law can similarly be established, even in the United States, to try persons for violations of such international law committed here. Such a law and such a judicial system would be international, not those of the United States. And the American citizen would be directly subject to such laws, just as he is to different levels of law under the American system—*i.e.*, federal and state.[28] Neither law nor tribunals would have to be concerned with any limitations in the United States Constitution which can apply only to United States laws and United States governmental bodies.

The arguments against this suggestion are much the same as in the case of international administrative law discussed in the preceding chapter. Perhaps here additional weights in the balance against the broad view might be the argument that criminal law in particular is peculiarly an aspect of a nation's sovereignty and responsibility; that the Constitution evinces especially tender concern for American citizens and residents accused of crime, as reflected in the Constitution's original provisions as well as in several of the amendments. There can be no criminal law in the United States, it would be argued, which is not United States criminal law, subject to the Constitution's limitations on its enforcement. To make acts of Americans in the United States unlawful, to bring them to trial for such acts, to convict and punish them are functions of United States government in relation to its citizens. The United States cannot, even by treaty, delegate them to another sovereignty and wash its hands of them.[29]

Again, as with many suggestions which rely on the uncertain breadth of the treaty power, no ground exists for a clear choice between arguments for and against. This is true also, then, for other arguments to support international criminal tribunals, based primarily on the treaty power.

A second point of departure, not unrelated to the one just discussed, starts from the position that the law of nations is part of the law of the United States. This was true of the law of nations as it antedated the

International Tribunals 135

Constitution, and is so also, it would be urged, for such law of nations as may have been developed and accepted since the Constitution. It is so also as to any law of nations which is based on treaties. This law must be given effect by federal and state judges in the United States wherever it is applicable.[30] But the law of nations could provide for special international tribunals to try offenses against this law. Congress could, of course, reject the law of nations and the proposed tribunals. But if Congress, on the contrary, accepted such law and such tribunals of nations, these would be supreme and independent of limitations and procedures which apply to national laws and tribunals. International tribunals applying the law of nations, although accepted by Congress, thus need not abide by all the provisions of the Constitution governing criminal trials in the federal courts.

The argument to the contrary might distinguish between the law of nations which antedated the Constitution (and might be deemed to be incorporated into it) and that which has followed. It might distinguish also what has been done by treaty, arguing that the treaty makers, like other branches of the federal government, are subject to United States constitutional limitations. In any event, criminal law, even if based on the law of nations, could become law in the United States only if defined as such by Congress, and such criminal laws would stand no better against constitutional requirements than those adopted under other congressional powers.[31] Finally, whatever crimes might be established pursuant to the law of nations could only be tried in courts of the United States subject to Article III and the Bill of Rights—not in international courts responsible to some other sovereignty.

We pass to other arguments, somewhat narrower, though also based on the breadth and sweep of the treaty power. A third approach, the strongest perhaps, would urge that without asserting the power to establish in the United States a new law under a new sovereignty, the treaty makers may properly agree that cases based on certain laws, part of or incorporated in the law of the United States, may be tried by special tribunals not courts of the United States. The treaty power is separate, independent; within its domain it is paramount; it is subject to specific prohibitions in the Constitution, but is not to be limited by exegesis from radiations of other powers in the Constitution.[32] The treaty power, for example, is not limited by the legislative power of Congress and may deal with matters otherwise assigned by the Constitution to that power.[33] The treaty power, similarly, may deal with matters which in other contexts are within the judicial power of the United States under Article III, and deal with them without regard to the limits of the judicial power under the Constitution. The United States may then by treaty agree to have offenses against certain of the laws of nations which are incorporated into United States law tried by courts which are not United States courts, and by judges not United States judges. These judges do not have to meet the tenure and compensation requirements of Article III or the other constitutional requirements applicable to United States officials—presidential appointment, confirmation, and oath.

The argument may go further and suggest that these "treaty courts," not being United States courts, need not concern themselves with the Bill of Rights, which applies only to federal authorities. The United States would of course wish to assure a fair trial, but it would not be necessary to meet all the special requirements of Article III or of the first nine amendments to the Constitution, *e.g.*, jury trial, privilege against self-incrimination, trial in the state and district where the act was committed.

And for lack of other precedent, it may be suggested that the role of courts of the States of the Union affords some authority. Although these are not courts of the United States, from the very beginning of the republic Congress has on numerous occasions provided that state courts may carry out judicial functions on behalf of the United States, including even the trial of persons for violations of federal law.[34] Whether or not Congress could require these state courts to carry out such functions, there seems to have been little question that Congress could request them to do so, that it would not be unconstitutional for Congress to delegate such United States judicial power to state courts or for the state courts to exercise it.[35] In doing so the state courts do not become courts of the United States; their judges are not judges of the United States; and they are not subject to all the requirements and limitations which the Constitution imposes on courts of the United States.

The counterargument for more limited scope for the treaty power would of course begin by asserting that the treaty power is subject to the Constitution and the Bill of Rights. It would be pointed out that the only provision in the original Constitution in regard to the trial of crimes is contained in Article III, which provides:

The Trial of all Crimes, except in Cases of Impeachment, shall be by Jury; and such Trial shall be held in the State where the said Crimes shall have been committed; but when not committed within any State, the Trial shall be at such Place or Places as the Congress may by Law have directed.

International Tribunals

That some of these provisions were subsequently repeated in the Bill of Rights, was not intended to affect the basic pattern of the Constitution that criminal trials shall be by a United States court meeting the requirements of Article III including life tenure and assured compensation. On this question, the cases are not wholly silent. There are suggestions in the cases that a person accused of crime in the United States is entitled to trial in such a court.[36] These suggestions would appear to treat the requirement as an implied addition to the other safeguards of the Bill of Rights; in one form, it may be stated as a right of an accused to be tried by a court whose judges offer the additional assurance of independence and impartiality that come from life tenure and compensation not subject to reduction. The Supreme Court, also, has said that Congress can devolve judicial power of the United States—which surely includes criminal trials for violation of United States law—only on courts ordained and established by Congress.[37] There is no basis for finding that the treaty power can devolve such judicial power on courts not created by Congress. In any event it has never been held that an American in the United States could be subjected, for an act committed here, to trial before a court which is not a United States court at all, by judges who are not United States judges at all, not appointed by the President, not confirmed by the Senate, not sworn to uphold the Constitution. There may be no explicit prohibition in the Constitution against subjecting American citizens in the United States, charged with violations here of United States law, to trial in non–United States courts; but surely such a prohibition is clearly and strongly implied.

The state courts, it would be pointed out, are hardly a persuasive analogy. Entrusting federal judicial power to state courts, has the sanction of long practice and has support in the history of the development and negotiation of the Constitution.[38] In addition, support for the practice may derive from the supremacy of the federal government in federal matters, so that state courts may be deemed to act by assignment from the federal government even if for many purposes the courts do not thereby become United States courts.[39] International tribunals, on the other hand, would include foreign judges selected by international machinery; the statute governing their functions would be an international document to which the United States is but one party. These tribunals would not be an inextricable part of the federal system; they would not be subject to "supremacy" of the federal government.

The above, then, are three series of arguments for and against the constitutionality of entrusting criminal jurisdiction to international tribunals. We do not venture to choose here between the thesis and its contrary, or to appraise the relative weights of the various arguments on each side. One point may be worth noting, however. If it is decided that international courts may exercise criminal jurisdiction in the United States, the theory and basis on which this is justified will make a difference. On the last approach suggested, for example, there is a stronger basis for saying that international tribunals are acting in lieu of United States courts and that as such they must afford the protections contained in the Bill of Rights, including indictment, jury trial, and right to counsel.

It has been suggested in another context that these requirements be met by provision that criminal jurisdiction be exercised by United States courts, which would accord the protections of the Bill of Rights, and that an appeal be provided to an international tribunal.[40] In regard to arms control this may not be acceptable internationally. In any event it would raise constitutional questions perhaps as difficult as those it would eliminate. An appeal from the federal judiciary to an international tribunal was hardly contemplated by Article III of the Constitution.[41] And if in the United States trial court a jury acquits the accused, to permit the prosecution to appeal to an international tribunal, and allow the latter to reverse the acquittal and direct a new trial, would probably violate the safeguards against double jeopardy in the Fifth Amendment.[42]

INTERNATIONAL CRIMINAL COURTS AS COURTS OF THE UNITED STATES

Proponents of international tribunals seeking additional support even under narrow views of the treaty power might suggest that if a treaty creates international tribunals, these should be viewed as United States courts.

ARTICLE III COURTS. Those who argue thus might say that while Article III of the Constitution speaks of "such inferior Courts as the Congress may from time to time ordain and establish," and Article I specifically authorizes Congress "to constitute Tribunals inferior to the supreme Court," the treaty power, which, within its proper sphere, is also a legislative power, can also "ordain and establish" such courts; it could ordain and establish international tribunals as such courts. Or Congress, in implementation of a treaty, could ordain and establish these international tribunals as inferior courts of the United States.

Attempts to treat the international tribunals as United States courts

International Tribunals

would encounter formidable obstacles, formal and substantive. Assuming that the treaty makers or Congress sought to establish international tribunals as inferior courts of the United States, the tribunals would become part of the United States judicial system. They would be subject to all its rules and limitations, including the appellate jurisdiction of the Supreme Court and the requirement that there be a "case or controversy."[43] The judges would have to enjoy life tenure, and their compensation must remain undiminished during their continuance in office. For criminal cases Article III requires jury trial. In addition to the requirements of this article there are also the other constitutional requirements, explicit or implied, applicable to all United States bodies and United States officials. The judges presumably would be officers of the United States, appointed by the President in accordance with the Constitution.[44] Their tenure, the terms of their office, the right to remove them, would have to be determined in accordance with United States law pursuant to the United States Constitution. The international tribunal, on the other hand, would surely include judges who are foreign nationals, and its judges would be selected by some international body or machinery. Its jurisdiction and rules would be determined by international agreement. It is difficult to see that international tribunals of this kind could be formed and fashioned so as to meet the requirements for United States courts. It is inconceivable that the steps necessary even to approximate these requirements would meet with acquiescence by the other parties to the treaty.

INTERNATIONAL TRIBUNALS AS LEGISLATIVE COURTS. Finally, it may be suggested that since there are United States courts other than those established pursuant to Article III, an international tribunal might qualify as such a United States court.

It is no longer open to question that Congress may establish "courts" which are not subject to the limitations of Article III relating to tenure and compensation, the requirement that there be a "case or controversy," or other limitations which may be implicit.[45] Thus, Congress has created courts to deal with patents, customs, and revenue, whose judges do not enjoy life tenure or guaranteed compensation.[46] *Ex parte Quirin* upheld the right of Congress to establish a military commission in the United States to try aliens and apparently even citizens for violations of the law of war.[47] Congress has also established such courts abroad, where consular courts for many years exercised jurisdiction granted to the United States by treaty.[48] And courts have been established in the territories pursuant to the power of Congress to make all needful rules and regulations respecting the territory of the United States.[49] Why not then treaty courts, or another kind of legislative court, under the power of Congress to adopt legislation necessary and proper for the implementation of treaties, or under its power to define offenses against the law of nations? Why could not an international tribunal be so treated?

There is some learning and much confusion about the place of legislative courts in the constitutional pattern. It has been suggested that properly viewed there is no distinction in character between "legislative courts" and "constitutional courts." The power to establish courts is one power, and it is subject to the requirements of Article III. The power in Congress, in Article I, to "constitute tribunals inferior to the Supreme Court" is the same power referred to in Article III. Where courts established by Congress do not meet some of the requirements of Article III, this can be justified only on one of two grounds for distinction. Congress might create a body which, while it is called a "court," is not really exercising judicial functions. Such a body, like the Court of Claims as to some of its functions, is really exercising legislative or administrative power by delegation from Congress.[50] Of course, not being a court, not exercising judicial power, such a "tribunal" need not take account of the provisions of Article III. The second distinction suggests that all courts exercising judicial functions must satisfy Article III; but, as a matter of sound constitutional interpretation, one may imply exceptions from the tenure and compensation provisions of Article III in circumstances where these requirements could not have been intended, and would not have been if the framers had anticipated special situations. Thus, for example, courts in the territories of the United States could not have been intended to be permanent since the territories would probably become states; the Constitution, therefore, could not sensibly be deemed to require life tenure for their judges.[51]

Justices of the Supreme Court, on the other hand, have also described the "doctrine" of "legislative courts" in different, broader terms. It has been asserted that there is a power in Congress to establish special courts as necessary and proper for the implementation of its other powers, independent of its power to establish the courts contemplated by Article III. Hence the various kinds of courts created in implementation of various congressional powers, such as those mentioned—revenue, patents, territorial courts, consular courts, and others. Of course, it is admitted, within the territory of the States of the Union, Congress could not circumvent the requirements of Article III by establishing other courts, not satisfying these limitations, to do the work intended for Article III courts—*e.g.,* for the trial of criminal offences.[52]

If a clearly federal court could not exercise criminal jurisdiction, then, in the United States unless it satisfied Article III, the most liberal legislative court analogy offers little support for treaty courts exercising such jurisdiction. On the other hand, the fact that criminal jurisdiction, for example, can be exercised in other "legislative courts" outside the territory of the States of the Union may suggest an argument for vesting such criminal jurisdiction—even in the United States—in special courts dealing with a limited field like foreign relations. For whatever its worth, the argument might be stated as follows: the territorial courts, clearly legislative courts, may be granted true judicial functions including the exercise of criminal jurisdiction, by virtue of the power of Congress to govern those areas.[53] Other courts outside the United States—the consular courts—have also been accorded judicial power of the United States.[54] These suggest a geographic line: legislative courts may exercise judicial functions outside the territory of the States of the Union. The geographic line, however, reflects political realities in the federal system. It reflects that in so far as the federal judicial power was being carved out of judicial powers which might otherwise be exercised by the states, its scope was confined as set forth in Article III. One might suggest, then, that a "functional" line, analogous to the accepted geographic line, would accord with the same fundamentals of federal-state relationships. International affairs are, like the territories, an "area" from which the states are, and have always been, excluded.[55] When by treaty, or under the power of Congress to define offenses against the law of nations, courts are created to deal with matters of international concern, these courts may also be accorded judicial functions without regard to the limitations inferred from Article III. Such judicial functions arising out of international affairs would not, in principle, infringe on the judicial area left to the states or enlarge the area intended for the federal government. The international area has always been intended for the federal government even if hitherto the occasion for federal judicial functions in that area did not arise.[56] That Congress, as held in the *Quirin* case, could set up military commissions under the law of war, even within the United States, even, it seems, to try an American citizen, may support other "exceptions" to Article III.

If the suggestion that international tribunals might be viewed as analogous to United States legislative courts were made, the arguments against it would not be wanting. All federal criminal law is enacted by Congress in implementation of its various enumerated powers, yet criminal jurisdiction, within the territory of the States of the Union, cannot be given to legislative courts. There is no basis for selecting from among the powers of Congress the power to implement treaties or legislate on foreign relations, and for saying then that these powers alone may be implemented by criminal law enforced in courts which are not Article III courts. That the states never had control over foreign relations is not an adequate basis for such an exception. Article III prescribes the courts which shall deal with "all cases . . . arising under . . . the laws of the United States." These include all federal criminal laws equally whether in implementation of foreign affairs, or naturalization, or interstate commerce. And all federal crimes in the territory of the States of the Union must be tried in Article III courts subject to the safeguards contained in that article and in the Bill of Rights. The exercise of criminal jurisdiction in territorial and consular courts, the military commission in time of war, are exceptions by virtue of their character, and this exception should not be extended on the basis of unwarranted distinctions.

Another complete answer might be that even if the analogy and distinctions suggested have any validity, the formal obstacles would remain. Other legislative courts are still United States courts; if they need not meet the prescriptions for Article III constitutional courts, they must still satisfy other constitutional requirements applicable to all United States bodies, agencies, and officials—*e.g.,* appointment by the President, Senate confirmation, and oath of office. It would take special arrangements, convolutions, and fictions to make judges selected by international machinery and responsible to an international body into United States officials. If it be suggested that the treaty power and the area of foreign relations are so broad, independent, and special that they may support the creation of United States courts which are not subject to formalities of other United States bodies, one would be calling the international tribunal a "United States court" in order to justify conferring upon it United States judicial power without requiring it to possess the principal characteristics of a United States court. If the treaty power can effect that, it could, perhaps more easily, justify the grant of criminal jurisdiction in the United States to international tribunals openly and avowedly not United States courts.

One distinction among the various arguments for international crimi-

International Tribunals

nal tribunals should be reemphasized. The broadest arguments, those which might support an international tribunal which is not a United States tribunal, applying international law which is not United States law, would be free of the limitations and requirements of the Bill of Rights. If an international tribunal were viewed as a United States court, whether a "treaty court" or a "legislative court," it would have to grant jury trial, sit in the state and district where the crime was committed, and accord other guarantees which the Bill of Rights affords to all persons accused of crime under federal authority.

SPECIAL CASES

The previous section indicates some of the problems which would have to be faced in providing criminal trials by an international tribunal for American citizens charged with committing violations in the United States. Normally, we have seen, the enforcement of criminal law by judicial proceedings in the United States is a function of the United States Government, surrounded by safeguards and limitations for the protection of the individual. It cannot be easily delegated, except on the broadest views of the treaty power, and probably not without assuring the protections of the Bill of Rights. If a case of strong national interest should in the future suggest the need for international tribunals, a constitutional amendment might be in order, whether or not strictly required.

In regard to arms control, it was suggested earlier, there may be peripheral areas of enforcement where international cooperation to suppress arms trade might with greater probability suggest a system of international criminal tribunals. If these are to deal with private arms violations on the high seas or elsewhere outside United States territory, international tribunals may receive more serious consideration. As we shall now suggest, these cases may also raise far fewer difficulties under the Constitution. We shall consider whether different rules might apply if the act with which the accused is charged were committed outside the United States; if it were committed in the territory, or by a national, of another country party to the arms control treaty; if the international tribunal were sitting outside the United States, or at the United Nations Headquarters in New York.

ACTS BY AMERICANS ABROAD. Suppose the act violating the arms control plan were performed by a United States citizen not in the United States but in a foreign country or on the high seas—for example, someone running arms forbidden by the treaty. If a statutory or treaty provision makes such acts by Americans abroad violations of United States law, can the United States agree that such violator be tried before an international tribunal?

This case may be less difficult because the act of the United States citizen was committed abroad. Under the law as it was understood for many years, the United States could provide, in the case of Americans committing violations of American law either on the high seas or on foreign soil, for trial before American legislative courts, *e.g.*, consular courts. And such courts sitting abroad must accord to the accused a fair trial but need not accord him the specific provisions of the Bill of Rights. This was the doctrine of *In re Ross*.[57]

If these persons can be tried by United States consular courts abroad, the United States might perhaps also make them available for trial before an international tribunal abroad. In regard to acts abroad, United States jurisdiction is exercised pursuant to the law of nations or by grant from a host state.[58] For trial of such violations abroad, the Constitution may not even require United States courts; or an international tribunal might be adequately a "United States court" for this purpose. And if the United States consular court need not accord the privileges and guarantees of the constitutional amendments, there would be no reason for finding that the United States must obtain such rights for Americans from an international tribunal. If the American had since come back to the United States, there might be no constitutional objection to arranging by treaty that he should be "extradited" for trial before an international tribunal abroad.[59]

Such violations abroad might also be tried, perhaps, by an international tribunal sitting in the United States. It might be suggested that since, the act having been committed abroad, the United States could have agreed that the persons be tried before an international tribunal sitting abroad, moving the international tribunal here should not make a constitutional difference. If so, whether the tribunal might have to accord the protections of the Bill of Rights, as would a United States court sitting in the United States, would present another and different issue. Perhaps since the international tribunal would be trying the accused for a violation of United States law, it would be exercising United States judicial power in United States territory, and would have to afford the same procedures and protections which obtain in United States courts in the United States.

These suggestions cannot be stated with confidence. Indeed, the entire basis for the distinction between trials of Americans for acts committed abroad and trials for those committed in the United States may have crumbled with *Reid v. Covert,* decided in 1957.[60] In that case the Supreme Court held that Congress could not authorize trial by court-martial for dependents accompanying members of the armed forces, charged with having committed murder on foreign soil. There was no opinion on which a majority of the court agreed.[61] Speaking for himself and three other judges, however, Mr. Justice Black asserted, "At the beginning we reject the idea that when the United States acts against citizens abroad it can do so free of the Bill of Rights." At some points his language suggests a constitutional doctrine of the character of *noblesse oblige;* the United States must act in accordance with the Bill of Rights at all times, no matter who the accused, where the act was committed, where the trial is held. Later in the opinion, after stating that the fact that the trials in question were conducted pursuant to an international agreement made no constitutional difference, Mr. Justice Black concluded "that the Constitution in its entirety applied to the trials." In addition, sufficient aspersions were cast on *In re Ross* both in this opinion of four Justices and in the concurring opinion of Mr. Justice Frankfurter to leave its continued validity in all cases in doubt.[62] The *Covert* decision owes its majority to the fact that the accused was charged with a capital crime. Noncapital cases were reserved, and one can only speculate whether in the future a court might go further and hold that any trial by a United States tribunal for a violation of United States law, even if the act was committed outside United States territory, must conform to the provisions of the Bill of Rights. In that event, even if in the situation we assumed a case were made for holding such a trial before an international tribunal, where the trial was in fact for a violation of United States law, the tribunal would be sitting as a United States court and all the protections would have to be afforded.

ARMS CONTROL INFRINGEMENTS AS VIOLATIONS OF FOREIGN LAW. In regard to violations of international arms control committed abroad, and even as to those committed on American soil by certain persons, it is possible to work out a basis on which an international tribunal might try American citizens or residents even without according them the specific guarantees of the Bill of Rights.

Assume that an arms control treaty is accepted almost universally, or, at least, that it is in effect in the territory of a country where a violation is committed. The treaty, therefore, is presumably part of the law of that land, and its violation is a violation of that local law. An act committed there by anyone, including a national of the United States, which violated the arms control agreement, therefore would violate the law of the host country. The host nation could try him in its own courts.[63] Or it could in accordance with its own laws and treaties have him tried instead by an international tribunal established pursuant to treaty. If basic principles of fair procedure are observed, the United States would have no basis for objecting, particularly if the United States had itself accepted the statute of the international tribunal. If the violator, United States national or no, were now in the United States, the United States could, so far as the Constitution may be concerned, agree to his extradition for trial by the foreign or international tribunal—by extension from traditional extradition practices. And if the United States agreed that an international tribunal sit in the United States, it could, pursuant to treaty, probably make such violators abroad, even American citizens, available for trial before this international tribunal. In this situation, that court would be trying the accused not for a violation of United States law but for a violation of the law of the country where it was committed. The court would be sitting, not as a United States court exercising United States judicial power, but as a court of that country or of an international community. As such, even though the court sat in the United States, with the consent of the United States, it would not be acting under United States authority and therefore need not accord the privileges of the Bill of Rights.

This suggestion becomes clearer if we consider another group of cases subject to the same principle, *i.e.,* aliens in the United States. The alien who while in the United States committed an act which violated the international control agreement would of course be violating the law of the United States. He might also, however, be violating the law of his country of nationality, if it had accepted the arms control plan and made it applicable to its citizens everywhere. So far as that country would be concerned, its national who violated the control plan in the United States might be in the same situation as if he had committed the violation in his homeland. True, the United States could bring the alien to trial here for violation of its laws in its own courts and he would be entitled to the full protection of the Bill of Rights.[64] The United States might, however, agree to allow the country of his nationality to try him for violating its laws, even if the act were com-

International Tribunals 147

mitted in the United States, even if it were also a violation of United States law.[65] The United States could agree to let a foreign court try him here—as is done by foreign consuls in regard to seamen, or by friendly foreign forces to their military personnel. Similarly, the United States might give effect to the desires or agreement of the foreign country to have its national tried by an international tribunal here or elsewhere.[66] And the United States could even assist in the alien's arrest, hand him over to the international tribunal here, or extradite him abroad.[67] In this context, we emphasize, the same international tribunal would be trying him not on behalf of the United States for a violation of United States law, but at the behest of his own country of nationality for violation of its law. The international tribunal would be in the character of a foreign court rather than a United States court and would not have to respect the guarantees of the Bill of Rights.

ARMS VIOLATIONS AS INTERNATIONAL CRIMES

In the light of the special cases just discussed, we may now consider the extent to which the United States could join with other nations to establish violations of armaments control as international crime triable in international tribunals. At the beginning of this chapter we discussed and laid aside this proposal as it might relate to acts by American citizens within the United States. This proposal, however, has important possibilities as regards action on the high seas, or elsewhere not subject to the territorial jurisdiction of any national state, perhaps even in the stratosphere or outer space.

A long-established precedent is the traditional pattern of international law for dealing with the international crime of piracy. By the law of nations, piracy is a crime wherever committed on the high seas. The nation capturing the pirate tries him as for a violation of its own laws—before its own tribunals and in accordance with its own procedures.[68] By analogy, nations could agree that violations of armaments control when committed on the high seas, or elsewhere outside the territory of any state, shall be treated on the same basis as piracy. A person charged with a violation in such circumstances could be tried by the courts of the capturing country in the same manner as for other violations of its own laws. Presumably nations could agree instead to establish international tribunals for the trial of arms violators, which would apply international procedures and international penalties. The

Nuremberg trials and their counterparts in Japan, international tribunals applying "international criminal law," offer some precedent.

The United States could constitutionally agree to such arrangements for persons captured by other nations, even as applied to United States citizens, since the accused would be tried for a violation not of United States law but of a foreign law, whether it be viewed as the law of a nation or as the law of nations.[69] On that basis even if the violator were seized by United States authorities, or had escaped to United States authorities, or to the United States, the United States could probably turn him over for trial by a foreign or international tribunal, as akin to extradition. If, on the other hand, the United States undertook to deal with a person captured by the United States as for a violation of United States laws, it might have to accord him the protections of the Bill of Rights, if *Reid v. Covert* has indeed replaced *In re Ross*. Certainly the Bill of Rights would apply if the United States brought the accused to trial in this country, even if he were an alien. If the United States presented him for trial before an international tribunal, particularly one sitting in the United States, the rights of the accused before this tribunal might depend on whether in these circumstances the tribunal must be viewed as in the nature of a United States court applying law of the United States.

An international criminal law for arms violations on the high seas might develop from the conviction of nations that this is a problem requiring cooperative, uniform handling through international machinery. Eventually this might suggest to nations that arms control even within and across the territories of national states requires enforcement through international law and international tribunals. States willing, and able under their constitutions, might then agree to establish an international criminal law enforceable in international tribunals against arms violations even within their own territories. Without a constitutional amendment, we have said, the United States might not be able to agree to have such a system applicable in United States territory, at least so far as American citizens are concerned. The United States might, however, agree, on the basis earlier indicated, to join or cooperate in such a system to apply to acts anywhere outside United States territory, even those of American citizens. The constitutional problems for the United States would not be substantially different from those raised by a system limited to the high seas.

A TRIBUNAL AT UNITED NATIONS HEADQUARTERS

At several points in this chapter we have mentioned that whether an international tribunal sits in the United States or abroad may have constitutional significance. A probable site for an international tribunal is the United Nations Headquarters in New York, and question may arise as to whether a tribunal sitting there and exercising criminal jurisdiction has special constitutional qualities.

What is the status of the United Nations Headquarters? Is the Headquarters District United States territory so far as that is relevant to the present constitutional inquiry? More directly, in what circumstances and to what extent does the United States Constitution apply to an international court sitting there?

The territory occupied by the United Nations—the "Headquarters District"—has not, in terms at least, been ceded to the United Nations by the United States.[70] The Headquarters Agreement between the United Nations and the United States[71] seems carefully to avoid the conceptual question—who retains "sovereignty" in the Headquarters District. Instead, the agreement distributed authority and function between the United States and the United Nations on a practical, empirical basis without labeling the result. In its most relevant provisions, the agreement provides that "the headquarters district shall be under the control and authority of the United Nations as provided in this agreement." On the other hand, except as otherwise provided, "the federal, state and local law of the United States shall apply within the headquarters district," and "the federal, state and local courts of the United States shall have jurisdiction over acts done and transactions taking place in the headquarters district as provided in applicable federal, state and local laws." The United Nations, however, "shall have the power to make regulations, operative within the headquarters district, for the purpose of establishing therein conditions in all respects necessary for the full execution of its functions. No federal, state, or local law or regulation of the United States which is inconsistent with a regulation of the United Nations authorized by this section shall, to the extent of such inconsistency, be applicable within the headquarters district."

In the light of these provisions, one may argue over whether the United States has retained full sovereignty in the Headquarters District, or whether there has been, in effect, a partial cession of the territory to the United Nations. What appears, from the sum of the provisions quoted and others in the agreement which have some relevance, is that United States laws (including the United States Constitution) continue to apply in the Headquarters District as in other United States territory. We leave aside for the present the significance of the power of the United Nations, within limits, to supersede United States laws in the Headquarters District.

If the United States Constitution and United States laws normally apply, how would they affect an international tribunal established there? Resuming the previous discussion, we may summarize—with the tribunal at the United Nations Headquarters in mind—the following different cases:

1. Except on the broadest views of the treaty power, where an American citizen, or an alien, is charged with an act in the United States violating United States law (incorporating an international control agreement), he must be tried in the United States by a United States court and accorded all the protections of the Bill of Rights. If on some theory discussed above the United States might perhaps agree to his trial before an international tribunal, such a tribunal, for purposes of the United States Constitution, might be deemed to be sitting as a court of the United States and thus must give the accused the protections he would enjoy in a court of the United States. And, under the Sixth Amendment, one of these is trial in the state and district in which the act was committed. On that basis an international tribunal sitting at the United Nations Headquarters could try only persons accused of committing a crime in the State of New York and in the federal district in which the United Nations Headquarters is situated; of course, it might seek agreement to sit in another district for the purposes of a case.

2. In other circumstances, an international tribunal sitting at the United Nations Headquarters might be sitting not as a United States court administering United States law but as a foreign court administering the law of another nation which had jurisdiction and has agreed to international trial, say in the following cases: any American or alien who while abroad violated arms control provisions incorporated into the law of the host country; anyone charged with violation on the high seas, at least where captured and prosecuted by a nation other than the United States; an alien who, whether abroad or in the United States, violated arms control provisions in the law of his country of nationality. In these circumstances, although the accused were now in the United States, the United States might agree that he be tried by a foreign or inter-

International Tribunals 151

national tribunal and might "extradite" or otherwise make him available for such trial. That the United States was a party to the statute of the tribunal, or had otherwise accepted it, would not impose constitutional limitations on the tribunal or grant the person tried by it full constitutional rights. Nor would the fact that it sits in the United States—and the United Nations Headquarters presents the *a fortiori* case.

3. The close case might be that of the American citizen who is prosecuted by the United States for violating an arms control agreement forming part of United States law, where such violation took place outside of the United States. In such cases, it may still be true, if anything of the *Ross* case survives, that the United States could have him tried by an American court abroad without according him all the protections of the Bill of Rights. The United States, then, could perhaps have him tried by an international tribunal, but in this instance the international tribunal would be sitting in lieu of a United States court, administering United States law. If the tribunal were sitting outside the United States, it need accord the American citizen in these circumstances no greater protection than he would enjoy, say, in a United States consular court. Where, however, the court would be sitting in United States territory, it might be argued that since it was akin to an American court administering American law and sitting in American territory, it must abide by the same constitutional requirements and accord the same constitutional protections as other American courts in the United States. At this point, as to a tribunal sitting at the United Nations Headquarters, the character of the United Nations Headquarters District might become crucial. If the district were United States territory for this purpose, the international tribunal might have to accord the same protections as, say, the Federal District Court in New York. Probably, the question should be framed not as a subsidiary, conceptual question—whether the United Nations Headquarters is United States territory—but rather as whether the United States Constitution applies in these circumstances in the Headquarters District. We have seen that it normally does. We have seen also that the United Nations can supersede United States law in certain cases. The United Nations might decide that it is not feasible for an international tribunal sitting at United Nations Headquarters to accord all the protections of the Bill of Rights. It might therefore by regulation establish its own trial procedures. If these were "in all respects necessary" for the full execution of the functions of the United Nations within the meaning of the United Nations Headquarters Agree-

ment, they might prevail over the requirements of the Constitution. The argument that the United States cannot by international agreement eliminate the applicability of the Constitution, or give the United Nations the power to do so, might be met by suggesting that the international agreement was a partial cession of the territory; the power of the United States to cede territory to a foreign government has not been seriously questioned, even though thereby the Constitution is rendered inapplicable in such ceded territory.

The discussion in this chapter appears to warrant certain conclusions about proposals for international tribunals. There may be useful functions for such tribunals in the general implementation of arms control. They might be used by governments and by international bodies to find facts, to examine charges of violations, and to determine monetary claims arising out of the operation of the plan. Such tribunals might also be given auxiliary functions such as the issuance of subpoenas, the administration of oaths, perhaps even the issuance of warrants in selected cases.

As courts of criminal jurisdiction to punish individuals for those violations of arms control which are intrinsically violations by governments, such international tribunals appear to be neither feasible nor acceptable, either in the United States or elsewhere. To introduce such criminal tribunals into the United States would make a constitutional amendment perhaps necessary, and probably desirable. Without such amendment, complicated and perhaps oversubtle analysis like that essayed in this chapter might develop arguments for squeezing such international tribunals into the scheme of the Constitution. But except on very broad views of the treaty power, the arguments are both complex and artificial, reflecting that we are seeking to fit an international tribunal, part of an international system applicable to different kinds of situations in different countries, Procrustes-fashion into the United States Constitution, a national document concerned primarily with national needs and interests. On the other hand, for international cooperation to prevent private arms smuggling on the high seas or across national boundaries, the international criminal tribunal may have useful possibilities. And here since it would not, in the main, be a substitute for United States criminal jurisdiction, it would more easily fit into the pattern of the Constitution.

Chapter IX. CONCLUSION

This study represents analysis and conclusions, reached and stated with varying degrees of confidence, about the legal implications of an arms control plan as applied in the United States. We have stressed the provisions which make no or few inroads into accepted constitutional limitations. We have examined also more radical proposals strange to constitutional concepts and traditions.

One may put aside the extreme positions. In general, political, practical, and legal problems will be avoided or mitigated if the United States Government stands responsible to an international body established to administer arms control, and if the government regulates the activities of its citizens to assure the nation's compliance with its international undertakings. This would avoid the new and difficult issues which might be raised by a proposal for a system of international administrative process applied directly to the citizen. Any international tribunals which might be proposed also could avoid sharp conflict with traditional constitutional concepts if they decided between governments, or between a government and an international body, but did not seek to exercise in the United States basic governmental functions like criminal jurisdiction.

In sum, it may be said that the probable characteristics of an arms control plan lie largely within the framework of the United States Constitution. Although new elements may be introduced, those which are in the realm of foreseeable negotiation do not violate constitutional limitations, nor do they seriously disturb traditional concepts. International control of armaments, in degrees and by methods reflecting the circumstances and the times, was not unknown in the early days of the country, or in the early days of world wars. The Constitution has accommodated all the arrangements that have been adopted by the United States in the past; it is adequate to the needs and efforts of the United States to solve problems of peace and security in the age of atomic energy and earth satellites.

The crux of arms control for this study, as it has been in recent years of negotiations between nations, is international inspection. If direct inspection by international officials is called for, one may conclude that, even on a conservative view of the flexibility of the constitutional pattern, such inspection, for the most part, would not do it violence. The essentials of the inspection system—the reports from government and industry, interrogations of officials and citizens, inspection of governmental installations and private industrial establishments related to armaments, perhaps even of any industrial establishment suspected—will not turn the litmus paper of the Constitution. It is the eccentric, perhaps, the extreme suggestion—the improbable incursion into the home—which raises serious warning signals, and this may prove to be only an imaginary dragon. It does not appear necessary to effective investigation of arms control; it would raise major constitutional questions if applied in the United States; it should not lightly materialize in negotiations, in demands by or of other nations.

Congressional implementation will vary, of course, with the details of a plan, and with the extent to which the treaty adopting the plan is not itself self-executing. In general, Congress will be required to establish a system of regulation not unlike that which applies to existing regulated industries. The Atomic Energy Act, for an important example, may require extensive revision. Privileges, immunities, and facilities, generally of a diplomatic character, will have to be accorded the inspection body. And legislation should protect the citizen and the rights of industry subject to inspection from damage or loss due to abuse of the inspection process. For most of the legislation envisaged there is precedent in existing laws.

Arms control may require the cooperation of state and local as well as federal officials, but it promises no grave or novel problems vis-à-vis the rights of the states. In its impact on the citizen, control should not prove more onerous, more jarring to traditional behavior and liberties than control of narcotics, or liquor, or firearms, or filled milk.

If its legal implications need not reach far or wide, arms control will nevertheless contain new elements. The novel aspects in law, as in our traditions, will be the presence of international officials observing operations of the United States Government and its citizens. This may be a grating, even a wrenching concept, which opponents of arms control may exploit. The "foreign" character of the inspectorate and of international control may create some problems like those which earlier in our history resulted from federal operations in areas of the country where "federal"

Conclusion

meant "foreign." But the nation survived these tests, and has prevailed. In peripheral respects, the United States, with other nations, may have to accept minor international intrusion for the sake of peace and its own security. Yet the degree of intrusion may prove rather less than we may be asked to imagine. Few Americans would, in probability, hear of international inspectors; fewer still would have contact with them. And few of these might ever be subjected to adversary, antagonistic requirements, to hostile interrogation, to subpoenas, or to unwelcome nonroutine inspection. The citizen is already accustomed to federal, state, county, and city officials; another small, special group, under federal auspices, should not disturb him. The contacts with international inspectors may be fewer than those with the inspectors of whom he is aware; they need not be more startling or onerous.

The major impact of control of armaments will be on national policy and on governmental activity. If comprehensive arms control and limitation are achieved, they will signify and reflect fundamental change. Recent experience, and the only experience many Americans have known, is of an America laden with heavy military expenditures, engrossed in tremendous defense production, committed to large standing armies. One tends to forget that these are not inevitable, that they are not essential to the ways of nations, especially the ways of this nation. It may be necessary to remind ourselves that this nation does not have a military tradition, that peacetime armies are not natural to us, and that large-scale production need not mean military production. Probably, a control plan would be introduced gradually, however, and there would be some time for adjustments in the economy and in national psychology.

Perhaps the most striking aspect of arms control is the projected effect on secrecy and security. There is an air of unreality, redolent of Utopia, in a discussion which assumes freedom of access, even to foreigners, to United States installations and offices, which may even entail the virtual abolition of security classification and with them security checks, and investigations, and prosecutions for espionage or related crime. And, indeed, if arms control comes, it may still take years to replace habits of secrecy and withholding with easy and free habits of openness and cooperation. It will take legislation to educate the public and education to make legislation possible. It will take bold leadership, enjoying popular confidence, to bring it about and make it work. Again, it is useful to stress that secrecy is not a constitutional principle; to recall times not beyond the memory of living men when "security" was not a living concept, when there was not a single prosecution for espionage in any form in many years, when classifications were few and relaxed. To remind of this is not to dream idly of better, old days before total war, warm or cold, but rather to recall that openness and freedom have at least as good a claim in the American tradition as secrecy and fear.

Arms control, then, would not present a daunting challenge for American law. The important obstacles to control of armaments are not in law, and the adjustments which such control would ask of our laws are neither radical nor distorting, the new elements not foreign or unassimilable. If arms control has not been achieved, the reasons must be sought in the foreign policies of nations. Perhaps arms control is not needed, or desirable, or feasible, but if it is all these, it is urgent to know why it has not been achieved, how it can be achieved.

A major obstacle to the control of armaments, of course, has been the attitude of the Soviet Union. But we must guard also against obstacles in ourselves. If the Soviet Union were to make important concessions toward reasonable agreement, there might still be reluctance in the United States, and opposition in important circles, to substantial reduction and control of armaments. There is a confidence and reliance in the possession of our own weapons perhaps greater than is warranted in an age of new weapons; they afford a sense of security that may be false. Fear and distrust of the Soviet Union, which go deeper perhaps than toward any other country in our history, may have succeeded in frightening the United States into actions and attitudes not ultimately consistent with the interests and security of this country. It will be necessary to educate ourselves in new habits of thought, free ourselves from suspicion and secretiveness. The purpose of a defense policy is to forestall and, if possible, remove danger. The United States may do that more effectively by disarming its enemies than by frantically building up for itself armaments of uncertain comparative effectiveness. The best defense may be to remove the offensive power of those whom this country fears.

Achieving this security will require effective inspection, and reciprocal inspection. If indeed an agreement to disarm is in the interest of both the United States and the Soviet Union, the continued effectiveness of such an agreement would also seem to be in the interest of both, and inspection should be possible, and desired, to assure that the other side does not fear violations and discontinue the agreement. If to give the United

Conclusion 157

States this security there must be control and inspection in Russia and elsewhere, this country will have to accept them here too. These limitations on the citizen would be minimal as compared to the restrictions and regulations (not excluding inspection) which the American people have accepted in the interest of national defense through armament, as compared to the limitations and restrictions in time of cold war, and those which might be required in the event of a new war.

But the limitations must be necessary, and the citizen must be persuaded that they are necessary. If he must be assured that we are learning enough to be satisfied of Soviet compliance, he must be assured also that his rights are being protected against unnecessary harassment here. Inspection proposals must be scrutinized not merely to determine how much we can learn of what goes on in the Soviet Union; there must be inquiry also into the burdens which they would place on the United States citizen and into their acceptability to the American people. Examination in the light of the Constitution and of legal institutions affords an important index of the impact of a particular provision or plan on the life of the nation. Where it appears that a proposal could not be assimilated or accepted, surely it could not be lightly or sincerely urged on other nations; and rejection by them need not necessarily be evidence of a refusal to disarm or to permit effective corroboration of compliance with disarmament. One may properly ask that the makers of policy reexamine whether such a proposal is indeed essential to United States security. The need then is to consider methods of control and verification carefully. The Columbia Inspection Study is one effort at this. These efforts should concentrate on what one needs to limit and what one needs to know to assure timely detection at some point of a pattern of action which may suggest preparation for war. In this and other ways, proposals for international regulatory and investigative activity may have to be adjusted to fit more easily into the institutions of this nation and of other nations. To this process, we hope, this study will make its contribution.

The law cannot bring about arms control. It is the citizen and his leaders who must be sufficiently shaken by danger to realize that arms control may not be a duty, only a necessity. If they and if our political institutions reflect sufficient initiative, intelligence, foresight, courage, and restraint to do the utmost needed to achieve arms control, the United States Constitution, its laws and legal institutions will not fail.

NOTES

NOTES TO I: INTRODUCTION

1. A preliminary study of the technical feasibility of inspection as it relates to the control of armaments has been concluded by Professor Seymour Melman of Columbia University for the University's Institute of War and Peace Studies. That project too has been made possible by a grant from the Institute for International Order. The report has been published as INSPECTION FOR DISARMAMENT (Melman ed. 1958). It is referred to in this volume as the "Inspection Study."

For an examination of existing and projected weapons, see 1970 WITHOUT ARMS CONTROL (1958), a report of the National Planning Association Special Project Committee on Security Through Arms Control.

2. Indeed, they are said to be quite old, including an instance in China during the sixth century B.C. See U.S. EXECUTIVE OFFICE OF THE PRESIDENT, DISARMAMENT STAFF, REFERENCE DOCUMENTS ON DISARMAMENT MATTERS, BACKGROUND SERIES 1 (1957).

Although the literature on disarmament efforts of the past is voluminous, there appears to be no comprehensive up-to-date history of such attempts. A history of the earlier efforts is contained in TATE, THE DISARMAMENT ILLUSION: THE MOVEMENT FOR A LIMITATION OF ARMAMENTS TO 1907 (1942), and in *Background Paper on Disarmament,* U.N. Doc. ST/DPI/Ser.A/75/Rev. 1 (1955). For a review of the post-1920 efforts see MYERS, WORLD DISARMAMENT: ITS PROBLEMS AND PROSPECTS (1932). American attitudes are reviewed in TATE, THE UNITED STATES AND ARMAMENTS (1948). A shorter, more recent review, emphasizing disarmament efforts made under United Nations auspices is contained in the United Nations *Background Paper on Disarmament, op. cit. supra.* See also Subcommittee on Disarmament, Senate Foreign Relations Committee, *Disarmament and Security: A Collection of Documents, 1919–55,* 84th Cong., 2d Sess. (1956), and the accompanying *Staff Studies,* particularly No. 2, *Disarmament: A Selected Chronology,* and No. 3, *Control and Reduction of Armaments: A Decade of Negotiations.* See also NOEL-BAKER, THE ARMS RACE: A PROGRAMME FOR WORLD DISARMAMENT (1958).

3. Nations, including the United States, did in the past agree to limit elements of their own armaments, *e.g.,* the number and size of their warships. The Rush-Bagot Agreement With Great Britain, an early example, limited naval armament on the Great Lakes. Agreement of April 28, 1817, 8 STAT. 231, T.S. No. 110½. The post–First World War naval treaties are discussed in note 5 below.

Where nations voluntarily assumed limitations on armaments, they usually agreed also to supply information indicating their compliance with such limitations. See, *e.g.,* art. 6 of the Convention on the Limitation of Armaments of Central American States, Feb. 27, 1923; arts. 10, 21 of the London Treaty on Limitation and Reduction of Naval Armament, April 22, 1930, 46 STAT. 2858, T.S. No. 830; art. 11 of the London Limitation of Naval Armament, March 25, 1936, 50 STAT. 1363, T.S. No. 919; all are reprinted in *Disarmament and Security, op. cit. supra* note 2, at 29, 41, 47.

There appears, however, to be no instance of voluntary and mutual submission to inspection to assure compliance with arms control limitations until the creation of the Agency of Western European Union for the Control of Armaments. The seven members of this union pledged to the inspection agency "free access on demand to plants and depots, and the relevant accounts and documents." Paris Protocols Relating to the Brussels Treaty, Oct. 23, 1954, Protocol No. IV, art. 12, reprinted in *Disarmament and Security, op. cit. supra* at 515. Art. 81 of the Treaty Establishing the European Atomic Energy Community, 25 March 1957, provides that the commission may send inspectors into the territories of the members and the inspectors shall at all times have access to the plants subject to EURATOM control.

Also of interest are the recent bilateral treaties between the United States and more than thirty nations concerning cooperation for peaceful uses of atomic energy. Such agreements provide for representatives of the United States Atomic Energy Commission "to observe from time to time the condition and use of any leased Material." See, *e.g.,* the Agreement for Cooperation Between the Government of the United States of America and the Government of the United States of Brazil Concerning Civil Uses of Atomic Energy, Aug. 3, 1955, art. VIc, 6 U.S. TREATIES AND OTHER INT'L AGREEMENTS (hereinafter cited as U.S. TREATIES) 2583, 2586, T.I.A.S. No. 3303. Similarly, the Statute of the International Atomic Energy Agency, art. XIIA-(6), 8 U.S. TREATIES 1093 (1957), T.I.A.S. No. 3873, would permit the agency to send into the territory of member states which had been allotted fissionable materials, inspectors "who shall have access at all times to all places and data and to any person who by reason of his occupation deals with materials, equipment, or facilities . . . as necessary to account for source and special fissionable materials supplied and fissionable products and to determine whether there is compliance with the undertaking against use in furtherance of any military purpose . . . with the health and safety measures . . . and with any other conditions prescribed in the agreement between the Agency and the State or States concerned."

In another setting the United States joined in the General Act for the Repression of African Slave Trade, July 2, 1890, 27 STAT. 886, T.S. No. 383, which regulated the importation of arms into certain sections of Africa. The provisions included control of transportation of armaments, inspection of vessels, and a promise by the signatories to pass laws punishing violators.

Of course, enforced and supervised disarmament was frequently imposed by victors upon the vanquished in war. The Treaty of Versailles of 1919

Notes to I: Introduction

established an Inter-Allied Commission of Control to assure compliance with the treaty's ceilings on German military strength. See *Disarmament and Security, op. cit. supra* note 2, at 1–12. Arms restrictions of even greater severity were applied to Germany after the Second World War. See Declaration Regarding Germany, June 5, 1945, 60 STAT. 1649, T.I.A.S. No. 1520. Total disarmament was provided for Japan by the Allies, and the arms prohibition was incorporated into art. 9 of the postwar Japanese Constitution, reprinted in U.S. DEP'T OF STATE PUB. NO. 2836, FAR EASTERN SER. 22 (1947).

4. See "Findings on the Safeguards to Ensure the Use of Atomic Energy Only for Peaceful Purposes," in *The International Control of Atomic Energy: First Report of the United Nations Atomic Energy Commission to the Security Council,* U.N. Doc. No. AEC/18/Rev. 1 (1947), also reprinted in U.S. DEP'T OF STATE PUB. NO. 2737 (1947). This plan substantially embodied the United States proposal known as the "Baruch Plan," which, in turn, was based on the proposals of the Acheson-Lilienthal Report, U.S. Dep't of State Special Committee on Atomic Energy, *A Report on the International Control of Atomic Energy,* U.S. DEP'T OF STATE PUB. NO. 2498 (1946). See also *International Control of Atomic Energy,* U.S. DEP'T OF STATE PUB. NOS. 2702 (1946), 3161 (1948).

5. While the United States had shunned the League of Nations, it participated in efforts to achieve disarmament before and between the World Wars. It had, for example, taken part in disarmament discussions at the Hague in 1899 and 1907. B. WILLIAMS, THE UNITED STATES AND DISARMAMENT 121–25 (1931); U.S. EXECUTIVE OFFICE OF THE PRESIDENT, DISARMAMENT STAFF, *op. cit. supra* note 2, at 4, 5. However, neither of these conferences achieved a significant reduction in armaments. See Hague Convention, July 29, 1899, 32 STAT. 1779, T.S. No. 392; Hague Convention, Oct. 18, 1907, 36 STAT. 2199, T.S. No. 536.

Multilateral attempts to control armaments in the period between the World Wars included:

The Peace Treaty of Versailles, June 28, 1919, GREAT BRITAIN TREATY SERIES, 1919, No. 4, which contained several references to disarmament, *e.g.,* part I, art. 8, and part V. The United States signed this treaty but the Senate refused consent to its ratification.

The Convention for the Control of Arms, Sept. 10, 1919, GREAT BRITAIN TREATY SERIES, 1919, No. 12, which was an attempt to restrict international trade in arms. The United States signed, but again the Senate declined to consent.

The Washington Naval Treaty, Feb. 6, 1922, 43 STAT. 1655, T.S. No. 671, which was signed and ratified by the United States. This treaty, *inter alia,* obligated the parties to restrict their capital ship tonnage.

The Arms Traffic Convention, June 17, 1925, which had as its purpose the limitation of world arms trade. This convention was not ratified by the Senate until June 6, 1935, and never came into force because the requisite number of ratifications was not obtained. See Trenwith, 4 *Treaties, Con-*

ventions, International Acts, and Agreements Between the United States of America and Other Powers 4903, S. Doc. No. 134, 75th Cong., 3d Sess. (1938).

The Preparatory Commission on Disarmament of the League of Nations in which the United States participated from 1926 to 1930. The commission's purpose was to prepare a draft treaty for a world disarmament conference. On February 2, 1932, such a conference met at Geneva, with the United States one of sixty nations represented. This conference or its bureaus held sessions until May 31, 1937. No final convention was ever presented for the signature of the conference participants.

The London Naval Agreement, April 22, 1930, 46 STAT. 2858, T.S. No. 830, which placed some limits on cruiser tonnage and submarine warfare.

Another treaty restricting naval armaments, which the United States signed on March 25, 1936, at London, and which it later ratified, 50 STAT. 1363, T.S. No. 919. This was principally an extension of the naval treaties of 1922 and 1930.

For a brief outline of United States participation in these efforts see *Disarmament: A Selected Chronology, op. cit. supra* note 2.

6. For example, the Baruch Plan added one element to the proposals in the Acheson-Lilienthal Report: it insisted that for violation of the proposed control agreement there must be United Nations sanctions and that to the imposition of such sanctions the veto of the Security Council should not apply. This insistence by the United States on the elimination of the veto undoubtedly raised still another obstacle to Soviet acceptance of the control plan. Yet one is not persuaded that Soviet insistence on retaining the veto in this field was responsible for the impasse; it is difficult to believe now that nations expected that a serious breach of the atomic control plan would be dealt with principally by action of the United Nations Security Council.

Indeed, it has been suggested that serious negotiations were not taking place, and were not possible as long as the United States alone had the atomic bomb. They became possible only later, when the United States monopoly in atomic weapons terminated and, in turn, Soviet superiority in conventional weapons was sharply reduced as a result of Western rearmament. Evidence in 1957 of probable Soviet superiority in guided missiles again disturbed comparative negotiating strength of East and West.

7. See *Control and Reduction of Armaments, op. cit. supra* note 2; Cavers, *Arms Control in the United Nations: A Decade of Disagreement,* 12 BULL. ATOM. SCI. 105 (1956). More recent official statements of the positions of both the Soviet Union and the United States may be found in 36 DEP'T STATE BULL. 89 and 225 (1957). See also Secretary of State Dulles, News Conference of May 14, 29, June 11, and June 25 (1957), in 36 DEP'T STATE BULL. 894 and 961 (1957), and 37 DEP'T STATE BULL. 9 and 96 (1957). The efforts of the United Nations Disarmament Commission are reviewed in *Disarmament—Continued Narrowing of Differences Sought,* 3 U.N. REV. No. 2, at 53 (1956), and in *Disarmament: The Continuing Quest for Agreement,* 3 U.N. REV. No. 11, at 6 (1957). For a statement of the

Notes to I: Introduction 163

American position in mid-1957, see Baldwin, *World Arms Picture—The Dangers and Proposals to Meet Them,* N.Y. Times, July 28, 1957, § 4, p. 5, col. 1. See also NOEL-BAKER, *op. cit. supra* note 2.

8. The Soviet Union's launching of its earth satellite gave proof of highly advanced scientific knowledge and technology, pertinent particularly to the development of long-range missiles. Although smaller United States satellites soon followed, the result was new stature for the Soviet Union, neutral nations impressed, uncertainty and confusion in the West. The impact was deep and multivaried, not least in regard to disarmament—in the comparative negotiating postures, in an enhanced sense of urgency in the West, perhaps also in a greater willingness to re-examine positions and make concessions. For the Soviet's part, on the other hand, with new confidence and prestige came, at the start at least, new intransigence as to the terms, conditions, and circumstances in which it would discuss arms control. In 1958, however, the Soviet Union announced unilateral suspension of nuclear tests and challenged the United States to do likewise. See note 11 below. Shortly thereafter the Soviet Union vetoed a resolution in the Security Council proposing international inspection in the Arctic.

9. The Eisenhower blueprint and aerial-inspection plan was first made public at the 1955 Geneva "summit" conference. The full text of the proposal is reprinted in 33 DEP'T STATE BULL. 171, 173 (1955) and *The Geneva Conference of Heads of Government* 56–59, DEP'T OF STATE PUB. No. 6046 (1955). See discussion in chapter IV note 7. See also Leghorn, *How Aerial Inspection Would Work,* U.S. News and World Report, July 29, 1955, p. 83; Baldwin, *Arms Control: Can U.S. Plan Work?,* N.Y. Times, Sept. 18, 1955, § 4, p. 6, col. 1.

The suspension of nuclear tests, while it might prove a first step toward arms control has been viewed largely as the elimination of a hazard to health, rather than a disarmament measure. See note 11 below.

10. See, *e.g.,* Kissinger, *Controls, Inspection, and Limited War,* The Reporter, June 13, 1957, p. 14; Leghorn, *The Approach to a Rational World Security System,* 13 BULL. ATOM. SCI. 195 (1957).

11. Beginning in 1956 there was sharp disagreement in the United States over a proposal to seek agreement for the cessation of nuclear tests. The United States position was that it would agree to stop these tests only if the Soviet Union agreed also to cease production of additional nuclear materials and accepted effective inspection. After the launching of the earth satellites United States officials began apparently to give serious thought to at least a moratorium on tests for an agreed period. See, *e.g.,* Stassen, N.Y. Times, Feb. 26, 1958, p. 1, col. 2. Behind United States reluctance to stop tests appeared to be the fear that this might prevent the United States from catching up with the Soviets in missile technology. There was some fear also that the Soviets might develop means for concealing tests held in violation of the agreement. See Baldwin, *Halt in Nuclear Tests?, The Arguments Pro and Con,* N.Y. Times, March 30, 1958, § 4, p. 6, col. 1; the arguments on both sides—before Sputnik—may also be found in 13 BULL. ATOM. SCI. 201

et seq. (1957). Scientists seemed to differ as to whether clandestine tests in violation of an agreement could be detected. Compare Professor Orear's paper in the Inspection Study, with TELLER AND LATTER, OUR NUCLEAR FUTURE, chapter XV, especially at 139–40 (1958); see *Hearings before the Subcommittee on Disarmament of the Senate Committee on Foreign Relations,* 85th Cong., 2d Sess., pts. 15–17 (1958). In August, 1958, however, a conference of scientists from eight nations, including Russia and the United States, concluded that an agreement to eliminate the testing of nuclear weapons could be effectively supervised and that the detection of violations was technically feasible. N.Y. Times, Aug. 22, 1958, p. 4, col. 4.

On August 22, 1958, President Eisenhower announced that the United States was prepared to negotiate for the suspension of nuclear tests, and was ready to suspend further tests when the negotiations began, if the Soviet Union also refrained. N.Y. Times, Aug. 23, 1958, p. 2, col. 4.

12. Most would agree that it is proper and even desirable to use the threat of massive retaliation to deter a would-be aggressor. There may be less agreement as to whether, if this deterrence fails, the threat should in fact be carried out, especially if it means the end of man. The dilemma, of course, is that insofar as the threat is necessary to deter, its effect would be vitiated if the enemy believed that it would not be carried out.

Perhaps the moral problem is posed in the form of an improbable extreme. For it is likely that even a major attack on the United States would not cause immediate, complete destruction, and neither would our retaliation. Presumably, a United States counterattack would begin—and few would say it should not—as soon as word of an enemy attack arrived, and attack and counterattack might then continue for some time. The result might be nearly total destruction of both sides, but the manner in which it occurred would not pose the moral problem in clear and sharp form.

For a brief discussion of the moral issue, see the letter of James R. Newman to the Editor of the Washington Post and Times-Herald, July 19, 1956, p. 12, col. 3. See also Szilard, *Disarmament and the Problem of Peace,* 11 BULL. ATOM. SCI. 297, 298 (1955).

13. Or perhaps the false claimant to the living baby before Solomon: "Let it be neither mine nor thine, but divide it."

14. See *e.g.,* Millis, *Disarmament: A Dissenting View,* N.Y. Times, July 28, 1957, § 6, p. 8.

15. See, *e,g.,* CLARK & SOHN, WORLD PEACE THROUGH WORLD LAW xi–xii, 203 *et seq.* (1958).

16. "The danger of world war is in some respects less than it has been for several centuries. Science speaks equally to all who will listen. The conquest of the air has been made available to many countries and increasingly to all. The Prometheus-like seizure of the atom has placed unlimited destruction in the power of at least four great nations. Combined with air power, it has made war almost useless as a means of accomplishing any human end save mass suicide. Fifteen years ago general staffs could advise and politicians could accept war as an instrument of policy and could advance a dubious claim to predict the probable results of war. Today, neither statesman nor

Notes to I: Introduction

general dares predict any result save universal catastrophe." BERLE, TIDES OF CRISIS: A PRIMER OF FOREIGN RELATIONS 220 (1957). Quoted with the permission of the publisher, Reynal & Company, Inc., New York.

17. Most of the earlier American disarmament proposals were related to plans for settlement of political differences. Thus disarmament proposals submitted to the United Nations General Assembly in 1946 envisaged simultaneous provisions for placement of armed forces at the disposal of the Security Council pursuant to art. 43 of the Charter and international control of atomic energy. See, *e.g.,* U.N. General Assembly Res. 41(I) (1947), *Principles Governing the General Regulation and Reduction of Armaments,* U.N. GENERAL ASSEMBLY RESOLUTIONS, 1st–4th Sess.; Statement by Secretary of State Byrnes, U.N. GENERAL ASSEMBLY OFF. REC., 1st Sess. 2d pt., 62d Pl. Mtg., at 1289 (1946). A 1951 Tripartite (United States, United Kingdom, and France) proposal to the General Assembly called for disarmament in both conventional and atomic weapons, to be verified by effective international inspection, but this was made contingent upon a Korean truce and a concurrent settlement of the major political issues dividing the world. U.N. Doc. No. A/C.1/667/Rev. 1 (1951) and Statement by Secretary of State Acheson, U.N. GENERAL ASSEMBLY OFF. REC. 6th Sess., 335th Pl. Mtg. at 13 (1951). Other statements of Western policy have related disarmament to the settlement of other political problems, for example, the unification of Germany. *Compare* N.Y. Times, July 15, 1955, p. 2, col. 5, and July 17, 1955, § 1, p. 1, col. 7, *with* N.Y. Times, July 18, 1955, p. 1, col. 8.

At different times the Soviet position appeared to be that disarmament plans must include the settlement of political issues. See *e.g., Union of Soviet Socialist Republics: Proposal on the Reduction of Armaments,* U.N. DISARMAMENT COMM'N OFF. REC., Supp. for April–Dec. 1955, at 17, 23 (U.N. Doc. No. DC/SC./1/26/Rev. 2) (1955); *Union of Soviet Socialist Republics: Proposal Submitted by Mr. N. A. Bulganin,* U.N. DISARMAMENT COMM'N OFF. REC., Supp. for April–Dec. 1955, at 33, 34 (U.N. Doc. No. DC/SC.1/29/Rev. 1) (1955). But see the statement by Soviet U.N. Representative Kuznetsov that "to make disarmament contingent on the solution of international political problems was tantamount to abandoning all hope of an agreement on disarmament." U.N. GENERAL ASSEMBLY OFF. REC., 11th Sess., 1st Comm., 821st Mtg., at 44 (1957).

Compare, for example: "Competition for armaments reflects, and is an instrument of, competition for power. So long as nations advance contradictory claims in the contest for power, they are forced by the very logic of the power contest to advance contradictory claims for armaments. Therefore, a mutually satisfactory settlement of the power contest is a precondition for disarmament." MORGENTHAU, POLITICS AMONG NATIONS 387 (2d ed. 1954). Quoted with the permission of the publisher, Alfred A. Knopf, Inc., New York. And see BERLE, *op cit. supra* note 16, at 256: "Save in certain limited aspects, disarmament is more likely to be a result of world peace than a cause of it."

18. See CLARK & SOHN, *op. cit. supra* note 15. *Cf.* BLUM, PEACE AND DIS-

ARMAMENT 200 (1932) ("disarmament is a cause, and not an effect, a condition and not a result of 'security' "). See also NOEL-BAKER, *op. cit. supra* note 2, especially chapters 6 and 7.

19. The "confidence-building" rationale for limited inspection proposals was suggested by both Prime Minister Eden and President Eisenhower in their respective plans submitted to the 1955 Geneva Heads of Government Conference. See *Proposal Submitted by the Delegation of the United Kingdom*, U.N. DISARMAMENT COMM'N OFF. REC., Supp. for April–Dec. 1955 at 35 (U.N. Doc. No. DC/SC.1/30) (1955); *Memorandum Supplementing Outline Plan for the Implementation of the Proposal Made by the President of the United States on 21 July 1955 at the Conference of Heads of Government of the Four Great Powers*, U.N. DISARMAMENT COMM'N OFF. REC., Supp. for April–Dec. 1955 at 45 (U.N. Doc. No. DC/SC.1/36) (1955).

20. See KISSINGER, NUCLEAR WEAPONS AND FOREIGN POLICY (1957), particularly chapters IV and VI; Finletter, *Facing Disarmament*, 13 BULL. ATOM. SCI. 154 (1957).

21. See Statement of U.S. Representative Lodge, U.N. GENERAL ASSEMBLY OFF. REC., 10th Sess., 1st Comm., 798th Mtg., at 216 (1955) (detection of all of the dangerous nuclear-weapon materials is not feasible); article by the French Representative to the U.N. Disarmament Commission, Moch, *Towards A Disarmed Peace*, 11 INT'L JOURNAL 85, 89 (1956) (if inspection is not put into effect now it may become forever impossible); Finletter, *Should U.S. Risk Unenforced Disarmament?*, 34 FOREIGN POLICY BULL. 181 (1955) (inspection will not detect all Russian fissionable material). The Russians have also recognized that inspection will not assure the discovery of all nuclear weapons. *Union of Soviet Socialist Republics: Proposal on the Reduction of Armaments, supra* note 17, at 23–24.

22. See, *e.g.*, Szilard, *supra* note 12, at 300.

23. See, *e.g.*, Cavers, *The Challenge of Planning Arms Control*, 34 FOREIGN AFFAIRS 50, 54 (1955).

24. See letter of James R. Newman to the Washington Post of Jan. 9, 1954, reprinted in 100 CONG. REC. A308 (1954), saying, in part:

"If an international agreement fixes levels of armaments production, levels thought to be adequate for defense but inadequate for waging war, it is important to know whether the levels are being adhered to.

"These levels will be reflected in certain critical indices: steel and aluminum production, the use of electric power, shipbuilding, mining of strategic metals, the manufacture of machine tools, airframes, jet and internal combustion engines, electronics equipment. . . . The economy of a large industrial nation is so integrated, its parts are so interdependent, that a sharp increase in rate of output at one point is visible at every point. The inspectors need not concern themselves over leaks; their task is to watch for floods. War mobilization is a flood. The notion of hidden preparations for a major war is absurd."

In one of the papers of the Inspection Study, Professor Boley stresses: "It is . . . unrealistic to hope to find a single item that can be used as a sole criterion of clandestine operations. It is rather necessary to search . . . a

Notes to III: Under the Constitution

number of separate components for possible adverse evidence, final proof of malpractice being provided by the weight of accumulated discoveries." Inspection Study 140.

25. See Inspection Study 3. See also p. 48 and note 11 above.

NOTES TO II: ARMS CONTROL PROVISIONS

1. Inspection might cover also commercial planes and commercial vessels entering and leaving the United States, and perhaps other national and international transportation as well. Such inspection would be part of the network designed to assure that the United States, like the Soviet Union and other governments in their respective territories, is not violating controls to which it has agreed. The control of transportation, moreover, might achieve an additional purpose. The "suitcase bomb" may be farfetched and not a serious object of international control, but the introduction of weapons or materials into a country for purposes hostile to that country may not be out of the question. International inspection would also afford the United States some protection against this threat.

2. President Eisenhower's "open skies" proposal did not necessarily contemplate a treaty. See chapter I note 9, chapter IV note 7.

3. Various arms plans have recognized the need to impose some limitations on inspection and to afford safeguards against its abuse. See *Report to the Security Council,* U.N. ATOMIC ENERGY COMM'N OFF. REC., 1st Year, Special Supp., at 46 (1946); *United States Memorandum No. 2—Functions and Powers of Proposed Atomic Development Authority,* 15 DEP'T STATE BULL. 98, 102 (1946); *United States of America—General Views on Item 3—"Safeguards" of the Plan of Work Adopted by the Commission for Conventional Armaments,* U.N. Doc. No. S/C.3/43 (1950); *United States of America—Working Paper Setting Forth Proposals for Progressive and Continuing Disclosure and Verification of Armed Forces and Armaments,* U.N. Doc. No. DC/C.2/1 (1952). The latter two are reprinted in *Disarmament and Security, op. cit. supra* chapter I note 2, at 279 and 318.

4. See, *e.g.,* Federal Firearms Act, 52 STAT. 1250 (1938), 15 U.S.C. §§ 901–9 (1952); Federal Explosives Act, 55 STAT. 863 (1941), 50 U.S.C. §§ 121–43 (1952); Mutual Security Act of 1954, § 414, 68 STAT. 848, 22 U.S.C. § 1934 (Supp. V, 1958); Atomic Energy Act of 1954, 68 STAT. 936, 42 U.S.C. §§ 2121, 2122 (Supp. V, 1958); Armed Forces Code, 10 U.S.C. §§ 4501, 4502 (Supp. V, 1958).

NOTES TO III: ARMS CONTROL AND THE CONSTITUTION

1. Wherever in this or succeeding chapters a serious constitutional obstacle or doubt is suggested, this could, of course, be eliminated by constitu-

tional amendment. An amendment might be desirable, also, as a means of assuring the support of the American people for any arms control plan having radical features. *Cf., e.g.,* CLARK & SOHN, WORLD PEACE THROUGH WORLD LAW 200–1 (1958). Compare their earlier suggestion in PEACE THROUGH DISARMAMENT AND CHARTER REVISION 141–42 (Prelim. Print, 1953).

There would appear to be no agreed limitation on what can be done by constitutional amendment. Attempts to impose limitations on the amending power were made and rejected both at the time of the Constitutional Convention and just prior to the Civil War. See MADISON, JOURNAL OF THE FEDERAL CONVENTION 737 (Scott ed. 1893); CONG. GLOBE, 36th Cong., 2d Sess. 1263–64 (1861). The Supreme Court has not heeded arguments that the Eighteenth Amendment was invalid as dealing with a subject beyond the scope of the amending power, National Prohibition Cases, 253 U.S. 350 (1920), or that the Nineteenth Amendment was void for depriving the states of their constitutional rights, Leser v. Garnett, 258 U.S. 130 (1922).

2. Atomic Energy Act of 1946, 60 STAT. 755; Atomic Energy Act of 1954, 68 STAT. 919, 42 U.S.C. §§ 2011–2281 (Supp. V, 1958).

3. Compare, *e.g.*: "It was one of the main objects of the Constitution to make us, so far as regarded our foreign relations, one people, and one nation; and to cut off all communication between foreign governments, and the several state authorities. The power now claimed for the states, is utterly incompatible with this evident intention; and would expose us to one of those dangers, against which the framers of the Constitution have so anxiously endeavored to guard." Taney, C. J., in Holmes v. Jennison, 14 Pet. 540, 575–76 (U.S. 1840). See also Mr. Justice Johnson, concurring in Gibbons v. Ogden, 9 Wheat. 1, 222, 228 (U.S. 1824) ("the states are unknown to foreign nations"). *Cf.,* CALHOUN, A DISCOURSE ON THE CONSTITUTION AND GOVERNMENT OF THE UNITED STATES, reprinted in I Works 111, 200 *et seq.* (Crallé ed. 1854). And see cases note 5.

4. See, *e.g.,* Penhallow v. Doane's Administrators, 3 Dall. 54, 80–82 (U.S. 1795).

5. 299 U.S. 304, 316–18 (1936). See also Chinese Exclusion Case, 130 U.S. 581, 604 (1889); Legal Tender Cases, 12 Wall. 457, 554, 555 (U.S. 1871) (concurring opinion). For a recent expression, see Perez v. Brownell, 356 U.S. 44 (1958).

6. *Id.* at 58. Mr. Justice Frankfurter said: "Broad as the power in the National Government to regulate foreign affairs must necessarily be, it is not without limitation. The restrictions confining Congress in the exercise of any of the powers expressly delegated to it in the Constitution apply with equal vigor when that body seeks to regulate our relations with other nations."

7. Holmes, J., in Missouri v. Holland, 252 U.S. 416, 433–34 (1920). Compare Home Building & Loan Ass'n v. Blaisdell, 290 U.S. 398, 442–43 (1934); McCulloch v. Maryland, 4 Wheat. 316, 407, 415 (U.S. 1819).

8. 133 U.S. 258, 266 (1890). Mr. Justice Field added: "The treaty power, as expressed in the Constitution, is in terms unlimited except by those

Notes to III: Under the Constitution

restraints which are found in that instrument against the action of the government or of its departments, and those arising from the nature of the government itself and of that of the States. It would not be contended that it extends so far as to authorize what the Constitution forbids, or a change in the character of the government or in that of one of the States, or a cession of any portion of the territory of the latter, without its consent. . . . But with these exceptions, it is not perceived that there is any limit to the questions which can be adjusted touching any matter which is properly the subject of negotiation with a foreign country." *Id.* at 267. See note 15 below.

9. 23 PROC. AM. SOC'Y INT'L L. 194 (1929). At that time he was not yet Chief Justice. Mr. Hughes also said: "So I come back to the suggestion I made at the start, that this is a sovereign nation; from my point of view the nation has the power to make any agreement whatever in a constitutional manner that relates to the conduct of our international relations, unless there can be found some express prohibition in the Constitution, and I am not aware of any which would in any way detract from the power as I have defined it in connection with our relations with other governments. But if we attempted to use the treaty-making power to deal with matters which did not pertain to our external relations but to control matters which normally and appropriately were within the local jurisdictions of the States, then I again say there might be ground for implying a limitation upon the treaty-making power that it is intended for the purpose of having treaties made relating to foreign affairs and not to make laws for the people of the United States in their internal concerns through the exercise of the asserted treaty-making power." *Id.* at 195–96. Compare CALHOUN, *op. cit. supra* note 3.

10. In 1817 the Rush-Bagot Agreement limited naval armaments on the Great Lakes for both the United States and Great Britain. In 1936 the second London Naval Treaty provided for additional limitations on the size of naval vessels. This was the last arms control agreement to which the United States adhered. See chapter I notes 3 and 5.

11. *Ibid.*

12. U.N. CHARTER art. 11, ¶ 1; art. 26.

13. The constitutional requirement of a "case or controversy," and other constitutional limitations on the judicial power, render it unlikely that most treaty provisions would come before a court of the United States for examination. A substantial number, however, have been involved in cases before United States courts and none of them has been struck down. See Corwin, *The Constitution of the United States of America,* S. Doc. No. 170, 82d Cong., 2d Sess. 428 (1953). But compare COWLES, TREATIES AND CONSTITUTIONAL LAW 294–95 (1941), whose thesis is that the Supreme Court has in fact declined to enforce treaty provisions where they infringed on private property rights.

14. (*a*) Generally, the only authority cited for this proposition is the suggestion of Mr. Justice Holmes, based on his reading of art. VI, cl. 2, of the Constitution. Mr. Justice Holmes said: "Acts of Congress are the supreme law of the land only when made in pursuance of the Constitution, while treaties are declared to be so when made under the authority of the

United States. It is open to question whether the authority of the United States means more than the formal acts prescribed to make the convention." Missouri v. Holland, 252 U.S. 416, 433 (1920).

Shortly after that case was decided Professor Thomas Reed Powell said of the opinion: "Its hint that there may be no other test to be applied than whether the treaty has been duly concluded indicates that the court might hold that specific constituional limitations in favor of individual liberty and property are not applicable to deprivations wrought by treaties." Powell, *Constitutional Law in 1919–20,* 19 MICH. L. REV. 1, 13 (1920).

The possibility of such an interpretation was recognized also in Stinson, *The Treaty-Making Power and the Restraint of the Common Law,* 1 B.U.L. REV. 111, 112 (1921), and in 6 CORNELL L.Q. 91, 92 (1920). See also United States v. Reid, 73 F.2d 153, 155 (9th Cir. 1934), *cert. denied for untimeliness,* 299 U.S. 544 (1936); the case was rejected on other grounds in Perkins v. Elg, 307 U.S. 325, 349 n. 31 (1939).

In fact, however, Mr. Justice Holmes himself continued, "We do not mean to imply that there are no qualifications to the treaty-making powers; but they must be ascertained in a different way." 252 U.S. at 433. And later in the case he stressed that "the treaty in question does not contravene any prohibitory words to be found in the Constitution. The only question is whether it is forbidden by some invisible radiation from the general terms of the Tenth Amendment." *Id.* at 433–34.

It is now commonly accepted that the distinction in Article VI, Clause 2, of the Constitution, to which Mr. Justice Holmes referred, was intended to give supremacy also to treaties which antedated the Constitution; specifically, the Treaties of Peace with Great Britain, 1782–83, 8 STAT. 54–60, 80, T.S. No. 102–4, which were not, of course, treaties "in pursuance of the Constitution." The distinction was not intended to establish a different standard of constitutionality, so that laws of the United States need be, but treaties need not be, "in pursuance" of the Constitution. See Mr. Justice Black, in Reid v. Covert, 354 U.S. 1, 16 (1957). See also 2 FARRAND, THE RECORDS OF THE FEDERAL CONVENTION OF 1787, at 417 (1911); RAWLE, A VIEW OF THE CONSTITUTION 66–67 (2d ed. 1829). That Article VI refers also to treaties "which shall be made" does not necessarily negative this explanation; this may have appeared to be the most felicitous way of including all treaties past and future. It may also have been designed to obviate any doubts as to inclusion of treaties concluded between the drafting of the Constitution and its coming into effect.

That a treaty is not subject to constitutional limitation has been suggested, in addition, on the ground that under international law a sovereign nation may enter into any treaty of proper international concern, and that this international law, antedating the Constitution, was not modified by the adoption of the Constitution. It has even been argued that the Constitution could not effectively limit the treaty powers of a sovereign nation. See Potter, *Inhibitions Upon the Treaty-Making Power of the United States,* 28 AM. J. INT'L L. 456 (1934).

Notes to III: Under the Constitution 171

Sutherland, *Restricting the Treaty Power,* 65 HARV. L. REV. 1305, 1319 (1952), notes that the President and the Senate evidently thought that they had the authority to contravene by treaty the Eighteenth Amendment of the Constitution when they ratified the Smuggling of Intoxicating Liquors Agreement, Jan. 23, 1924, 43 STAT. 1761, T.S. No. 685.

In the hearings on the Bricker Amendment some proponents argued that it was not clear that the Constitution could not be abridged by treaty. They, however, cited little authority for the view they feared. See, *e.g.*, Statements of Frank Holman, *Hearings Before a Subcommittee of the Senate Committee on the Judiciary,* 83d Cong., 1st Sess. at 142–49, 1219 (1953). See note 17 below.

John Foster Dulles, shortly before he became Secretary of State, said: "The treatymaking power is an extraordinary power, liable to abuse. Treaties make international law and also they make domestic law. Under our Constitution, treaties become the supreme law of the land. They are, indeed, more supreme than ordinary laws for congressional laws are invalid if they do not conform to the Constitution, whereas treaty law can overrule the Constitution. Treaties, for example, can take powers away from the Congress and give them to the President; they can take powers from the States and give them to the Federal Government or to some international body, and they can cut across the rights given the people by their constitutional Bill of Rights." Address at the regional meeting of the ABA, April 11, 1952, reprinted in *Hearings Before a Subcommittee of the Senate Committee on the Judiciary, op. cit. supra* at 862.

Later, when Secretary of State, Mr. Dulles explained that he did not believe the treaty power to be unlimited and that the only personal rights which could be limited by treaties would be "property" rights through the exercise of eminent domain. *Hearings Before a Subcommittee of the Senate Committee on the Judiciary,* 84th Cong., 1st Sess. at 177–79 (1955).

(*b*) A different but related argument might be made that even if a treaty as domestic law is subject to constitutional limitations, the United States may by treaty join with other nations to establish international law which has validity independent of the Constitution and does not derive authority from it. This law would be the law of the international community and would be applicable to Americans and others alike; it is not the law of the United States and is not subject to any of the constitutional limitations which govern United States law. This argument will be considered in chapters VII and VIII in relation to special issues to which it is relevant.

(*c*) It may be urged that in view of the possible international consequences of declaring a treaty provision unconstitutional, courts should not consider the validity of a treaty provision but treat that as a political question not for judicial determination. One commentator has said: "It is difficult to imagine anything more anomalous than a lawsuit between private litigants becoming the means of upsetting an international engagement." MCCLURE, INTERNATIONAL EXECUTIVE AGREEMENTS 223 (1941). *Cf.* United States v. Reid, *supra.* Compare Mr. Justice Chase, in Ware v. Hylton, 3 Dall. 199,

237 (U.S. 1796). "If the court possesses a power to declare treaties void, I shall never exercise it, but in a very clear case indeed." Other questions involving treaties, *e.g.,* whether power remains in a foreign state to carry out its treaty provisions, or whether a treaty continues to be effective in view of changed circumstances, have been deemed political questions, and not for judicial consideration. See Terlinden v. Ames, 184 U.S. 270, 288 (1902); Clark v. Allen, 331 U.S. 503, 514 (1947). On the proper role of the judiciary in relation to the political departments as to the interpretation of a treaty see Chief Justice Marshall in Foster v. Neilson, 2 Pet. 253, 307 (U.S. 1829).

Of course, whatever the courts might do, the President who makes treaties and the Senate which consents to them are bound to observe the Constitution as they see it, until and unless the Supreme Court has seen it otherwise. There appears, however, to be no authoritative precedent or declaration by either President or Senate which might indicate a standard for testing the validity of a treaty. Earlier in United States history, questions were raised, on a number of occasions, about the validity of treaties considered or entered into by the United States. See, generally, HOLT, TREATIES DEFEATED BY THE SENATE (1933). There were questions in Congress about the validity of treaties which required an appropriation of funds. See, *e.g.,* Speech of Albert Gallatin in the House of Representatives, March 9, 1796, 5 ANNALS OF CONG. 464, 467 (1796); CRANDALL, TREATIES: THEIR MAKING AND ENFORCEMENT 164–82 (2d ed. 1916). The Senate refused consent to a commercial treaty with the German States in 1844 because of lack of "constitutional competency." Senate Committee on Foreign Relations, *On the Convention With Prussia,* 8 REPORTS OF SENATE COMMITTEE ON FOREIGN RELATIONS, 28th Cong., 1st Sess. 36, 38 (1844). President Jefferson himself seriously questioned the constitutionality of the treaty whereby the United States acquired Louisiana. 10 JEFFERSON, WORKS 2–12, 28–30 (Ford ed. 1905). Treaties on these, and other subjects as to which questions were raised, have been entered into in later years by the United States. See WRIGHT, THE CONTROL OF AMERICAN FOREIGN RELATIONS 102–3 (1922).

15. Geofroy v. Riggs, 133 U.S. 258, 267 (1890) ("it would not be contended that it [the treaty power] extends so far as to authorize what the Constitution forbids"); Holden v. Joy, 17 Wall. 211, 243 (U.S. 1872) ("it must be assumed that the framers of the Constitution intended that it [the treaty power] should extend to all those objects which in the intercourse of nations had usually been regarded as the proper subjects of negotiation and treaty, if not inconsistent with the nature of our government and the relation between the States and the United States"); The Cherokee Tobacco, 11 Wall. 616, 620–21 (U.S. 1871) ("It need hardly be said that a treaty cannot change the Constitution or be held valid if it be in violation of that instrument. This results from the nature and fundamental principles of our government"); Doe v. Braden, 16 How. 635, 657 (U.S. 1853) ("The treaty is therefore a law . . . and the courts of justice have no right to annul or disregard any of its provisions, unless they violate the Constitution of the

Notes to III: Under the Constitution 173

United States"); New Orleans v. United States, 10 Pet. 662, 736 (U.S. 1836) ("Congress cannot, by legislation, enlarge the federal jurisdiction, nor can it be enlarged under the treaty-making power"); *cf.* Asakura v. Seattle, 265 U.S. 332, 341 (1924) ("The treaty-making power of the United States is not limited by any express provision of the Constitution, and, though it does not extend 'so far as to authorize what the Constitution forbids,' it does extend to all proper subjects of negotiation between our government and other nations"). See also 1 WILLOUGHBY, THE CONSTITUTIONAL LAW OF THE UNITED STATES §§ 310–13 (2d ed. 1929).

16. 354 U.S. 1, 16–17 (1957). Mr. Justice Black explains the Supremacy Clause along the lines given above, note 14(*a*).

17. 354 U.S. at 16–17. The opinion also states, "It would be manifestly contrary to the objectives of those who created the Constitution, as well as those who were responsible for the Bill of Rights—let alone alien to our entire constitutional history and tradition—to construe Article VI [the Supremacy Clause] as permitting the United States to exercise power under an international agreement without observing constitutional prohibitions. In effect, such construction would permit amendment of that document in a manner not sanctioned by Article V." *Id.* at 17. The two concurring and the two dissenting Justices did not concern themselves with this issue. This opinion is discussed in a different context in chapter VIII below.

It has been noted that in the Judiciary Act of 1789, 1 STAT. 73, 85–87, the Supreme Court was given jurisdiction over suits "where is drawn in question the validity of a treaty or a statute," suggesting that the Congress of the time of adoption of the Constitution thought a treaty might be invalid. Of course, it may have referred to a procedural invalidity where a treaty was not properly made by the President with the consent of two thirds of the Senators present. Or they may have had in mind limitations on the subject matter of treaties. See notes 8, 9, 15 above. On the other hand, the cases dealing with this phrase in the Judiciary Act, long after it was settled that federal statutes could be declared invalid, gave no indication that the validity of a treaty was to be tested in ways different from those for testing the validity of a statute. See, *e.g.,* Erie R.R. v. Hamilton, 248 U.S. 369 (1919).

In the controversy over the proposed Bricker Amendment, both sides supported a position that a treaty provision is of no domestic effect if it is contrary to any provision of the Constitution. *Compare, e.g.,* the statement of Manion supporting the amendment, *Hearings Before a Subcommittee of the Senate Committee on the Judiciary,* 84th Cong., 1st Sess. at 263 (1955), *with* the statement of Perlman opposing the amendment, *id.* at 237–38.

18. For the concept that a treaty cannot distort the basic division of power contemplated by the Constitution, see the discussion in WRIGHT, *op. cit. supra* note 14(*c*), at 101 *et seq.*

19. Foster v. Neilson, 2 Pet. 253, 314 (U.S. 1829).

20. 124 U.S. 190, 194 (1888). This view of the relation between the legislative power and the treaty power has been explained as an application of the maxim *leges posteriores priores contrarias abrogant* ("the last expres-

sion of the sovereign will must control"). Chinese Exclusion Case, 130 U.S. 581, 600 (1889). Implicit is the view that, in the area of jurisdiction common to both, the treaty power and the legislative power are distinct but equal. Either may enter the field but may be superseded by the other.

21. Prior treaty provisions have been held to have been superseded in numerous cases, *e.g.,* Chinese Exclusion Case, 130 U.S. 581 (1889); Whitney v. Robertson, 124 U.S. 190 (1888); Head Money Cases 112 U.S. 580 (1884); The Cherokee Tobacco, 11 Wall. 616 (U.S. 1871); and see Moser v. United States, 341 U.S. 41 (1951) (dictum). The only case in which the Supreme Court upheld a treaty provision in the face of inconsistent prior congressional legislation is Cook v. United States, 288 U.S. 102 (1933), which held that § 581 of the Tariff Act of 1922, pertaining to the enforcement of prohibition, had been modified by a treaty with Great Britain signed in 1924. This result was obtained although the relevant provisions of the Tariff Act of 1922 had been re-enacted without change in the Tariff Act of 1930. A lower court also recently applied the rule to allow a treaty provision to prevail over earlier legislation. Hannevig v. United States, 84 F. Supp. 743 (Ct. Cl. 1949).

There has been little question about the authority of Congress to refuse to honor earlier treaty provisions and by legislation to "repeal" them, at least so far as concerns their application in the United States. On the other hand, writers have questioned the converse—whether a treaty should prevail in the face of earlier inconsistent legislation by Congress. See Corwin, *The Constitution of the United States of America,* S. Doc. No. 170, 82d Cong., 2d Sess. 422–23 (1953); 1 WILLOUGHBY, *op. cit. supra* note 15, § 306. Cook v. United States, *supra,* in this view, is an aberration, perhaps to be explained by the low estate of the prohibition laws and the exigencies of diplomacy. Nevertheless, the rule of the *Cook* case could muster argument in its support. Indeed, as an original proposition it may be easier to sustain than its converse, *i.e.,* that an act of Congress can supersede a treaty provision. The treaty power was given to the President and the Senate, and a role in treatymaking for the Congress as a whole was refused during the constitutional negotiations. See MADISON, JOURNAL OF THE FEDERAL CONVENTION 548, 680 (Scott ed. 1893). It might have been argued that within the limited domain of the treaty power, the treaty makers were intended to be supreme and that a treaty should prevail over an inconsistent statutory provision regardless of which came first. See THE FEDERALIST No. 64, at 363 (Glazier ed. 1826) (Jay). This view, of course, has not prevailed. And, if Congress has plenary power in the field of foreign relations and may by legislation or joint resolution join powers with the President and do virtually all that could be done alternatively by the treaty makers, there can be little basis for arguing for a special and superior status for treaties. See note 67 below. The effect of conflict between national law and treaty provisions may be limited by compensation provisions like those in the treaties discussed in chapter VIII note 41.

22. See cases cited in first paragraph of note 21.

Notes to III: Under the Constitution

23. It is this abiding power in Congress which may dispose, for instance, of any challenge to the validity of key provisions of the United Nations Charter. It has been argued that the provision in the Charter whereby the United States agreed to "refrain . . . from the threat or use of force" (art. 2, ¶ 4) is invalid because it would deprive Congress of its power "to declare war." One answer is that while this provision in the Charter, a treaty of the United States, imposes an international obligation not to go to war in violation of the Charter, Congress continues to have its constitutional power to violate this treaty provision, "repeal" it, and declare war. Whether the President, in circumstances where his constitutional power to use force is recognized, may do so in violation of the United Nations Charter is a more difficult question. His power to use force may perhaps be limited by treaty as in other areas it may be limited by specific prohibition of Congress. *Cf.* the various concurring opinions, especially that of Mr. Justice Frankfurter, in Youngstown Sheet & Tube Co. v. Sawyer, 343 U.S. 579, 593 (1952). But perhaps treaties, being more in the executive domain, are less a restriction on the President than is congressional legislation. The Executive may have the power to denounce a treaty. See WRIGHT, *op. cit. supra* note 14(*c*), at 256–62, especially 259–60; CORWIN, THE PRESIDENT: OFFICE AND POWERS, 435–36 (4th rev. ed. 1957). A recent instance of the abrogation of a treaty by the President alone occurred in 1939, when the Executive Department notified Japan that the United States was terminating the Japanese-American Treaty of Commerce and Navigation, Feb. 21, 1911, 37 STAT. 1504, T.S. No. 558. Letter from the Secretary of State to Japanese Ambassador, [1931–41] 2 FOREIGN REL. U.S.: JAPAN 189 (1943). At the time of the treaty's abrogation Congress was considering resolutions to the same effect. S. RES. 166, 76th Cong., 1st Sess. (1939); H.R. RES. 264, 76th Cong., 1st Sess. (1939).

Similarly, despite American participation in treaties on limitations of naval armaments (see chapter I note 5), this country was soon building ships in excess of these limitations. Act to Establish the Composition of the United States Navy, 52 STAT. 401 (1938). Of course, the United Nations Charter permits action in self-defense. U.N. CHARTER art. 51. And as to any treaty, there are always reservations (specific or implied) permitting "breach" when other signatories have breached their pledges. This country was a party to the Kellogg-Briand Pact, Treaty Providing for the Renunciation of War, Aug. 27, 1928, 46 STAT. 2343, T.S. No. 796, by whose terms the signatories condemned recourse to war and agreed to pacific settlement of disputes. But when Japan attacked, and Germany and Italy declared war on the United States, this country was, by the terms of the treaty itself, not bound to refrain from declaring war on the three Axis nations.

Perhaps the power of Congress to declare war in the face of a treaty is of a character different from its power to disregard a treaty provision and enact inconsistent domestic legislation. The latter, while it may compel the United States to violate its treaty, deals with a matter of domestic character in the United States. A declaration of war in the face of a treaty is not strictly an exercise of domestic congressional legislation, but primarily an international act entrusted by the Constitution to the Congress, even if it may have far-reaching domestic consequences as well.

24. Of course, if such a provision has desirable psychological effect, as an expression of United States sincerity and earnest intention, the United States can include it in a treaty. In other circumstances, the United States has in effect agreed not to adopt certain legislation, indicating in the agreement the international consequences should Congress so do. See General Agreement on Tariffs and Trade, Oct., 1947, 61 STAT. A3, T.I.A.S. No. 1700. The General Agreement is an executive agreement which may have congressional authorization in general legislation authorizing trade agreements. See § 350 of the Tariff Act of 1930, as amended, 19 U.S.C. § 1351 (1952). But compare the reference to GATT in the Trade Agreements Extension Act of 1955, 69 STAT. 162, 163.

25. See, *e.g.*, Jefferson, *Manual of Parliamentary Practice*, H.R. Doc. No. 1019, 66th Cong., 3d Sess. § 587 (1921). Finch, *The Need to Restrain the Treaty-making Power of the United States Within Constitutional Limits*, 48 AM. J. INT'L L. 57, 61 (1954), contends that the majority of the Founding Fathers held the Jeffersonian view on this issue. Hayden, *The States' Rights Doctrine and the Treaty-Making Power*, 22 AM. HIST. REV. 566 (1917), presents evidence that the Executive and Legislative Branches of the government in the period 1830–60 believed that treaties could not deal with matters not otherwise in the federal domain. A few commentators also adopted this narrow view of the treaty power. 5 MOORE, A DIGEST OF INTERNATIONAL LAW § 736 (1906); J. Williams, *Federal Usurpations*, 32 ANNALS 185, 207–8 (1908); Mikell, *The Extent of the Treaty-Making Power of the President and Senate of the United States*, 57 U. PA. L. REV. 435, 528, 535 (1909).

Even before the Supreme Court settled the issue, in Missouri v. Holland, 252 U.S. 416 (1920), these authorities represented a minority view. Compilations of commentators may be found in Wright, *The Constitutionality of Treaties*, 13 AM. J. INT'L L. 242, 256 & n.51, 257 (1919), and WRIGHT, THE CONTROL OF AMERICAN FOREIGN RELATIONS 92 & n.97 (1922). For two of the views in the majority, see: Root, *The Real Questions Under the Japanese Treaty and the San Francisco School Board Resolution*, 1 AM. J. INT'L L. 273 (1907); Corwin, *The Constitution of the United States of America*, S. Doc. No. 170, 82d Cong., 2d Sess. 426–27 (1933).

In the past, the narrow view of the treaty power was also officially adopted by United States representatives on a number of occasions. For a review of these, see Potter, *Inhibitions Upon the Treaty-Making Power of the United States*, 28 AM. J. INT'L L. 456 (1934). Indeed, United States representatives at various times specifically denied that the United States could regulate the production of armaments by treaty; this they did on the ground that treaties are powerless to regulate matters which are otherwise within the domain of the states. LEAGUE OF NATIONS DOC. No. C. 219 M. 142 (1927) IX, at 13; *id.* at No. C.F.A./2 Sess./P.V. 1 (1928), at 12; *id.* at No. A. 30 (1929) IX, at 7. This position was officially abandoned by the Department

Notes to III: Under the Constitution

of State in 1932. BUREAU OF THE DISARMAMENT CONFERENCE, MINUTES OF THE 30TH MEETING, Nov. 18, 1932, I, at 100. Several commentators agreed that this paralysis was self-imposed and unnecessary. Hudson, *The Treaty-Making Power of the United States in Connection With the Manufacture of Arms and Ammunition,* 28 AM. J. INT'L L. 736, 738 (1934); Potter, *supra* at 468, 473; Butler, *Speech,* 23 PROC. AM. SOC'Y INT'L L. 176, 177 (1929).

26. 252 U.S. 416 (1920).

27. 3 Dall. 199 (U.S.); *cf.* Georgia v. Brailsford, 3 Dall. 1 (U.S. 1794).

28. See, *e.g.,* the treaties upheld in Asakura v. Seattle, 265 U.S. 332 (1924); Hauenstein v. Lynham, 100 U.S. 483 (1880); *cf.* United States v. Belmont, 301 U.S. 324 (1937).

29. Holmes, J., in Missouri v. Holland, 252 U.S. 416, 433–34 (1920).

30. See note 15 above. One limitation on the treaty power frequently cited is that the United States cannot by treaty give away the territory of a state without its consent. See Geofroy v. Riggs, 133 U.S. 258, 267 (1890), citing Fort Leavenworth R.R. v. Lowe, 114 U.S. 525, 541 (1885). *Cf.* art. V of the Webster-Ashburton Treaty, Aug. 9, 1842, 8 STAT. 575, T.S. No. 119, where the consent of two states was obtained to the settlement of a boundary with Canada. See WRIGHT, *op. cit. supra* note 25, at 88–89. This proposition has not been unquestioned. While it was early supported by Jefferson, 5 WRITINGS 441, 443–44 n.2, 476 (FORD ed. 1892), others took an opposite view. CRANDALL, *op. cit. supra* note 14, § 99. See also 5 MOORE, *op. cit. supra* note 25, at 171–75. Corwin, *The Constitution of the United States of America,* S. DOC. No. 170, 82d Cong., 2d Sess. 430 n.3. There would seem to be little doubt that in case of necessity, *e.g.,* if the United States lost a war, a peace treaty ceding state territory could not be challenged on constitutional grounds. Letter of Jefferson, 1 AM. STATE PAPERS: FOREIGN RELATIONS 252 (1833). In time of peace it is open to question whether state territory can be ceded without its consent. The settlement of boundary disputes may be distinguished since the authority of the state over the territory is basically in dispute.

31. U.S. CONST. art. I, § 10.

32. U.S. CONST. art. I, § 8.

33. The militia has been described as "civilians primarily, soldiers on occasion. . . . [It] comprised all males physically capable of acting in concert for the common defense." United States v. Miller, 307 U.S. 174, 179 (1939), and materials cited *id.* at 179–82.

34. See Scott, *Militia Debates,* S. DOC. No. 695, 64th Cong., 2d Sess. (1917), for a summary of the comments about the militia at the Constitutional Convention of 1787 and at the various state ratifying conventions. That the militia would be a state bulwark against an overbearing central government was suggested by Dickinson and Elsworth, *id.* at 33–34, and by Henry, at 47–48. *But cf.* Pinckney, at 33, and Langdon, at 36. THE FEDERALIST No. 29 (Hamilton), and No. 46 (Madison), also viewed the militia as a protection for the states. See also People v. Brown, 253 Mich. 537, 235 N.W.

245 (1931); 2 STORY, COMMENTARIES ON THE CONSTITUTION 646 (5th ed. 1891); Haight, *The Right to Keep and Bear Arms*, 2 BILL OF RIGHTS REV. 31 (1941).

35. Congress has apparently required that the organized militia must be part of the National Guard, which in turn has been assimilated to the United States Army Reserve. See 10 U.S.C. §§ 101, 311 (Supp. V, 1958); 32 U.S.C. § 101 (Supp. V, 1958). See also FINAL REPORT OF THE NEW YORK STATE JOINT LEGISLATIVE COMMITTEE TO STUDY THE MILITARY LAW 109, 115 (1953); Wiener, *The Militia Clause of the Constitution*, 54 HARV. L. REV. 181, 208 (1940). Congress has directed that a state may "in time of peace . . . maintain no troops other than those of its National Guard and State defense forces." 32 U.S.C. § 109 (Supp. V, 1958).

36. Wiener, *supra* note 35, at 217: "the power of Congress to prohibit the raising of home guards is . . . clear. The short answer is that the power to provide for organizing the militia includes the power to provide how it shall not be organized."

37. *Compare* Wiener, *supra* note 35, *with* McKenna, *The Right to Keep and Bear Arms*, 12 MARQ. L. REV. 138, 143 (1928), "the Federal Government exercises a paramount control over, but may not destroy, the militia of the states."

38. New York v. United States, 326 U.S. 572 (1946).

39. California v. Taylor, 353 U.S. 553 (1957); United States v. California, 297 U.S. 175 (1936).

40. University of Illinois v. United States, 289 U.S. 48 (1933).

41. See St. Louis v. Western Union Tel. Co., 148 U.S. 92, 101 (1893). *Cf.* Missouri *ex rel.* Camden County v. Union Elec. Light & Power Co., 42 F.2d 692 (W.D. Mo. 1930), noted in 44 HARV. L. REV. 305.

In the *Western Union* case, Mr. Justice Brewer appears to imply that federal eminent domain might be available even against "statehouse grounds." 148 U.S. at 101. In New York v. United States, 326 U.S. 572, 582 (1946), Mr. Justice Frankfurter suggests that for tax purposes the "Statehouse" may "partake of uniqueness from the point of view of intergovernmental relations" and to tax it might be to tax "the State as a State."

42. Case v. Bowles, 327 U.S. 92 (1946). We have suggested that the war power may itself support federal arms control, see p. 43 above and note 67 this chapter; on that basis if rent control under the war power applies to state activities, so it might be said would arms control under this power. In any event, language in Case v. Bowles is authority for the proposition that the states enjoy no constitutional immunity from federal regulation under any power, if such immunity would interfere with the full realization of that federal power. The Court said: "For reasons to which we have already adverted, an absence of federal power to fix maximum prices for state sales or to control rents charged by a State might result in depriving Congress of ability effectively to prevent the evil of inflation at which the Act was aimed. The result would be that the constitutional grant of the power to make war would be inadequate to accomplish its full purpose. And this result would im-

Notes to III: Under the Constitution

pair a prime purpose of the Federal Government's establishment." 327 U.S. at 102. The control of arms under the treaty, foreign-relations, and other federal powers also should not be rendered "inadequate to accomplish its full purpose," and the "prime purpose" of the federal government to maintain peace should not be frustrated by radiations of state "immunity" and "sovereignty."

43. See p. 60 above.

44. This is now generally assumed, although there appears to be no clear holding by the Supreme Court. The First Amendment was one of a number invoked in Joint Anti-Fascist Refugee Comm. v. McGrath, 341 U.S. 123 (1951), but the Court's judgment did not necessarily rest on it, and the opinions of the Court did not examine the applicability of the amendment to the Executive. In his concurring opinion, however, Mr. Justice Black said, "In my judgment the executive has no constitutional authority, with or without a hearing, officially to prepare and publish the lists challenged by petitioners. In the first place, the system adopted effectively punishes many organizations and their members merely because of their political beliefs and utterances, and to this extent smacks of a most evil type of censorship. This cannot be reconciled with the First Amendment as I interpret it." *Id.* at 143. Mr. Justice Reed's dissent dealt with the First Amendment so as to imply that in a proper case the amendment would limit the powers of the Executive. *Id.* at 199.

There are also broad statements in other opinions of Justices of the Supreme Court. Recently, in Watkins v. United States, 354 U.S. 178, 188 (1957), Chief Justice Warren wrote for the Court: "The Bill of Rights is applicable to investigations as to all forms of governmental action. Witnesses cannot be compelled to give evidence against themselves. They cannot be subjected to unreasonable search and seizure. Nor can the First Amendment freedoms of speech, press, religion, or political belief and association be abridged." Earlier, in an opinion of the Court, Mr. Justice Jackson said: "If there is any fixed star in our constitutional constellation, it is that no official, high or petty, can prescribe what shall be orthodox in politics, nationalism, religion, or other matters of opinion or force citizens to confess by word or act their faith therein." West Virginia Bd. of Educ. v. Barnette, 319 U.S. 624, 642 (1943). The case itself involved state action, not action by the Federal Executive under the First Amendment, although the First Amendment is much mentioned in the opinion. See also Mr. Justice Douglas dissenting, in Beauharnais v. Illinois, 343 U.S. 250, 284, 286 (1952): "The First Amendment says that freedom of speech, freedom of press, and the free exercise of religion shall not be abridged. That is a negation of power on the part of each and every department of government." Compare also Mr. Justice Black, in Reid v. Covert, 354 U.S. 1 (1957). See generally Maslow, *Is the President Bound by the First Amendment, Hearings Before A Subcommittee of the Senate Committee on the Judiciary,* 83d Cong., 1st Sess. at 314 (1953).

It may be urged that in any event the Fifth Amendment denies the Executive as well as other branches the right to deprive a citizen of "liberty" without due process of law, and that the "liberty" protected includes the freedoms specified in the First Amendment.

45. 307 U.S. 174, 178 (1939).

46. See Cases v. United States, 131 F.2d 916, 921–23 (1st Cir. 1942), cert. denied, 319 U.S. 770 (1943).

47. 291 U.S. 502, 525 (1934). Although the doctrine grew and ramified pursuant to the Fourteenth Amendment and has been invoked more frequently in regard to state action, substantive due process has been frequently sought and applied under the Fifth Amendment in regard to acts of Congress. A single famous instance, before the Fourteenth Amendment existed, is, of course, Scott v. Sandford, 19 How. 393 (U.S. 1857), which, in fact, involved federal legislation in implementation of a treaty. Later the Court measured federal statutes by the yardstick of substantive due process in numerous cases, *e.g.*, Virginian Ry. v. Federation, 300 U.S. 515, 558 (1937); Lottery Case, 188 U.S. 321, 356–57 (1903). For the development and scope of the doctrine of substantive due process, see, *e.g.*, Cushman, *Social and Economic Interpretation of the Fourteenth Amendment*, 20 MICH. L. REV. 737 (1922), and Brown, *Due Process of Law, Police Power, and the Supreme Court*, 40 HARV. L. REV. 943 (1927).

48. Williamson v. Lee Optical, Inc., 348 U.S. 483, 488 (1955).

49. Day-Brite Lighting, Inc. v. Missouri, 342 U.S. 421, 423 (1953). Referring to these cases Judge Learned Hand said: "One would suppose that these decisions and the opinions that accompanied them had put an end—at least when economic interests only were at stake—to any judicial review of a statute because the choice made between the values and sacrifices in conflict did not commend itself to the court's notions of justice. That would, however, be too hasty a conclusion because in one of its most recent decisions the Court did intervene and annulled a state statute for just such reasons. It is true that this was by virtue of the 'Equal Protection Clause,' but the language used applied as well to the 'Due Process Clause.' " Judge Hand then quoted from Morey v. Doud, 354 U.S. 457, 466 (1957): "Of course, distinctions in the treatment of business entities engaged in the same business activity may be justified by genuinely different characteristics of the business involved. This is so even where the discrimination is by name. But distinctions cannot be so justified if the 'discrimination has no reasonable relation to these differences.' " HAND, THE BILL OF RIGHTS 44–45 (1958).

In addition to "unreasonable" discrimination, the Court would probably still strike down measures which are "confiscatory" when no compensation is provided. See p. 43 above. Compare chapter VII note 41. And however little may be left of the protection of substantive due process as regards "economic" and "property" rights, some rights continue to be vindicated by the courts against "unreasonable" deprivation. *E.g.*, Schware v. Board of Bar Examiners, 353 U.S. 232 (1957); Butler v. Michigan, 352 U.S. 380 (1957). The view that some freedoms have a "preferred position" justifying, if not requiring, greater judicial curbs on the legislature, has been expressed in a number of opinions. They were collected by Mr. Justice Frankfurter (who

Notes to III: Under the Constitution

does not share the view) in Kovacs v. Cooper, 336 U.S. 77, 89, 90–94 (1949). And see HAND, *op. cit. supra* at 50 *et seq.*

50. That a corporation is a "person" under the Fourteenth Amendment was considered so obvious that it was a question on which "the court [did] not wish to hear argument"—when it first arose in relation to the equal protection clause. Santa Clara County v. Southern Pac. R.R., 118 U.S. 394, 396 (1886). This was soon applied also in regard to corporate property under the due process clause of the Fourteenth Amendment. Covington and Lexington Turnpike Road Co. v. Sandford, 164 U.S. 578 (1896); Smyth v. Ames, 169 U.S. 466 (1898); Grosjean v. American Press Co., 297 U.S. 233 (1936). While Mr. Justice Black at one time sought to have this interpretation overruled—see dissenting opinion, Connecticut Gen. Life Ins. Co. v. Johnson, 303 U.S. 77, 83, 85 (1938)—it appears to be firmly fixed. That a corporation is a "person" whose property is protected by the due process clause of the Fifth Amendment does not appear to have been seriously questioned and has been held, in effect, in numerous cases. In Sinking-Fund Cases, 99 U.S. 700, 718–19 (1879), the Court said that the United States "equally with the States . . . are prohibited from depriving persons or corporations of property without due process of law."

51. "That Congress had the power to sacrifice the *rights* and *interests* of *private* citizens to secure the safety or prosperity of the public, I have no doubt; but the immutable principles of justice; the public faith of the States, that confiscated and received *British* debts, pledged to the debtors; and the rights of the debtors violated by the treaty; all combine to prove, that ample compensation ought to be made to all the debtors who have been injured by the treaty for the benefit of the *public*. This principle is recognized by the Constitution, which declares, 'that *private* property shall not be taken for *public* use without *just compensation.*' " Chase, J., 3 Dall. 199, 245 (U.S. 1796). See also the opinion of Mr. Justice Iredell, at 256, 279. Mr. Justice Cushing, at 281, 283, suggests that the state should be responsible to the debtor. *Cf.* Cities Serv. Co. v. McGrath, 342 U.S. 330 (1950), discussed below note 68. John Foster Dulles, who, prior to becoming Secretary of State, had suggested that treaties can "cut across the rights given the people by their constitutional Bill of Rights," later took the position that the only personal rights that could be affected by treaties would be "property rights" and that this would constitute an exercise of eminent domain. See note 14(*a*). See also p. 44 above.

52. Whether there is a denial of due process is a question related to but different from whether there has been a public taking requiring compensation. See Mr. Justice Chase in Ware v. Hylton, 3 Dall. 199 (U.S. 1796), discussed above note 51. This difference is examined at p. 43 above.

The settlement by treaty of claims of American citizens against a foreign country, which might be deemed to raise questions both of due process and of taking for public use, involves special considerations, which are discussed in another connection in chapter VII.

53. COWLES, *op. cit. supra* note 13, at 292–95, suggests that this case

would not be followed today. His argument, however, does not lead to the conclusion that the treaty is invalid, but rather that to bring it into effect domestically in the United States Congress would have to meet the requirements of the Fifth Amendment and provide compensation. A court might well, however, follow Ware v. Hylton, leaving the debtor to an action in the Court of Claims on a claim "founded upon the Constitution." See p. 44 above. *Cf.* Cities Serv. Co. v. McGrath, 342 U.S. 330 (1952), discussed in note 68. And see chapter VII note 20.

If in a situation such as Ware v. Hylton the courts were to decide in favor of the American citizen whose property rights are involved, the United States might fulfill its international obligations by compensating the foreign claimant. Compare the treaty discussed in chapter VIII note 41.

54. North American Cold Storage Co. v. Chicago, 211 U.S. 306 (1908), citing, *inter alia,* Lawton v. Steele, 152 U.S. 133 (1894).

55. Miller v. Schoene, 276 U.S. 272 (1928).
56. Hadacheck v. Sebastian, 239 U.S. 394 (1915).
57. Reinman v. Little Rock, 237 U.S. 171 (1915).
58. Powell v. Pennsylvania, 127 U.S. 678 (1888).
59. Mugler v. Kansas, 123 U.S. 623 (1887).
60. Buttfield v. Stranahan, 192 U.S. 470 (1904).
61. Stutz v. Bureau of Narcotics, 56 F. Supp. 810 (N.D. Cal. 1944), sustaining the constitutionality of the Opium Poppy Control Act of 1942, 56 STAT. 1045, 21 U.S.C. §§ 188–188n (1952).
62. United States v. Carolene Products Co., 304 U.S. 144 (1938).
63. United States v. Miller, 307 U.S. 174 (1939), *supra* p. 37; Cases v. United States, 131 F.2d 916 (1st Cir. 1943), *cert. denied,* 319 U.S. 770 (1943) (upholding the constitutionality of the act forbidding interstate transportation of certain arms, Federal Firearms Act, 52 STAT. 1250 (1938), 15 U.S.C. § 902 (1952)).
64. Legal Tender Cases, 12 Wall. 457 (U.S. 1871).
65. Woods v. Miller Co., 333 U.S. 138, 146 (1948); Fleming v. Rhodes, 331 U.S. 100, 107 (1947). *Cf.* Mulford v. Smith, 307 U.S. 38, 49–51 (1939).
66. Atomic Energy Act of 1946, 60 STAT. 755; Atomic Energy Act of 1954, 68 STAT. 919, 42 U.S.C. §§ 2011–2281 (Supp. V, 1958). For an analysis of the later act, see MARKS & TROWBRIDGE, FRAMEWORK FOR ATOMIC INDUSTRY (1955).
67. While a treaty would support congressional legislation without regard to other powers of Congress, the power of Congress to regulate armaments in the absence of treaty would be substantial, and perhaps even plenary; such legislation under other powers of Congress would, of course, also be supreme. Congress could regulate, and even forbid, the interstate transportation of armaments, or their import or export. United States v. Miller, 307 U.S. 174 (1939); United States v. Curtiss-Wright Export Corp., 299 U.S. 304 (1936). By invoking the taxing power and imposing taxes on engaging

Notes to III: Under the Constitution

in the manufacture or traffic in armaments, Congress could also impose strict and far-reaching controls, including registration, reporting, and inspection, in order to protect the revenue. Sonzinsky v. United States, 300 U.S. 506 (1937); United States v. Doremus, 249 U.S. 86 (1919). See also chapter IV below. In order to make such regulation effective, Congress could reach both behind the interstate or international transportation of armaments and subsequent to it, and could regulate manufacture, possession, or local transportation to the extent that this is reasonably related to the regulation of the interstate or foreign commerce in armaments. NLRB v. Jones & Laughlin Steel Corp., 301 U.S. 1 (1937). Congress may even regulate strictly intrastate transactions in arms if it can be reasonably claimed to be necessary for the effective regulation of interstate or foreign commerce in armaments. Shreveport Case, 234 U.S. 342 (1914).

There may be other powers of Congress adequate to support armaments control legislation. The inherent power of the nation to deal with foreign relations, propounded by Mr. Justice Sutherland in the *Curtiss-Wright* case, *supra,* carries the implication that the Legislative Branch of the nation has power to deal with foreign relations by legislation. Such a legislative power was given effect in Perez v. Brownell, 356 U.S. 44 (1958). Compare the Chinese Exclusion Case, 130 U.S. 581 (1889), and later decisions which recognize in Congress far-reaching power over aliens, as an aspect of inherent national sovereignty. Such an implied power, independent of the foreign commerce or other explicit powers of Congress, might itself support legislation dealing with the regulation of arms in the United States, even without a treaty, as having reasonable relation to the conduct of foreign relations.

One may also invoke the power of Congress to act in the national defense, rooted in the express powers to declare war, to raise and support armies, and to provide and maintain a navy. This power is broad and sturdy enough to support the extensive and far-reaching controls of the Atomic Energy Act. It is broad enough to support legislation designed to achieve the national defense by arming the United States for defense against would-be enemies. It might be broad enough to support legislation designed to achieve the national defense by controlling United States arms so as to bring about the disarmament of would-be enemies. Of course, Congress would presumably not wish to do so in the absence of an agreement with such potential enemies. If there is such an agreement, the power of Congress is joined to that of the President, and still another power of Congress may be invoked. Where the Executive has negotiated such an agreement (even if it is not a treaty), Congress can pass legislation necessary and proper for carrying the agreement into execution. See U.S. CONST. art. I, § 8. An executive agreement authorized or approved by Congress is deemed the equivalent of a treaty. 40 OPS. ATT'Y GEN. 469 (1946). *Compare* McDougal and Lans, *Treaties and Congressional-Executive or Presidential Agreements: Interchangeable Instruments of National Policy,* 54 YALE L.J. 181, 534 (1945), *with*

Borchard, *Shall the Executive Agreement Replace the Treaty?*, 53 YALE L.J. 664 (1944), and Borchard, *Treaties and Executive Agreements—A Reply*, 54 YALE L.J. 616 (1945).

68. In Cities Serv. Co. v. McGrath, 342 U.S. 330 (1952), the Court upheld the power of Congress to authorize the Alien Property Custodian to seize certain obligations owned by enemy aliens, where the obligor was in the United States but the negotiable debenture was not. The Court said that if the obligor should in the future be compelled by a foreign court to make payment on the debenture to a holder in due course, the obligor would be entitled to compensation from the United States under the Fifth Amendment to the extent of any double liability. For the majority, Mr. Justice Clark said: "Only with this assurance against double liability can it fairly be said that the present seizure is not itself an unconstitutional taking of petitioners' property." *Id.* at 336. See also the opinion below, 189 F.2d 744, 747 (2d Cir. 1951) (L. Hand, J.). *Cf.* Yearsley v. W. A. Ross Constr. Co., 309 U.S. 18, 21 (1940); Hurley v. Kincaid, 285 U.S. 95 (1932).

69. There appears, however, to be no case which held a "taking" to be not for a public use where the legislature, or the executive pursuant to legislation, either of the nation or of a state, said that it was. Compare the various opinions in United States *ex. rel.* TVA v. Welch, 327 U.S. 546 (1946). The question was considered and the taking held to be for "public use" in numerous cases, *e.g.*, Brown v. United States, 263 U.S. 78 (1923); United States v. Gettysburg Elec. Ry., 160 U.S. 668 (1896). *Cf.* Cincinnati v. Vester, 281 U.S. 439 (1930), where the Court refused to rule whether a taking was in violation of the Fourteenth Amendment, holding the challenged use to be unauthorized by the state statute from which the city derived its power of eminent domain.

70. Omnia Commercial Co. v. United States, 261 U.S. 502 (1923); Peabody v. United States, 231 U.S. 530 (1913); Legal Tender Cases, 12 Wall. 457, 551 (U.S. 1871).

In United States v. Caltex, Inc., 344 U.S. 149 (1952), the majority of the Court found no constitutional right to compensation where the United States Army in time of war destroyed private property to prevent its taking and use by the enemy. The Court's opinion emphasizes that there is no obligation to compensate private losses incurred as a result of war. It is not clear whether the Court is saying that there was no "taking" within the meaning of the Fifth Amendment, or that it was a taking but not for public use. There is no discussion in terms of the due process clause—whether compensation might be necessary in order that the owner not be deprived of property "without due process of law." That the action was by military authorities not pursuant to legislation or executive order should not render the due process clause inapplicable. Presumably it is implied that destruction of property in war operations, without compensation, is within the limits of substantive due process; or that in any event suits against the United States, in this area, can only be maintained in situations which fall within the "public use" clause. *But cf.* Seery v. United States, 127 F. Supp. 601 (Ct. Cl. 1955).

The Court also found no "taking" by the United States when the War

Notes to III: Under the Constitution

Production Board ordered the closing of nonessential gold mines to release personnel, equipment, and materials for essential defense production. United States v. Central Eureka Mining Co., 357 U.S. 155 (1958).

The Court has sometimes divided as to whether a governmental regulation or restriction goes so far as to be a "taking." *Ibid.;* United States v. Kansas City Life Ins. Co., 339 U.S. 799 (1950); *cf.* United States v. Causby, 328 U.S. 256 (1946). Compare also Pennsylvania Coal Co. v. Mahon, 260 U.S. 393, 416 (1922).

71. The Tucker Act, 62 STAT. 940 (1948), as amended, 28 U.S.C. § 1491 (Supp. V, 1958). There is also concurrent jurisdiction in the district courts for claims which do not exceed $10,000. 28 U.S.C. § 1346(a)(2) (1952).

72. Compare notes 51, 53, 68 above.

73. Whether the power to exercise "eminent domain" might be conferred on an international body see chapter VII note 27.

74. United States v. Caltex, 344 U.S. 149 (1952), note 70 above.

75. 35 U.S.C. §§ 1–160, 162–293 (1952); 35 U.S.C. § 161 (Supp. V, 1958).

76. 35 U.S.C. § 101 (1952) requires, *inter alia,* that an invention to be patentable must be useful. Based on this requirement, courts have denied the validity of patents which could be used only for gambling purposes. Brewer v. Lichtenstein, 278 Fed. 512 (7th Cir. 1922); Schultze v. Holtz, 82 Fed. 448 (C.C.N.D. Cal. 1897); National Automatic Device Co. v. Lloyd, 40 Fed. 89 (C.C.N.D. Ill. 1889). In view of the statutory requirement of utility, a court would also strike down a patent which had only an illegal or pernicious use. See Rickard v. Du Bon, 103 Fed. 868, 873 (2d Cir. 1900). The Atomic Energy Act imposes drastic limitations on patents in the atomic field. See note 77.

77. Atomic patents and inventions are now governed by the Atomic Energy Act of 1954, 68 STAT. 943, 42 U.S.C. §§ 2181–90 (Supp. V, 1958). The act bars patents "for any invention or discovery which is useful solely in the utilization of special nuclear material or atomic energy in an atomic weapon"; patents already granted are revoked, and "just compensation" provided. 42 U.S.C. §§ 2181(a), (b). The act also requires inventions relating to described atomic purposes to be reported to the Atomic Energy Commission, unless a patent has been applied for. 42 U.S.C. § 2181(c). Inventions conceived under contract or other relationship to the commission are deemed to have been conceived by the commission. 42 U.S.C. § 2182. The commission may use, or license to others, atomic patents "affected with the public interest," the owner to be paid a "reasonable royalty fee." 42 U.S.C. § 2183. For a commentary on these sections of the act and the changes from the provisions of the 1946 Act, see MARKS & TROWBRIDGE, *op. cit. supra* note 66, at 25–33 (1955).

Compare 35 U.S.C. §§ 181–83 (1952), which requires withholding the grant of a patent on an invention whenever publication or disclosure might be "detrimental to the national security." The act provides procedural safeguards and compensation to the inventor.

78. There was no opinion of the Court in Sweezy v. New Hampshire, 354

U.S. 234 (1957). For himself and three other Justices, Chief Justice Warren said: "We believe that there unquestionably was an invasion of petitioner's liberties in the areas of academic freedom and political expression—areas in which government should be extremely reticent to tread. . . . Teachers and students must always remain free to inquire, to study and to evaluate, to gain new maturity and understanding; otherwise our civilization will stagnate and die." *Id.* at 250.

Mr. Justice Frankfurter, joined by Mr. Justice Harlan, said: "Progress in the natural sciences is not remotely confined to findings made in the laboratory. Insights into the mysteries of nature are born of hypothesis and speculation. . . . Political power must abstain from intrusion into this activity of freedom, pursued in the interest of wise government and the people's well-being, except for reasons that are exigent and obviously compelling. . . . This means the exclusion of governmental intervention in the intellectual life of a university. It matters little whether such intervention occurs avowedly or through action that inevitably tends to check the ardor and fearlessness of scholars, qualities at once so fragile and so indispensable for fruitful academic labor." *Id.* at 255, 261–62.

An earlier case which involved a form of academic freedom was Meyer v. Nebraska, 262 U.S. 390 (1923).

79. Mr. Justice Frankfurter in Sweezy v. New Hampshire, 354 U.S. 234, 255, 262 (1957).

80. See note 77 above.

NOTES TO IV: INVESTIGATION OF COMPLIANCE WITH ARMS CONTROL

1. Skepticism and near-despair about the effectiveness and practicability of extensive inspection have evoked ingenious and perhaps silly suggestions for determining whether a country is violating an arms control agreement and preparing for war. Thus, it has been suggested that the President of the United States (and the chiefs of other states) submit periodically to a lie detector test or be given "truth serum" and be required to answer questions about the extent of national armaments and the nature of national war plans. Whatever may be said of the desirability, effectiveness, and practicability of such a suggestion, it would not run afoul of any provision of the Constitution if the President by treaty agreed to do so. If the President, or a successor President, refused to submit to such tests, although required by treaty, he could not, of course, be compelled to do so. He could, perhaps, denounce the treaty. See chapter III note 23. The President himself is probably immune to the process of the courts. *Cf.* Mississippi v. Johnson, 4 Wall. 475 (U.S. 1868). He is, however, subject to impeachment for a "high crime" or "misdemeanor" under Article II, Section 4, of the Constitution.

Other suggestions—for example, an elaborate system for encouraging in-

Notes to IV: Investigation of Compliance 187

formers, paying them large, tax-free fees for information of violations by fellow citizens or government officials—would also raise more questions as to desirability and practicability than of constitutional validity. In some areas Congress has offered payment to informers. See, *e.g.,* Act of June 17, 1930, 46 STAT. 758, 19 U.S.C. § 1619 (1952); Act of July 15, 1955, 69 STAT. 365, 50 U.S.C. §§ 47a, c (Supp. V, 1958). See chapter V note 17.

2. Basically, of course, some measure of assurance that a nation is complying with its treaty provisions derives from the existence of the treaty itself. While all nations may at some time have violated treaties, that a nation has entered a treaty has, in most instances, reflected a prima facie intention to comply.

Past efforts to control armaments included provisions for voluntary reporting on the part of governments, *e.g.,* the London Naval Treaty of 1936, 50 STAT. 1363, T.S. No. 919. Treaties on other subjects also provided for such reporting, *e.g.,* the Convention for the Suppression of the Abuse of Opium and Other Drugs of 1912, 38 STAT. 1912, T.S. No. 612; Convention for Limiting the Manufacture and Regulating the Distribution of Narcotic Drugs of 1931, 48 STAT. 1543, T.S. No. 863. See chapter I note 3.

3. See p. 15 above.
4. See pp. 85–86 above.
5. See the discussion of regulated industries pp. 66–68, 69–70 above.
6. See pp. 45, 75–76 above.
7. The President proposed that the United States and Russia agree "to give each other a complete blueprint of our military establishments, from beginning to end, from one end of our countries to the other; lay out the establishments and provide the blueprints to each other.

"Next, to provide within our countries facilities for aerial photography to the other country." 33 DEP'T STATE BULL. 171, 174 (1955).

It is not clear whether President Eisenhower intended that the proposal be incorporated into a treaty. None would be required in so far as the agreement involved subjects exclusively within the constitutional power of the President, in his capacity as Commander in Chief, or as director of our foreign relations; or which are left to the President by delegation of Congress. If, on the other hand, there were involved *pro tanto* modification of federal statutes—*e.g.,* those dealing with security information, the right to fly in and out of the United States, the immigration laws (see chapter V)— such an executive agreement might require congressional approval. *Cf.* Youngstown Sheet & Tube Co. v. Sawyer, 343 U.S. 579 (1952); United States v. Guy W. Capps, Inc., 204 F.2d 655 (4th Cir. 1953), *aff'd on other grounds,* 348 U.S. 296 (1955). A joint resolution of Congress authorizing or approving such an executive agreement would, of course, eliminate questions as to the adequacy of the executive power, eliminate problems of conflict with existing federal law, and serve to repeal *pro tanto* any limitations in existing law which might otherwise preclude implementation of the executive agreement. See chapter III note 67.

The early American agreement with Great Britain limiting armaments on the Great Lakes, the Rush-Bagot Agreement, April 28, 1817, 8 STAT. 231, T.S. No. 110½, was originally accomplished by a mere exchange of notes. It was not until nearly a year later that it was suggested that the agreement might partake of the nature of a treaty and so require Senate consent. President Monroe on April 6, 1818, forwarded the notes to the Senate, which expressed its concurrence on April 16. No exchange of ratifications with Great Britain ever took place, however, and the British never treated the agreement as a treaty. When the agreement was finally printed in the United States Statutes at Large in 1846, it was not called a treaty but was rather titled an "arrangement." For a history of the agreement pointing out its uncertain character, see Secretary of State Foster, *Naval Forces on the Great Lakes,* S. Ex. Doc. No. 9, 52d Cong., 2d Sess. (1893).

8. The Federal Civil Aeronautics Act of 1938, § 1107(i)(3), 52 STAT. 1028, 49 U.S.C. § 176(a) (1952), declares that the United States possesses and exercises "complete and exclusive national sovereignty in the air space above the United States." The Supreme Court has treated this provision as a declaration of sovereignty in relation to other nations, which did not exclude the sovereign power of the states. Respective national and state sovereignty in the air would seem generally the same as in the land beneath it. The state could exercise governmental power as to the air over its territory subject to the supremacy of action by the federal government under various powers. The Civil Aeronautics Act, the Court said, is "bottomed on the commerce power of Congress, not on national ownership of the airspace, as distinguished from sovereignty." Braniff Airways v. Nebraska State Bd., 347 U.S. 590, 596 (1954). In that case, the Court, upholding a state tax on the equipment of an interstate air carrier, compared flight through navigable airspace to commerce on navigable streams. Following Gibbons v. Ogden, 9 Wheat. 1 (U.S. 1824), the Court recognized the federal power to legislate regarding air commerce but upheld a power in the states to deal with local matters where the federal government had not acted.

With respect to air navigation the Commission on Uniform State Laws recognized that the federal government has covered most of the field. See *Report of Special Committee to Reexamine Uniform Aeronautical Code,* in [1956] HANDBOOK OF THE NATIONAL CONFERENCE OF COMMISSIONERS ON UNIFORM STATE LAWS 175, 179. In the International Civil Aviation Treaty of 1944, 61 STAT. 1180, T.I.A.S. No. 1591, the United States agreed to international regulations which applied also to flight over the United States, and thus over territory of the states. There would seem to be no question that in pursuance of various powers the federal government could authorize flights in connection with air inspection.

For an example of a state statute dealing with the use of the air, see PA. STAT. ANN. tit. 2, §§ 1467, 1468 (Supp. 1957): "The ownership of the space over and above the lands and waters of this Commonwealth is declared to be vested in the owner of the surface beneath, but such ownership exists only so far as is necessary to the enjoyment of the use of the surface without interference, and is subject to the right of passage or flight of aircraft. . . .

Notes to IV: Investigation of Compliance

"Flight in aircraft over the lands and waters of this Commonwealth is lawful, unless at such low altitude as to interfere with the then existing use to which the land or water, or the space over the land or water, is put by the owner, or unless so conducted as to be dangerous or damaging to persons or property lawfully on the land or water beneath."

9. The common law maxim, *Cujus est solum ejus est usque ad coelum* (Whose is the soil, his it is up to the sky), found in 1 COKE, INSTITUTES, c. 1, § 1(4a) (19th ed. 1832); 2 BLACKSTONE, COMMENTARIES 18 (Lewis ed. 1902); 3 KENT, COMMENTARIES 621 (Gould ed. 1896), has been declared to have "no place in the modern world" and to be revolting to common sense. See Douglas, J., in United States v. Causby, 328 U.S. 256, 261 (1946).

10. In United States v. Causby, 328 U.S. 256 (1946), the Supreme Court approved in principle recovery by a chicken farmer who claimed that the extremely low flights over his property by United States military aircraft had frightened his chickens and damaged his business. The Court, while recognizing that the "complete and exclusive" sovereignty of the United States over the airspace prevented the petitioner from objecting to the continuation of flights, nevertheless stressed that "the flight of airplanes, which skim the surface [of the land] but do not touch it, is as much an appropriation of the use of the land as a more conventional use of it." *Id.* at 264. If they prevented the owner's reasonable enjoyment of his land the flights would constitute taking of property for a public use requiring compensation under the Fifth Amendment.

11. Mr. Justice Holmes, dissenting in Olmstead v. United States, 277 U.S. 438, 469, 470 (1928). See also On Lee v. United States, 343 U.S. 747 (1952), in which several of the Justices consider at length the policies behind the use and admission of evidence obtained by police "dirty business."

12. Communications Act of 1934, § 605, 48 STAT. 1103, 47 U.S.C. § 605 (1952). The act has been held to forbid intercepting and disclosure even by federal officials. Nardone v. United States, 302 U.S. 379 (1937). It is quite clear, however, that some officials have been tapping wires; see, *e.g.,* United States v. Coplon, 185 F.2d 629 (2d Cir. 1950), *cert. denied,* 342 U.S. 920 (1952); Coplon v. United States, 191 F.2d 749 (D.C. Cir. 1951), *cert. denied,* 342 U.S. 926 (1952). Bills to permit wire tapping by federal officials in certain circumstances have been introduced but have not been adopted.

The federal courts will, however, exclude both evidence obtained from the tap itself and evidence obtained through "leads" given in the tap. Nardone v. United States, 308 U.S. 338 (1939). The evidence is not admissible in a federal court although it was obtained through a wire tap by a state officer. Benanti v. United States, 355 U.S. 96 (1957). But state courts may admit evidence obtained from an illegal tap. Schwartz v. Texas, 344 U.S. 199 (1952).

13. Olmstead v. United States, 277 U.S. 438 (1928).

14. Compare the requirement of the Atomic Energy Act of 1954 that all inventions pertaining to atomic weapons must be reported to the Atomic

Energy Commission, 68 STAT. 943, 42 U.S.C. § 2181(c) (Supp. V, 1958). See chapter III note 77.

15. 70 STAT. 899 (1956), 50 U.S.C. § 851–57 (Supp. V, 1958).

16. Compare Sweezy v. New Hampshire, 354 U.S. 234 (1957), chapter III, note 78.

Although there is no "equal protection" clause applicable to the federal government, see United States v. Carolene Products Co., 304 U.S. 144, 151 (1938), "discrimination may be so unjustifiable as to be violative of due process." Bolling v. Sharpe, 347 U.S. 497, 499 (1954). Cf. Hurd v. Hodge, 334 U.S. 24 (1948); Thiel v. Southern Pac. Co., 328 U.S. 217 (1946). See also Mr. Justice Jackson, concurring, in Railway Express Agency, Inc. v. New York, 336 U.S. 106, 111, 112 (1949).

17. 66 STAT. 224, 8 U.S.C. § 1302 (1952).

18. 56 STAT. 251, 255 (1952), as amended, 22 U.S.C. §§ 612, 614 (1952).

19. A special provision of the Selective Service Act required medical and allied specialists to register although they were beyond the age at which other citizens were required to register, 64 STAT. 826 (1950), 50 U.S.C. App. § 454(i)(1) (1952). The Supreme Court has not passed on the constitutionality of this classification of specialists although it underlay the case of Orloff v. Willoughby, 345 U.S. 83 (1953).

20. A federal tax on the business of accepting wagers which included a registration requirement was upheld in United States v. Kahriger, 345 U.S. 22 (1953), although such business is illegal in most states. The majority opinion dismissed the claim of privilege against self-incrimination on the ground that the registration is required of those who wish or intend to engage in gambling; one is not compelled to confess that he has so engaged in the past. Id. at 32–33. Mr. Justice Jackson, concurring, said the Fifth Amendment should not be used to impair the taxing power. Id. at 34–35. The privilege was properly asserted in the view of Justices Black and Douglas, dissenting. Id. at 36–37. See also Justice Frankfurter's dissent, id. at 37, 39–40.

21. The Columbia Inspection Study also stresses the importance of direct inspection. See the discussion earlier in this chapter.

22. For a fuller discussion of the problems raised by conferring functions normally those of branches of the United States Government on an international body, see chapters VII and VIII.

23. As regards inspection, some federal statutes permit the use of private persons (not themselves United States officials) to carry out inspections authorized by law. See, e.g., Act of Sept. 29, 1950, 64 STAT. 1079, 49 U.S.C. § 460 (1952).

24. Treaty Between the United States and Great Britain Relating to the Boundary Waters Between the United States and Canada, Jan. 11, 1909, 36 STAT. 2448, T.S. No. 548, as implemented by Act of Mar. 4, 1911, 36 STAT. 1364, as amended, 22 U.S.C. § 268 (1952), and 22 C.F.R. §§ 401.1–401.28 (1958).

25. FED. R. CIV. P. 45(f); 18 U.S.C. § 401 (1952).

Notes to IV: Investigation of Compliance 191

26. Act of July 3, 1930, § 1, 46 STAT. 1005, 22 U.S.C. §§ 270–270c (1952). Subsequent amendments to the act permitted the United States agent before such tribunals to invoke the aid of a federal court to order witnesses to appear before the court for examination by the agent. Act of June 7, 1933, 48 STAT. 117, 22 U.S.C. §§ 270d–270g (1952).

27. See, *e.g.*, Convention Between the United States of America and Greece Defining the Rights, Privileges and Immunities of Consular Officers in the Two Countries, Nov. 19, 1902, arts. II, IX, XII, 33 STAT. 2122, T.S. No. 424; the more recent Consular Convention Between the United States of America and Ireland, May 1, 1950, arts. 21–27, 5 U.S. TREATIES 949, T.I.A.S. No. 2984; and the enabling legislation in REV. STAT. §§ 4079–81 (1875), as amended, 22 U.S.C. §§ 256–58 (1952); 36 STAT. 1163 (1911), 22 U.S.C. § 258a (1952).

28. § 3, 58 STAT. 644 (1944), as amended, 22 U.S.C. § 703 (1952).

29. Presidents, as early as Washington, successfully resisted attempts of Congress to require production of Executive Department documents. For a thorough review, see Warren, *Presidential Declarations of Independence,* 10 B.U.L. REV. 1 (1930). See also CORWIN, THE PRESIDENT: OFFICE AND POWERS 110–18, 427–30 (4th rev. ed. 1957).

30. Assuming that the United States has agreed to arms control, and that either the arms treaty itself, or implementing legislation thereafter passed by Congress, provides for full disclosure of pertinent information or documents by the Legislative Branch of the government to the arms inspectorate, interrogation of members of Congress or subpoena of their documents should present no difficulty. The only question which might arise is whether Congressmen could claim an immunity from interrogation or disclosure on the grounds of the constitutional provision that "they shall in all Cases, except Treason, Felony and Breach of the Peace, be privileged from Arrest during their Attendance at the Session of their respective Houses . . . ; and for any Speech or Debate in either House, they shall not be questioned in any other Place." Art. I, § 6, cl. 1.

Neither the history nor the meager subsequent interpretation of this section indicates any basis for immunity from disclosure or interrogation in such a case. The constitutional provision confers immunity only from civil arrest, not from criminal arrest or any service of process. Long v. Ansell, 293 U.S. 76 (1934); Williamson v. United States, 207 U.S. 425 (1908). Thus, if failure to disclose information to the inspectorate were made a criminal offense, a Congressman could be held criminally liable for his contumacy. Williamson v. United States, *supra;* Burton v. United States, 202 U.S. 344 (1906); *cf. In re* Chapman, 166 U.S. 661, 669–70 (1897). Further, the immunity from questioning "in any other Place," would seem applicable only to "any Speech or Debate in either House," as a protection to a Congressman from libel suits or other liabilities arising from his exercise of speech on the floor of Congress or from other official acts in the discharge of his congressional duties. Kilbourn v. Thompson, 103 U.S. 168, 200 *et seq.* (1881); *cf.* Methodist Federation for Social Action v. Eastland, 141 F. Supp.

729 (D.D.C. 1956). See also the discussion of the history of the immunity by Mr. Justice Frankfurter in Tenney v. Brandhove, 341 U.S. 367, 372–78 (1951), and Judge Yankwich, *The Immunity of Congressional Speech—Its Origin, Meaning and Scope,* 99 U. PA. L. REV. 960 (1951).

The Constitution also provides that "Each House may determine the Rules of its Proceedings, punish its Members for disorderly Behaviour, and, with the Concurrence of two thirds, expel a Member." Art. I, § 5, cl. 2. If Congress were, by Rule, to require its members to testify before, or produce papers for, an international body, punishment and expulsion could follow failure to comply even if such failure were not otherwise a crime. See the discussion of the case of Senator Blount, expelled from the Senate in 1797 for noncriminal behavior deemed by his colleagues to be inconsistent with his office, in *In re* Chapman, 166 U.S. 661, 670 (1897). Any immunity from questioning "in any other Place" would also, probably, not apply to interrogations authorized by Congressional Rule. See Yankwich, *supra* at 972.

31. Pfitzinger v. United States Civil Serv. Comm'n, 96 F. Supp. 1, 2–3 (D.N.J.) (dictum), *aff'd,* 192 F.2d 934 (3d Cir. 1951); see Moyer v. Brownell, 137 F. Supp. 594, 608–10 (E.D. Pa. 1956) (dictum). Both courts appeared to recognize that the government employee could have availed himself of the privilege in a proper case, but rejected the claim of privilege in the instant proceedings.

32. Compare Davis v. United States, 328 U.S. 582 (1946), which held that gasoline coupons, property of the federal government, may be taken without warrant and used in a criminal prosecution of their custodian. Compare also Shapiro v. United States, 335 U.S. 1 (1948); and other cases note 51(*b*). While the Supreme Court does not appear to have considered a case involving official documents, it has held that officers of corporations may not refuse to surrender corporate books demanded of them, even though such books reveal criminal acts of the corporation or its officers. Wilson v. United States, 221 U.S. 361 (1911); Hale v. Henkel, 201 U.S. 43 (1906). See also Oklahoma Press Publishing Co. v. Walling, 327 U.S. 186, 205–8 (1946). The Court has extended the doctrine to the records of unincorporated associations as well, in the case of labor unions. United States v. White, 322 U.S. 694 (1944); see Curcio v. United States, 354 U.S. 118 (1957). But the *Curcio* case held that the privilege against self-incrimination might protect the officer who refused to reveal the whereabouts of required records.

While the corporation is not protected by the privilege against self-incrimination, it enjoys protections against unreasonable search and seizure. See pp. 65, 75 above.

33. It has been suggested that government officials be required to waive their privilege against self-incrimination in connection with any future investigations concerning their official activites as a condition to holding public office. See Address of Judge Seabury Before the American Law Institute, May 7, 1932, quoted in 8 WIGMORE, EVIDENCE § 2275a (3d ed. 1940); Note, *Denying the Privilege Against Self-Incrimination to Public Officers,* 64 HARV. L. REV. 987, 990 (1951). Another approach to the problem is that

Notes to IV: Investigation of Compliance

indicated by the New York State Constitution, art. I, § 6 (1949), which provides that any public officer refusing to testify before a grand jury concerning the performance of his official duties, shall by virtue of such refusal be disqualified from holding any other public office for five years and shall be removed from office. *But cf.* Slochower v. Board of Higher Educ., 350 U.S. 551 (1956).

34. See p. 37 above.

35. *Cf.* Kentucky v. Dennison, 24 How. 66 (U.S. 1861), for a discussion of the authority of the United States in relation to state officials. See also chapter VI.

36. McCarthy v. Arndstein, 266 U.S. 34, 40–41 (1924); Counselman v. Hitchcock, 142 U.S. 547, 563–64 (1892). Compare also Slochower v. Board of Higher Educ., 350 U.S. 551 (1956) (Senate committee); Ullmann v. United States, 350 U.S. 422 (1956) (federal grand jury); Brown v. Walker, 161 U.S. 591 (1896) (federal regulatory agency).

37. Grunewald v. United States, 353 U.S. 391, 421 (1957); Slochower v. Board of Higher Educ., 350 U.S. 551, 557–58 (1956); Ullmann v. United States, 350 U.S. 422, 426–27 (1956).

38. Although dissents have continued, the Supreme Court has consistently held that the Bill of Rights applies only to federal authorities and that it has not been automatically rendered applicable to the states by the Fourteenth Amendment. Whether a particular protection accorded by the Bill of Rights is also guaranteed against invasion by the states by virtue of the due process clause of the Fourteenth Amendment is a separate inquiry with different results in regard to different provisions in the Bill. Adamson v. California, 332 U.S. 46 (1947); Palko v. Connecticut, 302 U.S. 319 (1937); and *compare* Rochin v. California, 342 U.S. 165 (1952), *with* Irvine v. California, 347 U.S. 128 (1954). The privilege against self-incrimination has not been considered so basic to our concepts of liberty as to be inherent in "due process" guaranteed against invasion by the states. Twining v. New Jersey, 211 U.S. 78 (1908). Although the states have generally included this privilege in their own constitutions, some have permitted encroachments on the privilege which would not be permissible for the federal government under the Fifth Amendment. See, *e.g.,* Adamson v. California, *supra*. A state can compel testimony under a state immunity statute even though the testimony reveals violation of federal law. Knapp v. Schweitzer, 357 U.S. 371 (1958); Jack v. Kansas, 199 U.S. 372 (1905); *cf.* Feldman v. United States, 322 U.S. 487 (1944).

Even if the subpoena issued from an international tribunal, and contempt proceedings were instituted by such a tribunal, it may be argued that since this tribunal is in the United States and acts pursuant to authorization by treaty from the federal government, it is subject to the Fifth Amendment. See the discussion in chapter VIII.

39. Ullmann v. United States, 350 U.S. 422 (1956). *Cf.* Regan v. New York, 349 U.S. 58 (1955). The *Ullmann* case reaffirmed the earlier decision of the Court in Brown v. Walker, 161 U.S. 591 (1896).

40. Such provisions exist in numerous acts regulating economic activities and in internal security legislation. See, *e.g.,* Atomic Energy Act of 1954, 68 STAT. 948, 42 U.S.C. § 2201(c) (Supp. V, 1958); Securities Exchange Act of 1934, § 21(d), 48 STAT. 900, 15 U.S.C. § 78u(d) (1952); Interstate Commerce Act [amendment], 32 STAT. 904 (1903), 49 U.S.C. § 47 (1952); Compulsory Testimony Act of 1954, 18 U.S.C. § 3486 (Supp. V, 1958).

41. That the compelled testimony may reveal crimes under the law of another "sovereign" is not a valid ground for refusing to answer pertinent questions. United States v. Murdock, 284 U.S. 141 (1931). However, since witnesses may prefer to risk federal contempt citations to potential prosecution in a state court, Congress has the power to immunize a witness from both federal and state prosecution. See Adams v. Maryland, 347 U.S. 179 (1954). The legislative history of the Compulsory Testimony Act of 1954, 18 U.S.C. § 3486 (Supp. V, 1958), would seem to indicate that Congress sought to bar prosecutions in state courts based on evidence compelled pursuant to that statute. See H.R. REP. No. 2606, 83d Cong., 2d Sess. 7, 15 (1954). The constitutionality of such a provision was reasserted in the *Ullmann* case, 350 U.S. 422, 434–37 (1956).

42. In Brown v. Mississippi, 297 U.S. 278 (1936), the Court held physical coercion used to extort a confession to be a denial of due process under the Fourteenth Amendment; *cf.* Watts v. Indiana 338 U.S. 49 (1949); Payne v. Arkansas, 356 U.S. 560 (1958).

43. Frankfurter, J. concurring in *In re* Groban, 352 U.S. 330, 335, 337 (1957).

Speaking of an issue of negligence, Mr. Justice Holmes said: "I do not think we need trouble ourselves with the thought that my view depends upon differences of degree. The whole law does so as soon as it is civilized . . . and between the variations . . . that I suppose to exist and the simple universality of the rules in the Twelve Tables or the Leges Barbarorum, there lies the culture of two thousand years." LeRoy Fibre Co. v. Chicago, M. & St. P. Ry., 232 U.S. 340, 352, 354 (1914) (concurring opinion).

44. In *In re* Groban, *supra* note 43, at 333, the Court stated that "a witness before a grand jury cannot insist, as a matter of constitutional right, on being represented by his counsel," citing lower federal court decisions. As to counsel in preliminary stages of criminal proceedings, compare Crooker v. California, 78 S.Ct. 1287, 357 U.S.——(1958).

45. In United States *ex rel.* Bilokumsky v. Tod, 263 U.S. 149 (1923), it was held that an alien was not entitled to counsel while being interrogated prior to a statutory deportation proceeding. The scarcity of decisions regarding right of counsel in federal administrative hearings is due in part to the fact that the right to counsel is accorded by the Administrative Procedure Act, 60 STAT. 240 (1946), 5 U.S.C. § 1005(a) (1952); persons "compelled to appear in person before any agency or representative thereof shall be accorded the right to be accompanied, represented, and advised by counsel." The subject is considered in Note, *Representation as an Element of Due Process,* in GELLHORN & BYSE, ADMINISTRATIVE LAW: CASES AND COMMENTS 909–13 (1954 ed.).

Notes to IV: Investigation of Compliance

46. 352 U.S. 330 (1957).

47. *Id.* at 335, 337.

48. Some of the difficulties which might face a witness in his exercise of the privilege against self-incrimination, even in federal inquiries, are suggested, for example, by Quinn v. United States, 349 U.S. 155 (1955), and its companion cases, and Rogers v. United States, 340 U.S. 367 (1951). The majority in *Groban* did not deal with the witness's difficulty, although it was relied on by the dissent as a factor requiring the presence of counsel; the concurring opinion expressly rejected this argument.

While *Groban* involves state proceedings, "It ought not to require argument to reject the notion that due process of law meant one thing in the Fifth Amendment and another in the Fourteenth." Frankfurter, J., concurring in Adamson v. California, 332 U.S. 46, 59, 66 (1947).

49. In more than fifteen cases involving questions of search and seizure which have come before the Supreme Court since the Second World War, almost half have been decided by majorities of only five Justices, and no holding has received more than seven votes.

50. United States v. Rabinowitz, 339 U.S. 56 (1950). A majority of five justices supported the proposition that the constitutional reasonableness of a particular search without warrant depended upon "the total atmosphere" of the case. This overruled the decision, two years earlier, in Trupiano v. United States, 334 U.S. 699 (1948), in which the Court had held the absence of a warrant, where it was "reasonably practicable" to obtain it, rendered the search unreasonable.

51. United States v. Morton Salt Co., 338 U.S. 632, 652 (1950); *cf.* United States v. Bausch & Lomb Optical Co., 321 U.S. 707, 726–27 (1944).

Silverthorne Lumber Co. v. United States, 251 U.S. 385 (1920), is the leading case applying the Fourth Amendment to a search of the offices of a corporation. Nevertheless, the Court has not infrequently found the protection of the Fourth Amendment inapplicable to "searches" of business establishments or records, under one or another of the following theories:

(*a*) *Regulated industries.* This is considered at greater length later in this chapter. Briefly, if Congress "regulates" a business or occupation pursuant to one of the enumerated powers, the regulatory scheme may include provision for inspection of the premises without warrant. Numerous regulatory statutes with such inspection provisions exist, and the only one which troubled the Supreme Court did so on account of vagueness—although perhaps a desire to avoid issues under the Fourth Amendment underlay the Court's treatment of the case. United States v. Cardiff, 344 U.S. 174 (1952), note 65 below. Whether such inspection of regulated industries is deemed outside the Fourth Amendment, or is held to satisfy its requirements, is not clear. See p. 70 above.

(*b*) *Required records.* One of the means by which Congress may insure compliance with its regulations of commerce, or protect the revenue, is by requiring the filing of returns or the keeping of pertinent records. See notes 58, 61 below and chapter V note 10. Whether kept by an individual or a corporation, such records may be subject to examination. Shapiro v. United

States, 335 U.S. 1 (1948); see Wilson v. United States, 221 U.S. 361, 380 (1911); *cf.* Oklahoma Press Publishing Co. v. Walling, 327 U.S. 186 (1946). Compare also the right to inspect "public documents," Davis v. United States, 328 U.S. 582 (1946).

(*c*) *Waiver by invitation.* The protection of the Fourth Amendment may be deemed waived by express or implied invitation onto the premises thereafter searched, or by consent to inspection of records. See Davis v. United States, 328 U.S. 582 (1946); United States v. Sferas, 210 F.2d 69 (7th Cir.), *cert. denied,* 347 U.S. 935 (1954); United States v. Antonelli Fireworks Co., 155 F.2d 631 (2d Cir.), *cert. denied,* 329 U.S. 742 (1946).

The protection of the amendment may also be deemed partially waived by a person maintaining a store or other place to which the public is invited. Such a person may not complain of the entry on such premises by officials, who are thus enabled to "observe" the commission of a crime there, to arrest the owner, and to search the premises. On Lee v. United States, 343 U.S. 747 (1952); United States v. Rabinowitz, 339 U.S. 56 (1950).

(*d*) *Waiver by contract.* The Fourth Amendment may be deemed waived by a contract with the government in which the latter reserves a right to examine the contractor's books or premises. Zap v. United States, 328 U.S. 624 (1946).

(*e*) *Possession of contraband.* When Congress has declared particular products to be contraband, the government is said to have a superior claim to such goods against all the world; it may, therefore, retain such goods for forfeiture even when seized unlawfully, although they are subject to exclusion as evidence. United States v. Jeffers, 342 U.S. 48 (1951).

(*f*) *Elusive premises.* Presumably as an aspect of "reasonableness," a search warrant has not been required where illegal activities were suspected on "elusive premises," such as motor vehicles, Brinegar v. United States, 338 U.S. 160 (1949); Carroll v. United States, 267 U.S. 132 (1925), and ships, United States v. Lee, 274 U.S. 559 (1927).

The Court, in an opinion of Mr. Justice Holmes, has also held that the protection accorded by the Fourth Amendment to the people in their "persons, houses, papers, and effects" does not extend to open fields—the distinction between the latter and a house being "as old as the common law." Hester v. United States, 265 U.S. 57, 59 (1924).

52. Wolf v. Colorado, 338 U.S. 25, 27–28 (1949). *Cf.* Rochin v. California, 342 U.S. 165 (1952).

53. There appear to have been no cases in which a search was held invalid under the due process clause of the Fifth Amendment. However, language in Supreme Court opinions suggests that the concepts of "reasonableness" of the kind normally associated with due process will be applied in determining the reasonableness of a search and seizure under the Fourth Amendment. In ruling that there was no statutory authority for a search through the files of a corporation under investigation, Justice Holmes declared: "The interruption of business, the possible revelation of trade secrets, and the expense that compliance with the Commission's wholesale

Notes to IV: Investigation of Compliance 197

demand [for records] would cause are the least considerations. It is contrary to the first principles of justice to allow a search through all the respondents' records, relevant or irrelevant, in the hope that something will turn up. . . . We assume that the rule to be applied here is more liberal but still a ground must be laid and the ground and the demand must be reasonable." FTC v. American Tobacco Co., 264 U.S. 298, 306 (1924). An interpretation of the statute which permitted such a search would, he added, create serious questions under the Fourth Amendment.

In Oklahoma Press Publishing Co. v. Walling, 327 U.S. 186, 213 (1946), Mr. Justice Rutledge, although upholding the reasonableness under the Fourth Amendment of the search in the case before him, said: "Officious examination can be expensive, so much so that it eats up men's substance. It can be time consuming, clogging the processes of business. It can become persecution when carried beyond reason."

54. See the discussion at p. 70.

55. Of course, even under the Fourth Amendment abuse may render a search unreasonable although it would otherwise have been valid. See cases cited note 53 above.

56. *Cf.* United States v. Causby, 328 U.S. 256 (1946), discussed in note 10 above.

57. Some have considered exclusion of illegally seized evidence the sole effective means of vindicating Fourth Amendment rights. See note 91 below.

58. See note 51 above and the cases there cited, particularly Shapiro v. United States, 335 U.S. 1, 29, 34–36 (1948). The majority opinion sets forth an extensive list of statutes in which Congress has required the keeping of records. *Id.* at 6 n.4. See also United States v. Darby, 312 U.S. 100, 124–25 (1941).

59. See note 32 above. And see Meltzer, *Required Records, the McCarran Act, and the Privilege Against Self-Incrimination,* 18 U. CHI. L. REV. 687 (1951).

60. Although "fishing expeditions" among all "relevant or irrelevant" business records are proscribed, FTC v. American Tobacco Co., 264 U.S. 298 (1924), examinations of great breadth have been upheld. See, *e.g.,* United States v. Morton Salt Co., 338 U.S. 632 (1950); United States v. Bausch & Lomb Optical Co., 321 U.S. 707 (1944); Brown v. United States, 276 U.S. 134 (1928); Wheeler v. United States, 226 U.S. 478 (1913). *Cf.* Shapiro v. United States, 335 U.S. 1 (1948); Oklahoma Press Publishing Co. v. Walling, 327 U.S. 186 (1946).

61. See note 51(*b*) above and chapter V note 10. For some other examples see Communications Act of 1934, §§ 203, 211, 213(f), 220, 48 STAT. 1070, 1073, 1075, 1078, 47 U.S.C. §§ 203, 211, 213(f), 220 (1952); Federal Power Act, § 213, 49 STAT. 854, 855 (1935), 16 U.S.C. §§ 825 and 825c (1952). There are also requirements for special registrations and filing, *e.g.,* Securities Exchange Act of 1934, § 12, 48 STAT. 992, 15 U.S.C. § 78*l* (1952); Labor Management Relations Act of 1947, tit. 1, §§ 9(f)–(g), 61 STAT. 136, 29 U.S.C. §§ 159(f), (g) (1952).

62. See note 65 below and chapter V notes 11–13. For some other examples see Civil Aeronautics Act, § 605, 52 STAT. 1010 (1938), as amended, 49 U.S.C. § 555(b) (1952); Meat Inspection Act, 34 STAT. 1260 (1907), 21 U.S.C. §§ 71–92 (1952).

63. Statutes differ in this respect. See, *e.g.,* the Food, Drug, and Cosmetic Act, as amended, § 704, 67 STAT. 477 (1953), 21 U.S.C. § 374(a) (Supp. V, 1958), which provides for inspections "at reasonable times." On the other hand, the Meat Inspection Act, 34 STAT. 1261 (1907), 21 U.S.C. § 74 (1952), permits inspection of slaughterhouses at "all times, by day or night," and the INT. REV. CODE OF 1954, § 5196(b), makes similar provision for distilleries. See also chapter V note 11.

64. For examples see chapter V note 12. Compare also INT. REV. CODE OF 1954, § 5241(b) (Treasury storekeeper-gauger must have control over bonded liquor warehouse; and it may not be opened except in his presence).

65. For examples see chapter V note 13. *Cf.* United States v. Darby, 312 U.S. 100, 124–25 (1941); United States v. Barnes, 222 U.S. 513 (1912). In United States v. Cardiff, 344 U.S. 174 (1952), the Supreme Court was reviewing a conviction of the owner of a factory who had refused to admit food and drug inspectors and was convicted under a statute which was claimed to make such refusal criminal. The Court found that the statute was vague and left doubt whether it was intended to make it a crime for a person to refuse admission to inspectors, or only to make it a crime if, having agreed to inspection in advance, he then interfered with this inspection. The Court did not find that Congress could, or that Congress could not, make it a crime to refuse to submit to inspection in the first instance. It is not clear whether the Court held that to apply the statute in the case would deprive the accused of the due process of law because the statute was "vague," or whether the Court interpreted the statute as not applicable, perhaps to avoid constitutional doubts.

66. See, *e.g.,* INT. REV. CODE OF 1954, § 5196 (distilled spirits); see also the provision quoted in chapter V note 15. *Cf.* Dederick v. Smith, 88 N.H. 63, 184 Atl. 595, *appeal dismissed for want of substantial federal question,* 299 U.S. 506 (1936) (state statute permitting forcible entry of state health officials for purpose of testing cattle for tuberculosis, upheld).

67. The pleasure vehicle is generally subject to the same princples of search and seizure as dwellings, discussed below, except in so far as the mobile character of a vehicle may affect what is reasonable search in the circumstances. See note 51(*f*). Still, one may expect that even apart from its mobility the vehicle would not be respected to the same degree as the privacy of a dwelling.

68. U.S. CONST., amend. IV; FED. R. CRIM. P. 41. The learning that has gone into defining the terms of the constitutional and statutory provisions is discussed in Note, *Probable Cause in Searches and Seizures,* 3 ST. LOUIS U.L.J. 36 (1954); Note, *The "Probable Cause" Requirement for Search Warrants,* 46 HARV. L. REV. 1307 (1933).

69. The possibility of a warrant from an international tribunal is discussed in chapter VIII.

Notes to IV: Investigation of Compliance

70. The only Supreme Court case refusing enforcement to a federal inspection statute was United States v. Cardiff, 344 U.S. 174 (1952), discussed in note 65 above.

71. See Judge Holtzoff dissenting, in District of Columbia v. Little, 178 F.2d 13, 21, 24 (D.C. Cir. 1949); Givner v. State, 210 Md. 484, 124 A.2d 764 (1956). See note 73 below.

When Congress was considering the inspection provision of the Food, Drug, and Cosmetic Act, 67 STAT. 476 (1953), 21 U.S.C. § 374(a) (Supp. V, 1958), the Senate report accompanying the proposed amendment declared that routine inspections without warrants were "a necessary part of a regulatory scheme intended to protect the health and lives of the public." S. REP. No. 712, 83d Cong., 1st Sess. 3 (1953). Although the act is concerned with inspections of places in which foods, drugs, or cosmetics are prepared, and thus covers primarily factories, warehouses, and the like, it may even be broad enough to include private homes if the latter are used for the preparation of foods, drugs, or cosmetics for interstate commerce. *Cf. Developments in the Law—The Federal Food, Drug and Cosmetic Act,* 67 HARV. L. REV. 632, 690 (1954).

72. 339 U.S. 1 (1950). Once before, in 1936, the Court dismissed an appeal involving a related question as not presenting a substantial federal question; that case involved the right of a state veterinarian to force entry into a barn to test cattle. See Dederick v. Smith, 88 N.H. 63, 184 Atl. 595, *appeal dismissed for want of substantial federal question,* 299 U.S. 506 (1936). And see the opinion quoted in note 74. Compare the discussion of the character of the fire inspector in another context, *In re* Groban, p. 64 above.

73. 178 F.2d 13 (D.C. Cir. 1949). The majority (per Prettyman, J.) rejected the argument that health "inspections" were different in kind from police "searches" connected with the apprehension of criminals. The alleged distinction, said the Court, "has no basis in semantics, in constitutional history, or in reason." *Id.* at 18. That under existing law health inspectors could not obtain search warrants, the Court considered a "procedural omission" for the legislature to correct, and not an argument supporting official invasions of private dwelling houses without valid warrants.

Holtzoff, J., dissenting, on the other hand, thought that the Fourth Amendment's ban on "unreasonable" searches did not extend so far as to proscribe what is a reasonable exercise of the police power in the interests of public health. He emphasized that not one of thousands of similar health ordinances enacted throughout the United States required the issuance of a warrant for routine inspection of private homes.

State courts have upheld building inspection laws similar to the ordinance with which the *Little* case was concerned as not "unreasonable." Givner v. State, 210 Md. 484, 124 A.2d 764 (1956). *Cf.* Sunderman v. Warnken, 251 Wis. 471, 29 N.W.2d 496 (1947); Dederick v. Smith, *supra* note 72.

74. In a case upholding a municipal ordinance requiring property owners to bring their garbage at their own expense for cremation, the Supreme Court said: "The householder may be compelled to submit even to an in-

spection of his premises, at his own expense, and forbidden to keep them or allow them to be kept in such condition as to create disease." California Reduction Co. v. Sanitary Reduction Works, 199 U.S. 306, 321–22 (1905).

75. The relation between the first and second clauses of the Fourth Amendment has not always been clear. The courts have found some searches without warrant not "unreasonable," but, apart from the regulated industries, these have generally accompanied valid arrests. Thus, when police officers arrest a person pursuant to an arrest warrant, the premises under the latter's "immediate control" may be searched to uncover evidence of crime. *Compare* United States v. Rabinowitz, 339 U.S. 56 (1950), discussed *supra* note 50; Harris v. United States, 331 U.S. 145 (1947); Marron v. United States, 275 U.S. 192 (1927), *with* United States v. Lefkowitz, 285 U.S. 452 (1932); Go-Bart Importing Co. v. United States 282 U.S. 344 (1931); Agnello v. United States, 269 U.S. 20 (1925). The evidence thus discovered may relate to a crime other than the one for which the owner of the premises was arrested. Harris v. United States, *supra*.

A valid arrest, authorizing a consequent search, may be without an arrest warrant, if, for instance, a crime is committed in the presence of the officers. The officer must observe the commission of the crime prior to the arrest. The results of the search do not justify its inception. Johnson v. United States, 333 U.S. 10 (1948); *cf.* Miller v. United States, 357 U.S. 301 (1958); Giordenello v. United States, 357 U.S. 480 (1958); Jones v. United States, 357 U.S. 493 (1958). Further, the search will not be valid if officers have observed the commission of crimes through tortious or felonious conduct of their own, such as by illegal entry on the premises or illegal detention of the owner. United States v. Jeffers, 342 U.S. 48 (1951); McDonald v. United States, 335 U.S. 451 (1948).

76. Shapiro v. United States, 335 U.S. 1 (1948). For a different instance, where the war powers were held to authorize search and seizure without warrant, as to a United States citizen abroad, see Best v. United States, 184 F.2d 131 (1st Cir. 1950), *cert. denied,* 340 U.S. 939 (1951).

77. See, *e.g.,* NLRB v. Jones & Laughlin Steel Corp., 301 U.S. 1 (1937). *Cf.* Alstate Constr. Co. v. Durkin, 345 U.S. 13 (1953).

It might be suggested that arms inspection could be achieved indirectly through the commerce and taxing powers. Many industrial and commercial establishments could be regulated by Congress under the greatly expanded concepts of what is or affects interstate commerce. Congress could also impose taxes on industrial and commercial activities and products. If Congress did either, it could authorize inspection to implement its regulation or tax. And since the motive of the regulation or tax would hardly be scrutinized by the courts, Congress could, under such taxing or commerce powers, legislate inspection, even if the inspection had another purpose also—say, to assure arms inspectors of the character of the operations. But this suggestion would require that Congress in fact impose a tax, or perhaps some regulation related to interstate commerce to which inspection would be auxiliary. If the primary purpose were international arms control inspection, there would

Notes to IV: Investigation of Compliance

be involved fictions and indirection, which might render it invalid. *But cf.* United States v. Kahriger, 345 U.S. 22 (1953). There would be similar and stronger objections to having the arms inspector accompany a municipal health or building inspector.

78. Shreveport Case, 234 U.S. 342 (1914).
79. See note 89 below.
80. See United States v. Morton Salt Co., 338 U.S. 632, 652 (1950), quoted at p. 65 above.
81. See pp. 93–96 above.
82. See p. 60 above.
83. See the discussion at p. 37 above.

Treaties of Friendship, Commerce, and Navigation have conferred on nationals of another country the right to practice some professions, although these professions are normally regulated by the states. See, *e.g.,* the treaties with:

Honduras, Dec. 7, 1927, art. I, 45 STAT. 2618, T.S. No. 764; Italy, Feb. 2, 1948, art. I, 63 STAT. 2255, T.I.A.S. No. 1965 (all professions except law).

Recently, however, there has been a tendency to limit such reciprocal national treatment for professionals. Thus, for example, although the treaty with Israel, Aug. 23, 1951, art. VIII(2), 5 U.S. TREATIES 550, T.I.A.S. No. 2948, as signed, provided that nationals of either party may not be barred from practicing the professions solely on account of alienage; and the treaty with Greece, Aug. 3, 1951, art. XII(1), 5 U.S. TREATIES 1829, T.I.A.S. No. 3057, guaranteed national and most-favored-nation treatment to professions with some exceptions, the Senate ratifications contained reservations strictly limiting these provisions. The Senate declared these provisions inapplicable to "professions which, because they involve the performance of functions in a public capacity, or in the interest of public health and safety, are state-licensed and reserved by statute or constitution exclusively to citizens of the country." 5 U.S. TREATIES at 603, 1918. It was not claimed, however, that such reservations were required by the Constitution. One of the most recent of these treaties—that with the Federal Republic of Germany, Oct. 29, 1954, art. VIII(2), 7 U.S. TREATIES 1839 (1956), T.I.A.S. No. 3593—extends the national treatment guarantee to "scientific, educational, religious and philanthropic activities," but does not mention the professions.

84. The physician-patient privilege was unknown at common law. It seems to have first appeared in a New York statute of 1828. Since then, nearly two thirds of the states have enacted analogous legislation, while seventeen states have no such privilege. The statutes are compiled in 8 WIGMORE, EVIDENCE § 2380 n.5 (3d ed. 1940). Some modern opinion seems to favor the abolition of the privilege in all cases. See MCCORMICK, EVIDENCE § 108 (1954).

85. See pp. 45, 52–53 above.
86. See note 89 below.

87. An early case in which the Supreme Court considered the scope of the Fourth Amendment underscored its connections with the Fifth. Boyd v. United States, 116 U.S. 616 (1886). See also Mr. Justice Brandeis's statement in dissent in Olmstead v. United States, 277 U.S. 438 (1928), quoted above at p. 80. The majority in that case upheld a conviction based on evidence obtained by wire tapping because it found a wire tap to be neither a search nor a seizure; having found no violation of the Fourth Amendment, it found "no room" for applying the Fifth. *Id.* at 462.

88. Of course, strictly the Fifth Amendment too does not speak of incrimination but provides that no person "shall be compelled . . . to be a witness against himself." As an original matter it might have been argued, and was argued, that even if Congress confers immunity from prosecution and conviction for the crime, the accused cannot be compelled "to be a witness against himself." The argument would also recite undesirable consequences other than prosecution which the amendment might have been intended to prevent and which are not avoided if only immunity from prosecution is accorded. In the case of the Fifth Amendment, however, the cases have long ago limited the protection of the amendment to freedom from prosecution. See note 39 above.

In its origin and its purpose, also, there appears to be more justification for limiting the scope of the Fifth Amendment, as the courts have done, than for circumscribing the Fourth. The protection against unreasonable search and seizure has been eloquently defended as a fundamental liberty, basic to a free society. See, *e.g.,* Mr. Justice Frankfurter in Wolf v. Colorado, 338 U.S. 25, 27 (1949), and Mr. Justice Brandeis quoted at p. 80 above, and the materials in note 89 below. The Fifth Amendment, on the other hand, while having its champions, has also been deprecated. Wigmore has called it "a bequest of the 1600's, . . . a relic of controversies and convulsions which have long ceased." 8 WIGMORE, EVIDENCE § 2251 at 304 (3d ed. 1940). After reviewing the policies behind the privilege against self-incrimination, and considering the arguments of some of its most outspoken opponents (*e.g.,* Jeremy Bentham, who considered the "privilege an absurd obstruction to law enforcement"), Wigmore concluded that "the privilege . . . should be kept within limits the strictest possible." *Id.* at 318. Mr. Justice Cardozo, also, expressed the view that the privilege was not inherent in the concept of ordered liberty nor was it a traditional freedom of Western civilization. "Justice . . . would not perish if the accused were subject to a duty to respond to orderly inquiry." Palko v. Connecticut, 302 U.S. 319, 326 (1937). See also Adamson v. California, 332 U.S. 46, 54 (1947); MCCORMICK, EVIDENCE § 136 (1954).

89. Olmstead v. United States, 277 U.S. 438, 471, 478–79 (1928).

The Fourth Amendment was the result of unhappy memories of the general warrant. Searches under general warrant were frequently authorized to find evidence of evasion of unpopular taxes or of sedition. General search warrants issued to colonial revenue officers were called "the worst instrument of arbitrary power, the most destructive of English liberty, and the

Notes to IV: Investigation of Compliance

fundamental principles of law, that ever was found in an English law book . . . [placing] the liberty of every man in the hands of every petty officer." 2 CHAS. F. ADAMS (ed.), THE WORKS OF JOHN ADAMS 523–25 (1866); James Otis, Quincy's Reports 471, 479 (Mass. 1761) (*semble*); quoted by Mr. Justice Bradley in Boyd v. United States, 116 U.S. 616, 625 (1886). In opposing a provision for general warrants in a bill levying a tax on cider the Earl of Chatham was heard to remark: "The poorest man may in his cottage bid defiance to all the forces of the crown; it may be frail, its roof may shake, the wind may blow through it; the storm may enter, the rain may enter; but the King of England cannot enter; all his forces dare not cross the threshhold of the ruined tenement." Quoted in Miller v. United States, 357 U.S. 301, 307 (1958), probably from the speech of March 27, 1763, 15 PARL. HIST. OF ENG. 1307 (1813). A few years prior to the American Revolution a British court held general warrants contrary to the laws of England, in the celebrated case of Entick v. Carrington, 19 How. St. Tr. 1030, 95 Eng. Rep. 807 (K.B. 1765). See the discussion of this case by Judge Cardozo in People v. Defore, 242 N.Y. 13, 24–25, 150 N.E. 585, 588–89 (1926).

Following the Revolution and the adoption of the American Constitution, strong popular demand for a prohibition of general warrants compelled the very first Congress to consider a constitutional amendment limiting the federal government's search and seizure rights. STEVENS, SOURCES OF THE CONSTITUTION OF THE UNITED STATES, 213, 226 (2d ed. 1927). Thus, "to extinguish from the bosom of every member of the community, any apprehensions that there are those among his countrymen who wish to deprive [him] of the liberty for which [he] valiantly fought and honorably bled," James Madison introduced a series of amendments, including what became the Fourth. As Madison said of the proposed amendment: "[T]he great object in view is to limit and qualify the powers of Government, by excepting out of the grant of power those cases in which the Government ought not to act, or to act only in a particular mode . . . It is true, the powers of the General Government are circumscribed . . . but even if Government keeps within those limits, it has certain discretionary powers with respect to the means, which may admit of abuse. . . . The General Government has a right to pass all laws which shall be necessary to collect its revenue; the means for enforcing the collection are within the direction of the Legislature: may not general warrants be considered necessary for this purpose . . . ? . . . [There] is like reason for restraining the Federal Government [from exercising this power]." Speech of June 8, 1879, 1 ANNALS OF CONGRESS 449, 454, 455, 456 (1834).

90. 338 U.S. 25, 27–28 (1949).

91. In Wolf v. Colorado, 338 U.S. 25, 30–31 (1949), Mr. Justice Frankfurter suggests that there are ways in which a protection against unlawful search and seizure can be vindicated other than by exclusion of the evidence uncovered by it. As to the exclusionary rule itself, it has been stressed that: (*a*) it protects only those persons wrongfully searched who were in fact in possession of goods then seized, (*b*) it operates only after the wrongful

search has been completed rather than as a bar to it, (*c*) its effect is to let off both the criminal and the lawbreaking officer, rather than to give to both the punishments they deserve, and (*d*) its operation has no relation to the gravity of the wrongs of either the person searched or the searching officer. See Comment, *Juidicial Control of Illegal Search and Seizure,* 58 YALE L.J. 144 (1948).

On the other hand, some Justices of the Supreme Court have considered the exclusionary rule the only effective sanction against unauthorized police invasions of privacy. See dissents of Mr. Justice Murphy in Wolf v. Colorado, 338 U.S. 25, 41 (1949), and Mr. Justice Jackson in Brinegar v. United States, 338 U.S. 160, 180, 181 (1949). In support of their argument it may be noted that:

(*a*) Although it is a crime for an official of the United States to search private property without a warrant, 18 U.S.C. § 2236 (1952), no prosecutions under this act have been reported. One federal court cited this section in support of its decision suppressing evidence illegally seized. Baxter v. United States, 188 F.2d 119, 120 (6th Cir. 1951). For a state case, see State v. Wagstaff, 115 S.C. 198, 105 S.E. 283 (1920). See Edwards, *Criminal Liability for Unreasonable Searches and Seizures,* 41 VA. L. REV. 621 (1955).

(*b*) Although the federal courts have been held to have jurisdiction to entertain common law actions against government officers who have conducted an illegal search, Bell v. Hood, 327 U.S. 678 (1946), attempted recoveries against federal officials have been unsuccessful. See, *e.g.,* Bell v. Hood, 71 F. Supp. 813 (S.D. Cal. 1947).

(*c*) Suits against the federal government itself, on the basis of the Federal Tort Claims Act, are barred, as Congress has expressly denied consent to suit on any claims arising out of "detention of any goods or merchandise by any . . . law-enforcement officer," or out of the "assault, battery, false imprisonment, false arrest, malicious prosecution, abuse of process" or "a discretionary function or duty . . . whether or not the discretion involved be abused" by federal officials. 28 U.S.C. § 2680 (1952). See p. 94 above.

92. See chapter V.

93. Thus, compulsory process against a foreign consular officer and his documents, enjoying immunity under a treaty, was refused to a defendant claiming right to compulsory process for obtaining witnesses in his favor under Amendment VI of the Constitution. *In re* Dillon, 7 Fed. Cas. 710, No. 3914 (N.D. Cal. 1854). Nor are there valid constitutional objections to the doctrine of sovereign immunity. See Kawananakoa v. Polyblank, 205 U.S. 349, 353–54 (1907). Compare Larson v. Domestic & Foreign Commerce Corp., 337 U.S. 682 (1949); also Frankfurter, J., dissenting, *id.* at 705, 713–15. That immunity is extended to an international official rather than a representative of a particular nation would seem to raise no special constitutional issues. *Cf.* Keeney v. United States, 218 F.2d 843 (D.C. Cir. 1954); Curran v. City of New York, 191 Misc. 229, 77 N.Y.S.2d 206 (Sup. Ct. 1947), *aff'd,* 275 App. Div. 784, 88 N.Y.S.2d 924 (2d Dep't 1949).

A court might also decide that a decision to grant immunity in an area re-

Notes to V: Congressional Implementation

lated to foreign affairs is a political question not subject to judicial scrutiny. This judicial attitude in immunity cases is reflected in the fact that courts now will not look behind a suggestion of immunity presented on behalf of the Department of State. See, *e.g., Ex parte* Republic of Peru, 318 U.S. 578, 587–89 (1943); Republic of Mexico v. Hoffman, 324 U.S. 30, 35–36 (1945) (dictum) (cases involving vessels claimed by foreign governments); *cf.* also National City Bank v. Republic of China, 348 U.S. 356, 358, 359–61 (1955) ("the status of the Republic of China in our courts is a matter for determination by the Executive and is outside the competence of this Court").

The Court will not consider other political questions in the field of foreign affairs although private rights are asserted. See, *e.g.,* Oetjen v. Central Leather Co., 246 U.S. 297 (1918); Z. & F. Assets Realization Corp. v. Hull, 311 U.S. 470, 490–93 (1941) (concurring opinion); *cf.* United States v. Pink, 315 U.S. 203 (1942); Foster v. Neilson, 2 Pet. 253 (U.S. 1829). In other areas the Court has refused to consider "political questions" although a violation of constitutional rights was claimed, *e.g.,* Colegrove v. Green, 328 U.S. 549 (1946). See also pp. 119–20 above.

94. Compare the provision in the Statute of the International Atomic Energy Agency, Oct. 26, 1956, art. VIIF, 8 U.S. TREATIES 1093, T.I.A.S. No. 3873, which provides, *inter alia,* that "the Director General and the staff . . . shall refrain from any action which might reflect on their position as officials of the Agency; subject to their responsibilities to the Agency, they shall not disclose any industrial secret or other confidential information coming to their knowledge by reason of their official duties for the Agency."

Compare also the provisions in the Headquarters Agreement with the United Nations for removal of foreign or international personnel for "abuse of such privileges of residence"; see chapter V note 40.

NOTES TO V: CONGRESSIONAL IMPLEMENTATION OF ARMS CONTROL

1. In the footnotes to this chapter will appear citations to principal existing legislation which may require modification, as well as precedents which might serve also as samples for new legislation required. Most of the examples cited deal with atomic energy, alcohol, narcotics, munitions, firearms—which have been subjects of extensive regulation. There is of course no attempt at an exhaustive list of all existing regulations.

2. As, for example, the Universal Military Training and Service Act, 65 STAT. 75 (1951), 50 U.S.C. App. §§ 451–73 (1952). The Defense Production Act of 1950, 64 STAT. 798, as amended, 50 U.S.C. App. §§ 2061–2166 (Supp. V, 1958), has been extended and many of its provisions continue in effect. See also the Defense Mobilization Act of 1954, § 50, 68 STAT. 1244, 50 U.S.C. § 404 (Supp. V, 1958).

3. Among the security laws which would require reexamination and modi-

fication are: the Espionage and Censorship chapter of the Criminal Code, 18 U.S.C. §§ 791–98 (Supp. V, 1958), which makes it felonious, *inter alia,* to gather and transmit information regarding the national defense to the advantage of a foreign nation; the Internal Security Act of 1950, § 4, 64 STAT. 991, 50 U.S.C. §§ 783(b), (c) (1952), which makes it a felony for employees of the United States to communicate classified information to a foreign government and for agents of a foreign government to obtain or seek such information. The Atomic Energy Act of 1954, 68 STAT. 958, 42 U.S.C. §§ 2274–78b (Supp. V, 1958), prohibits communication, tampering with, disclosure of, and receipt of restricted atomic energy data by unauthorized persons, and makes trespass upon or photographing of atomic energy installations a crime. Unauthorized entry upon military, naval, or Coast Guard installations, or violation of the regulations applicable to them, is also criminal. See 18 U.S.C. §§ 1382–83 (1952); Defense Mobilization Act of 1954, § 50, 68 STAT. 1244, 50 U.S.C. § 404 (Supp. V, 1958), and the Executive Orders thereunder, *e.g.,* No. 10421, 3 C.F.R. 55 (Supp. 1953), as amended by EXEC. ORDER NO. 10438, 3 C.F.R. 67 (Supp. 1953), authorizing the Director of Defense Mobilization to make rules protecting the security of defense facilities.

It might be possible to maintain in large measure the present security and classification legislation, with the inspectors entitled to know classified information under injunction of secrecy. Compare the provision in the Statute of the International Atomic Energy Agency, chapter IV note 94.

4. For examples of acts punishing failure to report, compare the section of the criminal code making it a crime for any person "owing allegiance to the United States and having knowledge of the commission of any treason against them," to fail to report this knowledge to the proper official. 18 U.S.C. § 2382 (1952). See also the provision punishing misprision of felony, 18 U.S.C. § 4 (1952).

5. There are numerous provisions giving power to United States administrative agencies to apply to courts for orders compelling the attendance of witnesses and the production of books, etc., *e.g.,* 52 STAT. 1021 (1938), 49 U.S.C. § 644 (1952) (Civil Aeronautics Board). And see similar provisions in aid of the authority of international commissions, chapter IV note 26. Failure to comply with court order is punishable as contempt of court. FED. R. CIV. P. 45(f); 18 U.S.C. § 401 (1952).

6. For a discussion of the problems raised by an immunity statute, see p. 62 above. Examples of immunity statutes are cited in chapter IV note 40.

7. Under different powers, Congress has regulated the manufacture, possession, transportation, or importation of various products: *e.g.,* atomic materials, alcoholic beverages, narcotics, firearms. The basic regulatory legislation concerning these goods may be found, respectively, in: Atomic Energy Act of 1954, 68 STAT. 919, 42 U.S.C. §§ 2011–2281 (Supp. V, 1958); INT. REV. CODE OF 1954, §§ 5001–5693 (distilled spirits, wine and beer); Opium Poppy Control Act of 1942, 56 STAT. 1045, 21 U.S.C. §§ 188–188n (1952);

Notes to V: Congressional Implementation 207

INT. REV. CODE OF 1954, §§ 4701–76 (narcotic drugs and marijuana); and Narcotic Control Act of 1956, c. 629, 70 STAT. 567 (codified in scattered sections of 8, 18, 21, 26 U.S.C.); Federal Firearms Act, 52 STAT. 1250 (1938), as amended, 15 U.S.C. §§ 901–9 (1952). For other legislation relating to arms, see note 19 below.

Perhaps the most extensive system of federal regulation reaching into virtually all commercial and industrial activities, local or national, was enacted during the Second World War, in the Emergency Price Control Act of Jan. 30, 1942, c. 26, 56 STAT. 23 (1952). It was terminated on June 30, 1947, pursuant to the provisions of the Act of July 25, 1946, c. 671, 60 STAT. 664. See p. 74 above.

8. The licensing requirement is a common form of control:

The Atomic Energy Act of 1954, 68 STAT. 936, as amended, 42 U.S.C. § 2131 (Supp. V, 1958), makes it unlawful for any person to transfer or receive in interstate commerce, manufacture, produce, transfer, acquire, possess, use, import, or export any utilization or production facility (as defined), except pursuant to license from the Atomic Energy Commission. Section 2122 has similar requirements of commission authorization in regard to atomic weapons, and § 2092 requires Atomic Energy Commission license for the transportation and sale of nuclear source material except for quantities "which, in the opinion of the Commission, are unimportant."

Pursuant to the INT. REV. CODE OF 1954, §§ 5171–77 (distilled spirits), the Treasury Department must receive and approve a bond of all persons engaged in the business of distilling, and must be notified of distilling apparatus by all persons having possession, custody, or control of such equipment. Section 5606 makes commercial distilling without prior submission of the required bond a felony, and provides for extensive forfeitures.

The Opium Poppy Control Act of 1942, 56 STAT. 1045, 21 U.S.C. §§ 188b–188f (1952), requires a Treasury license for production of poppies and manufacture of opium, and renders it criminal to produce, transport, or sell opium poppies or opium products except pursuant to license. The INT. REV. CODE OF 1954, § 4724 (narcotic drugs) declares it to be unlawful for persons to import, manufacture, produce, compound, sell, deal in, dispense, distribute, administer, or give away narcotic drugs without having registered with the Treasury Department. Unauthorized transportation is also made criminal.

Treasury Department licenses are required of all persons who manufacture or deal in firearms or ammunition in order to transport or receive them in interstate or foreign commerce. Federal Firearms Act, § 2, 52 STAT. 1250 (1938), 15 U.S.C. § 902 (1952). The Mutual Security Act of 1954, § 414, 68 STAT. 848, 22 U.S.C. § 1934 (Supp. V, 1958), requires registration of all persons manufacturing, exporting, or importing arms, ammunition, or implements of war.

9. Persons who act without Atomic Energy Commission license or authorization as required by the Atomic Energy Act may be punished by fines of up to $10,000 and imprisonment up to five years, with greater

penalties if there is involved a desire to injure the United States or to secure an advantage to a foreign country. 68 STAT. 958 (1954), 42 U.S.C. § 2272 (Supp. V, 1958). Persons may be fined $50 for any failure to register with the Secretary of the Treasury as required. INT. REV. CODE OF 1954, § 7272. Numerous and various penalties and forfeitures are provided for different violations of the liquor chapter of the INT. REV. CODE, §§ 5601–93. Prison terms up to 40 years and fines up to $20,000 are provided for violations of the laws relating to narcotic drugs and marijuana. INT. REV. CODE OF 1954, § 7237. A two-year prison term and $25,000 fine may be imposed on persons willfully violating the license requirements and regulations for the export and import of arms, ammunition, and implements of war. Mutual Security Act of 1954, § 414, 68 STAT. 848, 22 U.S.C. § 1934(c) (Supp. V, 1958). Five-year prison terms and $2,000 fines may be imposed on violators of the license provisions of the Federal Firearms Act, § 5, 52 STAT. 1252 (1938), as amended, 15 U.S.C. § 905(a) (1952).

10. Maintaining such records as the regulatory agency may prescribe is a common requirement in United States regulatory legislation. See, *e.g.*, Atomic Energy Act of 1954, 68 STAT. 933, 42 U.S.C. § 2095 (Supp. V, 1958), authorizing the Atomic Energy Commission to require reports of ownership, possession, extraction, refining, shipment, or other handling of nuclear source material. See also 42 U.S.C. § 2201(p); INT. REV. CODE OF 1954, § 5197, requiring extensive records of distilling and the submission of monthly returns on the operations to the Treasury Department; INT. REV. CODE OF 1954, § 4732, requiring similar records, statements, and monthly returns of importers, manufacturers, and wholesale dealers of narcotic drugs, as well as returns from others registered for possession of drugs; Federal Firearms Act, § 3, 52 STAT. 1251 (1938), 15 U.S.C. § 903(d) (1952), requiring maintenance of records of importation, shipment, and other disposal of firearms and ammunition by all licensed dealers. A list of statutes in which Congress has required the keeping of records is set forth in Shapiro v. United States, 335 U.S. 1, 6 n.4 (1948). Statutes requiring the keeping of records generally require also that they be available for inspection.

11. Revenue officers may inspect all premises used for the business of distilling "at all times, as well by night as by day," and if denied entrance, an officer may "break open by force any of the doors or windows, or . . . break through any of the walls of such distillery . . . to enable him to enter such distillery." INT. REV. CODE OF 1954, § 5196. The Secretary of the Treasury or his agents are authorized "to enter upon any land (but not a dwelling house, unless pursuant to a search warrant issued according to law) where opium poppies are being produced or stored." Opium Poppy Control Act, § 8, 56 STAT. 1047 (1942), 21 U.S.C. § 188g(c) (1952). Officers of the Food and Drug Administration are authorized upon written notice to "enter, at reasonable times, any factory, warehouse or establishment in which food, drugs, devices, or cosmetics are manufactured, processed, packed, or held, for introduction into interstate commerce." Federal Food, Drug, and Cosmetics Act, § 704, 67 STAT. 476 (1953), 21 U.S.C.

Notes to V: Congressional Implementation

§ 374(a) (Supp. V, 1958). The Atomic Energy Commission is authorized to provide for such inspections pursuant to various sections of the act "as may be necessary to effectuate the purposes of this Act," Atomic Energy Act of 1954, 68 STAT. 948, 42 U.S.C. § 2201(p) (Supp. V, 1958). Other inspection statutes are cited in chapter IV note 62.

12. Federal storekeeper-gaugers are permanently stationed on the premises of distilleries, INT. REV. CODE OF 1954, § 5191(a); and slaughterhouses where meat is prepared for shipment in interstate or foreign commerce are subject to various inspections, Meat Inspection Act, 34 STAT. 1260 (1907), 21 U.S.C. §§ 71–91 (1952). Manufacturers of filled cheese, oleomargarine, opium, process butter, or white phosphorus matches conduct their businesses under such surveillance of officers or employees of the Treasury Department as the Secretary may require. INT. REV. CODE OF 1954, § 7641.

13. Any person who willfully fails to keep records or supply information at the time and place required by the Internal Revenue Code is subject to a $10,000 fine and a year in prison in addition to any other penalties imposed by law. INT. REV. CODE OF 1954, § 7203. Persons who refuse to aid inspections, or who willfully obstruct inspections of distilleries, are subject to $500 and $1,000 fines, respectively, for each such action. INT. REV. CODE OF 1954, §§ 5615–17. Licensees' failures to provide information and to permit inspection of books or facilities by the Atomic Energy Commission are punishable by fines of $5,000 and two-year imprisonment, and persons committing this offense "with intent to injure the United States or . . . to secure an advantage to any foreign nation" may be fined up to $20,000 and imprisoned for up to twenty years. Atomic Energy Act of 1954, 68 STAT. 958, 42 U.S.C. § 2273 (Supp. V, 1958).

All conspiracies to prevent an officer of the United States from discharging his duties are felonies, 18 U.S.C. § 372 (1952), and forcible interferences with lawful searches and seizures are also felonious, 18 U.S.C. §§ 2231–33 (1952). Moreover, it is a felony to bribe or to attempt to bribe an employee or other person acting on behalf of the United States, 18 U.S.C. § 201 (1952).

14. Compare the provisions for acts of commission and omission by federal, state, and city officials in respect of an international organization in the Agreement Between the United States of America Regarding the Headquarters of the United Nations, June 26, 1947, 61 STAT. 3416, T.I.A.S. No. 1676. See chapter VI note 3. For a discussion of whether cooperation of local officials can be compelled, see p. 102 above.

REV. STAT. § 3071 (1875), 19 U.S.C. § 507 (1952), permits officers authorized to conduct searches and seizures under the customs laws, to demand of "any person within the distance of three miles" to assist them in making authorized arrests, searches, and seizures where necessary. Refusal so to assist is a misdemeanor.

15. Compare 18 U.S.C. § 3109 (1952). "The officer may break open any outer or inner door or window of a house, or any part of a house, or anything therein, to execute a search warrant, if, after notice of his authority

and purpose, he is refused admittance or when necessary to liberate himself or a person aiding him in the execution of the warrant." For a similar provision in the Internal Revenue Code, see note 11 above.

16. See, *e.g.*, INT. REV. CODE OF 1954, §§ 5601, 5606, 5626, providing for forfeiture of distillery equipment and liquor owned by persons violating the code. Section 5211 authorizes revenue agents temporarily to detain packages or containers which they have reason to suspect contain distilled spirits on which no tax has been paid or determined. The Internal Revenue Code also has provisions for forfeiture of narcotic drugs on which no tax has been paid or which is being used in violation of the code. INT. REV. CODE OF 1954, §§ 4706, 4714, 4745.

Other forfeiture statutes include: 67 STAT. 577 (1953), 22 U.S.C. § 401 (Supp. V, 1958) (illegal arms or munitions exports); 49 STAT. 32 (1935), 15 U.S.C. § 715f (1952) (contraband oil shipped in interstate commerce); Sherman Act, § 6, 26 STAT. 210 (1890), 15 U.S.C. § 6 (1952) (property in transit "owned under any contract" or by any combination in restraint of trade).

17. The Atomic Weapons Rewards Act of 1955, § 2, 69 STAT. 365, 50 U.S.C. § 47a (Supp. V, 1958), provides for rewards of up to $500,000 to persons providing information leading to the detection of nuclear material or atomic weapons manufactured or acquired or introduced into the United States contrary to law, or information concerning attempts to do such unlawful acts. Informers regarding violations of the customs laws may be awarded up to 25 percent of the value of the goods recovered by federal authorities, but not to exceed $50,000. Tariff Act of 1930, § 619, 46 STAT. 758, 19 U.S.C. § 1619 (1952). Awards of compensation are also authorized to persons informing federal authorities of attempted exports of arms or munitions contrary to law. 67 STAT. 577 (1953), 22 U.S.C. § 401(b) (Supp. V, 1958).

18. The Atomic Energy Act of 1954, 68 STAT. 959, 42 U.S.C. § 2280 (Supp. V, 1958), authorizes the United States Attorney General to apply for an injunction from an "appropriate court" whenever the Atomic Energy Commission finds a person engaging in, or about to engage in, practices violating the act. Other statutes authorizing government agencies to secure preventive injunctions include the Sherman Anti-Trust Act, § 4, 26 STAT. 209 (1890), as amended, 15 U.S.C. § 4 (1952), and the Fair Labor Standards Act of 1938, § 17, 52 STAT. 1069, as amended, 29 U.S.C. § 217 (1952). See also the Civil Rights Act of 1957, § 131(c), 71 STAT. 637, 42 U.S.C. § 1971(c) (Supp. V, 1958).

19. As, for example, the munitions, firearms, and atomic control legislation, cited above in notes 7 and 8. See also the Federal Explosives Act, § 2, 55 STAT. 864 (1941), 50 U.S.C. § 122 (1952), prohibiting the manufacture, possession, transit, or disposal of explosives except under license from and regulation by the Bureau of Mines in times of national emergency. Depending upon the details of the disarmament plan, other statutes, such as the Act of Aug. 10, 1956, 10 U.S.C. § 4681 (Supp. V, 1958), authorizing

Notes to V: Congressional Implementation

army disposal of surplus war material to foreign nations, may also require revision.

20. Atomic Energy Act of 1954, 68 STAT. 919, 42 U.S.C. §§ 2011–2281 (Supp. V, 1958). See MARKS & TROWBRIDGE, FRAMEWORK FOR ATOMIC INDUSTRY (1955).

21. Atomic Energy Act of 1954, 68 STAT. 943, 42 U.S.C. §§ 2181–90 (Supp. V, 1958). See chapter III note 77.

22. See, *e.g.,* U.N. CHARTER arts. 104, 105, providing that the United Nations, as well as its officials and the representatives of the member nations, are to be accorded such privileges and immunities as are necessary to enable them to exercise their respective functions. An American court has held this provision to be self-executing. Curran v. City of New York, 191 Misc. 229, 77 N.Y.S.2d 206 (Sup. Ct. 1947), *aff'd,* 275 App. Div. 784, 88 N.Y.S.2d 924 (2d Dep't 1949). These general provisions were to be implemented by the Convention on Privileges and Immunities of the United Nations, note 24 below.

For a study of the status of international organizations under American law, see Note, 71 HARV. L. REV. 1300 (1958).

23. See, *e.g.,* International Monetary Fund, Articles of Agreement (1944), art. IX, 60 STAT. 1401, T.I.A.S. No. 1501.

24. If the inspection agency were closely enough affiliated with the United Nations, it might be considered a subordinate body of the United Nations and partake of the juridical personality, privileges, and immunities accorded the organization in this country pursuant to the U.N. CHARTER, arts. 104, 105; the International Organizations Immunities Act, 59 STAT. 669 (1945), 22 U.S.C. § 288 (1952); and the Agreement Between the United States of America and the United Nations Regarding the Headquarters of the United Nations, June 26, 1947, 61 STAT. 3416, T.I.A.S. No. 1676. *Cf.* Convention on the Privileges and Immunities of the United Nations, 1 U.N. TREATY SERIES 15 (1946), to which the United States is not a party. If the agency were closely affiliated with the United Nations, the agency's officials and the inspectors might also be viewed as United Nations officials. However, it would seem important that the inspection agency and its inspectors have their status precisely defined. Their privileges and immunities would probably have to be greater than those of comparable United Nations civil servants.

For an example of a special agreement conferring privileges and immunities on a body established by the United Nations, see Agreement Between the United Nations and the Government of Egypt Concerning the Status of the United Nations Emergency Force in Egypt, U.N. Doc. A/3526 (Feb. 8, 1957). By its terms, the members of the UNEF are free of passport, immigration, and visa requirements, local taxes, and customs duties on supplies and equipment. Land used by the UNEF is inviolable, and its facilities, communications, and personnel enjoy the status, privileges, and immunities of the United Nations in accordance with the Convention on the Privileges and Immunities of the United Nations.

25. Whether the power of eminent domain might be conferred on the international inspecting body itself, see chapter VII note 27.

The State of New York has enacted legislation permitting the United Nations to take land by gift, grant, devise, or purchase, but not by condemnation. N.Y. STATE LAW § 59-j. In establishing the United Nations Headquarters District, the Headquarters Agreement required the "appropriate American authorities" (see chapter VI note 3) to acquire the territory by eminent domain and to guarantee title in the United Nations. The United Nations agreed to reimburse the American authorities. Agreement Between the United States of America and the United Nations Regarding the Headquarters of the United Nations, June 26, 1947, § 3, 61 STAT. 3417, T.I.A.S. No. 1676.

Other provisions have been designed for headquarters and facilities for the North Atlantic Treaty Organization. Article 10 of the Protocol on the Status of International Military Headquarters Set Up Pursuant to the North Atlantic Treaty, Aug. 28, 1952, 5 U.S. TREATIES 870, 883, T.I.A.S. No. 2978, provides that "each Supreme Headquarters shall . . . have the capacity . . . to acquire and dispose of property. The receiving State may, however, make the exercise of such capacity subject to special arrangements between it and the Supreme Headquarters."

United States regulatory agencies are frequently granted the power to acquire property by eminent domain. See, *e.g.,* Atomic Energy Act of 1954, 68 STAT. 933, 42 U.S.C. § 2096 (Supp. V, 1958) (Atomic Energy Commission may condemn nuclear source material, real property containing deposits of source material, and property deemed by the commission to have possibilities of containing such deposits); Civil Aeronautics Act, § 302, 52 STAT. 985 (1938), as amended, 49 U.S.C. § 452(c) (1952) (Administrator of Civil Aeronautics may condemn real property or interests therein to improve air-navigation facilities); Servicemen's Readjustment Act of 1944, § 100, 58 STAT. 284, as amended, 38 U.S.C. § 693 (1952) (Veterans' Administration given highest priority to acquire necessary space for extending benefits to veterans by means including condemnation or declaration of taking).

26. The Convention on the Privileges and Immunities of the United Nations, art. 5, § 19, 1 U.N. TREATY SERIES 15, 24–26 (1946), provides that "the Secretary-General and all Assistant Secretaries-General shall be accorded in respect of themselves, their spouses and minor children, the privileges and immunities, exemptions and facilities accorded to diplomatic envoys, in accordance with international law." A similar provision for the executive head of each of the United Nations Specialized Agencies is contained in the Convention on the Privileges and Immunities of the Specialized Agencies (1947), art. VI, § 21, 33 U.N. TREATY SERIES 261, 276 (1949). The United States has not ratified either convention.

The immunities and privileges accorded international officials by the United States are specifically enumerated. In some cases, these taken together approximate traditional diplomatic privileges and immunities. See, *e.g.,* Inter-

Notes to V: Congressional Implementation 213

national Monetary Fund, Articles of Agreement (1944), art. IX, § 8, 60 STAT. 1401, T.I.A.S. No. 1501, and International Bank for Reconstruction and Development, Articles of Agreement (1944), art. VII, § 8, 60 STAT. 1440, T.I.A.S. No. 1502. Most international officials in the United States, however, have only limited privileges. By the terms of the International Organizations Immunities Act, 59 STAT. 669 (1945), 22 U.S.C. §§ 288–288f (1952), the President has been authorized to extend a series of enumerated privileges and immunities to international organizations, to their officials, and to national representatives to these organizations. The principal difference, for our purposes, is that unlike diplomats they are not immune from arrest and all judicial process. Officials are immune only "from suit or legal process relating to acts performed by them in their official capacity and falling within their functions." See also note 28 below. This act has been applied to more than twenty organizations.

27. See, *e.g.*, the debate in the House of Representatives on H.R. 4489, 79th Cong., 1st Sess., which later became the International Organizations Immunities Act, in 91 CONG. REC. 12529–32 (1945). *Cf.* National City Bank v. Republic of China, 348 U.S. 356, 359 (1955), in which Mr. Justice Frankfurter writes: "Even the immunity enjoyed by the United States as territorial sovereign is a legal doctrine which has not been favored by the test of time. It has increasingly been found to be in conflict with the growing subjection of governmental action to the moral judgment." See also Federal Housing Administration v. Burr, 309 U.S. 242, 245 (1940); Mr. Justice Frankfurter dissenting in Larson v. Domestic & Foreign Commerce Corp., 337 U.S. 682, 705, 723–24 (1949).

If the international inspectorate includes American citizens, there may be strong reluctance to give them extensive privileges. International practice has not uniformly favored extension of broad privileges and immunities to officers or employees of an international agency who are nationals of the country in which they are employed on behalf of that agency. For example, the Articles of Agreement of the International Monetary Fund (1944), art. IX § 8, 60 STAT. 1401, T.I.A.S. No. 1501, grant immunity from legal process to all governors, directors, officers, and employees of the Fund, but extend limited diplomatic immunities from alien registration and national service obligations only to such employees as are not "local nationals." The International Organizations Immunities Act, § 7, 59 STAT. 671 (1945), 22 U.S.C. § 288d (1952), governing the status of employees of numerous international organizations in the United States, provides all officials with immunity from judicial process for their official acts, but grants tax, national service, alien registration, and similar exemptions only to United Nations personnel "other than nationals of the United States." The act's provision exempting even American officials from judicial process relating to their official acts was recognized as valid in Keeney v. United States, 218 F.2d 843 (D.C. Cir. 1954). That the United States would oppose extension of other immunities to American nationals employed by the United Nations was indicated in *Immunities for International Organizations,* S. REP. No. 861, 79th Cong.,

1st Sess. 5 (1945). See also Letter of Secretary of State George Marshall, in *Structure of the United Nations and the Relations of the United States to the United Nations, Hearings Before the House Committee on Foreign Affairs*, 80th Cong., 2d Sess. 507 (1948). American reluctance to extend diplomatic recognition to its own nationals, when the latter are in the service of a foreign power, was expressed by a number of Secretaries of State in the last century and was recognized by the Supreme Court (per Fuller, C.J.) in *In re* Baiz, 135 U.S. 403, 428–29 (1890).

On the other hand, the mentioned Conventions on the Privileges and Immunities of the United Nations, and of the Specialized Agencies, *op. cit. supra* note 26, at art. V, § 18, and art. VI, § 19, respectively, grant specific privileges and immunities to all "officials" of the United Nations and the Specialized Agencies irrespective of their nationality or place of employment. The term "officials" was, by General Assembly Resolution 76(I) (Dec. 1946), defined to include "all members of the staff of the United Nations, with the exception of those who are recruited locally and are assigned to hourly rates." These conventions were accepted without reservation regarding personal immunities by, among others, France, the United Kingdom, and the Union of Soviet Socialist Republics. Canada, New Zealand, and Turkey acceded with reservations excepting their nationals from the tax and/or military service immunities, when their nationals were employed within their respective home territories. 5 REPERTORY OF PRACTICE OF UNITED NATIONS ORGANS 371–74 (1955).

The conventions, furthermore, extend complete diplomatic immunity to the Secretary-General, Assistant Secretaries-General, and executive heads of the Specialized Agencies. See note 26 above. The United States, as said, is not a party to either of the conventions. In any event, it is doubtful whether the United States would agree to accord to an American serving as Secretary-General of the United Nations, or of a specialized agency, full diplomatic privileges in the United States.

28. 59 STAT. 669 (1945), 22 U.S.C. §§ 288–288f (1952). Among the privileges and immunities enumerated for officials of international organizations are: freedom from customs duties on baggage and effects, immunity from suit or legal process relating to acts performed in official capacity, and, in regard to alien registration and immigration laws, the privileges and immunities accorded officers of foreign governments in similar circumstances.

29. International Organizations Immunities Act, *supra* note 28, 28 U.S.C. § 288d(a); Immigration and Nationality Act, §§ 102, 221, 66 STAT. 173, 191, 8 U.S.C. §§ 1102(1), 1201(b) (1952).

30. Diplomats are required to obtain nonimmigrant visas. Immigration and Nationality Act, § 212, 66 STAT. 182, 8 U.S.C. § 1182(a)(26) (1952); 22 C.F.R. § 41.9 (1958); Coulter, *Visa Work of the Department of State and the Foreign Service*, 28 DEP'T STATE BULL. 195, 196, 235 (1953). This is generally a routine matter, and it is frequently handled on their behalf by the administrative officers of the particular foreign office involved. See 22 C.F.R. § 41.9(c) (Supp. 1957).

31. The United Nations *laissez-passer* is provided for in the Convention

Notes to V: Congressional Implementation

on the Privileges and Immunities of the United Nations, art. VII, 1 U.N. TREATY SERIES 15, 28 (1946), and the Convention on the Privileges and Immunities of the Specialized Agencies, art. VIII (1947), 33 U.N. TREATY SERIES 261, 278 (1949). The *laissez-passer* is recognized by the adherents to the conventions as a valid travel document for all United Nations officials entitled to use it. The United States, however, is neither a party to the conventions nor has it otherwise recognized the *laissez-passer* as a substitute for a passport. See *Privileges and Immunities of United Nations*, S. REP. NO. 559, 80th Cong., 1st Sess. 7 (1947); Brandon, *The United Nations Laissez-Passer*, 27 BRIT. Y.B. INT'L L. 448, 449 (1950).

32. In general, during times of peace, there are no restrictions on the departure of aliens from the United States. *But cf.* INT. REV. CODE OF 1954, § 6851(d), requiring aliens to procure a certificate attesting to their compliance with the income tax laws prior to their departure from the United States.

33. Traditionally, there has been no provision of law requiring a United States citizen to obtain a passport prior to departing from the United States. Since 1940, however, the President has had authority, during wartime or periods of national emergency, by proclamation to make it unlawful to leave the United States without a passport. This provision is now in the Immigration and Nationality Act, § 215, 66 STAT. 190, 8 U.S.C. § 1185 (1952). By Presidential Proclamation a national emergency has existed and passports have been required since before the entry of the United States into the Second World War. See Control of Persons Leaving or Entering the United States, Pres. Proc. No. 3004 (1953), 3 C.F.R. 20 (Supp. 1953).

For a recent decision involving the right of an American citizen to obtain a passport and to travel abroad, see Kent v. Dulles, 357 U.S. 116 (1958).

34. From the first criminal code in the United States it has been a federal offense to bring suit wrongfully against ambassadors or public ministers of foreign states or to assault them. Act of April 30, 1790, §§ 25, 26, 28, 1 STAT. 117–18, as amended, 22 U.S.C. §§ 252–53 (1952); 18 U.S.C. § 112 (1952).

35. The Air Commerce Act of 1926, as amended, 67 STAT. 489 (1953), 49 U.S.C. § 176(b) (Supp. V, 1958), prohibits operation in the United States of foreign nonmilitary aircraft without license from the Civil Aeronautics Board. The licenses are granted only on the basis of reciprocity with the nation whose planes seek permission to fly in the United States. When granted, the licenses and flights pursuant to them are subject to comprehensive CAB regulation. However, the statute provides that the CAB is to exercise its powers in accord wtih any treaties or international agreements to which the United States is a party. Nevertheless, specific exemption of the international inspectorate from CAB regulation would seem desirable. The inspectorate should also be given the express authority to enter the otherwise closed air space reserved by the national or state governments pursuant to the Air Commerce Act of 1926, § 4, 44 STAT. 570, 49 U.S.C. § 174 (1952).

36. The Tariff Act of 1930, § 308, 46 STAT. 690, as amended, 19 U.S.C.

§ 1308(5) (Supp. V, 1958), permits the temporary, free importation of means of transportation under bond for their exportation. Again, specific statutory authorization for inspectors to bring their own vehicles, airplanes, or ships might be desirable to avoid uncertainty and controversy.

The Anti-Smuggling Act, § 203, 49 STAT. 521 (1935), 19 U.S.C. § 1581 (1952), providing customs officers with wide powers of detention, search, and seizure of vessels or vehicles entering the United States, may also be inconsistent with the freedom necessary to effective disarmament inspection. Diplomatic immunity and inviolability would eliminate this obstacle.

37. A number of statutes prohibit or sharply curtail the importation of various products. See, *e.g.*, Atomic Energy Act of 1954, 68 STAT. 932, 42 U.S.C. § 2077(a)(2) (Supp. V, 1958), prohibiting import or export of special nuclear material; INT. REV. CODE OF 1954, § 5845, limiting the importation of firearms.

The Agreement on the Status of the North Atlantic Treaty Organization National Representatives and International Staff, Sept. 20, 1951, arts. 13, 18, 5 U.S. TREATIES 1094, 1098, T.I.A.S. No. 2992, exempts from customs duties and restrictions property of NATO imported for official use, as well as personal effects of its officials. There are comparable provisions in the United Nations Convention on Privileges and Immunities, *supra* note 26.

38. Foreign Agents Registration Act of 1938, as amended, 52 STAT. 631, 22 U.S.C. §§ 611–21 (1952); Immigration and Nationality Act, §§ 261–66, 66 STAT. 223, 8 U.S.C. §§ 1301–6 (1952).

39. The International Organizations Immunities Act, § 2, 59 STAT. 669 (1945), 22 U.S.C. § 288a(c) (1952), declares property and assets of the international organizations covered by the act to be immune from search and confiscation. The Agreement Between the United Nations and the United States of America Regarding the Headquarters of the United Nations, June 26, 1947, art. III, § 9(a), 61 STAT. 3422, T.I.A.S. No. 1676, declares, "The headquarters district shall be inviolable," and a similar provision regarding NATO property is contained in art. 13 of the Protocol on the Status of International Military Headquarters Set Up Pursuant to the North Atlantic Treaty, Aug. 28, 1952, 5 U.S. TREATIES 883, T.I.A.S. No. 2978, and in art. 6 of the Agreement on the Status of the North Atlantic Treaty Organization, National Representatives and International Staff, Sept. 20, 1951, 5 U.S. TREATIES 1092 (1954), T.I.A.S. No. 2992.

40. Strictly, a nation can declare *persona non grata* only a diplomat accredited to it. A nation which has agreed to act as host to an international organization could hardly assert that it retains a right to expel the officials of, or representatives of members to, that organization at the will or whim of the host government. Even member nations which are not hosts would normally be required to admit officials of the organization for activities necessary in connection with their official duties. The obligations which members undertook in the United Nations Charter and in the constitutions of other international organizations generally require them to accord to officials and member representatives the privileges and immunities necessary for the execution of their functions.

Notes to V: Congressional Implementation

In the Headquarters Agreement with the United Nations, the United States agreed to accord to member representatives diplomatic privileges "subject to corresponding conditions and obligations." 61 STAT. 3428 (1947), T.I.A.S. No. 1676. While the phrase is not defined, the United Nations at least could hardly agree that the price of these diplomatic privileges is that the United States may, as in the case of a diplomat accredited to this country, declare such a representative *persona non grata*. The Headquarters Agreement does contain specific provisions dealing with access to the headquarters district of enumerated categories of personnel (including international officials and member representatives). The right to expel or exclude these categories of personnel is, by the terms of the agreement itself, limited to cases of "abuse of such privileges of residence," and requires specific procedures. However, in authorizing the Headquarters Agreement, Congress, in effect, reserved for the United States the right to take measures necessary for its security which would presumably include the right to exclude any persons on this ground. See Section 6 of the Joint Resolution Authorizing Conclusion of the Agreement, 61 STAT. 756 (1947), T.I.A.S. No. 1676, at 27.

Apart from any obligations which the United States may have undertaken in other international agreements, the privileges which it gives to member representatives and international officials under the International Organizations Immunities Act may, under the terms of the statute, be terminated by the Secretary of State, and the person may be required to depart, 59 STAT. 669, 672 (1945), 22 U.S.C. §§ 288, 288e(b) (1952).

41. The Agreement Between the United Nations and the United States of America Regarding the Headquarters of the United Nations, June 26, 1947, art. II, § 4, 61 STAT. 3418, T.I.A.S. No. 1676, permits the United Nations to operate various wireless communications facilities within the Headquarters District and authorizes cooperation for circuit assignment and similar matters with appropriate United States authorities. In view of the wide discretion which the Federal Communications Commission may exercise over electronic communications pursuant to the Communications Act of 1934, 48 STAT. 1064, 47 U.S.C. §§ 151–609 (1952), it might be necessary, in the case of an arms inspection plan, to assure the inspectors freedom of communication by the passage of appropriate legislation. Such legislation would probably have to go further than § 4 of the Headquarters Agreement, and make the inspectors completely free of any interference by the Federal Communications Commission or other American authorities.

42. The Communications Act of 1934, § 605, 48 STAT. 1103, 47 U.S.C. § 605 (1952), makes wire tapping, and the divulgence of information obtained thereby, a crime. For a brief discussion of the constitutionality of wire tapping see pp. 51–52 above.

43. This assumes that Congress has legislated to authorize such forcible entry in the circumstances, as it has done, for example, in the INT. REV. CODE OF 1954, § 5196. See note 11 above.

44. *Cf.* North Atlantic Treaty Status of Forces Agreement, June 19, 1951, art. VIII, § 5, 4 U.S. TREATIES 1806 (1953), T.I.A.S. No. 2846,

which establishes proportional contribution between the host state and the sending state for certain damage caused by visiting armed forces.

Of course, the control agreement and the regulations of the inspectorate should prohibit and enjoin against abuse. Compare the provision in the Statute of the International Atomic Energy Agency quoted in chapter IV note 94.

45. 28 U.S.C. §§ 1346, 2671–80 (1952).

46. However, the act specifically exempts the United States from liability in a number of circumstances, 28 U.S.C. § 2680. See chapter IV note 91.

47. The act would not seem to warrant imposing liability on the United States for the torts of the inspectors of a foreign nation or international organization, even though they were inspecting pursuant to a treaty. The inspecting body would probably not be held a "federal agency," nor the inspector an "employee of the government," as defined in the act, 28 U.S.C. § 2671.

48. See p. 82 above. That a person could not, prior to the Tort Claims Act, sue the United States for damage inflicted by its agents did not deny him any constitutional rights, or at least none that he could assert in the courts. As to whether the Constitution requires that a remedy be afforded against a private person who caused "injury," *compare* Truax v. Corrigan, 257 U.S. 312 (1921), *with* Wilson v. Loew's Inc., 142 Cal. App. 2d 183, 298 P.2d 152 (1956), *cert. dismissed as improvidently granted*, 355 U.S. 597 (1958). *Cf.* also Joint Anti-Fascist Refugee Comm. v. McGrath, 341 U.S. 123 (1951).

49. A trade secret has been defined as "any formula, pattern, device or compilation of information which is used in one's business, and which gives him an opportunity to obtain an advantage over competitors who do not know or use it." 4 RESTATEMENT, TORTS § 757, Comment *b* (1939). This definition was used by the court in Sandlin v. Johnson, 141 F.2d 660, 661 (8th Cir. 1944).

50. See, *e.g.*, 18 U.S.C. § 1905 (1952), providing for a fine of $1,000 and imprisonment of up to one year for any officer of the United States who divulges without authorization any information relating to trade secrets coming to him in the course of his employment. Bank examiners, farm credit examiners, and National Agricultural Credit Corporation examiners who illegally disclose information obtained in the course of the inspections they are employed to conduct may be even more severely punished. 18 U.S.C. §§ 1906–8 (1952).

51. See, *e.g.*, Securities Exchange Act of 1934, § 24, 48 STAT. 901, 15 U.S.C. § 78x(a) (1952); see also Federal Explosives Act, 55 STAT. 866 (1941), 50 U.S.C. § 131 (1952).

52. See, *e.g.*, War and Defense Contract Act. § 2, 54 STAT. 676 (1940), 50 U.S.C. App. § 1152(a)(4) (1952).

53. Under the Mutual Security Act of 1954, § 506, 68 STAT. 852, 22 U.S.C. § 1758 (Supp. V, 1958), the United States has apparently assumed liability for certain trade secret disclosures and uses. The Mutual Security

Act of 1951, § 517, 65 STAT. 382, 22 U.S.C. § 1668 (1952) (now repealed) contained identical provisions. For a brief comment on the earlier act, see Beach, *A Question of Property Rights*, 41 A.B.A.J. 1024, 1085 (1955).

See also Atomic Energy Act of 1954, 68 STAT. 947, 42 U.S.C. § 2187(b)(3) (Supp. V, 1958), providing for Atomic Energy Commission awards to persons, not otherwise entitled to compensation under the act, who submitted reports of their inventions or discoveries in the utilization or production of special nuclear material or atomic energy.

54. Compare chapter IV note 94.

55. Two cases have considered the problem. In Fulmer v. United States, 83 F. Supp. 137 (N.D. Ala. 1949), it was held that the United States was not liable for use of the plaintiff's trade secret—a telescope bomb sight. The court held that as the plaintiff's action was based on contract, it was not cognizable under the Tort Claims Act; nor was the government's use of his unpatented invention tortious damage or taking of his property within the meaning of that act. And in Aktiebolaget Bofors v. United States, 194 F.2d 145 (D.C. Cir. 1951), it was held that the facts did not present a question of trade secret use, but the court implied that tort recovery against the United States for use of a trade secret might be possible. *Id.* at 148. The case is criticized in Case Notes in 20 GEO. WASH. L. REV. 802 (1952) and 24 TEMP. L.Q. 495 (1951).

56. Unless it is a tort according to "the law of the place where the act or omission occurred," no action against the United States will lie under the act, 28 U.S.C. §§ 1346(b), 2674 (1952). No case has been found involving a suit against a state, or a state employee, which was based on an improper disclosure or use of a trade secret learned in the course of an inspection. 4 RESTATEMENT, TORTS § 757(b) (1939), providing that "one who discloses or uses another's trade secret, without a privilege to do so, is liable to the other if . . . his disclosure or use constitutes a breach of confidence reposed in him by the other in disclosing the secret to him," might provide some argument in such a suit.

57. Emergency Detention Act of 1950, §§ 101–16, 64 STAT. 1019, 50 U.S.C. §§ 811–26 (1952), providing for "emergency" internment of suspected security risks in the event of a declaration of war, an invasion or an insurrection; Armed Forces Code, 10 U.S.C. §§ 4501, 4502 (Supp. V, 1958), granting to the President special powers for industrial mobilization, which powers are to be exercised only in time of war.

NOTES TO VI: STATE LAWS AND LOCAL COOPERATION

1. See National Commission on Law Observance and Enforcement, 1 *Report on the Enforcement of the Prohibition Laws of the United States (The Wickersham Report)*, H.R. DOC. No. 722, 71st Cong., 3d Sess. 12 (1931). "Efficiency in law enforcement depends in exceptional degree on

the temper of public opinion," MILLSPAUGH, CRIME CONTROL BY THE NATIONAL GOVERNMENT 5 (1937). See also A.B.A. COMMISSION ON ORGANIZED CRIME, 2 ORGANIZED CRIME AND LAW ENFORCEMENT 6 (1953).

2. See, *e.g.*, the addresses before the Attorney General's Conference of J. Howard McGrath, Attorney-General of the United States, and Alan Bible, then Attorney-General of Nevada, in U.S. DEP'T OF JUSTICE, ATTORNEY GENERAL'S CONFERENCE ON ORGANIZED CRIME 5 *et seq.* (1950).

3. See Agreement Between the United Nations and the United States of America Regarding the Headquarters of the United Nations, June 26, 1947, §§ 3, 4(c), 11, 14, 16, 17, 18, 25, 61 STAT. 3416, T.I.A.S. No. 1676. Some provisions impose obligations on "appropriate American authorities" (see §§ 3, 4(c), 14, 16, 17, 18, 25). That phrase is defined in section 1(b) as meaning "such federal, state, or local authorities in the United States as may be appropriate in the context and in accordance with the laws and customs of the United States, including the laws and customs of the state and local government involved." In some sections there is specific limitation on state and local authorities or officials, *e.g.*, prohibitions on interfering with proper access to the Headquarters (§ 11), or on entry into the Headquarters (§ 9). It is also provided that "federal, state and local courts . . . shall take into account the regulations enacted by the United Nations." (§ 7(d)). See notes 15, 19 below.

4. Both the State and City of New York have enacted laws in aid of the United Nations. These are of three kinds:

(1) Laws to enable the United Nations to acquire, control, and maintain land: N.Y. STATE LAW §§ 59-i-1; N.Y. REAL PROP. LAW § 10(3); N.Y. CITY CHARTER AND ADMIN. CODE § D41-28.0 (1952 Supp.).

(2) Laws granting tax immunities to the organization and its staff: N.Y. UNCONSOL. LAWS § 10006(c); N.Y. TAX LAW §§ 4(20), 4(20-a), 5-e, 350(9), 359(j), 366(1); N.Y. PUBLIC HOUSING LAW § 113 1-(c); N.Y. CITY CHARTER AND ADMIN. CODE N41-2.0(b)(3) (1952 Supp.).

(3) Laws making the unauthorized use of the name "United Nations," or the United Nations identification card, criminal offenses: N.Y. PENAL LAW §§ 964-a, 966

In addition, a number of miscellaneous laws pertain to the United Nations, *e.g.*, N.Y. CITY CHARTER AND ADMIN. CODE § D41-28.0(d) (1952 Supp.), relating to the control of billboards and other advertising in the vicinity of United Nations Headquarters.

5. U.S. CONST. art. I, § 8, cl. 17.

6. See pp. 34–36, 60–61 above.

7. The Constitution provides that "the Congress shall have Power . . . To constitute Tribunals inferior to the supreme Court." In a later article, "The judicial Power of the United States, shall be vested in one supreme Court, and in such inferior Courts as the Congress may from time to time ordain and establish." Art. I, § 8, cl. 9; art. III, § 1.

At the Constitutional Convention some doubt was expressed as to the need for separate federal inferior courts, and there was objection to granting

Notes to VI: State Laws

power to Congress to create such courts. One of the delegates favoring the grant of power nevertheless hoped Congress would "make use of the State tribunals, whenever it could be done with safety to the general interest." See remarks of Butler of South Carolina and Sherman of Connecticut in MADISON, JOURNAL OF THE FEDERAL CONVENTION 378–79 (Scott ed. 1893).

The debate was renewed at the first session of Congress, when the Judiciary Act, 1 STAT. 73 (1789), came under consideration. Representatives Tucker of Virginia and Livermore of New Hampshire argued that the state courts were fully competent and that a federal judiciary would be both a useless expense and a burdensome imposition on the population. 1 ANNALS OF CONG. 813–14 (1789). The opposition stressed that the Constitution *commanded* the creation of a federal judiciary, in the words "shall be vested," *id.* at 850, and Madison, echoing the views expressed by his associate from Virginia, Edmund Randolph, at the convention, supported the Judiciary Act on the grounds that "many States . . . cannot be trusted with the execution of the Federal laws." *Id.* at 844; MADISON, *op. cit. supra* at 379. Hamilton expressed what was probably the dominant view: "concurrent jurisdiction of the state tribunals . . . appears to me the most defensible construction." THE FEDERALIST No. 82, at 460 (Glazier ed. 1826). For a discussion of the origins of the federal courts, see Warren, *New Light on the History of the Federal Judiciary Act of 1789,* 37 HARV. L. REV. 49 (1923).

8. Judiciary Act, 1 STAT. 73 (1789). A further joint resolution "recommended to the legislatures of the several States to pass laws, making it expressly the duty of the keepers of their gaols, to receive and safe keep therein all prisoners committed under the authority of the United States." 1 STAT. 96 (1789).

9. Early federal regulatory acts provided for enforcement proceedings in state courts. See, *e.g.,* Carriage Tax Act § 10, 1 STAT. 373 (1794); Alien Enemies Act, § 2, 1 STAT. 577 (1798). And in 1815 Congress conferred upon the state courts jurisdiction over federal tax claims, including prosecutions for fines, penalties, forfeitures, and regulated state judicial proceedings in such cases. 3 STAT. 244 (1815).

10. The concept that one sovereign does not have to enforce the penal statutes of another is well accepted in international law. The Antelope, 10 Wheat. 66, 123 (U.S. 1825). Mr. Justice Story sought to apply this principle to the federal-state relationship in dicta in various cases. See Prigg v. Pennsylvania, 16 Pet. 539, 615–16 (U.S. 1842); Houston v. Moore, 5 Wheat. 1, 69 (U.S. 1820) (dissent); *cf.* Martin v. Hunter's Lessee, 1 Wheat. 304, 337 (U.S. 1816). Under this principle, it has been said that the states need not give full faith and credit to the penal laws of sister states. Huntington v. Attrill, 146 U.S. 657, 672 (1892); see Wisconsin v. Pelican Ins. Co., 127 U.S. 265, 291 (1888).

In the early days of the republic numerous state courts expressed a marked hostility to the enforcement of federal law. See, *e.g.,* Davison v. Champlin, 7 Conn. 244 (1828); Ely v. Peck, 7 Conn. 239 (1828); United

States v. Lathrop, 17 Johns. 4, 8 (N.Y. 1819). Thus, while originally fear for state sovereignty led some to oppose the creation of a federal judiciary, see note 7 above, similar fears apparently underlay this later resistance to federal utilization of state courts, lest the practice lead to undue federal control over them. See Warren, *Federal Criminal Laws and State Courts,* 38 HARV. L. REV. 545 (1925); Warren, *New Light on the History of the Federal Judiciary Act of 1789,* 37 HARV. L. REV. 49 (1923); Note, *Utilization of State Courts to Enforce Federal Penal and Criminal Statutes: Development in Judicial Federalism,* 60 HARV. L. REV. 966, 967 (1947).

11. 330 U.S. 386 (1947). This case involved a suit by a buyer against a seller for violation of a price ceiling under the Emergency Price Control Act. The act provided for recovery in such suit of up to three times the overcharge and gave jurisdiction of such suits to state and federal courts. In broad language, the Court (per Mr. Justice Black) said that the premise that a state court "has no more obligation to enforce a valid penal law of the United States than it has to enforce a penal law of another state or a foreign country. . . . flies in the face of the fact that the States of the Union constitute a nation." *Id.* at 389.

The *Testa* case was not the first—indeed it may be considered the capstone of a series of cases dating from 1876—in which the Court had rejected the concept that the state courts were tribunals of a truly independent sovereign, in the international sense, vis-à-vis federal law. In Claflin v. Houseman, 93 U.S. 130, 136–37 (1876), the Court, in holding that state courts could enforce rights under federal law, said that the Supremacy Clause required a state court to regard federal law no less than the enactments of its own state legislature: both formed the state's jurisprudence. Later cases held refusals by state courts to hear actions arising under federal regulatory laws to be unconstitutional discriminations against federally created rights. McKnett v. St. Louis & S.F. Ry., 292 U.S. 230 (1934). Conflicting state public policies or extreme inconvenience were held insufficient to excuse state courts from hearing such cases. Second Employers' Liability Cases, 223 U.S. 1 (1912). See also Miles v. Illinois Cent. R.R., 315 U.S. 698, 703–4 (1942). *Cf.* Brownell v. Union & New Haven Trust Co., 143 Conn. 662, 124 A.2d 901 (1956).

In any event, it is clear that throughout the history of the country the state courts voluntarily accepted jurisdiction and heard most private actions based on federal laws, including regulatory and quasi-penal statutes. See, *e.g.,* Desper v. Warner Holding Co., 219 Minn. 607, 19 N.W.2d 62 (1945); Adair v. Traco Div., 192 Ga. 59, 14 S.E.2d 466 (1941). See also Teal v. Felton, 12 How. 284, 292 (U.S. 1851); Ward v. Jenkins, 10 Metcalf 583 (Mass. 1846); United States v. Dodge, 14 Johns. 95 (N.Y. 1817).

12. When a state court enforces federal law it does not become a federal court subject to federal rules and procedures. *Compare* Minneapolis & St. L.R.R. v. Bombolis, 241 U.S. 211 (1916) (unanimous jury verdict required in federal courts by Seventh Amendment not required in state trial of federally created cause of action), *with* Dice v. Akron, C. & Y.R.R.,

Notes to VI: State Laws

342 U.S. 359 (1952) (state rule on finality of jury verdict may not be applied in state court to defeat federally created right), American Ry. Express Co. v. Levee, 263 U.S. 19 (1923) (state rule of burden of proof may not be used in state trial where effect is to permit party to escape liability otherwise imposed by federal law), and Davis v. Wechsler, 263 U.S. 22 (1923) (same with respect to state procedural rule on pleading defense).

13. FED. R. CRIM. P. 41(a). But searches by federal officers pursuant to state warrants must come up to strict federal standards. Byars v. United States, 273 U.S. 28, 29 (1927). *Cf.* Lustig v. United States, 338 U.S. 74, 78–79 (1949) (Frankfurter, J.). Warrants authorized by the rule include those issued by "a judge . . . of a state . . . court of record." There are cases, before the rules, which held invalid search pursuant to unauthorized state warrants. Salata v. United States, 286 Fed. 125 (6th Cir. 1923) (warrant issued by clerk of municipal court); United States v. Johnstone, 6 Alaska 323 (1920) (municipal magistrate).

14. The Constitution requires state officials to swear support of the Federal Constitution, art. VI, cl. 3. It imposes on the states the duty of providing procedures for congressional elections, although Congress has the power to alter such state procedures. Art. I, § 4, cl. 1. The Constitution also authorizes Congress to call forth the state militia to execute the laws of the Union, suppress insurrections, and repel invasions. Art. I, § 8, cl. 15.

15. The Headquarters Agreement with the United Nations may purport to impose duties on state and local officials as well. See note 3 above.

The cases, so far as they have spoken to this point, would seem to deny the power of the federal government to impose duties on state officials. In Kentucky v. Dennison, 24 How. 66 (U.S. 1861), Chief Justice Taney held it to be the moral obligation of a governor of a state to perform a duty (extradition of a fugitive) imposed upon him by Congress, but found no power in the federal government to compel the governor to do so should he disregard the obligation. Taney added that were the federal government to possess this power, "it might overload the officer with duties which would fill up all his time, and disable him from performing his obligations to the State, and might impose on him duties of a character incompatible with the rank and dignity to which he was elevated by the State." *Id.* at 108. See also Prigg v. Pennsylvania, 16 Pet. 539, 615–16 (U.S. 1842). It may be argued, however, that these cases are contrary to the intentions of the Founding Fathers. For Hamilton, speaking of the states, said: "Thus the legislatures, courts, and magistrates, of the respective members, will be incorporated into the operations of the national government, *as far as its just and constitutional authority extends;* and it will be rendered auxiliary to the enforcement of its laws." THE FEDERALIST No. 27, at 148 (Glazier ed. 1826). See also *id.* Nos. 44–45 (Madison); Holcombe, *The States as Agents of the Nation,* reprinted in 3 SELECTED ESSAYS ON CONSTITUTIONAL LAW 1187, 1189 (1938).

Even if the rule expressed by Taney were rejected, the problem of enforcing affirmative action by a recalcitrant state government would remain. It has been said that the framers of the Constitution were aware of the delicacy and difficulty of enforcing the affirmative mandates of the federal government against the states, so that both the Constitution's provisions and most subsequent legislation directed at the states have generally been framed in the form of "Do not do . . ." (thus leaving alternative methods of doing open) rather than in the command form of "Do this . . . ," H. Hart, *The Relations Between State and Federal Law,* 54 COLUM. L. REV. 489, 515 (1954).

The federal government may still punish a state officer, in his individual capacity, who has refused to obey applicable federal law. *Ex parte* Virginia, 100 U.S. 339 (1880).

Federal courts can also direct the actions of state officers to respect rights asserted under the Federal Constitution, *e.g.,* by writs of mandamus or habeas corpus. And the Supreme Court has from the beginning directed its mandate to state courts. Martin v. Hunter's Lessee, 1 Wheat. 304 (U.S. 1816).

16. See, *e.g.,* Guss v. Utah Labor Relations Board, 353 U.S. 1 (1957); Bethlehem Steel Co. v. New York State Labor Relations Bd., 330 U.S. 767 (1947).

17. See, *e.g.:*

(*a*) Federal Food, Drugs, and Cosmetics Act, 52 STAT. 1056 (1938), as amended, 21 U.S.C. § 372(a) (Supp. V, 1958), and N.Y. AGRICULTURAL AND MARKETS LAW § 16(25) (joint food inspection).

(*b*) Migratory Bird Conservation Act, 45 STAT. 1222 (1929), 16 U.S.C. § 715(p) (1952), and N.Y. CONSERVATION LAW §§ 360(1)(d), 364 (migratory bird conservation). United States treaty obligations concerning migratory bird conservation are executed almost entirely by the states, one report indicating that at one time only twenty-seven federal agents were assigned to this task, and then only to supervise state efforts. Koenig, *Federal and State Cooperation Under the Constitution,* 36 MICH. L. REV. 752, 775–76 (1938).

(*c*) Federal Coal Mine Safety Act, 55 STAT. 177 (1941), as amended, 30 U.S.C. §§ 451–83 (Supp. V, 1958) (joint mine inspections). State inspectors are authorized to conduct investigations on behalf of the Federal Bureau of Mines, and state inspection plans, if as rigorous as those of the federal bureau, may be substituted for the latter's own. State inspectors operating under such bureau-approved plans are then given authority, by the federal law, to enter mines subject to the act on the same terms as federal inspectors.

For a general discussion on the breadth of modern "cooperative federalism," see COMMISSION ON INTERGOVERNMENTAL RELATIONS, REPORT TO THE PRESIDENT FOR TRANSMITTAL TO THE CONGRESS (1955).

18. The Emergency Price Control Act of 1942, c. 26, § 201, 56 STAT. 29 (1952), authorized the administrator to utilize "services of Federal, State, and local agencies." Local implementing statutes were upheld in most cases. See, *e.g.,* People v. Sell, 310 Mich. 305, 17 N.W.2d 193 (1945); People v. Mailman, 293 N.Y. 887, 59 N.E.2d 790, *affirming* 182 Misc. 870, 49 N.Y.S.2d

Notes to VII: International Regulation 225

733 (App. Part, Sp. Sess. 1944). See also Teeval Co. v. Stern, 301 N.Y. 346, 93 N.E.2d 884, *cert. denied,* 340 U.S. 876 (1950); Wasservogel v. Meyerowitz, 300 N.Y. 125, 89 N.E.2d 712 (1949). The importance of municipal cooperation in price control may be gathered from the fact that in some four years, New York City courts heard 96,308 cases involving violations of the New York price control ordinances. Mermin, *"Co-operative Federalism" Again: State and Municipal Legislation Penalizing Violation of Existing and Future Federal Requirements,* 57 YALE L.J. 1, 201, 217–18 n. 68 (1947).

One state supreme court, however, held a local ordinance implementing federal price controls violative of the state constitution as an unauthorized delegation of legislative power to the federal government. Cleveland v. Piskura, 145 Ohio St. 144, 60 N.E.2d 919 (1945).

Of interest also is the Eighteenth Amendment to the Constitution, the Prohibition Amendment, which provided, "The Congress and the several States shall have concurrent power to enforce this article by appropriate legislation." Many states enacted "appropriate legislation," and an Executive Order (No. 4439 of May 8, 1926), authorized the commissioning of state peace officers as federal agents to assist in the enforcement of prohibition. See J. Hart, *Some Legal Questions Growing Out of the President's Executive Order for Prohibition Enforcement,* 13 VA. L. REV. 86 (1926). The results were not particularly efficacious, however: "Instead of the two governments each pressing vigorously toward a common end, as was contemplated in the Amendment, they allowed enforcement in large part to fall down between them." Roscoe Pound, in 1 *Report on the Enforcement of Prohibition Laws, op. cit. supra* note 1, at 159.

19. There are examples of such cooperation between local authorities and foreign diplomatic, as well as United Nations, officials. These have not been tested in the courts but it is unlikely that such informal "housekeeping" arrangements would be considered a violation of the prohibition that "no State shall, without the Consent of Congress . . . enter into any Agreement or Compact . . . with a foreign Power." U.S. CONST. art. I, § 10, cl. 3. Also, the courts may find or infer congressional consent in some cases, *e.g.,* when Congress by joint resolution approved the United Nations Headquarters Agreement. See note 3 above.

NOTES TO VII: INTERNATIONAL ADMINISTRATIVE REGULATION

1. The early plans for international control and development of atomic energy and the prohibition of nuclear weapons are set forth in the first three reports of the Atomic Energy Commission of the United Nations. U.N. Doc. Nos. AEC/18/Rev. 1 (1947); AEC/26 (1947); AEC/31 (1948). These plans were based on the Baruch Plan, submitted by the United States, which,

in turn, was substantially the proposal of the Acheson-Lilienthal Report—U.S. Dep't of State Committee on Atomic Energy, *A Report on the International Control of Atomic Energy,* DEP'T OF STATE PUB. NO. 2498 (1946). See p. 5 above.

2. There is legend that one United States official expressed confidence that even if agreement were reached, "the United States Senate would save us from it."

3. Treaty Constituting the European Coal and Steel Community (1951) (Official Translation by the High Authority, 1956), Treaty Establishing the European Atomic Energy Community (1957), and Treaty Establishing the European Economic Community (1957) (Provisional Translations of the European Community Information Service, 1957); unofficial translations may be found in 46 AM. J. INT'L L. 107 (Supp. 1952), and 51 AM. J. INT'L L. 865, 955 (1957). In different degrees similar developments may be seen in other European organizations like the Western European Union and the Organization for European Economic Cooperation. Others may develop from the new International Atomic Energy Agency, 8 U.S. TREATIES 1093 (1957), T.I.A.S. No. 3873.

An important innovation in the European Coal and Steel Community, which has been incorporated into the Atomic Energy and Economic Communities (EURATOM and Common Market) as well, is the establishment of a Court of Justice with a limited power to review the decisions of the executive and rulemaking arms of these supranational organizations. For a discussion of the court's role in the operations of the Coal and Steel Community, see VALENTINE, THE COURT OF JUSTICE OF THE EUROPEAN COAL AND STEEL COMMUNITY (1955); Stein, *The European Coal and Steel Community: The Beginning of Its Judicial Process,* 55 COLUM. L. REV. 985 (1955). And *cf.* Gros, *The Problems of Redress Against the Decisions of International Organisations,* and the following general discussion, 36 GROTIUS SOCIETY TRANSACTIONS 30–48 (1950).

4. The resolutions of the Security Council and of the General Assembly may impinge on activities in the United States. Some operate more or less automatically; others require the intervening action of the President or the President and Congress. See United Nations Participation Act of 1945, 63 STAT. 734, 22 U.S.C. §§ 287–287e (1952).

Under the Trusteeship system of the United Nations also, the United States has undertaken important commitments to the United Nations. These include making reports and permitting inspections, and, perhaps, acting in accordance with United Nations resolutions in administering the Trust Territories. The United States administers only Pacific islands which are considered "strategic," and these come under the supervision of the Security Council rather than the General Assembly. As the Trusteeship Council functions with regard to "strategic" areas also, the reporting and visiting provisions have operated in the same manner as with the territories where the Assembly has the plenary authority. However, a United States veto could prevent the Security Council from adopting any rules for the adminis-

Notes to VII: International Regulation

tration of these islands to which the United States might object. The United States is required to make reports to the Trusteeship Council only for the Pacific islands, but has voluntarily made them for other non-self-governing territories such as Alaska, Hawaii, and Guam.

Under the terms of the Charter it is not certain whether the administering authority is required to permit visits to trust terrritories, because these must be "at times agreed upon with the administering authority"; the better interpretation would seem to be that this provision was designed to prevent surprise inspections but not to permit the administrator to avoid inspection altogether. At the least, there is strong moral pressure to permit visits.

5. See the Articles of Agreement of the International Monetary Fund, (1944), 60 STAT. 1401, T.I.A.S. No. 1501, and Articles of Agreement of the International Bank for Reconstruction and Development (1944), 60 STAT. 1440, T.I.A.S. No. 1502, particularly arts. V and IV, respectively, defining the powers and describing the operations of these agencies.

6. Constitution of the World Health Organization (1946), art. 21, 62 STAT. 2685 (1948), T.I.A.S. No. 1808.

7. See the Documents of the Paris Congress of the Universal Postal Union including the Universal Postal Convention, July 5, 1947, 62 STAT. 3301, T.I.A.S. No. 1850.

8. See the [Geneva] Convention for Limiting the Manufacture and Regulating the Distribution of Narcotic Drugs, July 13, 1931, 48 STAT. 1543, T.S. No. 863. For a recent discussion of this subject see Renborg, *International Control of Narcotics,* 22 LAW & CONTEMP. PROB. 86 (1957).

The international obligations of the United States are recognized in the Opium Poppy Control Act of 1942, 56 STAT. 1045, 21 U.S.C. §§ 188–188n (1952), and in the act establishing the Narcotics Bureau, 46 STAT. 587 (1930), 21 U.S.C. § 197 (1952). A recent congressional report also reaffirmed the importance of international control of narcotics, calling it "the most effective means of eliminating illicit traffic in narcotic drugs." *Narcotic Control Act of 1956,* H.R. REP. No. 2388, 84th Cong., 2d Sess. 68 (1956).

9. International Wheat Agreement, March 23, 1949, arts. IX, X, 63 STAT. 2186, T.I.A.S. No. 1957, implemented by the International Wheat Agreement Act of 1949, 63 STAT. 945, 7 U.S.C. §§ 1641–42 (1952); International Agreement Regarding the Regulation of Production and Marketing of Sugar, May 6, 1937, arts. 20, 21, 59 STAT. 931, T.S. No. 990.

10. Convention Between the United States of America and Canada Concerning the Sockeye Salmon Fisheries, May 26, 1930, 50 STAT. 1355, T.S. No. 918, implemented by the Sockeye Salmon Fishing Act of 1947, 61 STAT. 511, 16 U.S.C. §§ 776–776f (1952). A 1957 protocol extended the coverage of the convention to other types of salmon but also rendered most regulations of the Sockeye Commission subject to the approval of both governments. 8 U.S. TREATIES 1057 (1957), T.I.A.S. No. 3867.

Halibut too has been the subject of conventions with Canada. The earlier conventions established the International Fisheries Commission with both investigatory and regulatory powers: See 43 STAT. 1841 (1924), T.S. No.

701; 47 Stat. 1872 (1930), T.S. No. 837; 50 Stat. 1351 (1937), T.S. No. 917. The name and composition of the commission were modified by the 1953 Convention, 5 U.S. Treaties 5 (1953), T.I.A.S. No. 2900. The regulations of the new International Pacific Halibut Commission are subject to approval by the President of the United States and the Governor General in Council of Canada. United States implementation was provided by successive Northwest Pacific Halibut Acts, 43 Stat. 648 (1924); 47 Stat. 142 (1932); and 50 Stat. 325 (1937), as amended, 67 Stat. 494 (1953), 16 U.S.C. §§ 772–772i (Supp. V, 1958).

Compare also the Convention With Canada and Japan on High Sea Fisheries of the North Pacific Ocean, May 9, 1952, 4 U.S. Treaties 380, T.I.A.S. No. 2786; also the Interim Convention on North Pacific Fur Seals (United States, Canada, Japan, and the Soviet Union), Feb. 9, 1957, T.I.A.S. No. 3948.

11. International Convention for the Northwest Atlantic Fisheries, Feb. 8, 1949, 1 U.S. Treaties 477, T.I.A.S. No. 2089. The commission makes proposals which, if accepted, have the force of law, enforceable by penal sanctions, within the United States. Northwest Atlantic Fisheries Act of 1950, 64 Stat. 1069, 16 U.S.C. §§ 988, 989 (1952). The Secretaries of State and of the Interior are authorized by the statute to accept on behalf of the United States, and are thus, in effect, empowered to promulgate penal regulations without having to make any additional reference to Congress.

Compare the Tuna Conventions Act of 1950, 64 Stat. 777, 16 U.S.C. §§ 951–61 (1952), implementing the 1949 Tropical Tuna Fishing Conventions with Costa Rica and Mexico, 1 U.S. Treaties 230, 513 (1950), T.I.A.S. Nos. 2044, 2094. The rulemaking powers of the Inter-American Tropical Tuna Commissions appear to be fewer than those of the Northwest Atlantic Fisheries Commission. See the discussion when all three conventions came before the Senate for ratification, 95 Cong. Rec. 11632 et seq. (1949).

12. Convention for the Regulation of Whaling, Dec. 2, 1946, 62 Stat. 1716, T.I.A.S. No. 1849, implemented by the Whaling Convention Act of 1949, 64 Stat. 421, 16 U.S.C. §§ 916–916l (1952).

13. The International Joint Commission was established by Treaty With Great Britain Relating to the Boundary Waters Between the United States and Canada, Jan. 11, 1909, 36 Stat. 2448, T.S. No. 548, modified in respects not here relevant by convention between the United States and Canada, 1 U.S. Treaties 694, T.I.A.S. No. 2130 (1950). The commission's principal duties concern the disposition and use of boundary waters, but the treaty provides that if both countries agree, the commission is empowered to decide disputes between them; the approval of the Senate is required to effectuate United States consent. The usual practice, however, is for the commission to make recommendations without receiving prior consent, which recommendations may later be embodied in a new treaty. For the history of such a proceeding, see Olson v. United States, 292 U.S. 246, 248–50 (1934).

Notes to VII: International Regulation

14. For example, the International Wheat Agreement, March 23, 1949, art. XIII(c), 63 STAT. 2189, T.I.A.S. No. 1957, provides that wheat-importing nations shall have a total of one thousand votes and wheat-exporting nations will have an equal number. Compare the Articles of Agreement of the International Monetary Fund (1944), art. XII, § 5, 60 STAT. 1418, T.I.A.S. No. 1501, providing for a weighted voting system based upon contribution to the Fund's capital. See Metzger, *Settlement of International Disputes by Non-Judicial Methods*, 48 AM. J. INT'L L. 408 (1954).

15. For example, the regulations of the World Health Organization, enacted pursuant to art. 21 of the WHO constitution, 62 STAT. 2685 (1948), T.I.A.S. No. 1808. In authorizing the President to accept membership in WHO, Congress emphasized its "understanding that nothing in the Constitution of the World Health Organization in any manner commits the United States to enact any specific legislative program regarding any matters referred to in said Constitution." Act of June 14, 1948, § 5, 62 STAT. 442, 22 U.S.C. § 290d (1952).

16. This includes most of the decisions of the Security Council, the recommendations of the General Assembly, and the resolutions of the Specialized Agencies. But in some limited respects, international organizations have dealt with the individual. The Trusteeship Council of the United Nations, for example, has liberal procedures for receiving petitions from inhabitants of Trust Territories and other parties. U.N. Trusteeship Council, Rules of Procedure 76–93, U.N. Doc. No. T/1/Rev. 1 (1947). The European Convention for the Protection of Human Rights and Fundamental Freedoms (1950), art. 25 (Official Translation of the Directorate of Information of the Council of Europe, 1952), provides for petition by aggrieved individuals to the European Commission of Human Rights. Article 48 of the convention, however, prevents individuals from presenting grievances before the European Court of Human Rights.

In the Coal and Steel Community international judicial review has been allowed to industrial enterprises and workers' organizations aggrieved by individual decisions and recommendations affecting them, and by general decisions and recommendations which they deem to involve an abuse of power affecting them, by the High Authority of the Community. Treaty Constituting the European Coal and Steel Community, art. 33, *supra* note 3. Similar rights of appeal are granted to individuals and corporations by the Treaty Establishing the European Economic Community (1957), art. 174, and the Treaty Establishing the European Atomic Energy Community (1957), art. 144, *supra* note 3. See JESSUP, LANDE & LISSITZYN, INTERNATIONAL REGULATION OF ECONOMIC AND SOCIAL QUESTIONS, in CHAMBERLAIN, INTERNATIONAL ORGANIZATION 15–35, 73–76 (1955); Bebr, *Protection of Private Interests Under the European Coal and Steel Community*, 42 VA. L. REV. 879 (1956).

For a general discussion of the theme that the individual has become a proper subject and object of international law, see JESSUP, A MODERN LAW OF NATIONS 15–42 (1948). And see pp. 132–33 above.

17. See the Convention Between the United States of America and Canada Concerning the Sockeye Salmon Fisheries, May 26, 1930, art. IX, 50 STAT. 1359, T.S. No. 918, *supra* note 10.

18. See, *e.g.*, Convention Between the United States of America and the Republic of Mexico for the Adjustment of Claims, July 4, 1868, art. II, 15 STAT. 682, T.S. No. 212; Agreement Between the United States and Germany for a Mixed Commission, Aug. 10, 1922, art. VI, 42 STAT. 2200, T.S. No. 665. Professor Hudson, writing in 1944, stated that the United States had participated in twenty-six such tribunals in the past one hundred years, HUDSON, INTERNATIONAL TRIBUNALS 196 (1944).

19. A leading early case in which the Supreme Court considered the conclusiveness of an award by an international commission to an American citizen is Comegys v. Vasse, 1 Pet. 193 (U.S. 1828). While the plaintiff did not object to the award on constitutional grounds, the Court said that so far as concerned the validity of a claim against Spain the decision of the commissioners was final and could not be reviewed by any judicial tribunal. *Id.* at 212. Compare Meade v. United States, 9 Wall. 691 (U.S. 1870). In the treaty there involved the United States took over obligations of Spain to American citizens and established a United States commission to consider them. The Court affirmed a judgment of the Court of Claims which dismissed a suit by an American citizen for failure to state a cause of action against the United States. The plaintiff's claims had been dismissed by the commission on the ground that it was not within the commission's jurisdiction; under the treaty it had authority only to consider unliquidated claims against Spain at the time of signature of the treaty. See also Ware v. Hylton, 3 Dall. 199 (U.S. 1796), discussed at pp. 40–41 above, involving a treaty confirming obligations of American citizens to British nationals.

But *cf.* Seery v. United States, 127 F. Supp. 601 (Ct. Cl. 1955).

20. See Gray v. United States, 21 Ct. Cl. 340 (1886), the principal case dealing with claims of American citizens arising out of French spoliation in the early days of the republic. The claims had been renounced by the United States in 1800, in a treaty which also relieved this government of liabilities to France. However, no recovery for American shipowners was possible without legislative authorization, and eighty-five years elapsed before such an act received the approval of Congress and the President. Although the *Gray* case recognized that the right of the government to bargain away the claims of its citizens "is too clear for discussion," the court asserted that there was an obligation on the part of the government, moral, and, under the Fifth Amendment, legal, to compensate these citizens. But the court also recognized that the right to compensation was not enforceable without appropriate legislation. *Id.* at 392–93. See also Buchanan v. United States, 24 Ct. Cl. 74, 82 (1889), dealing with similar claims. *Cf.* Meade v. United States, 9 Wall. 691 (U.S. 1870), *supra* note 19.

For a series of modern cases arising out of the Yugoslav Claims Agreement of 1948, 62 STAT. 2658, T.I.A.S. No. 1803, implemented in the International Claims Settlement Act of 1949, 64 STAT. 12, 22 U.S.C. §§ 1621–27

Notes to VII: International Regulation

(1952), see American and European Agencies, Inc. v. Gillilland, 247 F.2d 95 (D.C. Cir.), *cert. denied,* 355 U.S. 884 (1957); Haas v. Humphrey, 246 F.2d 682 (D.C. Cir.), *cert. denied,* 355 U.S. 854 (1957); Dayton v. Gillilland, 242 F.2d 227 (D.C. Cir.), *cert. denied,* 355 U.S. 813 (1957); De Vegvar v. Gillilland, 228 F.2d 640 (D.C. Cir. 1955), *cert. denied,* 350 U.S. 994 (1956).

21. Even when the United States has received payment on the basis of award by an international commission, it may refuse to turn the proceeds over to the claimant. See the cases concerning the La Abra mining claims litigation, in which the Court upheld the refusal of the United States Government to remit payments received from the Mexican government to Americans about whose claims this government had suspicions of fraud. La Abra Silver Mining Co. v. United States, 175 U.S. 423 (1899); United States *ex rel.* Boynton v. Blaine, 139 U.S. 306 (1891); Frelinghuysen v. Key, 110 U.S. 63 (1884). *Cf.* Z. & F. Assets Realization Corp. v. Hull, 311 U.S. 470 (1941).

22. See cases cited in note 20 above. In Z. & F. Realization Corp. v. Hull, 311 U.S. 470 (1941), Mr. Justice Black concurred on the ground that the propriety of the awards by the German-American Mixed Claims Commission was a question "constitutionally committed exclusively to the legislative and executive departments." *Id.* at 490.

23. "Administrative law has not come like a thief in the night. It is not an innovation; its general recognition is." Frankfurter, *Foreword to a Symposium on Administrative Law,* 47 YALE L.J. 515, 517 (1938).

The history of the growth of the administrative process and the development of administrative law is set out in *Final Report of the Attorney-General's Committee on Administrative Procedure* 1–24 (1941); DAVIS, ADMINISTRATIVE LAW §§ 2–4 (1951).

24. Attacks on administrative agencies came from commentators, courts, and members of Congress. Among the chief critics were former Solicitor General BECK, OUR WONDERLAND OF BUREAUCRACY (1932), Dean POUND, CONTEMPORARY JURISTIC THEORY (1940) (and many essays), and some leaders of the organized bar. See the *Reports of the Special Committee on Administrative Law of the American Bar Association,* in 59 ANNUAL REPORT OF THE ABA 539 (1934); 61 ANNUAL REPORT 720 (1936).

The courts scrutinized and set limits to the administrative process. See, *e.g.,* St. Joseph Stockyards Co. v. United States, 298 U.S. 38 (1936); Panama Refining Co. v. Ryan, 293 U.S. 388 (1935); Crowell v. Benson, 285 U.S. 22 (1932). Congress, which had created the administrative agencies, sought to curb their power in the Walter-Logan Bills, S. 915 and H.R. 6324, 76th Cong., 3d Sess. (1940).

But the administrative process has had its strong defenders. See, *e.g.,* Mr. Justice Stone, *The Common Law in the United States,* 50 HARV. L. REV. 4, 16–18 (1936); FRANK, IF MEN WERE ANGELS (1942); *Final Report of the Attorney-General's Committee on Administrative Procedure, op. cit. supra* note 23; GELLHORN, FEDERAL ADMINISTRATIVE PROCEEDINGS

(1941). And President Roosevelt vetoed the Walter-Logan Bills, H.R. Doc. No. 986, 76th Cong., 3d Sess. (1940). Today, administrative agencies are many, and firmly established, and administrative law is firmly a part of American government and jurisprudence.

A reevaluation of the administrative process, however, has been going on for some time. See, for example, Jaffe, *The Effective Limits of the Administrative Process: A Reevaluation,* 67 HARV. L. REV. 1105 (1954). See also B. Schwartz, *Administrative Justice and Its Place in the Legal Order,* 30 N.Y.U.L. REV. 1390 (1955). Compare GELLHORN, INDIVIDUAL FREEDOM AND GOVERNMENTAL RESTRAINTS (1956), especially chapters 1 and 3; L. B. Schwartz, *Legal Restriction of Competition in the Regulated Industries: An Abdication of Judicial Responsibility,* 67 HARV. L. REV. 436 (1954).

25. See, *e.g.,* United States v. Curtiss-Wright Export Corp., 299 U.S. 304, 318 (1936); Mackenzie v. Hare, 239 U.S. 299, 311 (1915); Fong Yue Ting v. United States, 149 U.S. 698, 705 (1893). See also Perez v. Brownell, 356 U.S. 44 (1958). And see p. 27 above.

26. See also discussion at p. 134 above.

Cf. Hirota v. MacArthur, 338 U.S. 197 (1948), which held that an international military tribunal in which the United States had participated was not a "tribunal of the United States," whose judgments could be subject to review by the Supreme Court or by other federal courts. Mr. Justice Douglas, concurring, was of the opinion that there was no power of review because the military tribunal "was solely an instrument of political power" as to which the President, spokesman for the United States in its foreign affairs, had the final say. *Id.* at 199, 215. See chapter VIII, note 69.

27. In the case of requisition, the owner of property may raise the question whether the taking is for a public use, but the decision of Congress in authorizing it "is entitled to deference until it is shown to involve an impossibility." Old Dominion Land Co. v. United States, 269 U.S. 55, 66 (1925). See also chapter III note 69. However, the transfer could probably not be challenged in a taxpayer's suit. *Cf.* Massachusetts v. Mellon, 262 U.S. 447 (1923). For suits seeking to prevent expenditure of tax funds for defense and foreign affairs purposes alleged to be unconstitutional, see Lee v. Humphrey, 352 U.S. 904 (1956) (motion for leave to file bill of complaint in original Supreme Court proceeding denied); Farmer v. Rountree, 149 F. Supp. 327 (M.D. Tenn. 1956).

For a discussion of the validity of a grant of power to an international agency itself to exercise eminent domain, see Deutsch, *Eminent Domain Under a Treaty: A Hypothetical Supreme Court Opinion,* 43 A.B.A.J. 699 (1957).

28. The nature of the remedies available to the international agency, *e.g.,* cease and desist orders, license cancellation, would depend on the scope of the regulative powers granted to it. As long as the required standards of fairness are met, to allow the international agency the types of remedy available to regulatory bodies of the United States would appear to raise no special constitutional problems. Neither would it be invalid to empower

Notes to VII: International Regulation

the agency to petition national courts for enforcement of their orders. The agency and the courts would, as we have assumed it, be applying United States law.

29. For an excellent discussion, see Jaffe, *An Essay on Delegation of Legislative Power,* 47 COLUM. L. REV. 359, 561 (1947).

30. Carter v. Carter Coal Co., 298 U.S. 238 (1936); Schechter Poultry Co. v. United States, 295 U.S. 495 (1935); Panama Refining Co. v. Ryan, 293 U.S. 388 (1935).

31. Nor is it likely that congressional action in these fields would be struck down on the grounds of undue delegation to the Executive. The power of the President, even without any delegation from Congress, is so broad in these areas that in the absence of a prohibition by Congress few powers are likely to be denied him. When Congress not only refrains from prohibiting presidential action but indeed authorizes it, the broad powers of the President are added to those of the Congress. "It is important to bear in mind that we are here dealing not alone with an authority vested in the President by an exertion of legislative power, but with such an authority plus the very delicate, plenary and exclusive power of the President as the sole organ of the federal government in the field of international relations—a power which does not require as a basis for its exercise an act of Congress." United States v. Curtiss-Wright Export Corp., 299 U.S. 304, 319–20 (1936). See also United States *ex rel.* Knauff v. Shaughnessy, 338 U.S. 537, 542 (1950); The Thomas Gibbons, 8 Cranch 421, 428–29 (U.S. 1814).

32. Within the context of the United States Government, this is the standard for determining whether Congress has unduly delegated its legislative power. It was suggested by Chief Justice Marshall in Wayman v. Southard, 10 Wheat. 1, 43 (U.S. 1825). Since the cases cited in note 30 above, the Supreme Court has applied this standard broadly and has upheld numerous, extensive delegations. See, *e.g.,* Lichter v. United States, 334 U.S. 742 (1948); Yakus v. United States, 321 U.S. 414 (1944); Sunshine Anthracite Coal Co. v. Adkins, 310 U.S. 381 (1940). And see generally GELLHORN & BYSE, ADMINISTRATIVE LAW: CASES AND COMMENTS 98 *et seq.* (1954).

33. See, *e.g.,* United States v. Rock Royal Co-operative, Inc., 307 U.S. 533 (1939) (setting milk marketing quotas); Currin v. Wallace, 306 U.S. 1 (1939) (setting tobacco marketing quotas), distinguishing Carter v. Carter Coal Co., 298 U.S. 238 (1936), on the ground that the instant scheme was not one "where a group of producers may make the law and force it upon a minority," as in the latter case. Currin v. Wallace, *supra* at 15–16. And see Jaffe, *Law Making by Private Groups,* 51 HARV. L. REV. 201 (1937).

34. *Cf.* Sunshine Anthracite Coal Co. v. Adkins, 310 U.S. 381, 394 (1940); Mulford v. Smith, 307 U.S. 38, 48 (1939). *But see* Note, *Judicial Acquiescence in the Forfeiture of Constitutional Rights Through Expansion of the Conditioned Privilege Doctrine,* 28 IND. L.J. 520 (1953), for a critique of this rule based on the observation of Mr. Justice Sutherland in Frost & Frost Trucking Co. v. Railroad Comm'n, 271 U.S. 583, 593 (1926),

that a state could not impose conditions upon the grant of the privilege of using state highways which would necessitate the surrender of the corporation-petitioner's constitutional rights.

35. *Cf.* notes 10–12 above. And see Migratory Bird Treaty Act, 40 STAT. 755 (1918), 16 U.S.C. §§ 703–11 (1952).

36. The Administrative Procedure Act, 60 STAT. 237 (1946), as amended, 5 U.S.C. §§ 1001–11 (1952), is the basic statute establishing administrative procedural standards, but the various acts setting up individual agencies also prescribe procedures. The courts generally review administrative proceedings on the basis of these statutes, but their approach frequently has a constitutional flavor. See, *e.g.,* Wong Yang Sung v. McGrath, 339 U.S. 33 (1950); Morgan v. United States, 304 U.S. 1 (1938).

37. The Supreme Court has frequently distinguished between "rights" and "privileges" in determining the nature of the hearing required and the scope of review. See, *e.g.,* United States *ex rel.* Milwaukee Social Democratic Publishing Co. v. Burleson, 255 U.S. 407 (1921). Thus, aliens subject to exclusion or deportation need not be accorded procedural safeguards granted by regulatory agencies in other circumstances. See Jay v. Boyd, 351 U.S. 345 (1956); United States *ex rel.* Knauff v. Shaughnessy, 338 U.S. 537 (1950). For discussion of the "right-privilege" dichotomy and its limitations, see Davis, *The Requirement of a Trial-Type Hearing,* 70 HARV. L. REV. 193 (1956).

38. See note 36 above.

39. A leading early case is American School of Magnetic Healing v. McAnnulty, 187 U.S. 94 (1902). See also Stark v. Wickard, 321 U.S. 288 (1944); Morgan v. United States, 298 U.S. 468 (1936); Lester v. Parker, 235 F.2d 787 (9th Cir. 1956); Parker v. Lester, 227 F.2d 708 (9th Cir. 1955). *But cf.* Aircraft & Diesel Equipment Co. v. Hirsch, 331 U.S. 752 (1947); Myers v. Bethlehem Shipbuilding Corp., 303 U.S. 41 (1938).

40. See Crowell v. Benson, 285 U.S. 22, 54 (1932). And Brandeis, J., concurring in St. Joseph Stock Yards Co. v. United States, 298 U.S. 38, 73, 84 (1936). Also, Yakus v. United States, 321 U.S. 414, 442–43 (1944). For a full discussion, see Jaffe, *The Right to Judicial Review,* 71 HARV. L. REV. 401, 769 (1958).

41. The Court's decisions have given considerable leeway to regulatory agencies in the formulation of substantive standards, generally on the basis of statutory interpretation without reference to constitutionality. See, *e.g.,* Federal Power Comm'n v. Hope Natural Gas Co., 320 U.S. 591 (1944); National Broadcasting Co. v. United States, 319 U.S. 190 (1943). And see the cases involving state administrative bodies in note 42 below. But at least as to some regulatory bodies, the Court appears to have felt increasingly free to disregard the conclusions of the agency. Federal Maritime Bd. v. Isbrandtsen Co., 356 U.S. 481 (1958); Public Serv. Comm'n v. United States, 356 U.S. 421 (1958); *cf., e.g.,* County of Marin v. United States, 356 U.S. 412 (1958); Schaffer Transp. Co. v. United States, 355 U.S. 83 (1957). The doctrine that the courts have the power to review the reason-

Notes to VII: International Regulation

ableness of substantive administrative determinations retains its vitality. In Federal Power Comm'n v. Natural Gas Pipeline Co., 315 U.S. 575 (1942), Mr. Justice Black, speaking also for two other Justices, sought to scuttle this doctrine in ratemaking cases, where it had its origin, see Chicago M. & St. P. Ry. v. Minnesota, 134 U.S. 418 (1890), but the majority reviewed the commission's decision to determine whether the rate is confiscatory; and the doctrine has not since been seriously challenged. See the discussion of substantive due process at pp. 39 ff. above.

42. See note 40 above. See also cases involving state administrative procedures: Brinkerhoff-Faris Trust & Sav. Co. v. Hill, 281 U.S. 673 (1930); Oklahoma Operating Co. v. Love, 252 U.S. 331 (1920); *Ex parte* Young, 209 U.S. 123 (1908).

43. U.S. *ex rel.* Knauff v. Shaughnessy, 338 U.S. 537 (1950); Gegiow v. Uhl, 239 U.S. 3 (1915); Gonzales v. Williams, 192 U.S. 1 (1904).

44. The standard of review may vary, at least verbally, with the statute being administered. *Compare* Universal Camera Corp. v. NLRB, 340 U.S. 474 (1951) (requiring "substantial evidence on the record as a whole" to support Labor Board findings under the Labor-Management Relations Act), *with* United States *ex rel.* Vajtauer v. Commissioner, 273 U.S. 103 (1927) (requiring only "some evidence" to sustain a deportation order). See also Jaffe, *Judicial Review: Question of Fact,* 69 HARV. L. REV. 1020, 1050 (1956).

45. See notes 40 and 42 above.

46. For an unusual instance, in extraordinary circumstances, of a treaty providing judicial review in United States courts of determinations of an international body, see Abrey v. Reusch, 153 F. Supp. 337 (S.D.N.Y. 1957).

47. United States v. Pink, 315 U.S. 203 (1942); Z. & F. Assets Realization Corp. v. Hull, 311 U.S. 470, 490 (1941) (concurring opinion); Oetjen v. Central Leather Co., 246 U.S. 297 (1918); Foster v. Neilson, 2 Pet. 253 (U.S. 1829). In other areas the Court has refused to consider "political questions" although a violation of constitutional rights was claimed, *e.g.,* Colegrove v. Green, 328 U.S. 549 (1946). Compare the international claims cases, *supra* notes 19–22. And see Hirota v. MacArthur, 338 U.S. 197 (1948), *supra* note 26, and the discussion below in chapter VIII. See also chapter IV note 93.

48. See cases cited by Frankfurter, J., in his dissent in Larson v. Domestic & Foreign Commerce Corp., 337 U.S. 682, 705, 711–12 (1949). In Youngstown Sheet & Tube Co. v. Sawyer, 343 U.S. 579 (1952), a vigorously litigated case, sovereign immunity was not even offered as a defense by the Secretary of Commerce, acting on behalf of the United States under an executive order, in an injunction proceeding challenging the constitutionality of his order.

49. Compare the cases dismissing suits because the United States was an indispensable party, *e.g.,* Minnesota v. United States, 305 U.S. 382 (1939). As is pointed out in Block, *Suits Against Government Officers and the Sovereign Immunity Doctrine,* 59 HARV. L. REV. 1060 (1946), the doctrines

of sovereign immunity and indispensability of party are frequently confused.

50. See pp. 82–83 above.

51. *Cf.* Estep v. United States, 327 U.S. 114 (1946).

NOTES TO VIII: INTERNATIONAL TRIBUNALS

1. U.N. GENERAL ASSEMBLY RESOLUTIONS, 1st Sess., part 2, p. 188, Dec. 11, 1946. See also *id.*, 1st Sess., part 1, p. 9, Feb. 13, 1946.

2. For discussions of such proposals, see Wright, *Proposal for an International Criminal Court,* 46 AM. J. INT'L L. 60 (1952); Yuen-li Liang, *Notes on Legal Questions Concerning the United Nations: The Establishment of an International Criminal Jurisdiction: The First Phase,* 46 AM. J. INT'L L. 73 (1952); Pella, *Towards an International Criminal Court,* 44 AM. J. INT'L L. 37 (1950); Parker, *An International Criminal Court: The Case for Its Adoption,* 38 A.B.A.J. 641 (1952); Finch, *An International Criminal Court: The Case Against Its Adoption,* 38 A.B.A.J. 644 (1952); Ely, *The Treaty-Making Power: The Constitutionality of International Courts,* 36 A.B.A.J. 738 (1950). These articles deal primarily with courts established in connection with an international criminal code relating to international crimes such as genocide or acts against the peace, particularly U.N. Committee on International Criminal Jurisdiction, *Draft Statute for an International Criminal Court,* U.N. Doc. A/AC.48/4 (1951), reprinted in 46 AM. J. INT'L L. 1 (Supp. 1952). Some of the constitutional issues discussed in this chapter are considered at length in the Ely article, and in passing by Parker and Finch. Douglas, J., concurring in Hirota v. MacArthur, 338 U.S. 197, 199, 205 (1948), also alludes to them. See note 69 below.

3. See, *e.g., Ex parte* Bakelite Corp., 279 U.S. 438 (1929); United States v. Ferreira, 13 How. 40 (U.S. 1851); Hayburn's Case, 2 Dall. 409 (U.S. 1792) and reporter's note there; compare the various opinions in National Mut. Ins. Co. v. Tidewater Transfer Co., 337 U.S. 582 (1949).

4. See p. 109 above.

5. 61 STAT. 1218 (1946), T.I.A.S. No. 1598.

6. The statute, REV. STAT. § 4079 (1875), 22 U.S.C. § 256 (1952), confers jurisdiction on a consul only where by treaty the nation he represents gives reciprocal rights to United States consuls in its territory. 22 U.S.C. § 258a provides for enforcement by federal courts or commissioners of consular awards and decrees in differences between captains and crews of the vessels of the nation the consul represents.

Lower federal courts have given effect to foreign consular jurisdiction: The Koenigin Luise, 184 Fed. 170 (D.N.J. 1910) (dismissing alien seaman's libel against vessel, because of exclusive jurisdiction of consul). See The Neck, 138 Fed. 144 (W.D. Wash. 1905) (refusing to dismiss suit for wages by United States citizen who was seaman serving under flag of country whose consul claimed exclusive jurisdiction under a treaty). See also The

Notes to VIII: International Tribunals

Betsey, 3 Dall. 6 (U.S. 1794) (implying that the United States has the power by treaty to permit foreign countries to establish courts in the United States).

7. See NATO Status of Forces Agreement, June 19, 1951, 4 U.S. TREATIES 1792, T.I.A.S. No. 2846; The Service Courts of Friendly Foreign Forces Act, 58 STAT. 643 (1944), 22 U.S.C. §§ 701–6 (1952); see p. 57 above.

8. See pp. 109–10 above.

9. Compare chapter IV note 94.

10. On legislative power to compel testimony and administer oaths, see 52 STAT. 942 (1938), 2 U.S.C. §§ 191–92 (1952). *Cf.* Watkins v. United States, 354 U.S. 178 (1957); Adams v. Maryland, 347 U.S. 179 (1954); McGrain v. Daugherty, 273 U.S. 135 (1927).

11. For administrative agencies empowered to compel testimony and administer oaths, see, *e.g.*, 38 STAT. 722 (1914), 15 U.S.C. § 49 (1952) (FTC); 49 STAT. 455 (1935), as amended, 29 U.S.C. § 161 (1952) (NLRB). See also Oklahoma Press Publishing Co. v. Walling, 327 U.S. 186 (1946).

12. See p. 57 above.

13. 46 STAT. 1006 (1930), 22 U.S.C. §§ 270a, c (1952). Foreign service courts, on the other hand, must request the issuance of subpoenas from the federal district courts. 58 STAT. 644 (1944), 22 U.S.C. § 703(a) (1952).

14. Barron v. Baltimore, 7 Pet. 243 (U.S. 1833). *Cf.* Adamson v. California, 332 U.S. 46 (1947). See p. 55 above.

15. "A search warrant authorized by this rule may be issued by a judge of the United States or of a state or territorial court of record or by a United States commissioner within the district wherein the property sought is located." FED. R. CRIM. P. 41(a). And see chapter VI, note 13.

United States commissioners are court officers but not judges; they do not exercise "judicial power." *Cf., e.g.,* Go-Bart Importing Co. v. United States, 282 U.S. 344, 352–54 (1931); Rice v. Ames, 180 U.S. 371 (1901); United States v. Casino, 286 Fed. 976 (S.D.N.Y. 1923); United States v. Berry, 4 Fed. 779 (D. Colo. 1880). Compare also Collins v. Miller, 252 U.S. 364, 369 (1920); Ocampo v. United States, 234 U.S. 91 (1914); Robertson v. Baldwin, 165 U.S. 275 (1897). The commissioner is not deemed to be exercising judicial power even when he is trying persons for petty offenses. See note 49 below.

16. To resist lawful search by United States officers is a federal offense. 18 U.S.C. § 2231 (1952). It was suggested that it might be made criminal to resist lawful search by international officials. See p. 87 above.

17. The victim of unlawful search could bring civil suit against a person performing unlawful search, if the latter is not immune. See p. 82 above.

18. See Watkins v. United States, 354 U.S. 178 (1957); McGrain v. Daugherty, 273 U.S. 135 (1927). *Cf.* Oklahoma Press Publishing Co. v. Walling, 327 U.S. 186 (1946). Legislative courts, discussed later in the chapter, may also cite for contempt. The statute giving contempt power to

the courts, 18 U.S.C. § 401 (1952), speaks of "a court of the United States." This term is defined elsewhere to include, *inter alia,* the district courts for Hawaii and Puerto Rico, the Court of Claims, the Court of Customs and Patent Appeals, and the Customs Court. *Cf. Ex parte* Bakelite Corp., 279 U.S. 438 (1929).

It is important also to distinguish between different types of contempt. Contempt may involve an act of disrespect to the body; more usually it consists of noncompliance with its process or orders. With respect to courts, at least, a distinction is drawn between contempt committed within the presence of the court and contempt outside it. There are also important differences between an order holding the accused in civil contempt, which may involve indefinite imprisonment until the court's order is complied with, and criminal contempt, a penalty for past noncompliance. These distinctions are discussed in Moskovitz, *Contempt of Injunctions, Civil and Criminal,* 43 COLUM. L. REV. 780 (1943). The contempt of international tribunals which would be of importance for arms control enforcement would be failure to obey their commands.

19. *Cf.* Watkins v. United States, 354 U.S. 178 (1957); Michaelson v. United States *ex rel.* Chicago, St. P.,M., & O. Ry., 266 U.S. 42, 65–67 (1924); Gompers v. Bucks Stove & Range Co., 221 U.S. 418 (1911). *But cf.* Green v. United States, 356 U.S. 165 (1958).

While the legislative power also may not be freely delegated (see chapter VII), power to punish for contempt, it would be argued, is intrinsically neither legislative nor judicial, and may be granted in support of other powers which may be conferred upon international tribunals.

20. The act authorizing friendly foreign forces to try their members in the United States provides a penalty for American citizens who commit an act of contempt or perjury before such a court, but this is a United States offense to be tried in a United States court. 58 STAT. 644 (1944), 22 U.S.C. § 703(c) (1952). The general perjury statute, 18 U.S.C. § 1621 (1952), is applicable by its terms to any oath before a competent tribunal, officer, or person authorized to administer oaths by a law of the United States. Such authorization has been given to international bodies, *e.g.,* the International Joint Commission, 36 STAT. 1364 (1911), 22 U.S.C. § 268 (1952).

21. Piracy as defined by the law of nations is punishable under 18 U.S.C. § 1651 (1952). See discussion later in this chapter at p. 147. Counterfeiting within the United States of securities of other nations is punishable under 18 U.S.C. §§ 478–79 (1952). Such counterfeiting is an offense against the law of nations. United States v. Arjona, 120 U.S. 479 (1887). The law of war, as part of the law of nations, has to some extent been made part of United States criminal law. See *Ex parte* Quirin, 317 U.S. 1, 28 (1942). Anyone who swears out a writ or executes process against an immune foreign diplomat is guilty under United States law as a "violator of the laws of nations and a disturber of the public repose." 1 STAT. 117 (1790), as amended, 22 U.S.C. 252–53 (1952). Congress has made it an offense for anyone to assault a foreign diplomat "in violation of the law of nations." 18 U.S.C. § 112 (1952). Violations of regulations of international administra-

Notes to VIII: International Tribunals 239

tive agencies in the fishing industries are violations of federal law under certain circumstances. See chapter VII note 12. See generally Radin, *International Crimes*, 32 IOWA L. REV. 33 (1946).

22. Compare JACKSON, THE NÜRNBERG CASE (1947); Glueck, *The Nuernberg Trial and Aggressive War*, 59 HARV. L. REV. 396 (1946); Meltzer, *A Note on Some Aspects of the Nuremberg Debate*, 14 U. CHI. L. REV. 455 (1947); Wechsler, *The Issues of the Nuremberg Trial*, 62 POL. SCI. Q. 11 (1947), with *The Nürnberg Novelty*, Fortune, Dec. 1945, p. 140; Rheinstein, Book Review, 14 U. CHI. L. REV. 319 (1947).

23. See, *e.g.*, JESSUP, A MODERN LAW OF NATIONS 15–42 (1948). See chapter VII note 16.

24. Procedures for giving effect to these treaties are contained in 18 U.S.C. § 3184 (1952). See Valentine v. United States *ex rel.* Neidecker, 299 U.S. 5 (1936); Charlton v. Kelly, 229 U.S. 447 (1913).

The power to extradite even American citizens under a treaty was upheld in an early case which aroused wide public interest. United States v. Robins, 27 Fed. Cas. 825, No. 16175 (D.S.C. 1799). (There is some doubt as to whether Robins was in fact an American citizen, but it was apparently assumed that he was.) John Marshall, then a member of the House of Representatives, made a major speech supporting Robins's extradition, with emphasis on the international obligations of the United States. The speech is reprinted as note 1 in the appendix to 5 Wheat. (18 U.S.).

25. 4 U.S. TREATIES 1798 (1953), T.I.A.S. No. 2846, art. VII. See notes 65–67 below.

26. Another problem would be the manner of punishment for persons convicted by the international court. Unless international prisons were established, which might create serious political and administrative difficulties, it would be necessary to turn offenders over to national prisons. In this connection the provision for implementing imprisonment of Americans convicted outside of the United States by consular courts is instructive: "Every person who refuses or neglects to comply with the sentence passed upon him shall stand committed until he does comply." REV. STAT. § 4101 (1875), 22 U.S.C. § 155 (1952). Seamen convicted by foreign consuls in the United States (see note 6 above) may be confined in United States prisons. 22 U.S.C. § 258 (1952). Compare also art. VII, § 7(b) of the NATO Status of Forces Treaty, *supra* note 25.

The police and prosecutorial functions would, presumably, also be in an international body. These might raise constitutional problems in regard to arrest and interrogation.

27. See p. 112 above.

28. Judge Parker approximated this view in his article *An International Criminal Court: The Case for Its Adoption*, 38 A.B.A.J. 641, 643 (1952): "There is nothing in the Constitution, however, which limits the power of the United States to join with other nations in setting up a court to try those who have committed crimes against the law of nations. The fact that Congress may provide for the trial of such crimes does not mean that the creation of an international criminal court would impinge upon the power of

Congress, just as the punishment of larceny by the states is no infringement of the power of Congress to punish larceny in interstate commerce. . . .

"So far as requirement of indictment by grand jury and trial by jury are concerned, these apply only to trials in federal courts and can have no application to an international court set up by a group of nations in the exercise of their treaty making power. . . . They do not apply in consular courts or in a court established by the United States by international agreement in China. *In re Ross,* 140 U.S. 453; . . . They do not apply to military tribunals set up to try violations of the laws of war. *Ex parte Quirin,* 317 U.S. 1, 45. If courts may be created in the exercise of the legislative power to which these provisions do not apply (see *Ex parte Bakelite Corporation,* 279 U.S. 438), there is no reason why such courts may not be created in the exercise of the treaty making power."

The precedents cited by Judge Parker, however, did not involve the trial of United States citizens in courts sitting in the United States for acts done in the United States (except perhaps as to one defendant in the *Quirin* case). These would seem to be elements which might be critical, as discussed in this chapter. The cases mentioned by Judge Parker are cited and discussed below.

29. Compare the Chinese Exclusion Case, 130 U.S. 581, 609 (1889). Arguing that, despite an earlier treaty, the United States retained its sovereign power to exclude aliens, the Court said: "The powers of government are delegated in trust to the United States, and are incapable of transfer to any other parties. They cannot be abandoned or surrendered."

30. See, *e.g.,* Mr. Justice Gray in The Paquete Habana, 175 U.S. 677, 700 (1900): "International law is part of our law, and must be ascertained and administered by the courts of justice of appropriate jurisdiction as often as questions of right depending upon it are duly presented for their determination."

Chief Justice Marshall said earlier, in deciding in favor of private claims in a prize case, that in the absence of an act of Congress "the Court is bound by the law of nations which is a part of the law of the land." The Nereide, 9 Cranch 388, 423 (U.S. 1815).

A local court in an early case even convicted a person for assaulting the French Consul General in Philadelphia, on the ground that this was an offense against the law of nations which was *ipso facto* part of the municipal law of Philadelphia. Respublica v. De Longchamps, 1 Dall. 111 (Pa. O. & T. 1784).

In the federal courts such an offense could not be punished unless defined by Congress. In United States v. Hudson & Goodwin, 7 Cranch 32 (U.S. 1812), the Court ruled that there is no federal criminal common law, and that federal courts have jurisdiction only over crimes defined by Congress. See also United States v. Coolidge, 1 Wheat. 415 (U.S. 1816). *But see* Warren, *New Light on the History of the Federal Judiciary Act of 1789,* 37 HARV. L. REV. 49, 73 (1923).

31. See note 30 above.

32. See Holmes, J., in Missouri v. Holland, 252 U.S. 416, 433 (1920). And see chapter III note 14.

33. See pp. 28, 29–31 above. *Cf.* Missouri v. Holland, *supra* note 32.

34. For a discussion of the power of Congress to use the state courts to enforce federal law see p. 101 above.

35. The Federal Employers' Liability Act, 35 STAT. 65 (1908), as amended, 45 U.S.C. § 51 (1952), is presently perhaps the most important instance of concurrent state court jurisdiction under an act of Congress. See, especially, 35 STAT. 66 (1908), 45 U.S.C. § 56 (1952). Early federal criminal laws gave concurrent jurisdiction to state courts, *e.g.,* the Post Office Act, 1 STAT. 733, 740 (1799). See also p. 101 above and materials in chapter VI notes 9–12. See HART & WECHSLER, THE FEDERAL COURTS AND THE FEDERAL SYSTEM 395–99 (1953).

36. United States *ex rel.* Toth v. Quarles, 350 U.S. 11, 15–17, 22–23 (1955); *Ex parte* Milligan, 4 Wall. 2, 121–22 (U.S. 1866).

One of the grievances in the Declaration of Independence was that the King had "made Judges dependent on his Will alone, for the tenure of their offices, and the amount and payment of their salaries." Hamilton also urged the enjoyment of judicial tenure as a barrier to oppression and as the best expedient for a steady, upright, and impartial administration of the laws. THE FEDERALIST No. 78. Petty offenses on the other hand have been tried before United States commissioners who do not enjoy life tenure and secured compensation. See note 49 below.

37. See Williams v. United States, 289 U.S. 553, 566 (1933); Martin v. Hunter's Lessee, 1 Wheat. 304, 331 (1816); *cf.* Robertson v. Baldwin, 165 U.S. 275 (1897).

38. See chapter VI notes 7–10.

39. Testa v. Katt, 330 U.S. 386 (1947); Mondou v. New York, N.H. & H.R.R., 223 U.S. 1 (1912). See p. 101 above.

40. See, Ely, *The Treaty-Making Power: The Constitutionality of International Courts,* 36 A.B.A.J. 738 (1950).

The reverse, *i.e.,* appeal from an international court to a United States court, would probably not satisfy constitutional requirements for trial of criminal offenses before an appropriate United States court, perhaps even if on appeal the United States court accorded the accused a trial *de novo. Cf.* Callan v. Wilson, 127 U.S. 540, 556–57 (1888). Compare also Crowell v. Benson, 285 U.S. 22 (1932); *id.* at 65, 86–87 (Brandeis, J., dissenting); Ng Fung Ho v. White, 259 U.S. 276, 283 (1922).

41. *Cf.* Gordon v. United States, 2 Wall. 561 (U.S. 1865), and the opinion of Chief Justice Taney prepared for this case and printed in 117 U.S. 697 (appendix). This difficulty is given consideration in Ely, *supra* note 40, at 739–40. When the United States adhered to the International Court of Prize, it did so only with the stipulation that the international court would not "reverse or affirm" national tribunals. See Butte, *The "Protocole Additionnel" to the International Prize Court Convention,* 6 AM. J. INT'L L. 799 (1912).

A solution to such difficulties was adopted in a treaty between Sweden and Finland which establishes methods for settling claims between the nations. By its terms these procedures may not be invoked until the courts of the nation against which the claim is made have adjudicated the question, if that nation's laws so require (art. 7). But the treaty provides that if the judgment of that court is found to be contrary to international law in a subsequent international proceeding and the constitution of the "defendant nation" does not permit annulment or modification of the judgment, that nation agrees to compensate the claimant in some other manner (art. 8). Convention for the Pacific Settlement of Disputes Between Sweden and Finland, Jan. 29, 1926, LEAGUE OF NATIONS TREATY SERIES No. 1192. See also similar treaties between Denmark and Sweden, Denmark and Finland, Norway and Sweden, LEAGUE OF NATIONS TREATY SERIES Nos. 1235, 1242, 1417.

42. See Kepner v. United States, 195 U.S. 100 (1904); United States v. Sanges, 144 U.S. 310 (1892). *But cf.* Palko v. Connecticut, 302 U.S. 319 (1937). See also Green v. United States, 355 U.S. 184 (1957); ORFIELD, CRIMINAL APPEALS IN AMERICA, c. 3 (1939).

43. The "case or controversy" requirement has been recognized since the beginning of the republic. The leading case cited is the earliest, Hayburn's Case, 2 Dall. 409 (U.S. 1792), although it was not decided by the Supreme Court. (The reporter's notes set forth the views of several lower courts including Justices of the Supreme Court sitting as circuit justices.) The various aspects and complexities of the requirement are considered in HART & WECHSLER, THE FEDERAL COURTS AND THE FEDERAL SYSTEM, c. II (1953).

Congress could, however, probably deny the Supreme Court appellate jurisdiction. See *Ex parte* McCardle, 7 Wall. 506 (U.S. 1869).

44. U.S. CONST. art. II, § 2, cl. 2.

45. For a full discussion see Katz, *Federal Legislative Courts*, 43 HARV. L. REV. 894 (1930). See also Note, *The Restrictive Effect of Article Three on the Organization of Federal Courts*, 34 COLUM. L. REV. 344 (1934); Note, *The Judicial Power of Federal Tribunals Not Organized Under Article Three*, 34 COLUM. L. REV. 746 (1934).

46. *E.g.*, 28 U.S.C. §§ 1541–43 (1952). See *Ex parte* Bakelite Corp., 279 U.S. 438 (1929). Legislative courts to implement various powers of Congress are frequently called "Article I courts," after the article of the Constitution vesting legislative power in Congress. The term "legislative courts" originated apparently in American Ins. Co. v. Canter, 1 Pet. 511 (U.S. 1828).

47. 317 U.S. 1 (1942). See 10 U.S.C. § 821 (Supp. V, 1958).

48. 20 STAT. 131 (1878), repealed, 70 STAT. 774 (1956). See *In re* Ross, 140 U.S. 453 (1891), discussed later and in notes 54 and 62.

49. *E.g.*, 39 STAT. 965 (1917), as amended, 48 U.S.C. § 863 (1952). These courts may be described as "Article IV courts" since Congress derives its power over territories from Article IV, Section 3. *Cf.* Balzac v. Porto Rico, 258 U.S. 298 (1922); Downes v. Bidwell, 182 U.S. 244 (1901). The President as Commander in Chief has established courts in occupied terri-

Notes to VIII: International Tribunals

tory for the trial of crimes committed there even by American citizens. His power to do so without legislative approval was upheld even though Congress had provided for an alternative judicial system, the court-martial. Madsen v. Kinsella, 343 U.S. 341 (1952). There are thus, also, "Article II courts."

The trial of petty offenses appears also to be exempt from the constitutional requirements of Article III. Such offenses were tried by magistrates and police officials even before the adoption of the Constitution, and may apparently be tried before United States commissioners who do not have life tenure and secured compensation within the meaning of Article III. At least some provisions of the Constitution applicable to trials for criminal offenses do not apply to petty offenses, for example, the requirement of a jury trial. *Compare* District of Columbia v. Clawans, 300 U.S. 617 (1937), and Schick v. United States, 195 U.S. 65 (1904), *with* District of Columbia v. Colts, 282 U.S. 63 (1930); see *Ex parte* Quirin, 317 U.S. 1, 39–40 (1942); *cf.* Wong Wing v. United States, 163 U.S. 228 (1895). See Frankfurter and Corcoran, *Petty Federal Offenses and the Constitutional Guaranty of Trial by Jury,* 39 HARV. L. REV. 917 (1926); L. B. Schwartz, *Federal Criminal Jurisdiction and Prosecutors' Discretion,* 13 LAW & CONTEMP. PROB. 64, 81–82 (1948).

50. See Williams v. United States, 289 U.S. 553 (1933).

51. Compare O'Donoghue v. United States, 289 U.S. 516, 536–38 (1933). See also HART & WECHSLER, *op. cit. supra* note 43, at 348–51.

The same argument might also support exemption of international tribunals from the tenure and compensation requirements, as not appropriate to their circumstances. But on this argument these are the only requirements from which they would be exempt, and they would have to meet all the other requirements for United States constitutional courts. To exempt such courts from other requirements on the ground of "inappropriateness" would render the suggestion that they are United States courts virtually meaningless.

52. See Downes v. Bidwell, 182 U.S. 244, 267 (1901); Benner v. Porter, 9 How. 235, 244 (U.S. 1850); American Ins. Co. v. Canter, 1 Pet. 511, 546 (U.S. 1828); *cf.* United States *ex rel.* Toth v. Quarles, 350 U.S. 11 (1955) (discharged serviceman residing in United States may not be tried by court-martial for offense committed during military service); *Ex parte* Milligan, 4 Wall. 2 (U.S. 1866) (military commission may not try citizen in state where federal courts are open). See Katz, *Federal Legislative Courts,* 43 HARV. L. REV. 894, 916–24 (1930). *But cf. Ex parte* Quirin, 317 U.S. 1 (1942), which upheld the power of Congress to provide for trial by military commission in the United States of violations of the law of war, apparently even by United States citizens.

53. Balzac v. Porto Rico, 258 U.S. 298 (1922); *cf.* American Ins. Co. v. Canter, 1 Pet. 511 (U.S. 1828).

The constitutional guarantees apply to criminal trials in the District of Columbia. Callan v. Wilson, 127 U.S. 540 (1888). With regard to United States territories the distinction has been made between territories which are "incorporated" into the United States, where the Constitution applies, *cf., e.g.,* Thompson v. Utah, 170 U.S. 343, 349 (1898), and those which are not, where these rights are not automatically operative, Balzac v. Porto Rico, 258 U.S. 298 (1922); Hawaii v. Mankichi, 190 U.S. 197 (1903); *cf.* Downes v. Bidwell, 182 U.S. 244 (1901). The territories acquired by early conquest from the Indians or by purchase were apparently automatically incorporated. But the treaty with Spain after the war of 1898 expressly provided that there should be no "incorporation," that the rights of the inhabitants should be determined by Congress, and the Supreme Court upheld the provision. *Ibid.*

54. *In re* Ross, 140 U.S. 453 (1891). The consular courts exercised jurisdiction over American civilians for offenses in many "uncivilized" countries under treaties by which these nations granted exclusive jurisdiction to the United States. The history of these courts is given in Justice Frankfurter's concurring opinion in Reid v. Covert, 354 U.S. 2, 41, 56–64 (1957). Their constitutionality was upheld in the *Ross* case, in which their purpose is discussed at length, 140 U.S. at 463. For the current status of the *Ross* case, see note 62 below.

The courts sustained in Madsen v. Kinsella, 343 U.S. 341 (1952), discussed in note 49 above, were also, of course, located outside of the United States.

55. The point is strongly made by Justice Sutherland in United States v. Curtiss-Wright Export Corp., 299 U.S. 304, 316–18 (1936). The Constitution itself expressly bars the states from areas of foreign affairs: "No State shall enter into any Treaty, Alliance, or Confederation." U.S. CONST. art. I, § 10, cl. 1. See also *id.* cl. 3. And see pp. 25–27 above.

56. Drawing in particular on suggestions by Mr. Justice Jackson in the *Tidewater* case below, the argument may be put this way. In Article III the Constitution granted to the federal government judicial power carved out of the judicial powers of the states and limited in regard to parties, subject matter, and the pattern of organization of the federal courts. These limitations were imposed by the states because they did not wish to give up more than was here agreed. The establishment of the federal government, however, entailed the exercise of judicial powers by the United States other than those derived from the states and described, and circumscribed, in Article III. These other judicial powers of the United States stem from the national sovereignty and the various powers accorded to the federal government elsewhere in the Constitution. Such judicial power in implementation of other, national functions of the United States does not derive from the states, is not dealt with in Article III, and is not subject to any of the limitations prescribed or implied in Article III. Indeed, there has been auxiliary judicial power pursuant to each of the other articles of the Constitution conferring governmental powers. Under Article I, for example, there is the Court of Claims whose jurisdiction has included judicial functions. Under his Article II power as Commander in Chief, the President has established courts in conquered areas occupied by the United States which exercise

criminal jurisdiction over United States citizens, surely a judicial function. Madsen v. Kinsella, 343 U.S. 341 (1952). The United States also exercises judicial power in the territories pursuant to Article IV. This judicial power, too, is not derived from the states but is part of the "general right of sovereignty which exists in the government, or in virtue of that clause which enables Congress to make all needful rules and regulations, respecting the territory belonging to the United States." American Ins. Co. v. Canter, 1 Pet. 511, 546 (U.S. 1828). Similarly, judicial power in implementation of the power over foreign affairs would also be a judicial power not derived from the states but one exercised under the "general right of sovereignty" of the federal government in foreign affairs, or under the treaty power.

The Court of Claims would be cited to illustrate this argument. Congress has given it jurisdiction over certain suits against the United States in which the United States was prepared to waive its sovereign immunity. This is judicial power, and for that reason only, judgments of the Court of Claims in such cases are reviewable in the Supreme Court. United States v. Jones, 119 U.S. 477 (1886); *cf.* Gordon v. United States, 2 Wall. 561 (U.S. 1865), 117 U.S. 697 (appendix). However, these functions could not have been within the judicial power of the states, since suits against the federal government had no meaning before it was created by the Constitution. In addition, the Court of Claims has been accorded nonjudicial functions which Congress need not have accorded to a court, and which could not have been accorded to courts established under Article III. Hayburn's Case, 2 Dall. 409 (U.S. 1792). See also Williams v. United States, 289 U.S. 553 (1933).

There has been controversy as to whether the courts of the District of Columbia are established under Article I or Article III. See the various opinions in National Mutual Ins. Co. v. Tidewater Transfer Co., 337 U.S. 582 (1949). But to the extent that these courts partake of the Article III limitations they may be said to do so because the District was created out of two states. In O'Donoghue v. United States, 289 U.S. 516, 535–45 (1933), the Supreme Court distinguished between the District of Columbia and territorial courts on this basis.

57. 140 U.S. 453 (1891).

58. See Wilson v. Girard, 354 U.S. 524 (1957); The Schooner Exchange v. M'Faddon, 7 Cranch 116 (U.S. 1812).

59. Strictly, and historically, "extradition" has meant the rendition of an accused by one nation to another for trial in the receiving nation's courts for crime committed in areas under its jurisdiction; the concept could probably, without constitutional difficulty, be extended to rendition for trial by international tribunal. In the example here assumed, however, the accused would be sent abroad for trial by an international tribunal for a violation of United States law; this would be less like extradition to a different sovereign, and more like a transfer of venue by the United States, looking at the international tribunal as being in the nature of a United States court.

60. 354 U.S. 1 (1957).

61. On the precedent value of decisions where there is no opinion of the

Court, see Comment, *Supreme Court No-Clear-Majority Decisions*, 24 U. CHI. L. REV. 99 (1956).

62. Justice Black (for himself and Chief Justice Warren, Justice Douglas, and Justice Brennan) termed the *Ross* case "a relic from a different era," 354 U.S. 1, 12 (1957), and used other language which suggests that the Constitution might govern almost all acts of the United States overseas. Justice Frankfurter, in his opinion, also emphasized the historical context of the *Ross* case, but said only that the Constitution applied in some situations, leaving precise definition to the future. *Id*. at 41, 64. Justice Harlan found that *In re* Ross did not apply to the case before him but emphasized that the applicability of constitutional requirements for United States action abroad would depend on the "particular circumstances, the practical necessities, and the possible alternatives which Congress had before it," in a future situation. *Id*. at 65, 75. Justices Clark and Burton said that *In re* Ross controlled Reid v. Covert; presumably they would place few specific constitutional limitations on the United States acting abroad.

The opinions leave doubt as to whether the applicability of the Bill of Rights abroad is viewed as an obligation on the United States to all who come within its power, or whether it is considered a right of the United States citizen vis-à-vis the United States. While there is language in Justice Black's opinion implying that the United States can never act outside constitutional limitations, he lays stress on the fact that American citizens are involved in the case before him. For the Justices who take a more limited view of constitutional rights abroad, the citizenship of the claimant might be a critical factor.

Opinions in Reid v. Covert also distinguished the Insular Cases, *e.g.*, Balzac v. Porto Rico, 258 U.S. 298 (1922), and Dorr v. United States, 195 U.S. 138 (1904). In those cases, the Court upheld the power of Congress under Article IV, Section 3, to establish courts in the territories acquired after the Spanish-American War without affording all the protections of the Bill of Rights. Justice Harlan particularly saw in these cases important examples of the impropriety of transferring all constitutional protections outside the United States. Although Justice Black sought to limit their authority, the Insular Cases appear still to have considerable vitality.

Even Justice Black distinguished military occupation of conquered territory, as to which the Court has held that United States occupation courts do not have to observe the Bill of Rights even in regard to United States citizens; Madsen v. Kinsella, 343 U.S. 341 (1952). In that case Justice Black had dissented.

63. See note 58 above.

64. Wong Wing v. United States, 163 U.S. 228 (1896). See Comment, *The Alien and the Constitution*, 20 U. CHI. L. REV. 547, 564–69 (1953).

65. A foreigner becomes subject to United States law even if he is only temporarily in United States territory, Wildenhus's Case, 120 U.S. 1 (1887), but the United States may decline to apply its laws to him. In a recent civil case the Court said: "The exercise of that jurisdiction is not mandatory but

Notes to VIII: International Tribunals

discretionary. Often, because of public policy, or for other reasons, the local sovereign may exert only limited jurisdiction and sometimes none at all." Benz v. Compania Naviera Hidalgo, 353 U.S. 138, 142 (1957).

If the accused is tried by one sovereign and acquitted, he would presumably not be tried again by the other, where they have concurrent jurisdiction. The NATO Status of Forces Agreement, June 19, 1951, art. VII, § 8, 4 U.S. TREATIES 1802, T.I.A.S. No. 2846, provides that the accused having been tried by one of the contracting parties may not be re-tried "for the same offence within the same territory" by another contracting party. (That would accord to an American soldier a right against his own government: the right not to be tried by the United States if he has already been tried by the host country for the same offense.) A dictum in an early piracy case expressed the view that the plea of double jeopardy would be accepted "in any civilized state, though resting on a prosecution instituted in the courts of any other civilized state." United States v. Furlong, 5 Wheat. 184, 197 (U.S. 1820).

66. Under the NATO Status of Forces Agreement, where the receiving state has relinquished primary jurisdiction there is no requirement that the sending state try the accused in the receiving country. And it has been suggested in this context that where trial by court-martial is not constitutionally permissible the United States district courts may be given jurisdiction to try Americans for offenses committed abroad. United States *ex rel.* Toth v. Quarles, 350 U.S. 11, 21 (1955).

67. The NATO Status of Forces Agreement requires sending and receiving states to assist each other in arresting offenders and handing them over for trial. The Service Courts of Friendly Foreign Forces Act, 58 STAT. 643 (1944), 22 U.S.C. § 702 (1952), authorized United States military officials to arrest offending visiting troops in the United States upon request of the commanding officer of the visiting force.

68. Thus, Congress has provided: "Whoever, on the high seas, commits the crime of piracy as defined by the law of nations and is afterwards brought into or found in the United States, shall be imprisoned for life." 18 U.S.C. § 1651 (1952). The application of earlier similar provisions even to noncitizens has been upheld in many cases, *e.g.,* United States v. Furlong, 5 Wheat. 184, 203 (U.S. 1820). See also United States v. Klintock, 5 Wheat. 144, 152 (U.S. 1820) (dictum), where Chief Justice Marshall said: "General piracy, or murder, or robbery, committed [on the high seas], by persons on board of a vessel, not at the time belonging to the subjects of any foreign power, but in possession of a crew acting in defiance of all law, and acknowledging obedience to no government whatever . . . is punishable in the courts of the United States. Persons of this description are proper objects for the penal code of all nations; and we think that the general words of the act of congress applying to all persons whatsoever, though they ought not to be so construed as to extend to persons under the acknowledged authority of a foreign state, ought to be so construed as to comprehend those who acknowledge the authority of no state. Those general terms ought not to

be applied to offences committed against the particular sovereignty of a foreign power; but we think they ought to be applied to offences committed against all nations, including the United States, by persons who by common consent are equally amenable to the laws of all nations."

See also 18 U.S.C. § 1653 (1952).

69. The Supreme Court was asked to review on habeas corpus the constitutionality of the trial of several Japanese for "war crimes" by an international commission which the Allied military commander, who was also United States commander, had established on behalf of the Allied Powers. In a brief *per curiam* opinion the Court ruled that it lacked jurisdiction to review the decision of the international tribunal because it was not a "tribunal of the United States." Justice Douglas concurred in the result on the ground that the agreement to try these particular defendants was a political decision of the President as Commander in Chief not subject to judicial scrutiny. He said, however, that in some instances prisoners held by American officials for trial by an international tribunal might challenge the validity of their detention on habeas corpus even though this would involve an indirect challenge to the validity of the tribunal's judgment. Hirota v. MacArthur, 338 U.S. 197 (1949).

70. The legislature of New York State authorized the governor to cede jurisdiction over the territory of the United Nations headquarters to the United States, presumably in the expectation that the United States might in turn cede jurisdiction to the United Nations. N.Y. STATE LAW § 59-*l*. Neither the governor nor the United States has to date executed such cession, except perhaps to the extent that some cession by the United States may be involved in the provisions of the Headquarters Agreement.

71. 61 STAT. 3416 (1947), T.I.A.S. No. 1676.

CASES CITED

Abrey v. Reusch, 153 F. Supp. 337 (S.D.N.Y. 1957): p. 235 (c. VII, n. 46)
Adair v. Traco Division, 192 Ga. 59, 14 S.E.2d 466 (1941): p. 222 (c. VI, n. 11)
Adams v. Maryland, 347 U.S. 179 (1954): pp. 194 (c. IV, n. 41), 237 (c. VIII, n. 10)
Adamson v. California, 332 U.S. 46 (1947): pp. 193 (c. IV, n. 38), 195 (c. IV, n. 48), 202 (c. IV, n. 88), 237 (c. VIII, n. 14)
Agnello v. United States, 269 U.S. 20 (1925): p. 200 (c. IV, n. 75)
Aircraft & Diesel Equipment Co. v. Hirsch, 331 U.S. 752 (1947): p. 234 (c. VII, n. 39)
Aktiebolaget Bofors v. United States, 194 F.2d 145 (D.C. Cir. 1951): p. 219 (c. V, n. 55)
Alstate Constr. Co. v. Durkin, 345 U.S. 13 (1953): p. 200 (c. IV, n. 77)
American and European Agencies, Inc. v. Gilliland, 247 F.2d 95 (D.C. Cir.), *cert. denied,* 355 U.S. 884 (1957): p. 231 (c. VII, n. 20)
American Ins. Co. v. Canter, 1 Pet. 511 (U.S. 1828): pp. 242 (c. VIII, n. 46), 243 (c. VIII, nn. 52, 53), 245 (c. VIII, n. 56)
American Ry. Express Co. v. Levee, 263 U.S. 19 (1923): p. 223 (c. VI, n. 12)
American School of Magnetic Healing v. McAnnulty, 187 U.S. 94 (1902): p. 234 (c. VII, n. 39)
Antelope, The, 10 Wheat. 66 (U.S. 1825): p. 221 (c. VI, n. 10)
Asakura v. Seattle, 265 U.S. 332 (1924): pp. 173 (c. III, n. 15), 177 (c. III, n. 28)

In re Baiz, 135 U.S. 403 (1890): p. 214 (c. V, n. 27)
Ex parte Bakelite Corp., 279 U.S. 438 (1929): pp. 236 (c. VIII, n. 3), 238 (c. VIII, n. 18), 242 (c. VIII, n. 46)
Balzac v. Porto Rico, 258 U.S. 298 (1922): pp. 242 (c. VIII, n. 49), 243 (c. VIII, n. 53), 246 (c. VIII, n. 62)
Barron v. Baltimore, 7 Pet. 243 (U.S. 1833): p. 237 (c. VIII, n. 14)
Baxter v. United States, 188 F.2d 119 (6th Cir. 1951): p. 204 (c. IV, n. 91)
Beauharnais v. Illinois, 343 U.S. 250 (1952): p. 179 (c. III, n. 44)
Bell v. Hood, 327 U.S. 678 (1946): p. 204 (c. IV, n. 91)
Bell v. Hood, 71 F. Supp. 813 (S.D. Cal. 1947): p. 204 (c. IV, n. 91)
Benanti v. United States, 355 U.S. 96 (1957): p. 189 (c. IV, n. 12)
Benner v. Porter, 9 How. 235 (U.S. 1850): p. 243 (c. VIII, n. 52)

Benz v. Compania Naviera Hidalgo, 353 U.S. 138 (1957): p. 247 (c. VIII, n. 65)
Best v. United States, 184 F.2d 131 (1st Cir. 1950), *cert. denied,* 340 U.S. 939 (1951): p. 200 (c. IV, n. 76)
Bethlehem Steel Co. v. New York State Labor Relations Bd., 330 U.S. 767 (1947): p. 224 (c. VI, n. 16)
Betsey, The, 3 Dall. 6 (U.S. 1794): pp. 236–37 (c. VIII, n. 6)
Bolling v. Sharpe, 347 U.S. 497 (1954): p. 190 (c. IV, n. 16)
Boyd v. United States, 116 U.S. 616 (1886): pp. 202 (c. IV, n. 87), 203 (c. IV, n. 89)
Braniff Airways v. Nebraska State Bd., 347 U.S. 590 (1954): p. 188 (c. IV, n. 8)
Brewer v. Lichtenstein, 278 Fed. 512 (7th Cir. 1922): p. 185 (c. III, n. 76)
Brinegar v. United States, 338 U.S. 160 (1949): pp. 196 (c. IV, n. 51), 204 (c. IV, n. 91)
Brinkerhoff–Faris Trust & Savings Co. v. Hill, 281 U.S. 673 (1930): p. 235 (c. VII, n. 42)
Brown v. Mississippi, 297 U.S. 278 (1936): p. 194 (c. IV, n. 42)
Brown v. United States, 276 U.S. 134 (1928): p. 197 (c. IV, n. 60)
Brown v. Walker, 161 U.S. 591 (1896): p. 193 (c. IV, nn. 36, 39)
Brownell v. Union & New Haven Trust Co., 143 Conn. 662, 124 A.2d 901 (1956): p. 222 (c. VI, n. 11)
Buchanan v. United States, 24 Ct. Cl. 74 (1889): p. 230 (c. VII, n. 20)
Burton v. United States, 202 U.S. 344 (1906): p. 191 (c. IV, n. 30)
Butler v. Michigan, 352 U.S. 380 (1957): p. 180 (c. III, n. 49)
Buttfield v. Stranahan, 192 U.S. 470 (1904): p. 182 (c. III, n. 60)
Byars v. United States, 273 U.S. 28 (1927): p. 223 (c. VI, n. 13)

California v. Taylor, 353 U.S. 553 (1957): p. 178 (c. III, n. 39)
California Reduction Co. v. Sanitary Reduction Works, 199 U.S. 306 (1905): p. 200 (c. IV, n. 74)
Callan v. Wilson, 127 U.S. 540 (1888): pp. 241 (c. VIII, n. 40), 243 (c. VIII, n. 53)
Carroll v. United States, 267 U.S. 132 (1925): p. 196 (c. IV, n. 51)
Carter v. Carter Coal Co., 298 U.S. 238 (1936): p. 233 (c. VII, nn. 30, 33)
Case v. Bowles, 327 U.S. 92 (1946): p. 178 (c. III, n. 42)
Cases v. United States, 131 F.2d 916 (1st Cir. 1942), *cert. denied,* 319 U.S. 770 (1943): pp. 180 (c. III, n. 46), 182 (c. III, n. 63)
In re Chapman, 166 U.S. 661 (1897): p. 191 (c. IV, n. 30)
Charlton v. Kelly, 229 U.S. 447 (1913): p. 239 (c. VIII, n. 24)
Cherokee Tobacco, The, 11 Wall. 616 (U.S. 1871): pp. 172 (c. III, n. 15), 174 (c. III, n. 21)
Chicago, M. & St. P. Ry. v. Minnesota, 134 U.S. 418 (1890): p. 235 (c. VII, n. 41)
Chinese Exclusion Case, 130 U.S. 581 (1889): pp. 168 (c. III, n. 5), 174 (c. III, nn. 20, 21), 183 (c. III, n. 67), 240 (c. VIII, n. 29)

Cases Cited

Cincinnati v. Vester, 281 U.S. 439 (1930): p. 184 (c. III, n. 69)
Cities Serv. Co. v. McGrath, 342 U.S. 330 (1950): pp. 181 (c. III, n. 51), 182 (c. III, n. 53), 184 (c. III, n. 68)
Claflin v. Housman, 93 U.S. 130 (1876): p. 222 (c. VI, n. 11)
Clark v. Allen, 331 U.S. 503 (1947): p. 172 (c. III, n. 14(*c*))
Cleveland v. Piskura, 145 Ohio St. 144, 60 N.E.2d 919 (1945): p. 225 (c. VI, n. 18)
Colegrove v. Green, 328 U.S. 549 (1946): pp. 205 (c. IV, n. 93), 235 (c. VII, n. 47)
Collins v. Miller, 252 U.S. 364 (1920): p. 237 (c. VIII, n. 15)
Comegys v. Vasse, 1 Pet. 193 (U.S. 1828): p. 230 (c. VII, n. 19)
Connecticut Gen. Life Ins. Co. v. Johnson, 303 U.S. 77 (1938): p. 181 (c. III, n. 50)
Cook v. United States, 288 U.S. 102 (1933): p. 174 (c. III, n. 21)
Coplon v. United States, 191 F.2d 749 (D.C. Cir. 1951), *cert. denied*, 342 U.S. 926 (1952): p. 189 (c. IV, n. 12)
Counselman v. Hitchcock, 142 U.S. 547 (1892): p. 193 (c. IV, n. 36)
Covington and Lexington Turnpike Road Co. v. Sandford, 164 U.S. 578 (1896): p. 181 (c. III, n. 50)
Crooker v. California, 78 S. Ct. 1287, 357 U.S. 433 (1958): p. 194 (c. IV, n. 44)
Crowell v. Benson, 285 U.S. 22 (1932): pp. 231 (c. VII, n. 24), 234 (c. VII, n. 40), 241 (c. VIII, n. 40)
Curcio v. United States, 354 U.S. 118 (1957): p. 192 (c. IV, n. 32)
Curran v. City of New York, 191 Misc. 229, 77 N.Y.S.2d 206 (Sup. Ct. 1947), *aff'd*, 275 App. Div. 784, 88 N.Y.S.2d 924 (2d Dep't 1949): pp. 204 (c. IV, n. 93), 211 (c. V, n. 22)
Currin v. Wallace, 306 U.S. 1 (1939): p. 233 (c. VII, n. 33)

Davis v. United States, 328 U.S. 582 (1946): pp. 192 (c. IV, n. 32), 196 (c. IV, n. 51)
Davis v. Wechsler, 263 U.S. 22 (1923): p. 223 (c. VI, n. 12)
Davison v. Champlin, 7 Conn. 244 (1828): p. 221 (c. VI, no. 10)
Day-Brite Lighting, Inc., v. Missouri, 342 U.S. 421 (1952): p. 180 (c. III, n. 49)
Dayton v. Gillilland, 242 F.2d 227 (D.C. Cir.), *cert. denied*, 355 U.S. 813 (1957): p. 231 (c. VII, n. 20)
Dederick v. Smith, 88 N.H. 63, 184 Atl. 595, *appeal dismissed*, 299 U.S. 506 (1936): pp. 198 (c. IV, n. 66), 199 (c. IV, nn. 72, 73)
Desper v. Warner Holding Co., 219 Minn. 607, 19 N.W.2d 62 (1945): p. 222 (c. VI, n. 11)
De Vegvar v. Gillilland, 228 F.2d 640 (D.C. Cir. 1955), *cert. denied*, 350 U.S. 994 (1956): p. 231 (c. VII, n. 20)
Dice v. Akron, C. & Y.R.R., 342 U.S. 359 (1952): pp. 222–23 (c. VI, n. 12)
In re Dillon, 7 Fed. Cas. 710, No. 3914 (N.D. Cal. 1854): p. 204 (c. IV, n. 93)

District of Columbia v. Clawans, 300 U.S. 617 (1937): p. 243 (c. VIII, n. 49)
District of Columbia v. Colts, 282 U.S. 63 (1930): p. 243 (c. VIII, n. 49)
District of Columbia v. Little, 339 U.S. 1 (1950): pp. 71, 72, 80, 199 (c. IV, n. 72)
District of Columbia v. Little, 178 F.2d 13 (D.C. Cir. 1949): pp. 71, 72, 80, 199 (c. IV, nn. 71, 73)
Doe v. Braden, 16 How. 635 (U.S. 1853): p. 172 (c. III, n. 15)
Dorr v. United States, 195 U.S. 138 (1904): p. 246 (c. VIII, n. 62)
Downes v. Bidwell, 182 U.S. 244 (1901): pp. 242 (c. VIII, n. 49), 243 (c. VIII, n. 52), 244 (c. VIII, n. 53)

Ely v. Peck, 7 Conn. 239 (1828): p. 221 (c. VI, n. 10)
Entick v. Carrington, 19 How. St. Tr. 1030, 95 Eng. Rep. 807 (K.B. 1765): p. 203 (c. IV, n. 89)
Erie R.R. v. Hamilton, 248 U.S. 369 (1919): p. 173 (c. III, n. 17)
Estep v. United States, 327 U.S. 114 (1946): p. 236 (c. VII, n. 51)

Farmer v. Rountree, 149 F. Supp. 327 (M.D. Tenn. 1956), *aff'd,* 252 F.2d 490 (6th Cir. 1958): p. 232 (c. VII, n. 27)
Federal Housing Administration v. Burr, 309 U.S. 242 (1940): p. 213 (c. V, n. 27)
Federal Power Comm'n v. Hope Natural Gas Co., 320 U.S. 591 (1944): p. 234 (c. VII, n. 41)
Federal Power Comm'n v. Natural Gas Pipeline Co., 315 U.S. 575 (1942): p. 235 (c. VII, n. 41)
Feldman v. United States, 322 U.S. 487 (1944): p. 193 (c. IV, n. 38)
Fleming v. Rhodes, 331 U.S. 100 (1947): p. 182 (c. III, n. 65)
Fong Yue Ting v. United States, 149 U.S. 698 (1893): p. 232 (c. VII, n. 25)
Fort Leavenworth R.R. v. Lowe, 114 U.S. 525 (1885): p. 177 (c. III, n. 30)
Foster v. Neilson, 2 Pet. 253 (U.S. 1829): pp. 172 (c. III, n. 14(*c*)), 173 (c. III, n. 19), 205 (c. IV, n. 93), 235 (c. VII, n. 47)
Frelinghuysen v. Key, 110 U.S. 63 (1884): p. 231 (c. VII, n. 21)
Frost & Frost Trucking Co. v. Railroad Comm'n, 271 U.S. 583 (1926): p. 233 (c. VII, n. 34)
FTC v. American Tobacco Co., 264 U.S. 298 (1924): p. 197 (c. IV, nn. 53, 60)
Fulmer v. United States, 83 F. Supp. 137 (N.D. Ala. 1949): p. 219 (c. V, n. 55)

Gegiow v. Uhl, 239 U.S. 3 (1915): p. 235 (c. VII, n. 43)
Geofroy v. Riggs, 133 U.S. 258 (1890): pp. 27, 168 (c. III, n. 8), 172 (c. III, n. 15), 177 (c. III, n. 30)

Cases Cited

Georgia v. Brailsford, 3 Dall. 1 (U.S. 1794): p. 177 (c. III, n. 27)
Gibbons v. Ogden, 9 Wheat. 1 (U.S. 1824): pp. 168 (c. III, n. 3), 188 (c. IV, n. 8)
Giordenello v. United States, 357 U.S. 480 (1958): p. 200 (c. IV, n. 75)
Givner v. State, 210 Md. 484, 124 A.2d 764 (1956): p. 199 (c. IV, nn. 71, 73)
Go-Bart Importing Co. v. United States, 282 U.S. 344 (1931): pp. 200 (c. IV, n. 75), 237 (c. VIII, n. 15)
Gompers v. Bucks Stove & Range Co., 221 U.S. 418 (1911): p. 238 (c. VIII, n. 19)
Gonzales v. Williams, 192 U.S. 1 (1904): p. 235 (c. VII, n. 43)
Gordon v. United States, 2 Wall. 561 (U.S. 1865), 117 U.S. 697 (appendix): pp. 241 (c. VIII, n. 41), 245 (c. VIII, n. 56)
Gray v. United States, 21 Ct. Cl. 340 (1886): p. 230 (c. VII, n. 20)
Green v. United States, 356 U.S. 165 (1958): p. 238 (c. VIII, n. 19)
Green v. United States, 355 U.S. 184 (1957): p. 242 (c. VIII, n. 42)
In re Groban, 352 U.S. 330 (1957): pp. 64, 194 (c. IV, nn. 43, 44, 46, 47), 199 (c. IV, n. 72)
Grosjean v. American Press Co., 297 U.S. 233 (1936): p. 181 (c. III, n. 50)
Grunewald v. United States, 353 U.S. 391 (1957): p. 193 (c. IV, n. 37)
Guss v. Utah Labor Relations Board, 353 U.S. 1 (1957): p. 224 (c. VI, n. 16)

Haas v. Humphrey, 246 F.2d 682 (D.C. Cir.), *cert. denied,* 355 U.S. 854 (1957): p. 231 (c. VII, n. 20)
Hadacheck v. Sebastian, 239 U.S. 394 (1915): p. 182 (c. III, n. 56)
Hale v. Henkel, 201 U.S. 43 (1906): p. 192 (c. IV, n. 32)
Hannevig v. United States, 84 F. Supp. 743 (Ct. Cl. 1949): p. 174 (c. III, n. 21)
Harris v. United States, 331 U.S. 145 (1947): p. 200 (c. IV, n. 75)
Hauenstein v. Lynham, 100 U.S. 483 (1880): p. 177 (c. III, n. 28)
Hawaii v. Mankichi, 190 U.S. 197 (1903): p. 244 (c. VIII, n. 53)
Hayburn's Case, 2 Dall. 409 (U.S. 1792): pp. 236 (c. VIII, n. 3), 242 (c. VIII, n. 43), 245 (c. VIII, n. 56)
Head Money Cases, 112 U.S. 580 (1884): p. 174 (c. III, n. 21)
Hester v. United States, 265 U.S. 57 (1924): p. 196 (c. IV, n. 51)
Hirota v. MacArthur, 338 U.S. 197 (1948): pp. 232 (c. VII, n. 26), 235 (c. VII, n. 47), 236 (c. VIII, n. 2), 248 (c. VIII, n. 69)
Holden v. Joy, 17 Wall. 211 (U.S. 1872): p. 172 (c. III, n. 15)
Holmes v. Jennison, 14 Pet. 540 (U.S. 1840): p. 168 (c. III, n. 3)
Home Building & Loan Ass'n v. Blaisdell, 290 U.S. 398 (1934): p. 168 (c. III, n. 7)
Houston v. Moore, 5 Wheat. 1 (U.S. 1820): p. 221 (c. VI, n. 10)
Huntington v. Attrill, 146 U.S. 657 (1892): p. 221 (c. VI, n. 10)
Hurd v. Hodge, 334 U.S. 24 (1948): p. 190 (c. IV, n. 16)
Hurley v. Kincaid, 285 U.S. 95 (1932): p. 184 (c. III, n. 68)

Irvine v. California, 347 U.S. 128 (1954): p. 193 (c. IV, n. 38)

Jack v. Kansas, 199 U.S. 372 (1905): p. 193 (c. IV, n. 38)
Jay v. Boyd, 351 U.S. 345 (1956): p. 234 (c. VII, n. 37)
Johnson v. United States, 333 U.S. 10 (1948): p. 200 (c. IV, n. 75)
Joint Anti-Fascist Refugee Comm. v. McGrath, 341 U.S. 123 (1951): pp. 179 (c. III, n. 44), 218 (c. V, n. 48)
Jones v. United States, 357 U.S. 493 (1958): p. 200 (c. IV, n. 75)

Kawanakoa v. Polyblank, 205 U.S. 349 (1907): p. 204 (c. IV, n. 93)
Keeney v. United States, 218 F.2d 843 (D.C. Cir. 1954): pp. 204 (c. IV, n. 93), 213 (c. V, n. 27)
Kentucky v. Dennison, 24 How. 66 (U.S. 1861): pp. 193 (c. IV, n. 35), 223 (c. VI, n. 15)
Kepner v. United States, 195 U.S. 100 (1904): p. 242 (c. VIII, n. 42)
Kilbourn v. Thompson, 103 U.S. 168 (1881): p. 191 (c. IV, n. 30)
Knapp v. Schweitzer, 357 U.S. 371 (1958): p. 193 (c. IV, n. 38)
Koenigin Luise, The, 184 Fed. 170 (D.N.J. 1910): p. 236 (c. VIII, n. 6)
Kovacs v. Cooper, 336 U.S. 77 (1949): p. 181 (c. III, n. 49)

La Abra Silver Mining Co. v. United States, 175 U.S. 423 (1899): p. 231 (c. VII, n. 21)
Larson v. Domestic & Foreign Commerce Corp., 337 U.S. 682 (1949): pp. 204 (c. IV, n. 93), 213 (c. V, n. 27), 235 (c. VII, n. 48)
Lawton v. Steele, 152 U.S. 133 (1894): p. 182 (c. III, n. 54)
Lee v. Humphrey, 352 U.S. 904 (1956): p. 232 (c. VII, n. 27)
Lee v. United States, 343 U.S. 747 (1952): p. 196 (c. IV, n. 51)
Legal Tender Cases, 12 Wall. 457 (U.S. 1871): pp. 168 (c. III, n. 5), 182 (c. III, n. 64), 184 (c. III, n. 70)
LeRoy Fibre Co. v. Chicago, M. & St. P. Ry., 232 U.S. 340 (1914): p. 194 (c. IV, n. 93)
Leser v. Garnett, 258 U.S. 130 (1922): p. 168 (c. III, n. 1)
Lester v. Parker, 235 F.2d 787 (9th Cir. 1956): p. 234 (c. VII, n. 39)
Lichter v. United States, 334 U.S. 742 (1948): p. 233 (c. VII, n. 32)
Long v. Ansell, 293 U.S. 76 (1934): p. 191 (c. IV, n. 30)
Lottery Case, 188 U.S. 321 (1903): p. 180 (c. III, n. 47)
Lustig v. United States, 338 U.S. 74 (1949): p. 223 (c. VI, n. 13)

Ex parte McCardle, 7 Wall. 506 (U.S. 1869): p. 242 (c. VIII, n. 43)
McCarthy v. Arndstein, 266 U.S. 34 (1924): p. 193 (c. IV, n. 36)
McCulloch v. Maryland, 4 Wheat. 316 (U.S. 1819): p. 168 (c. III, n. 7)
McDonald v. United States, 335 U.S. 451 (1948): p. 200 (c. IV, n. 75)
McGrain v. Daugherty, 273 U.S. 135 (1927): p. 237 (c. VIII, nn. 10, 18)
McGrath v. Cities Serv. Co., 189 F.2d 744 (2d Cir. 1951): p. 184 (c. III, n. 68)
MacKenzie v. Hare, 239 U.S. 299 (1915): p. 232 (c. VII, n. 25)

Cases Cited 255

McKnett v. St. Louis & S.F. Ry., 292 U.S. 230 (1934): p. 222 (c. VI, n. 11)
Madsen v. Kinsella, 343 U.S. 341 (1952): pp. 243 (c. VIII, n. 49), 244 (c. VIII, n. 54), 245 (c. VIII, n. 56), 246 (c. VIII, n. 62)
Marron v. United States, 275 U.S. 192 (1927): p. 200 (c. IV, n. 75)
Martin v. Hunter's Lessee, 1 Wheat. 304 (U.S. 1816): pp. 221 (c. VI, n. 10), 224 (c. VI, n. 15), 241 (c. VIII, n. 37)
Massachusetts v. Mellon, 262 U.S. 447 (1923): p. 232 (c. VII, n. 27)
Meade v. United States, 9 Wall. 691 (U.S. 1870): p. 230 (c. VII, nn. 19, 20)
Methodist Federation for Social Action v. Eastland, 141 F. Supp. 729 (D.D.C. 1956): pp. 191–92 (c. IV, n. 30)
Meyer v. Nebraska, 262 U.S. 390 (1923): p. 186 (c. III, n. 78)
Michaelson v. United States *ex rel.* Chicago, St. P.,M. & O. Ry., 266 U.S. 42 (1924): p. 238 (c. VIII, n. 19)
Miles v. Illinois Cent. R.R., 315 U.S. 698 (1942): p. 222 (c. VI, n. 11)
Miller v. Schoene, 276 U.S. 272 (1928): p. 182 (c. III, n. 55)
Miller v. United States, 357 U.S. 301 (1958): pp. 200 (c. IV, n. 75), 203 (c. IV, n. 89)
Ex parte Milligan, 4 Wall. 2 (U.S. 1866): pp. 241 (c. VIII, n. 36), 243 (c. VIII, n. 52)
Minneapolis & St. L.R.R. v. Bombolis, 241 U.S. 211 (1916): p. 222 (c. VI, n. 12)
Minnesota v. United States, 305 U.S. 382 (1939): p. 235 (c. VII, n. 49)
Mississippi v. Johnson, 4 Wall. 475 (U.S. 1868): p. 186 (c. IV, n. 1)
Missouri *ex rel.* Camden County v. Union Elec. Light & Power Co., 42 F.2d 692 (W.D. Mo. 1930): p. 178 (c. III, n. 41)
Missouri v. Holland, 252 U.S. 416 (1920): pp. 29, 33, 168 (c. III, n. 7), 170 (c. III, n. 14(*a*)), 176 (c. III, n. 25), 177 (c. III, nn. 26, 29), 241 (c. VIII, nn. 32, 33)
Mondou v. New York, N.H. & H.R.R., 223 U.S. 1 (1912): p. 241 (c. VIII, n. 39)
Morey v. Doud, 354 U.S. 457 (1957): p. 180 (c. III, n. 49)
Morgan v. United States, 304 U.S. 1 (1938): p. 234 (c. VII, n. 36)
Morgan v. United States, 298 U.S. 468 (1936): p. 234 (c. VII, n. 39)
Moser v. United States, 341 U.S. 41 (1951): p. 174 (c. III, n. 21)
Moyer v. Brownell, 137 F. Supp. 594 (E.D. Pa. 1956): p. 192 (c. IV, n. 31)
Mugler v. Kansas, 123 U.S. 623 (1887): p. 182 (c. III, n. 59)
Mulford v. Smith, 307 U.S. 38 (1939): pp. 182 (c. III, n. 65), 233 (c. VII, n. 34)
Myers v. Bethlehem Shipbuilding Corp., 303 U.S. 41 (1938): p. 234 (c. VII, n. 39)

Nardone v. United States, 308 U.S. 338 (1939): p. 189 (c. IV, n. 12)
Nardone v. United States, 302 U.S. 379 (1937): p. 189 (c. IV, n. 12)
National Automatic Device Co. v. Lloyd, 40 Fed. 89 (C.C.N.D. Ill. 1889): p. 185 (c. III, n. 76)

National Broadcasting Co. v. United States, 319 U.S. 190 (1943): p. 234 (c. VII, n. 41)
National City Bank v. Republic of China, 348 U.S. 356 (1955): pp. 205 (c. IV, n. 93), 213 (c. V, n. 27)
National Mut. Ins. Co. v. Tidewater Transfer Co., 337 U.S. 582 (1949): pp. 236 (c. VIII, n. 3), 244–45 (c. VIII, n. 56)
National Prohibition Cases, 253 U.S. 350 (1920): p. 168 (c. III, n. 1)
Nebbia v. New York, 291 U.S. 502 (1934): pp. 39, 180 (c. III, n. 47)
Neck, The, 138 Fed. 144 (W.D. Wash. 1905): p. 236 (c. VIII, n. 6)
Nereide, The, 9 Cranch 388 (U.S. 1815): p. 240 (c. VIII, n. 30)
New Orleans v. United States, 10 Pet. 662 (U.S. 1836): p. 173 (c. III, n. 15)
New York v. United States, 326 U.S. 572 (1946): p. 178 (c. III, nn. 38, 41)
Ng Fung Ho v. White, 259 U.S. 276 (1922): p. 241 (c. VIII, n. 40)
NLRB v. Jones & Laughlin Steel Corp., 301 U.S. 1 (1937): pp. 183 (c. III, n. 67), 200 (c. IV, n. 77)
North American Cold Storage Co. v. Chicago, 211 U.S. 306 (1908): p. 182 (c. III, n. 54)

Ocampo v. United States, 234 U.S. 91 (1914): p. 237 (c. VIII, n. 15)
O'Donoghue v. United States, 289 U.S. 516 (1933): pp. 243 (c. VIII, n. 51), 245 (c. VIII, n. 56)
Oetjen v. Central Leather Co., 246 U.S. 297 (1918): pp. 205 (c. IV, n. 93), 235 (c. VII, n. 47)
Oklahoma Operating Co. v. Love, 252 U.S. 331 (1920): p. 235 (c. VII, n. 42)
Oklahoma Press Publishing Co. v. Walling, 327 U.S. 186 (1946): pp. 192 (c. IV, n. 32), 196 (c. IV, n. 51), 197 (c. IV, nn. 53, 60), 237 (c. VIII, nn. 11, 18)
Old Dominion Land Co. v. United States, 269 U.S. 55 (1925): p. 232 (c. VII, n. 27)
Olmstead v. United States, 277 U.S. 438 (1928): pp. 189 (c. IV, nn. 11, 13), 202 (c. IV, nn. 87, 89)
Olson v. United States, 292 U.S. 246 (1934): p. 228 (c. VII, n. 13)
Omnia Commercial Co. v. United States, 261 U.S. 502 (1923): p. 184 (c. III, n. 70)
On Lee v. United States, 343 U.S. 747 (1952): p. 189 (c. IV, n. 11)
Orloff v. Willoughby, 345 U.S. 83 (1953): p. 190 (c. IV, n. 19)

Palko v. Connecticut, 302 U.S. 319 (1937): pp. 193 (c. IV, n. 38), 202 (c. IV, n. 88), 242 (c. VIII, n. 42)
Panama Refining Co. v. Ryan, 293 U.S. 388 (1935): pp. 231 (c. VII, n. 24), 233 (c. VII, n. 30)
Paquete Habana, The, 175 U.S. 677 (1900): p. 24 (c. VIII, n. 30)
Parker v. Lester, 227 F.2d 708 (9th Cir. 1955): p. 234 (c. VII, n. 39)

Cases Cited

Payne v. Arkansas, 356 U.S. 560 (1958): p. 194 (c. IV, n. 42)
Peabody v. United States, 231 U.S. 530 (1913): p. 184 (c. III, n. 70)
Penhallow v. Doane's Administrators, 3 Dall. 54 (U.S. 1795): p. 168 (c. III, n. 4)
Pennsylvania Coal Co. v. Mahon, 260 U.S. 393 (1922): p. 185 (c. III, n. 70)
People v. Brown, 253 Mich. 537, 235 N.W. 245 (1931): pp. 177–78 (c. III, n. 34)
People v. Defore, 242 N.Y. 13, 150 N.E. 585 (1926): p. 203 (c. IV, n. 89)
People v. Mailman, 293 N.Y. 887, 59 N.E.2d 790, *affirming* 182 Misc. 870, 49 N.Y.S.2d 733 (App. Part, Sp. Sess. 1944): pp. 224–25 (c. VI, n. 18)
People v. Sell, 310 Mich. 305, 17 N.W.2d 193 (1945): p. 224 (c. VI, n. 18)
Perez v. Brownell, 356 U.S. 44 (1958): pp. 168 (c. III, n. 5), 183 (c. III, n. 67), 232 (c. VII, n. 25)
Perkins v. Elg, 307 U.S. 325 (1939): p. 170 (c. III, n. 14(*a*))
Pfitzinger v. United States Civil Serv. Comm'n, 96 F. Supp. 1 (D.N.J.), *aff'd*, 192 F.2d 934 (3d Cir. 1951): p. 192 (c. IV, n. 31)
Powell v. Pennsylvania, 127 U.S. 678 (1888): p. 182 (c. III, n. 58)
Prigg v. Pennsylvania, 16 Pet. 539 (U.S. 1842): pp. 221 (c. VI, n. 10), 223 (c. VI, n. 15)

Quinn v. United States, 349 U.S. 155 (1955): p. 195 (c. IV, n. 48)
Ex parte Quirin, 317 U.S. 1 (1942): pp. 139, 141, 238 (c. VIII, n. 21), 243 (c. VIII, nn. 49, 52)

Railway Express Agency, Inc. v. New York, 336 U.S. 106 (1949): p. 190 (c. IV, n. 16)
Regan v. New York, 349 U.S. 58 (1955): p. 193 (c. IV, n. 39)
Reid v. Covert, 354 U.S. 1 (1957): pp. 29, 145, 148, 170 (c. III, n. 14(*a*)), 173 (c. III, nn. 16, 17), 179 (c. III, n. 44), 244 (c. VIII, n. 54), 245 (c. VIII, n. 60), 246 (c. VIII, n. 62)
Reinman v. Little Rock, 237 U.S. 171 (1915): p. 182 (c. III, n. 57)
Republic of Mexico v. Hoffman, 324 U.S. 30 (1945): p. 205 (c. IV, n. 93)
Ex parte Republic of Peru, 318 U.S. 578 (1943): p. 205 (c. IV, n. 93)
Respublica v. De Longchamps, 1 Dall. 111 (Pa. O. & T. 1784): p. 240 (c. VIII, n. 30)
Rice v. Ames, 180 U.S. 371 (1901): p. 237 (c. VIII, n. 15)
Rickard v. Du Bon, 103 Fed. 868 (2d Cir. 1900): p. 185 (c. III, n. 76)
Robertson v. Baldwin, 165 U.S. 275 (1897): pp. 237 (c. VIII, n. 15), 241 (c. VIII, n. 37)
Rochin v. California, 342 U.S. 165 (1952): pp. 193 (c. IV, n. 38), 196 (c. IV, n. 52)
Rogers v. United States, 340 U.S. 367 (1951): p. 195 (c. IV, n. 48)

In re Ross, 140 U.S. 453 (1891): pp. 144, 145, 148, 151, 242 (c. VIII, n. 48), 244 (c. VIII, n. 54), 245 (c. VIII, n. 57), 246 (c. VIII, n. 62)

St. Joseph Stockyards Co. v. United States, 298 U.S. 38 (1936): pp. 231 (c. VII, n. 24), 234 (c. VII, n. 40)
St. Louis v. Western Union Tel. Co., 148 U.S. 92 (1893): p. 178 (c. III, n. 41)
Salata v. United States, 286 Fed. 125 (6th Cir. 1923): p. 223 (c. VI, n. 13)
Sandlin v. Johnson, 141 F.2d 660 (8th Cir. 1944): p. 218 (c. V, n. 49)
Santa Clara County v. Southern Pac. R.R., 118 U.S. 394 (1886): p. 181 (c. III, n. 50)
Schechter Poultry Co. v. United States, 295 U.S. 495 (1935): p. 233 (c. VII, n. 30)
Schick v. United States, 195 U.S. 65 (1904): p. 243 (c. VIII, n. 49)
Schooner Exchange, The, v. M'Faddon, 7 Cranch 116 (U.S. 1812): p. 245 (c. VIII, n. 58)
Schultze v. Holtz, 82 Fed. 448 (C.C.N.D. Cal. 1897): p. 185 (c. III, n. 76)
Schware v. Board of Bar Examiners, 353 U.S. 232 (1957): p. 180 (c. III, n. 49)
Schwartz v. Texas, 344 U.S. 199 (1952): p. 189 (c. IV, n. 12)
Scott v. Sandford, 19 How. 393 (U.S. 1857): p. 180 (c. III, n. 47)
Second Employers' Liability Cases, 223 U.S. 1 (1912): p. 222 (c. VI, n. 11)
Seery v. United States, 127 F. Supp. 601 (Ct. Cl. 1955): pp. 184 (c. III, n. 70), 230 (c. VII, n. 19)
Shapiro v. United States, 335 U.S. 1 (1948): pp. 192 (c. IV, n. 32), 195–96 (c. IV, n. 51), 197 (c. IV, nn. 58, 60), 200 (c. IV, n. 76), 208 (c. IV, n. 10)
Shreveport Case, 234 U.S. 342 (1914): pp. 183 (c. III, n. 67), 201 (c. IV, n. 78)
Silverthorne Lumber Co. v. United States, 251 U.S. 385 (1920): p. 195 (c. IV, n. 51)
Sinking-Fund Cases, 99 U.S. 700 (1879): p. 181 (c. III, n. 50)
Slochower v. Board of Higher Educ., 350 U.S. 551 (1956): p. 193 (c. IV, nn. 33, 36, 37)
Smyth v. Ames, 169 U.S. 466 (1898): p. 181 (c. III, n. 50)
Sonzinsky v. United States, 300 U.S. 506 (1937): p. 183 (c. III, n. 67)
Stark v. Wickard, 321 U.S. 288 (1944): p. 234 (c. VII, n. 39)
State v. Wagstaff, 115 S.C. 198, 105 S.E. 283 (1920): p. 204 (c. IV, n. 91)
Stutz v. Bureau of Narcotics, 56 F. Supp. 810 (N.D. Cal. 1944): p. 182 (c. III, n. 61)
Sunderman v. Warnken, 251 Wis. 471, 29 N.W.2d 496 (1947): p. 199 (c. IV, n. 73)
Sunshine Anthracite Coal Co. v. Adkins, 310 U.S. 381 (1940): p. 233 (c. VII, nn. 32, 34)
Sweezy v. New Hampshire, 354 U.S. 234 (1957): pp. 185–86 (c. III, nn. 78, 79), 190 (c. IV, n. 16)

Cases Cited

Teal v. Felton, 12 How. 284 (U.S. 1851): p. 222 (c. VI, n. 11)
Teeval Co. v. Stern, 301 N.Y. 346, 93 N.E.2d 884, *cert. denied,* 340 U.S. 876 (1950): p. 225 (c. VI, n. 18)
Tenney v. Brandhove, 341 U.S. 367 (1951): p. 192 (c. IV, n. 30)
Terlinden v. Ames, 184 U.S. 270 (1902): p. 172 (c. III, n. 14(c))
Testa v. Katt, 330 U.S. 386 (1947): pp. 101, 222 (c. VI, n. 11), 241 (c. VIII, n. 39)
Thiel v. Southern Pac. Co., 328 U.S. 217 (1946): p. 190 (c. IV, n. 16)
Thomas Gibbons, The, 8 Cranch 421 (U.S. 1814): p. 233 (c. VII, n. 31)
Thompson v. Utah, 170 U.S. 343 (1898): p. 244 (c. VIII, n. 53)
Truax v. Corrigan, 257 U.S. 312 (1921): p. 218 (c. V, n. 48)
Trupiano v. United States, 334 U.S. 699 (1948): p. 195 (c. IV, n. 50)
TVA v. Welch, 327 U.S. 546 (1946): p. 184 (c. III, n. 69)
Twining v. New Jersey, 211 U.S. 78 (1908): p. 193 (c. IV, n. 38)

Ullmann v. United States, 350 U.S. 422 (1956): pp. 193 (c. IV, nn. 36, 37, 39), 194 (c. IV, n. 41)
United States v. Antonelli Fireworks Co., 155 F.2d 631 (2d Cir.), *cert. denied,* 329 U.S. 742 (1946): p. 196 (c. IV, n. 51)
United States v. Arjona, 120 U.S. 479 (1887): p. 238 (c. VIII, n. 21)
United States v. Barnes, 222 U.S. 513 (1912): p. 195 (c. IV, n. 65)
United States v. Bausch & Lomb Optical Co., 321 U.S. 707 (1944): pp. 195 (c. IV, n. 51), 197 (c. IV, n. 60)
United States v. Belmont, 301 U.S. 324 (1937): p. 177 (c. III, n. 28)
United States v. Berry, 4 Fed. 779 (D. Colo. 1880): p. 237 (c. VIII, n. 15)
United States *ex rel.* Bilokumsky v. Tod, 263 U.S. 149 (1923): p. 194 (c. IV, n. 45)
United States *ex rel.* Boynton v. Blaine, 139 U.S. 306 (1891): p. 231 (c. VII, n. 21)
United States v. California, 297 U.S. 175 (1936): p. 178 (c. III, n. 39)
United States v. Caltex, Inc., 344 U.S. 149 (1952): pp. 184 (c. III, n. 70), 185 (c. III, n. 74)
United States v. Cardiff, 344 U.S. 174 (1952): pp. 195 (c. IV, n. 51), 198 (c. IV, n. 65), 199 (c. IV, n. 70)
United States v. Carolene Products Co., 304 U.S. 144 (1938): p. 182 (c. III, n. 62)
United States v. Casino, 286 Fed. 976 (S.D.N.Y. 1923): p. 237 (c. VIII, n. 15)
United States v. Causby, 328 U.S. 256 (1946): pp. 185 (c. III, n. 70), 189 (c. IV, nn. 9, 10), 197 (c. IV, n. 56)
United States v. Central Eureka Mining Co., 357 U.S. 155 (1958): p. 185 (c. III, n. 70)
United States v. Coolidge, 1 Wheat. 415 (U.S. 1816): p. 240 (c. VIII, n. 30)
United States v. Coplon, 185 F.2d 629 (2d Cir. 1950), *cert. denied,* 342 U.S. 920 (1952): p. 189 (c. IV, n. 12)

United States v. Curtiss-Wright Export Corp., 299 U.S. 304 (1936): pp. 27, 168 (c. III, n. 5), 182 (c. III, n. 67), 232 (c. VII, n. 25), 233 (c. VII, n. 31), 244 (c. VIII, n. 55)
United States v. Darby, 312 U.S. 100 (1941): pp. 197 (c. IV, n. 58), 198 (c. IV, n. 65)
United States v. Dodge, 14 Johns. 95 (N.Y. 1817): p. 222 (c. VI, n. 11)
United States v. Doremus, 249 U.S. 86 (1919): p. 183 (c. III, n. 67)
United States v. Ferreira, 13 How. 40 (U.S. 1851): p. 236 (c. VIII, n. 3)
United States v. Furlong, 5 Wheat. 184 (U.S. 1820): p. 247 (c. VIII, nn. 65, 68)
United States v. Gettysburg Elec. Ry., 160 U.S. 668 (1896): p. 184 (c. III, n. 69)
United States v. Guy W. Capps, Inc., 204 F.2d 655 (4th Cir. 1953), *aff'd on other grounds,* 348 U.S. 296 (1955): p. 187 (c. IV, n. 7)
United States v. Hudson & Goodwin, 7 Cranch 32 (U.S. 1812): p. 240 (c. VIII, n. 30)
United States v. Jeffers, 342 U.S. 48 (1951): pp. 196 (c. IV, n. 51), 200 (c. IV, n. 75)
United States v. Johnstone, 6 Alaska 323 (1920): p. 223 (c. VI, n. 13)
United States v. Jones, 119 U.S. 477 (1886): p. 245 (c. VIII, n. 56)
United States v. Kahriger, 345 U.S. 22 (1953): pp. 190 (c. IV, n. 20), 201 (c. IV, n. 77)
United States v. Kansas City Life Ins. Co., 339 U.S. 799 (1950): p. 185 (c. III, n. 70)
United States v. Klintock, 5 Wheat. 144 (U.S. 1820): p. 247 (c. VIII, n. 68)
United States *ex rel.* Knauff v. Shaughnessy, 338 U.S. 537 (1950): pp. 233 (c. VII, n. 31), 234 (c. VII, n. 37), 235 (c. VII, n. 43)
United States v. Lathrop, 17 Johns. 4 (N.Y. 1819): pp. 221–22 (c. VI, n. 10)
United States v. Lee, 274 U.S. 559 (1927): p. 196 (c. IV, n. 51)
United States v. Lefkowitz, 285 U.S. 452 (1932): p. 200 (c. IV, n. 75)
United States v. Miller, 307 U.S. 174 (1939): pp. 37, 177 (c. III, n. 33), 180 (c. III, n. 45), 182 (c. III, nn. 63, 67)
United States *ex rel.* Milwaukee Social Democratic Publishing Co. v. Burleson, 255 U.S. 407 (1921): p. 234 (c. VII, n. 37)
United States v. Morton Salt Co., 338 U.S. 632 (1950): pp. 195 (c. IV, n. 51), 197 (c. IV, n. 60), 201 (c. IV, n. 80)
United States v. Murdock, 284 U.S. 141 (1931): p. 194 (c. IV, n. 41)
United States v. Pink, 315 U.S. 203 (1942): pp. 205 (c. IV, n. 93), 235 (c. VII, n. 47)
United States v. Rabinowitz, 339 U.S. 56 (1950): pp. 195 (c. IV, n. 50), 196 (c. IV, n. 51), 200 (c. IV, n. 75)
United States v. Reid, 73 F.2d 153 (9th Cir. 1934), *cert. denied,* 299 U.S. 544 (1936): p. 170 (c. III, n. 14(*a*))
United States v. Robins, 27 Fed. Cas. 825, No. 16175 (D.S.C. 1799): p. 239 (c. VIII, n. 24)

Cases Cited

United States v. Rock Royal Co-operative, Inc., 307 U.S. 533 (1939): p. 233 (c. VII, n. 33)
United States v. Sanges, 144 U.S. 310 (1892): p. 242 (c. VIII, n. 42)
United States v. Sferas, 210 F.2d 69 (7th Cir.), *cert. denied,* 347 U.S. 935 (1954): p. 196 (c. IV, n. 51)
United States *ex rel.* Toth v. Quarles, 350 U.S. 11 (1955): pp. 241 (c. VIII, n. 36), 243 (c. VIII, n. 52), 247 (c. VIII, n. 66)
United States *ex rel.* Vajtauer v. Commissioner, 273 U.S. 103 (1927): p. 235 (c. VII, n. 44)
United States v. White, 322 U.S. 694 (1944): p. 192 (c. IV, n. 32)
Universal Camera Corp. v. NLRB, 340 U.S. 474 (1951): p. 235 (c. VII, n. 44)
University of Illinois v. United States, 289 U.S. 48 (1933): p. 178 (c. III, n. 40)

Valentine v. United States *ex rel.* Neidecker, 299 U.S. 5 (1936): p. 239 (c. VIII, n. 24)
Ex parte Virginia, 100 U.S. 339 (1880): p. 224 (c. VI, n. 15)
Virginian Ry. v. Federation, 300 U.S. 515 (1937): p. 180 (c. III, n. 47)

Ward v. Jenkins, 10 Metcalf 583 (Mass. 1846): p. 222 (c. VI, n. 11)
Ware v. Hylton, 3 Dall. 199 (U.S. 1796): pp. 34, 40, 41, 44, 171–72 (c. III, n. 14(a)), 177 (c. III, n. 27), 181 (c. III, nn. 51, 52), 230 (c. VII, n. 19)
Wasservogel v. Meyerowitz, 300 N.Y. 125, 89 N.E.2d 712 (1949): p. 225 (c. VI, n. 18)
Watkins v. United States, 354 U.S. 178 (1957): pp. 179 (c. III, n. 44), 237 (c. VIII, nn. 10, 18), 238 (c. VIII, n. 19)
Watts v. Indiana, 338 U.S. 49 (1949): p. 194 (c. IV, n. 42)
Wayman v. Southard, 10 Wheat. 1 (U.S. 1825): p. 233 (c. VII, n. 32)
West Virginia Bd. of Educ. v. Barnette, 319 U.S. 624 (1943): p. 179 (c. III, n. 44)
Wheeler v. United States, 226 U.S. 478 (1913): p. 197 (c. IV, n. 60)
Whitney v. Robertson, 124 U.S. 190 (1888): pp. 31, 173 (c. III, n. 20), 174 (c. III, n. 21)
Wildenhus's Case, 120 U.S. 1 (1887): p. 246 (c. VIII, n. 65)
Williams v. United States, 289 U.S. 553 (1933): pp. 241 (c. VIII, n. 37), 243 (c. VIII, n. 50), 245 (c. VIII, n. 56)
Williamson v. Lee Optical, Inc., 348 U.S. 483 (1955): p. 180 (c. III, n. 48)
Williamson v. United States, 207 U.S. 425 (1908): p. 191 (c. IV, n. 30)
Wilson v. Girard, 354 U.S. 524 (1957): p. 245 (c. VIII, n. 58)
Wilson v. Loew's Inc., 142 Cal. App. 2d 183, 298 P.2d 152 (1956), *cert. dismissed,* 355 U.S. 597 (1958): p. 218 (c. V, n. 48)
Wilson v. United States, 221 U.S. 361 (1911): pp. 192 (c. IV, n. 32), 196 (c. IV, n. 51)

Wisconsin v. Pelican Ins. Co., 127 U.S. 265 (1888): p. 221 (c. VI, n. 10)
Wolf v. Colorado, 338 U.S. 25 (1949): pp. 80, 196 (c. IV, n. 52), 202 (c. IV, n. 88), 203 (c. IV, nn. 90, 91), 204 (c. IV, n. 91)
Wong Wing v. United States, 163 U.S. 228 (1896): p. 246 (c. VIII, n. 64)
Wong Yang Sung v. McGrath, 339 U.S. 33 (1950): p. 234 (c. VII, n. 36)
Woods v. Miller Co., 333 U.S. 138 (1948): p. 182 (c. III, n. 65)

Yakus v. United States, 321 U.S. 414 (1944): pp. 233 (c. VII, n. 32), 234 (c. VII, n. 40)
Yearsley v. W. A. Ross Constr. Co., 309 U.S. 18 (1940): p. 184 (c. III, n. 68)
Ex parte Young, 209 U.S. 123 (1908): p. 235 (c. VII, n. 42)
Youngstown Sheet & Tube Co. v. Sawyer, 343 U.S. 579 (1952): pp. 175 (c. III, n. 23), 187 (c. IV, n. 7), 235 (c. VII, n. 48)

Z. & F. Assets Realization Corp. v. Hull, 311 U.S. 470 (1941): pp. 205 (c. IV, n. 93), 231 (c. VII, nn. 21, 22), 235 (c. VII, n. 47)
Zap v. United States, 328 U.S. 624 (1946): p. 196 (c. IV, n. 51)

CONSTITUTIONAL PROVISIONS

Article I: pp. 138, 140, 245 (c. VIII, n. 56)
  Section 4: p. 223 (c. VI, n. 14)
  Section 5: p. 192 (c. IV, n. 30)
  Section 6: p. 191 (c. IV, n. 30)
  Section 8: pp. 39, 177 (c. III, n. 32), 183 (c. III, n. 67), 220 (c. VI, nn. 5, 7), 223 (c. VI, n. 14)
  Section 10: pp. 177 (c. III, n. 31), 225 (c. VI, n. 19), 244 (c. VIII, n. 55)
Article II: pp. 243 (c. VIII, n. 49), 244 (c. VIII, n. 56)
  Section 2: pp. 27, 242 (c. VIII, n. 44)
  Section 4: p. 186 (c. IV, n. 1)
Article III: pp. 125–28, 135–42, 243 (c. VIII, n. 49), 244–45 (c. VIII, n. 56)
  Section 1: p. 220 (c. VI, n. 7)
Article IV: p. 245 (c. VIII, n. 56)
  Section 3: pp. 242 (c. VIII, n. 49), 246 (c. VIII, n. 62)
Article V: p. 173 (c. III, n. 17)
Article VI: pp. 27, 169–70 (c. III, n. 14(a)), 173 (c. III, n. 17), 223 (c. VI, n. 14)
Amendment I: pp. 37, 45, 77, 179–80 (c. III, n. 44)
Amendment II: pp. 35, 37, 38
Amendment IV: pp. 51, 52, 64–67, 70–76, 78–82, 130, 195–96 (c. IV, n. 51), 196 (c. IV, n. 53), 197 (c. IV, nn. 55, 57), 198 (c. IV, n. 68), 199 (c. IV, n. 73), 200 (c. IV, n. 75), 202 (c. IV, nn. 87, 88), 202–3 (c. IV, n. 89)
Amendment V: pp. 39, 43, 53, 60–63, 67, 76, 77, 79–83, 86, 114, 130, 138, 179 (c. III, n. 44), 180 (c. III, n. 47), 181 (c. III, n. 50), 182 (c. III, n. 53), 184 (c. III, nn. 68, 70), 189 (c. IV, n. 10), 190 (c. IV, n. 20), 193 (c. IV, n. 38), 195 (c. IV, n. 48), 196 (c. IV, n. 53), 202 (c. IV, nn. 87, 88), 230 (c. VII, n. 20)
Amendment VI: pp. 63, 150, 204 (c. IV, n. 93)
Amendment VII: p. 222 (c. VI, n. 12)
Amendment X: pp. 33, 34, 170 (c. III, n. 14(a))
Amendment XIV: pp. 39–41, 45, 64, 65, 71, 80, 180 (c. III, n. 47), 181 (c. III, n. 50), 184 (c. III, n. 69), 193 (c. IV, n. 38), 194 (c. IV, n. 42), 195 (c. IV, n. 48)
Amendment XVIII: pp. 168 (c. III, n. 1), 171 (c. III, n. 14(a)), 225 (c. VI, n. 18)
Amendment XIX: p. 168 (c. III, n. 1)

SELECTED STATUTES

ALCOHOL CONTROL LEGISLATION

INTERNAL REVENUE CODE OF 1954—§§ *5001–5693:* p. 206 (c. V, n. 7); §§ *5171–77:* p. 207 (c. V, n. 8); § *5191(a):* p. 209 (c. V, n. 12); § *5196:* pp. 198 (c. IV, nn. 63, 66), 208 (c. V, n. 11), 210 (c. V, n. 15), 217 (c. V, n. 43); § *5197:* p. 208 (c. V, n. 10); § *5241(b):* p. 198 (c. IV, n. 64); § *5601:* p. 210 (c. V, n. 16); §§ *5601–93:* p. 208 (c. V, n. 9); § *5606:* p. 210 (c. V, n. 16); §§ *5615–17:* p. 209 (c. V, n. 13); § *5626:* p. 210 (c. V, n. 16)

ATOMIC ENERGY CONTROL LEGISLATION

Atomic Energy Act of 1946, 60 STAT. 755: pp. 168 (c. III, n. 2), 182 (c. III, n. 66)

Atomic Energy Act of 1954, 68 STAT. 919, 42 U.S.C. §§ 2011–2281 (Supp. V, 1958): pp. 167 (c. II, n. 4), 168 (c. III, n. 2), 182 (c. III, n. 66), 185 (c. III, n. 77), 194 (c. IV, n. 40), 206 (c. V, nn. 3, 7), 207 (c. V, n. 8), 207–8 (c. V, n. 9), 208 (c. V, n. 10), 209 (c. V, nn. 11, 13), 210 (c. V, n. 18), 211 (c. V, nn. 20, 21), 212 (c. V, n. 25), 216 (c. V, n. 37), 219 (c. V, n. 53)

Atomic Weapons Rewards Act of 1955, 69 STAT. 365, 50 U.S.C. § 47a (Supp. V, 1958): pp. 187 (c. IV, n. 1), 210 (c. V, n. 17)

FIREARMS AND MUNITIONS CONTROL LEGISLATION

Federal Explosives Act, 55 STAT. 863 (1941), 50 U.S.C. § 122 (1952): pp. 167 (c. II, n. 4), 210 (c. V, n. 19), 218 (c. V, n. 51)

Federal Firearms Act, 52 STAT. 1250 (1938), as amended, 15 U.S.C. §§ 901–9 (1952): pp. 167 (c. II, n. 4), 182 (c. III, n. 63), 207 (c. V, nn. 7, 8), 208 (c. V, nn. 9, 10)

INTERNAL REVENUE CODE OF 1954, § *5845:* p. 216 (c. V, n. 37)

67 STAT. 577 (1953), 22 U.S.C. § 401 (Supp. V, 1958): p. 210 (c. V, nn. 16, 17)

NARCOTICS CONTROL LEGISLATION

INTERNAL REVENUE CODE OF 1954—§§ *4701–4776:* p. 207 (c. V, n. 7); § *4706:* p. 210 (c. V, n. 16); § *4714:* p. 210 (c. V, n. 16); § *4724:* p. 207

Selected Statutes

(c. V, n. 8); *§ 4732:* p. 208 (c. V, n. 10); *§ 4745:* p. 210 (c. V, n. 16); *§ 7237:* p. 208 (c. V, n. 9); *§ 7641:* p. 209 (c. V, n. 12)

Narcotic Control Act of 1956, c. 629, 70 STAT. 567 (codified in scattered sections of 8, 18, 21, 26 U.S.C.): p. 207 (c. V, n. 7)

Opium Poppy Control Act of 1942, 56 STAT. 1045, 21 U.S.C. §§ 188–188n (1952): pp. 182 (c. III, n. 61), 206 (c. V, n. 7), 207 (c. V, n. 8), 208 (c. V, n. 11), 227 (c. VII, n. 8)

46 STAT. 585 (1930), 21 U.S.C. § 197 (1952): p. 227 (c. VII, n. 8)

OTHER LEGISLATION

Emergency Price Control Act of Jan 30, 1942, c. 26, 56 STAT. 23: pp. 74, 207 (c. V, n. 7), 224 (c. VI, n. 18)

Federal Tort Claims Act, 28 U.S.C. §§ 1346, 2671–80 (1952): pp. 94, 96, 204 (c. IV, n. 91), 218 (c. V, nn. 45, 46, 47, 48), 219 (c. V, nn. 55, 56)

Immigration and Nationality Act of 1952, 66 STAT. 163, 8 U.S.C. § 1101: pp. 190 (c. IV, n. 17), 214 (c. V, nn. 29, 30), 215 (c. V, n. 33), 216 (c. V, n. 38)

International Organizations Immunities Act, 59 STAT. 669 (1945), 22 U.S.C. § 288 (1952): pp. 90, 211 (c. V, n. 24), 213 (c. V, nn. 26, 27), 214 (c. V, nn. 28, 29), 216 (c. V, n. 39), 217 (c. V, n. 40)

Judiciary Act of 1789, 1 STAT. 73: pp. 173 (c. III, n. 17), 221 (c. VI, nn. 7, 8)

Mutual Security Act of 1954, 68 STAT. 832, 22 U.S.C. § 1751 (Supp. V, 1958): pp. 167 (c. II, n. 4), 207 (c. V, n. 8), 208 (c. V, n. 9), 218 (c. V, n. 53)

Service Courts of Friendly Foreign Forces Act, 58 STAT. 643 (1944), 22 U.S.C. § 701 (1952): pp. 57, 191 (c. IV, n. 28), 237 (c. VIII, n. 7), 247 (c. VIII, n. 67)

FEDERAL RULES OF CIVIL PROCEDURE, Rule 45(f): pp. 190 (c. IV, n. 25), 206 (c. V, n. 5)

FEDERAL RULES OF CRIMINAL PROCEDURE, Rule 41: pp. 198 (c. IV, n. 68), 223 (c. VI, n. 13), 237 (c. VIII, n. 15)

TREATIES AND OTHER INTERNATIONAL AGREEMENTS

Agreement Between the United States and Germany for a Mixed Commission, Aug. 10, 1922, 42 STAT. 2200, T.S. No. 665: p. 230 (c. VII, n. 18)

Agreement Between the United States of America and the United Nations Regarding the Headquarters of the United Nations, June 26, 1947, 61 STAT. 3416, T.I.A.S. No. 1676: pp. 98, 149, 205 (c. IV, n. 94), 209 (c. V, n. 14), 211 (c. V, n. 24), 212 (c. V, n. 25), 216 (c. V, n. 39), 217 (c. V, nn. 40, 41), 220 (c. VI, n. 3), 223 (c. VI, n. 15), 225 (c. VI, n. 19), 248 (c. VIII, nn. 70, 71)

    Joint Resolution Authorizing Conclusion of the Agreement, 61 STAT. 756 (1947), T.I.A.S. No. 1676: p. 217 (c. V, n. 40)

Agreement for Cooperation Between the Government of the United States of America and the Government of the United States of Brazil Concerning Civil Uses of Atomic Energy, Aug. 3, 1955, 6 U.S. TREATIES 2583, T.I.A.S. No. 3303: p. 160 (c. I, n. 3)

Agreement on the Status of the North Atlantic Treaty Organization, National Representatives and International Staff, Sept. 20, 1951, 5 U.S. TREATIES 1087, T.I.A.S. No. 2992: p. 216 (c. V, nn. 37, 39)

Articles of Agreement of the International Bank for Reconstruction and Development (1944), 60 STAT. 1440, T.I.A.S. No. 1502: pp. 213 (c. V, n. 26), 227 (c. VII, n. 5)

Articles of Agreement of the International Monetary Fund (1944), 60 STAT. 1401, T.I.A.S. No. 1501: pp. 211 (c. V, n. 23), 212–13 (c. V, n. 26), 213 (c. V, n. 27), 227 (c. VII, n. 5), 229 (c. VII, n. 14)

Constitution of the World Health Organization, July 22, 1946, 62 STAT. 2679, T.I.A.S. No. 1808: pp. 227 (c. VII, n. 6), 229 (c. VII, n. 15)

Consular Convention Between the United States of America and Ireland, May 1, 1950, 5 U.S. TREATIES 949, T.I.A.S. No. 2984: p. 191 (c. IV, n. 27)

Convention Between the United States and Canada, 1 U.S. TREATIES 694, T.I.A.S. No. 2130 (1950): p. 228 (c. VII, n. 13)

Convention Between the United States of America and Canada Concerning the Sockeye Salmon Fisheries, May 26, 1930, 50 STAT. 1355, T.S. No. 918: pp. 227 (c. VII, n. 10), 230 (c. VII, n. 17)

Convention Between the United States of America and Greece Defining the

Rights, Privileges and Immunities of Consular Officers in the Two Countries, Nov. 19, 1902, 33 STAT. 2122, T.S. No. 424: p. 191 (c. IV, n. 27)

Convention Between the United States of America and the Republic of Mexico for the Adjustment of Claims, July 4, 1868, 15 STAT. 679, T.S. No. 212: p. 230 (c. VII, n. 18)

Convention for the Control of Arms, Sept. 10, 1919, GREAT BRITAIN TREATY SERIES, 1919, No. 12: p. 161 (c. I, n. 5)

Convention for the Pacific Settlement of Disputes Between Sweden and Finland, Jan. 29, 1926, LEAGUE OF NATIONS TREATY SERIES No. 1192: p. 242 (c. VIII, n. 41)

Convention for the Regulation of Whaling, Dec. 2, 1946, 62 STAT. 1716, T.I.A.S. No. 1849: p. 228 (c. VII, n. 12)

Convention for the Suppression of the Abuse of Opium and Other Drugs, Jan. 23, 1912, 38 STAT. 1912, T.S. No. 612: p. 187 (c. IV, n. 2)

Convention on the Limitation of Armaments of Central American States, Feb. 27, 1923 (reprinted in *Disarmament and Security: A Collection of Documents, 1919–55,* 84th Cong., 2d Sess. 29 (1956)): p. 160 (c. I, n. 3)

Convention on the Privileges and Immunities of the Specialized Agencies (1947), 33 UNITED NATIONS TREATY SERIES 261 (1949): pp. 212 (c. V, n. 26), 214 (c. V, n. 27), 215 (c. V, n. 31)

Convention on the Privileges and Immunities of the United Nations, 1 UNITED NATIONS TREATY SERIES 15 (1946): pp. 211 (c. V, n. 24), 212 (c. V, n. 26), 214 (c. V, n. 27), 214–15 (c. V, n. 31), 216 (c. V, n. 37)

Convention With Canada and Japan on High Sea Fisheries of the North Pacific Ocean, May 9, 1952, 4 U.S. TREATIES 380, T.I.A.S. No. 2786: p. 228 (c. VII, n. 10)

Declaration Regarding Germany, June 5, 1945, 60 STAT. 1649, T.I.A.S. No. 1520: p. 161 (c. I, n. 3)

Documents of the Paris Congress of the Universal Postal Union Including the Universal Postal Convention, July 5, 1947, 62 STAT. 3301, T.I.A.S. No. 1850: p. 227 (c. VII, n. 7)

European Convention for the Protection of Human Rights and Fundamental Freedoms (1950) (Official Translation of the Directorate of Information of the Council of Europe, 1952): p. 229 (c. VII, n. 16)

General Act for the Repression of African Slave Trade, July 2, 1890, 27 STAT. 886, T.S. No. 383: p. 160 (c. I, n. 3)

General Agreement on Tariffs and Trade, Oct. 30, 1947, 61 STAT. A3, T.I.A.S. No. 1700: p. 176 (c. III, n. 24)

Geneva Convention for Limiting the Manufacture and Regulating the Distribution of Narcotic Drugs, July 13, 1931, 48 STAT. 1543, T.S. No. 863: pp. 187 (c. IV, n. 2), 227 (c. VII, n. 8)

Hague Convention, July 29, 1899, 32 STAT. 1779, T.S. No. 392: p. 161 (c. I, n. 5)

Hague Convention, Oct. 18, 1907, 36 STAT. 2199, T.S. No. 536: p. 161 (c. I, n. 5)

Interim Convention on North Pacific Fur Seals, Feb. 9, 1957, T.I.A.S. No. 3948: p. 228 (c. VII, n. 10)

International Agreement Regarding the Regulation of Production and Marketing of Sugar, May 6, 1937, 59 STAT. 922, T.S. No. 990: p. 227 (c. VII, n. 9)

International Civil Aviation Treaty (1944), 61 STAT. 1180, T.I.A.S. No. 1591: p. 188 (c. IV, n. 8)

International Convention for the Northwest Atlantic Fisheries, Feb. 8, 1949, 1 U.S. TREATIES 477, T.I.A.S. No. 2089: p. 228 (c. VII, n. 11)

International Wheat Agreement, March 23, 1949, 63 STAT. 2173, T.I.A.S. No. 1957: pp. 227 (c. VII, n. 9), 229 (c. VII, n. 14)

Japanese-American Treaty of Commerce and Navigation, Feb. 21, 1911, 37 STAT. 1504, T.S. No. 558: p. 175 (c. III, n. 23)

Kellogg-Briand Pact, Treaty Providing for the Renunciation of War, Aug. 27, 1928, 46 STAT. 2343, T.S. No. 796: p. 175 (c. III, n. 23)

London Limitation of Naval Armament, March 25, 1936, 50 STAT. 1363, T.S. No. 919: pp. 160 (c. I, n. 3), 162 (c. I, n. 5), 169 (c. III, n. 10), 187 (c. IV, n. 2)

London Treaty on Limitation and Reduction of Naval Armament, April 22, 1930, 46 STAT. 2858 (1931), T.S. No. 830: pp. 160 (c. I, n. 3), 162 (c. I, n. 5)

North Atlantic Treaty Status of Forces Agreement, June 19, 1951, 4 U.S. TREATIES 1792, T.I.A.S. No. 2846: pp. 127, 133, 217–18 (c. V, n. 44), 237 (c. VIII, n. 7), 239 (c. VIII, nn. 25, 26), 247 (c. VIII, nn. 65, 66, 67)

Paris Protocols Relating to the Brussels Treaty, Oct. 23, 1954, Protocol No. IV (reprinted in *Disarmament and Security: A Collection of Documents, 1919–55*, 84th Cong., 2d Sess. 515 (1956)): p. 160 (c. I, n. 3)

Peace Treaty of Versailles, June 28, 1919, GREAT BRITAIN TREATY SERIES, 1919, No. 4: p. 161 (c. I, n. 5)

Protocol on the Status of International Military Headquarters Set Up Pursuant to the North Atlantic Treaty, Aug. 28, 1952, 5 U.S. TREATIES 870, T.I.A.S. No. 2978: pp. 212 (c. V, n. 25), 216 (c. V, n. 39)

Rush-Bagot Agreement, April 28, 1817, 8 STAT. 231, T.S. No. 110½: pp. 159 (c. I, n. 3), 169 (c. III, n. 10), 188 (c. IV, n. 7)

Smuggling of Intoxicating Liquors Agreement, Jan. 23, 1924, 43 STAT. 1761, T.S. No. 685: p. 171 (c. III, n. 14)

Statute of the International Atomic Energy Agency, Oct. 26, 1956, 8 U.S. TREATIES 1093, T.I.A.S. No. 3873: pp. 160 (c. I, n. 3), 205 (c. IV, n. 94), 206 (c. V, n. 3), 218 (c. V, n. 44), 226 (c. VII, n. 3)

Treaties of Peace With Great Britain, 1782–83, 8 STAT. 54–60, T.S. Nos. 102–4: p. 170 (c. III, n. 14(*a*))

Treaty Between the United States and Great Britain Relating to the Boundary Waters Between the United States and Canada, Jan. 11, 1909, 36 STAT. 2448, T.S. No. 548: pp. 190 (c. IV, n. 24), 228 (c. VII, n. 13)

Treaty Constituting the European Coal and Steel Community (1951)

Treaties and Other Agreements 269

(printed in 46 AM. J. INT'L L. 107 (Supp. 1952)) (Official Translation by the High Authority, 1956): pp. 226 (c. VII, n. 3), 229 (c. VII, n. 16)

Treaty Establishing the European Atomic Energy Community (1957) (Provisional Translation of the Community Information Service, 1957) (reprinted in 51 AM. J. INT'L L. 865 (1957)): pp. 160 (c. I, n. 3), 226 (c. VII, n. 3), 229 (c. VII, n. 16)

Treaty Establishing the European Economic Community (1957) (Provisional Translation of the Community Information Service, 1957) (reprinted in 51 AM. J. INT'L L. 955 (1957)): pp. 226 (c. VII, n. 3), 229 (c. VII, n. 16)

Treaty With Greece, Aug. 3, 1951, 5 U.S. TREATIES 1829, T.I.A.S. No. 3057: p. 201 (c. IV, n. 83)

Treaty With Honduras, Dec. 7, 1927, 45 STAT. 2618 (1928), T.S. No. 764: p. 201 (c. IV, n. 83)

Treaty With Israel, Aug. 23, 1951, 5 U.S. TREATIES 550, T.I.A.S. No. 2948: p. 201 (c. IV, n. 83)

Treaty With Italy, Feb. 2, 1948, 63 STAT. 2255, T.I.A.S. No. 1965: p. 201 (c. IV, n. 83)

Treaty With the Federal Republic of Germany, Oct. 29, 1954, 7 U.S. TREATIES 1839 (1956), T.I.A.S. No. 3593: p. 201 (c. IV, n. 83)

1949 Tropical Tuna Fishing Conventions With Costa Rica and Mexico, 1 U.S. TREATIES 230, 513 (1950), T.I.A.S. Nos. 2044, 2094: p. 228 (c. VII, n. 11)

United Nations Charter, June 26, 1945, 59 STAT. 1031, T.S. No. 993: pp. 169 (c. III, n. 12), 175 (c. III, n. 23), 211 (c. V, nn. 22, 24)

Washington Naval Treaty, Feb. 6, 1922, 43 STAT. 1655, T.S. No. 671: p. 161 (c. I, n. 5)

Webster-Ashburton Treaty, Aug. 9, 1842, 8 STAT. 572, T.S. No. 119: p. 177 (c. III, n. 30)

Yugoslav Claims Agreement (1948), 62 STAT. 2658, T.I.A.S. No. 1803: p. 230 (c. VII, n. 20)

BOOKS AND ARTICLES

ABA Commission on Organized Crime, 2 Organized Crime and Law Enforcement (1953): p. 220 (c. VI, n. 1)
2 Adams, Charles Francis (ed.), The Works of John Adams (1866): p. 203 (c. IV, n. 89)
Alien and the Constitution, The, 20 U. Chi. L. Rev. 547 (1953), Comment: p. 246 (c. VIII, n. 64)
American Law Institute, 4 Restatement, Torts (1939) § 757(b): p. 219 (c. V, n. 56); § 757, Comment *b:* p. 218 (c. V, n. 49)
1 Am. State Papers: Foreign Relations (1833): p. 177 (c. III, n. 30)
Baldwin, *Arms Control: Can U.S. Plan Work?,* N.Y. Times, Sept. 18, 1955, § 4, p. 6, col. 1: p. 163 (c. I, n. 9)
—— *Halt in Nuclear Tests?, The Arguments Pro and Con,* N.Y. Times, March 30, 1958, § 4, p. 6, col. 1: p. 163 (c. I, n. 11)
—— *World Arms Picture—The Dangers and Proposals to Meet Them,* N.Y. Times, July 28, 1957, § 4, p. 5, col. 1: p. 163 (c. I, n. 7)
Beach, *A Question of Property Rights,* 41 A.B.A.J. 1024 (1955): p. 219 (c. V, n. 53)
Bebr, *Protection of Private Interests Under the European Coal and Steel Community,* 42 Va. L. Rev. 879 (1956): p. 229 (c. VII, n. 16)
Beck, Our Wonderland of Bureaucracy (1932): p. 231 (c. VII, n. 24)
Berle, Tides of Crisis: A Primer of Foreign Relations (1957): p. 165 (c. I, nn. 16, 17)
2 Blackstone, Commentaries (Lewis ed. 1902): p. 189 (c. IV, n. 9)
Block, *Suits Against Government Officers and the Sovereign Immunity Doctrine,* 59 Harv. L. Rev. 1060 (1946): p. 235 (c. VII, n. 49)
Blum, Peace and Disarmament (1932): p. 165–66 (c. I, n. 18)
Borchard, *Shall the Executive Agreement Replace the Treaty?,* 53 Yale L.J. 664 (1944): p. 184 (c. III, n. 67)
—— *Treaties and Executive Agreements—A Reply,* 54 Yale L.J. 616 (1945): p. 184 (c. III, n. 67)
Brandon, *The United Nations Laissez-Passer,* 27 Brit. Y.B. Int'l L. 448 (1950): p. 215 (c. V, n. 31)
Brown, *Due Process of Law, Police Power, and the Supreme Court,* 40 Harv. L. Rev. 943 (1927): p. 180 (c. III, n. 47)
Butler, *Speech,* 23 Proc. Am. Soc'y Int'l L. 176 (1929): p. 177 (c. III, n. 25)
Butte, *The "Protocole Additionnel" to the International Prize Court Convention,* 6 Am. J. Int'l L. 799 (1912): p. 241 (c. VIII, n. 41)

CALHOUN, DISCOURSE ON THE CONSTITUTION AND GOVERNMENT OF THE UNITED STATES, reprinted in 1 WORKS 111 (Crallé ed. 1854): pp. 168 (c. III, n. 3), 169 (c. III, n. 9)

Cavers, *Arms Control in the United Nations: A Decade of Disagreement,* 12 BULL. ATOM. SCI. 105 (1956): p. 162 (c. I, n. 7)

—— *The Challenge of Planning Arms Control,* 34 FOREIGN AFFAIRS 50 (1955): p. 166 (c. I, n. 23)

CLARK & SOHN, PEACE THROUGH DISARMAMENT AND CHARTER REVISION (Prelim. Print, 1953): p. 168 (c. III, n. 1)

—— WORLD PEACE THROUGH WORLD LAW (1958): pp. 164 (c. I, n. 15), 165 (c. I, n. 18), 168 (c. III, n. 1)

1 COKE, INSTITUTES (19th ed. 1832): p. 189 (c. IV, n. 9)

COLUMBIA UNIVERSITY INSTITUTE OF WAR AND PEACE STUDIES, INSPECTION FOR DISARMAMENT (Melman ed. 1958): pp. 16, 20, 48, 157, 159 (c. I, n. 1), 166 (c. I, n. 24), 167 (c. I, n. 25)

COMMISSION ON INTERGOVERNMENTAL RELATIONS, REPORT TO THE PRESIDENT FOR TRANSMITTAL TO THE CONGRESS (1955): p. 224 (c. VI, n. 17)

Constitutional Law: The Treaty Making Power and the Constitution, 6 CORNELL L.Q. 91 (1920): p. 170 (c. III, n. 14(*a*))

Correspondence of President Eisenhower and Premier Bulganin Concerning Reduction of International Tension and Disarmament, 36 DEP'T STATE BULL. 89 (1957): p. 162 (c. I, n. 7)

Corwin, *The Constitution of the United States of America,* S. DOC. No. 170, 82d Cong., 2d Sess. (1953): pp. 169 (c. III, n. 13), 176 (c. III, n. 25), 177 (c. III, n. 30)

—— THE PRESIDENT: OFFICE AND POWERS (4th rev. ed. 1957): pp. 175 (c. III, n. 23), 191 (c. IV, n. 29)

Coulter, *Visa Work of the Department of State and the Foreign Service,* 28 DEP'T STATE BULL. 195, 232 (1953): p. 214 (c. V, n. 30)

COWLES, TREATIES AND CONSTITUTIONAL LAW (1941): pp. 169 (c. III, n. 13), 181 (c. III, n. 53)

CRANDALL, TREATIES: THEIR MAKING AND ENFORCEMENT (2d ed. 1916): pp. 172 (c. III, n. 14(*c*)), 177 (c. III, n. 30)

Cushman, *Social and Economic Interpretation of the Fourteenth Amendment,* 20 MICH. L. REV. 737 (1922): p. 180 (c. III, n. 47)

DAVIS, ADMINISTRATIVE LAW (1951): p. 231 (c. VII, n. 23)

—— *The Requirement of a Trial-Type Hearing,* 70 HARV. L. REV. 193 (1956): p. 234 (c. VII, n. 37)

Denying the Privilege Against Self-Incrimination to Public Officers, 64 HARV. L. REV. 987 (1951), Note: p. 192 (c. IV, n. 33)

Deutsch, *Eminent Domain Under a Treaty: A Hypothetical Supreme Court Opinion,* 43 A.B.A.J. 699 (1957): p. 232 (c. VII, n. 27)

Developments in the Law—The Federal Food, Drug and Cosmetic Act, 67 HARV. L. REV. 632 (1954): p. 199 (c. IV, n. 71)

Disarmament and Security: A Collection of Documents, 1919–55, 84th Cong., 2d Sess. (1956): pp. 159 (c. I, n. 2), 160–61 (c. I, n. 3)

Disarmament—Continued Narrowing of Differences Sought, 3 U.N. REV. No. 2, at 53 (1956): p. 162 (c. I, n. 7)

Disarmament: The Continuing Quest for Agreement, 3 U.N. REV. No. 11, at 6 (1957): p. 162 (c. I, n. 7)

Dulles, *News Conferences,* 36 DEP'T STATE BULL. 894, 961 (1957); 37 DEP'T STATE BULL. 9, 96 (1957): p. 162 (c. I, n. 7)

Edwards, *Criminal Liability for Unreasonable Searches and Seizures,* 41 VA. L. REV. 621 (1955): p. 204 (c. IV, n. 91)

Ely, *The Treaty-Making Power: The Constitutionality of International Courts,* 36 A.B.A.J. 738 (1950): pp. 236 (c. VIII, n. 2), 241 (c. VIII, nn. 40, 41)

FARRAND, THE RECORDS OF THE FEDERAL CONVENTION OF 1787 (1911): p. 170 (c. III, n. 14)

FEDERALIST, THE (Glazier ed. 1826) No. 27: p. 223 (c. VI, n. 15); No. 29: p. 177 (c. III, n. 34); Nos. 44, 45: p. 223 (c. VI, n. 15); No. 46: p. 177 (c. III, n. 34); No. 64: p. 174 (c. III, n. 21); No. 78: p. 241 (c. VIII, n. 36); No. 82: p. 221 (c. VI, n. 7)

Federal Power of Eminent Domain Over State Property Devoted to a Public Use, 44 HARV. L. REV. 305 (1930): p. 178 (c. III, n. 41)

Federal Tort Claims Act—Trade Secrets—Breach of Confidence, 24 TEMP. L.Q. 495 (1951): p. 219 (c. V, n. 55)

Finch, *An International Criminal Court: The Case Against Its Adoption,* 38 A.B.A.J. 644 (1952): p. 236 (c. VIII, n. 2)

—— *The Need to Restrain the Treatymaking Power of the United States Within Constitutional Limits,* 48 AM. J. INT'L L. 57 (1954): p. 176 (c. III, n. 25)

Finletter, *Facing Disarmament,* 13 BULL. ATOM. SCI. 154 (1957): p. 166 (c. I, n. 20)

—— *Should U.S. Risk Unenforced Disarmament?,* 34 FOREIGN POLICY BULL. 181 (1955): p. 166 (c. I, n. 21)

FRANK, IF MEN WERE ANGELS (1942): p. 231 (c. VII, n. 24)

Frankfurter, *Foreword to a Symposium on Administrative Law,* 47 YALE L.J. 515 (1938): p. 231 (c. VII, n. 23)

Frankfurter and Corcoran, *Petty Federal Offenses and the Constitutional Guaranty of Trial by Jury,* 39 HARV. L. REV. 917 (1926): p. 243 (c. VIII, n. 49)

GELLHORN, FEDERAL ADMINISTRATIVE PROCEEDINGS (1941): pp. 231–32 (c. VII, n. 24)

—— INDIVIDUAL FREEDOM AND GOVERNMENTAL RESTRAINTS (1956): p. 232 (c. VII, n. 24)

GELLHORN & BYSE, ADMINISTRATIVE LAW: CASES AND COMMENTS (1954): pp. 194 (c. IV, n. 45), 233 (c. VII, n. 32)

Glueck, *The Nuernberg Trial and Aggressive War,* 59 HARV. L. REV. 396 (1946): p. 239 (c. VIII, n. 22)

Gros, *The Problems of Redress Against the Decisions of International Or-*

Books and Articles

ganisations, GROTIUS SOCIETY TRANSACTIONS 30 (1950): p. 226 (c. VII, n. 3)

Haight, *The Right to Keep and Bear Arms*, 2 BILL OF RIGHTS REV. 31 (1941): p. 178 (c. III, n. 34)

HAND, THE BILL OF RIGHTS (1958): pp. 180–81, (c. III, n. 49)

Hart, H., *The Relations Between State and Federal Law*, 54 COLUM. L. REV. 489 (1954): p. 224 (c. VI, n. 15)

HART, H., & WECHSLER, THE FEDERAL COURTS AND THE FEDERAL SYSTEM (1953): pp. 241 (c. VIII, n. 35), 242 (c. VIII, n. 43), 243 (c. VIII, n. 51)

Hart, J., *Some Legal Questions Growing Out of the President's Executive Order for Prohibition Enforcement*, 13 VA. L. REV. 86 (1926): p. 225 (c. VI, n. 18)

Hayden, *The States' Rights Doctrine and the Treaty-Making Power*, 22 AM. HIST. REV. 566 (1917): p. 176 (c. III, n. 25)

Hearings Before a Subcommittee of the Senate Committee on the Judiciary ("Bricker Amendment" Hearings), 83d Cong., 1st Sess. (1953): pp. 171 (c. III, n. 14(*a*)), 179 (c. III, n. 44); 84th Cong., 1st Sess. (1955): pp. 171 (c. III, n. 14(*a*)), 173 (c. III, n. 17)

Holcombe, *The States as Agents of the Nation*, reprinted in 3 SELECTED ESSAYS ON CONSTITUTIONAL LAW 1187 (1938): p. 223 (c. VI, n. 15)

HOLT, TREATIES DEFEATED BY THE SENATE (1933): p. 172 (c. III, n. 14 (*c*))

HUDSON, INTERNATIONAL TRIBUNALS (1944): p. 230 (c. VII, n. 18)

Hudson, *The Treaty-Making Power of the United States in Connection with the Manufacture of Arms and Ammunition*, 28 AM. J. INT'L L. 736 (1934): p. 177 (c. III, n. 25)

Hughes, *Statement*, 23 PROC. AM. SOC'Y INT'L L. 194 (1929): pp. 28, 169 (c. III, n. 9)

JACKSON, THE NÜRNBERG CASE (1947): p. 239 (c. VIII, n. 22)

Jaffe, *An Essay on Delegation of Legislative Power*, 47 COLUM. L. REV. 359 (1947): p. 233 (c. VII, n. 29)

—— *Judicial Review: Question of Fact*, 69 HARV. L. REV. 1020 (1956): p. 235 (c. VII, n. 44)

—— *Law Making by Private Groups*, 51 HARV. L. REV. 201 (1937): p. 233 (c. VII, n. 33)

—— *The Effective Limits of the Administrative Process: A Reevaluation*, 67 HARV. L. REV. 1105 (1954): p. 232 (c. VII, n. 24)

—— *The Right to Judicial Review*, 71 HARV. L. REV. 401, 769 (1958): p. 234 (c. VII, n. 40)

10 JEFFERSON, WORKS (Ford ed. 1905): p. 172 (c. III, n. 14(*c*))

5 JEFFERSON, WRITINGS (Ford ed. 1892): p. 177 (c. III, n. 30)

JESSUP, A MODERN LAW OF NATIONS (1948): pp. 229 (c. VII, n. 16), 239 (c. VIII, n. 23)

JESSUP, LANDE & LISSITZYN, INTERNATIONAL REGULATION OF ECONOMIC

AND SOCIAL QUESTIONS, in CHAMBERLAIN, INTERNATIONAL ORGANIZATION (1955): p. 229 (c. VII, n. 16)
Judicial Acquiescence in the Forfeiture of Constitutional Rights Through Expansion of the Conditioned Privilege Doctrine, 28 IND. L.J. 520 (1953), Note: p. 233 (c. VII, n. 34)
Judicial Control of Illegal Search and Seizure, 58 YALE L.J. 144 (1948), Comment: p. 204 (c. IV, n. 91)
Judicial Power of Federal Tribunals Not Organized Under Article Three, The, 34 COLUM. L. REV. 746 (1934), Note: p. 242 (c. VIII, n. 45)
Katz, *Federal Legislative Courts,* 43 HARV. L. REV. 894 (1930): pp. 242 (c. VIII, n. 45), 243 (c. VIII, n. 52)
3 KENT, COMMENTARIES (Gould ed. 1896): p. 189 (c. IV, n. 9)
Kissinger, *Controls, Inspection and Limited War,* The Reporter, June 13, 1957, p. 14: p. 163 (c. I, n. 10)
—— NUCLEAR WEAPONS AND FOREIGN POLICY (1957): p. 166 (c. I, n. 20)
Koenig, *Federal and State Cooperation Under the Constitution,* 36 MICH. L. REV. 752 (1938): p. 224 (c. VI, n. 17)
Leghorn, *How Aerial Inspection Would Work,* U.S. News and World Report, July 29, 1955, p. 83: p. 163 (c. I, n. 9)
—— *The Approach to a Rational World Security System,* 13 BULL. ATOM. SCI. 195 (1957): p. 163 (c. I, n. 10)
Lodge, *General Assembly Consideration of the Problem of Disarmament,* 36 DEP'T STATE BULL. 225 (1957): p. 162 (c. I, n. 7)
MCCLURE, INTERNATIONAL EXECUTIVE AGREEMENTS (1941): p. 171 (c. III, n. 14(*c*))
MCCORMICK, EVIDENCE (1954): pp. 201 (c. IV, n. 84), 202 (c. IV, n. 88)
McDougal and Lans, *Treaties and Congressional-Executive or Presidential Agreements: Interchangeable Instruments of National Policy,* 54 YALE L.J. 181, 534 (1945): p. 183 (c. III, n. 67)
McKenna, *The Right to Keep and Bear Arms,* 12 MARQ. L. REV. 138 (1928): p. 178 (c. III, n. 37)
MADISON, JOURNAL OF THE FEDERAL CONVENTION (Scott ed. 1893): pp. 168 (c. III, n. 1), 174 (c. III, n. 21), 221 (c. VI, n. 7)
MARKS & TROWBRIDGE, FRAMEWORK FOR ATOMIC INDUSTRY (1955): pp. 182 (c. III, n. 66), 185 (c. III, n. 77), 211 (c. V, n. 20)
Meeting of Heads of Government at Geneva, 33 DEP'T STATE BULL. 171 (1955): pp. 163 (c. I, n. 9), 187 (c. IV, n. 7)
MELMAN, *see* COLUMBIA UNIVERSITY INSTITUTE OF WAR AND PEACE STUDIES
Meltzer, *A Note on Some Aspects of the Nuremberg Debate,* 14 U. CHI. L. REV. 455 (1947): p. 239 (c. VIII, n. 22)
—— *Required Records, the McCarran Act and the Privilege Against Self-Incrimination,* 18 U. CHI. L. REV. 687 (1951): p. 197 (c. IV, n. 59)
Mermin, *"Co-operative Federalism" Again: State and Municipal Legislation Penalizing Violation of Existing and Future Federal Requirements,* 57 YALE L.J. 1, 201 (1947): p. 225 (c. VI, n. 18)

Metzger, *Settlement of International Disputes by Non-Judicial Methods,* 48 Am. J. Int'l L. 408 (1954): p. 229 (c. VII, n. 14)

Mikell, *The Extent of the Treaty-Making Power of the President and Senate of the United States,* 57 U. Pa. L. Rev. 435, 528 (1909): p. 176 (c. III, n. 25)

Millis, *Disarmament: A Dissenting View,* N.Y. Times, July 28, 1957, § 6, p. 8: p. 164 (c. I, n. 14)

Millspaugh, Crime Control by the National Government (1937): p. 220 (c. VI, n. 1)

Moch, *Towards a Disarmed Peace,* 11 Int'l Journal 85 (1956): p. 166 (c. I, n. 21)

5 Moore, A Digest of International Law (1906): p. 176 (c. III, n. 25)

Morgenthau, Politics Among Nations (2d ed. 1954): p. 165 (c. I, n. 17)

Moskovitz, *Contempt of Injunctions, Civil and Criminal,* 43 Colum. L. Rev. 780 (1943): p. 238 (c. VIII, n. 18)

Myers, World Disarmament: Its Problems and Prospects (1932): p. 159 (c. I, n. 2)

National Planning Association, Special Project Committee on Security Through Arms Control, 1970 Without Arms Control (1958): p. 159 (c. I, n. 1)

Noel-Baker, The Arms Race: A Programme for World Disarmament (1958): pp. 159 (c. I, n. 2), 163 (c. I, n. 7), 166 (c. I, n. 18)

Nuclear Weapon Test Ban, The, 13 Bull. Atom. Sci. 201 (1957): pp. 163–64 (c. I, n. 11)

Nürnberg Novelty, The, Fortune, Dec., 1945, p. 140: p. 239 (c. VIII, n. 22)

N.Y. Times, July 15, 1955, p. 2, col. 5; July 17, 1955, § 1, p. 1, col. 7; July 18, 1955, p. 1, col. 8: p. 165 (c. I, n. 17)

—— Aug. 22, 1958, p. 4, col. 4; Aug. 23, 1958, p. 1, col. 6 & p. 2, col. 4: p. 164 (c. I, n. 11)

Orfield, Criminal Appeals in America (1939): p. 242 (c. VIII, n. 42)

Parker, *An International Criminal Court: The Case for Its Adoption,* 38 A.B.A.J. 641 (1952): pp. 236 (c. VIII, n. 2), 239 (c. VIII, n. 28)

15 Parl. Hist. of Eng. 1307 (1813): p. 203 (c. IV, n. 89)

Pella, *Towards an International Criminal Court,* 44 Am. J. Int'l L. 37 (1950): p. 236 (c. VIII, n. 2)

Potter, *Inhibitions Upon the Treaty-Making Power of the United States,* 28 Am. J. Int'l L. 456 (1934): pp. 170 (c. III, n. 14(a)), 177 (c. III, n. 25)

Pound, Contemporary Juristic Theory (1940): p. 231 (c. VII, n. 24)

Powell, *Constitutional Law In 1919–20,* 19 Mich. L. Rev. 1 (1920): p. 170 (c. III, n. 14(a))

Probable Cause in Searches and Seizures, 3 St. Louis U.L.J. 36 (1954), Note: p. 198 (c. IV, n. 68)

"Probable Cause" Requirement for Search Warrants, The, 46 Harv. L. Rev. 1307 (1933), Note: p. 198 (c. IV, n. 68)

Radin, *International Crimes,* 32 Iowa L. Rev. 33 (1946): p. 239 (c. VIII, n. 21)

Rawle, A View of the Constitution (2d ed. 1829): p. 170 (c. III, n. 14(*a*))

Renborg, *International Control of Narcotics,* 22 Law & Contemp. Prob. 86 (1957): p. 227 (c. VII, n. 8)

Reports of the Special Committee on Administrative Law of the American Bar Association, 59 Annual Report of the ABA 539 (1934); 61 Annual Report 720 (1936): p. 231 (c. VII, n. 24)

Restrictive Effect of Article Three on the Organization of Federal Courts, The, 34 Colum. L. Rev. 344 (1934), Note: p. 242 (c. VIII, n. 45)

Rheinstein, Book Review, 14 U. Chi. L. Rev. 319 (1947): p. 239 (c. VIII, n. 22)

Root, *The Real Questions Under the Japanese Treaty and the San Francisco School Board Resolution,* 1 Am. J. Int'l L. 273 (1907): p. 176 (c. III, n. 25)

Schwartz, B., *Administrative Justice and Its Place in the Legal Order,* 30 N.Y.U.L. Rev. 1390 (1955): p. 232 (c. VII, n. 24)

Schwartz, L. B., *Federal Criminal Jurisdiction and Prosecutor's Discretion,* 13 Law & Contemp. Prob. 64 (1948): p. 243 (c. VIII, n. 49)

—— *Legal Restriction of Competition in the Regulated Industries: An Abdication of Judicial Responsibility,* 67 Harv. L. Rev. 436 (1954): p. 232 (c. VII, n. 24)

Stassen, N.Y. Times, Feb. 26, 1958, p. 1, col. 2: p. 163 (c. I, n. 11)

Status of International Organizations Under the Law of the United States, The, 71 Harv. L. Rev. 1300 (1958), Note: p. 211 (c. V, n. 22)

Stein, *The European Coal and Steel Community: The Beginning of Its Judicial Process,* 55 Colum. L. Rev. 985 (1955): p. 226 (c. VII, n. 3)

Stevens, Sources of the Constitution of the United States (2d ed. 1927): p. 203 (c. IV, n. 89)

Stinson, *The Treaty-Making Power and the Restraint of the Common Law,* 1 B.U.L. Rev. 111 (1921): p. 170 (c. III, n. 14(*a*))

Stone, *The Common Law in the United States,* 50 Harv. L. Rev. 4 (1936): p. 231 (c. VII, n. 24)

2 Story, Commentaries on the Constitution (5th ed. 1891): p. 178 (c. III, n. 34)

Supreme Court No-Clear-Majority Decisions, 24 U. Chi. L. Rev. 99 (1956), Comment: p. 246 (c. VIII, n. 61)

Sutherland, *Restricting the Treaty Power,* 65 Harv. L. Rev. 1305 (1952): p. 171 (c. III, n. 14(*a*))

Szilard, *Disarmament and the Problem of Peace,* 11 Bull. Atom. Sci. 297 (1955): pp. 164 (c. I, n. 12), 166 (c. I, n. 22)

Tate, The Disarmament Illusion: The Movement for a Limitation of Armaments to 1907 (1942): p. 159 (c. I, n. 2)

—— The United States and Armaments (1948): p. 159 (c. I, n. 2)

Teller and Latter, Our Nuclear Future (1958): p. 164 (c. I, n. 11)

Trade Secrets—Basis for Relief, 20 GEO. WASH. L. REV. 802 (1952): p. 219 (c. V, n. 55)

United States Memorandum No. 2—Functions and Powers of Proposed Atomic Development Authority, 15 DEP'T STATE BULL. 98 (1946): p. 167 (c. II, n. 3)

U.S. DEP'T OF JUSTICE, ATTORNEY GENERAL'S CONFERENCE ON ORGANIZED CRIME (1950): p. 220 (c. VI, n. 2)

Utilization of State Courts to Enforce Federal Penal and Criminal Statutes: Development in Judicial Federalism, 60 HARV. L. REV. 966 (1947), Note: p. 222 (c. VI, n. 10)

VALENTINE, THE COURT OF JUSTICE OF THE EUROPEAN COAL AND STEEL COMMUNITY (1955): p. 226 (c. VII, n. 3)

Warren, *Federal Criminal Laws and the State Courts,* 38 HARV. L. REV. 545 (1925): p. 222 (c. VI, n. 10)

—— *New Light on the History of the Federal Judiciary Act of 1789,* 37 HARV. L. REV. 49 (1923): pp. 221 (c. VI, n. 7), 222 (c. VI, n. 10), 240 (c. VIII, n. 30)

—— *Presidential Declarations of Independence,* 10 B.U.L. REV. 1 (1930): p. 191 (c. IV, n. 29)

Washington Post, Jan. 9, 1954: p. 166 (c. I, n. 24)

Washington Post and Times-Herald, July 19, 1956, p. 12, col. 3: p. 164 (c. I, n. 12)

Wechsler, *The Issues of the Nuremberg Trial,* 62 POL. SCI. Q. 11 (1947): p. 239 (c. VIII, n. 22)

Wiener, *The Militia Clause of the Constitution,* 54 HARV. L. REV. 181 (1940): p. 178 (c. III, nn. 35, 36, 37)

8 WIGMORE, EVIDENCE (3d ed. 1940): pp. 192 (c. IV, n. 33), 201 (c. IV, n. 84), 202 (c. IV, n. 88)

WILLIAMS, B., THE UNITED STATES AND DISARMAMENT (1931): p. 161 (c. I, n. 5)

Williams, J., *Federal Usurpations,* 32 ANNALS 185 (1908): p. 176 (c. III, n. 25)

1 WILLOUGHBY, THE CONSTITUTIONAL LAW OF THE UNITED STATES (2d ed. 1929): pp. 173 (c. III, n. 15), 174 (c. III, n. 21)

Wright, *Proposal for an International Criminal Court,* 46 AM. J. INT'L L. 60 (1952): p. 236 (c. VIII, n. 2)

—— *The Constitutionality of Treaties,* 13 AM. J. INT'L L. 242 (1919): p. 176 (c. III, n. 25)

—— THE CONTROL OF AMERICAN FOREIGN RELATIONS (1922): pp. 172 (c. III, n. 14(c)), 173 (c. III, n. 18), 175 (c. III, n. 23), 176 (c. III, n. 25), 177 (c. III, n. 30)

Yankwich, *The Immunity of Congressional Speech—Its Origin, Meaning and Scope,* 99 U. PA. L. REV. 960 (1951): p. 192 (c. IV, n. 30)

Yuen-li Liang, *Notes on Legal Questions Concerning the United Nations: The Establishment of an International Criminal Jurisdiction: The First Phase,* 46 AM. J. INT'L L. 73 (1952): p. 236 (c. VIII, n. 2)

INDEX

Academic freedom, 45, 185-86
Acheson-Lilienthal Report, 5, 161, 162, 226
Administrative law, American, 107, 112-21, 231-32
Adversary relation, between government and industry, 21
Aerial inspection: and Eisenhower proposal, 7, 22, 47, 163, 187; and American policy, 9; American attitudes toward, 14; United States laws and, 50-51; and introduction of weapons, 167; *see also* Inspection
Africa, regulation of importation of arms, 160
Agency of Western European Union for the Control of Armaments, 160
Air, sovereignty and ownership of, 51, 188
Alcohol industry, regulation of, 21, 66-67, 69-70, 74, 205-6, 208, 209, 210
Alien registration, exemptions for inspectors, 92
Aliens: and American law, 146-47, 150, 246-47; departure of, from United States, 215; and procedural safeguards, 234
Alien seamen, jurisdiction over, 57, 127, 147, 236-37
Alien servicemen, *see* Foreign Service courts
Amending power, U.S. Constitution, 168
Appeal, from international court to United States court, 241
Arctic, inspection, 47, 163
Armaments: manufacture of, as "regulated industry," 66-68, 205; and arms control, 86-88; and international administrative regulation, 110
Armed forces, abolition of, by treaty, 29-31
Arms control: United States government and, 2-3, 153-57; and inspection, 4, 53-83, 153-54; and national sovereignty, 5; and atomic energy control, 5, 104; and limited agreement, 8, 13; and Soviet Union, 10, 156-57; and cold war, 10-11; provisions for, postulated in this book, 17-24; violations of, 19, 122-24; Constitution and, 23, 25-46, 153-57; investigation of compliance with, 47-83; basic regulatory legislation necessary for, 84-88; immunity statutes in, 86; privileges and facilities for the inspectorate, 88-93; protection of citizens against abuse of inspection, 93-96; stand-by legislation suggested for, 96, and state laws and local cooperation, 98-103, 153-54; and criminal law, 123-24, 147-48; jurisdiction of international tribunal, in relation to United States government, 128-29; jurisdiction of international tribunal, in relation to United States residents, 129-31; and secrecy, 155-56; and negotiating strength of nations, 162, 163; and war power, 178-79; and Congress, 182-83, 191; and interstate commerce, 200-1; *see also* Disarmament; Inspection
Arms inspection, *see* Inspection
Arrest: of inspectors, 89-90; and search, 200
Article III, *see* Judicial power
Article III courts, international courts as, 138-39
Articles of Confederation, and foreign affairs, 26
Atomic energy: American proposal for controlling, 3; and United Nations, 5, 6; international regulation of, 104, 225-26; bilateral treaties for peaceful uses of, 160
Atomic Energy Act: assertion of broad governmental powers by, 26; establishment of monopoly in atomic energy by, 42; and patent rights, 45, 185; and arms control plan, 88, 154; prohibitions in, 206, 207-8; reporting under, 208; and injunctions, 210

Atomic Energy Commission: and monopoly in atomic energy, 42; licensing by, 88, 207-8; and bilateral treaties for peaceful uses of atomic energy, 160; and inventions, 185, 219; and reports, 208; and inspections, 209; and eminent domain, 212

Atomic weapons, 2, 7, 104-5, 162, 210

Attorney General, and Atomic Energy Act, 210

Aviation, regulation of, 51, 107, 188-89

Baruch Plan, 5, 161, 162, 225

Berle, A. A., Jr., quoted, 164-65

Bible, Alan, 220

Bill of Rights: as bulwark of rights against infringement by treaty, 37, 55; and international inspectors, 55; and international tribunals, 135, 136, 138, 143, 144, 146-48, 151; and criminal law, 142, 143; and Americans abroad, 143-45, 240; and investigations, 179; and federal officials, 193; and Fourteenth Amendment, 193; *see also* Constitution *and* appropriate Amendments

Biological weapons, 7, 45

Black, Justice Hugo L., 29, 170, 173, 181, 190; quoted, 29, 145, 179, 222, 231, 246

Blount, Senator William, 192

Boley, Bruno A., quoted, 166-67

Bomb tests, 6, 163

Brandeis, Justice Louis D., 80, 202; quoted, 80

Brennan, Justice William J. Jr., 246

Brewer, Justice David J., quoted, 178

Bricker Amendment, 33, 34, 171, 173

Bureau of Mines, 210, 224

Burton, Justice Harold H., 246

Butler, Pierce, 221

"Button factory," 68-72, 78

Caltex case, 184-85

Canada, United States agreements with, 108, 109, 214, 227-28

Cardiff case, 198

Cardozo, Justice Benjamin N., 202, 203; quoted, 202

"Case or controversy" limitation on judicial power, 169

Causby case, 185, 189

Chase, Justice Samuel, quoted, 171, 181

Chatham, Earl of, quoted, 203

Chemical warfare, 7, 45

China, 106, 159, 240

Chinese Exclusion Case, 30, 173-74, 183, 240

Chinese immigration, 30, 31

Cities Service case, 180, 181, 182

Citizens, in United States: and policy on arms control, 2, 10-11, 23, 153-57; and right to keep arms, 38-39; and international tribunals, 57-58, 129-52; protection against abuses of, 81-83, 93-96; and international administrative regulation, 105-6, 109, 112-15; arms control jurisdiction in relation to, 129-31; arms control violations by, 143-45, 151; and arms control infringements as violations of foreign law, 145-47; in international organizations, 213-14; claims of, 230; criminal trials of abroad, 243; *see also* Private Persons

Civil Aeronautics Act, 188

Civil Aeronautics Board, 91, 215

Claims, 109-10, 127, 204, 218, 230

Clark, Justice Tom C., 184, 246; quoted, 184

Classified security information, and arms control treaty, 85-86; *see also* Secrecy

Coercion of witnesses, 63, 194

Cold war, 6, 10-11

Columbia Inspection Study, *see Inspection for Disarmament*

Commissioners, United States, 236, 237, 243

Commission on Uniform State Laws, air navigation, 188

Communication, freedom of, for inspectors, 93

Compensation: and Fifth Amendment, 39, 43-45, 83, 114, 181-82, 184; for destruction of property by inspectors, 93-94; and war damage, 184; for disclosure of trade secrets, 94-96, 218-19; by Atomic Energy Commission, 219

Compliance, with arms control, investigation of, 47-83; with disarmament, reports on, 160

Compulsory military service, and arms control, 98

Concealment, 8, 15, 41, 163-64

Congress: and policy on arms control, 2, 10-11, 44, 182-83, 191; and policy on inspection, 23, 66-68, 198; and treaties, 30-31, 142, 172-73, 174, 176; and states, 35-36, 99-103, 223; and

Index

militia, 35-36, 178, 223; regulation of interstate commerce by, 37, 74, 200-1; and war power, 42-43, 175, 183; and reporting by government, 49-50; and international tribunals, 57, 136-52; and interrogation of private persons, 61; and privilege against self-incrimination, 62, 79, 202; regulation of industry by, 66-68; and inspection of private property and records, 68-70, 73-75; and inspection of hospitals and medical records, 75-76; and implementation of arms control, 84-96; delegation of power of, 114-16, 233; and President, 115, 175, 183, 187, 191, 233; and state courts, 136, 241; and foreign relations power, 174, 183; and Executive Department, 191; Constitution on, 192; and witnesses, 194; and record keeping, 197; and claims, 204; and courts, 221; and United Nations, 226; and Supreme Court, 242; and territories, 242; on piracy, 247; *see also* Senate

Constitution: and arms control plan, 3-4, 23, 25-46, 153-57; and inspection plan, 23, 186-87; and foreign relations, 25-27; and treaty power, 27, 29, 169-84, 201; and states, 33-37, 60-61, 97-103, 223, 225, 244; and reporting by government, 49; and external verification of arms control, 50; and aerial inspection, 50-51; and foreign inspectors, 55-58; and inspection of federal installations and documents, 59; and inspection of state enterprises and activities, 60-61; and inspection of private property and records, 68-75; and inspection of hospitals and medical records, 76; and states, 99-103; and international administrative regulation, 110-14; and the law of nations, 111-13, 133-35; and administrative process, 115-21; and international tribunals, 123-52; on courts, 125-26, 138-43, 220-26, 242-43, 244-45; on trial of crimes, 138-39; on Congress, 192; and claims, 218; *see also* Bill of Rights *and* various Amendments

Constitutional Convention, 26, 167, 177, 203, 220-21

"Constitutional" courts, *see* Article III courts

Consular courts, United States, 127, 141, 144, 244

Consuls, foreign, jurisdiction over seamen, 57, 127, 147, 236-37

Contempt citations, 87, 131, 237-38

Contraband, 44, 87, 196

Convention for Northwest Atlantic Fisheries, 108, 109

Convention for the Regulation of Whaling, 108

Convention on Privileges and Immunities of Specialized Agencies, 212-14

Convention on Privileges and Immunities of the United Nations, 210-15

Cook case, 174

Cooperation, by state and municipal officials, 101-3

Corporations: and federal due process, 40; and right to privacy, 65; and Fourth Amendment, 65, 192, 195-97; and Fourteenth Amendment, 181; and privilege against self-incrimination, 192

Counsel, right to, 63-64, 194-95

Counterfeiting, and the law of nations, 238

Court of Claims, 44, 244-45

Court of Justice, of European Coal and Steel Community, 226

Courts, United States: and arms control violations, 19, 122-24; and foreign inspectors, 23, 56-58; and treaties, 29, 169-72; and constitutional rights, 81-83; and international administrative regulation, 111, 118-21; and international tribunals, 122-52; Constitution on, 125-26, 132-52, 220-21, 242-43, 244-45; international tribunals as, 138-43; and wire tapping, 189; and administrative agencies, 206; and the states, 223-24; and perjury, 238; *see also* State courts; Supreme Court

Covert case, 29, 145, 148, 170, 173, 179, 244, 246

Criminal law: in United States, 19, 61-62, 134-37, 142, 143; early federal, 240-41; *see also* International criminal law

Criminal trials: in arms control, 87, 91, 123-24, 131; and international administrative regulation, 120-21; of American citizens abroad, 243; *see also* International criminal courts

Curtiss-Wright case, 27, 183, 232, 233, 244

Customs laws, 92

Customs officers, 216

Declaration of Independence, quoted, 241
Defense, national, power of Congress, see War power
Delegation of powers, in United States, 114-16, 233, 238
Department of State, 176-77, 205
Departure from United States, 90-91, 215
Detection, 8, 14, 15, 47-48
Detention, freedom of inspectors from, 89, 90
Diplomatic status: for inspectors, 89-93, 120, 154, 216-17; immunity in, 204-5; of international officials, 213; and Americans in service of foreign power, 213-14; visas and, 214
Director of Defense Mobilization, 206
Disarmament: since Second World War, 1-2; American policy on, since Second World War, 4-8, 60-62; changing issues in negotiations on, 7-8; American policy in years ahead, 8-9; issues behind American policy of, 10-13; literature on, 159; and reports on compliance, 160; and League of Nations, 161; and naval treaties, 169, 187-88; see also Arms control
Disclosure: of trade secrets, 94-96, 218-19; of intercepted communications, 189
Distilleries, see Alcohol industry
District of Columbia, 71-72, 99, 245
Documents, inspection of, 58-59
Douglas, Justice William O., 179, 190, 246; quoted, 179, 189, 232
Drugs, see Narcotics
Due process: "substantive," 39-43; personal and economic rights, 45, 180; and interrogation of private persons, 63-66; and search and seizure, 65-66, 73, 196-97; by international tribunals, 116-20; and "liberty," 180
Dulles, John Foster, 171, 181; quoted, 171
Dwelling house, inspection of, 77-79

Earth satellite, of Soviet Union, 6, 7, 163
East: relations of, with West, 4-8; negotiating strength of, 162
Economic rights, and due process, 39-40, 180; see also Compensation; Property

Eden, Anthony, 166
Educational institutions, inspection of, 77
Egress, freedom of, for inspectors, 90-91
Egypt, agreement with United Nations, 211
Eighteenth Amendment, 168, 171; quoted, 225
Eisenhower, Dwight D.: proposal of, for exchange of blueprints and aerial inspection, 7, 22, 47, 50, 163, 167, 187; and Geneva Conference, 166
Elusive premises, search of, 196
Emergency Price Control Act, 74, 102, 207, 222, 224-25
Eminent domain: international organizations and, 185, 212, 232; United States regulatory agencies and, 212
England, see Great Britain
Equity power, to enforce arms control, 87, 210
Espionage, 52-53, 85-86, 206
European Atomic Energy Community (EURATOM), 53, 107, 160, 226
European Coal and Steel Community, 107, 226, 229
European Commission of Human Rights, 229
European Economic Community (Common Market), 107, 226
Exclusion of evidence, and unauthorized search, 82, 203-4
Executive Branch: and Congress, 59, 191; and arms control treaty, 85-86; and treaties, 176; and First Amendment, 179; see also President
Exit, freedom of, for inspectors, 90-91
Expenditures, national, and arms control, 98
Expulsion of inspectors, 92-93
External verification, of arms control, 50
Extradition, 144, 239, 245

Fairness, and due process, 63
Federal Communications Commission, 98
Federal Tort Claims Act, 94, 96, 204, 218, 219
Field, Justice Stephen J., quoted, 27-28, 31, 168
Fifth Amendment: and compensation for public taking, 39, 43-45, 114, 182, 184; quoted, 39, 61; and Fourteenth Amendment, 39, 181, 195; and due

Index

process, 39-45, 179-80; and "liberty," 40, 180; and privilege against self-incrimination, 59-63, 79-81, 193, 202; and international inspection of governmental activities, 60; and interrogation of private persons, 61-63; and seizure and disclosure of records, 67; and control of scientific research, 77; and Fourth Amendment, 79-81; and search and seizure, 196-97; *see also* Due process; Self-incrimination
Finland, claims treaty of, 242
Firearms, regulation of, 21, 205, 207, 208, 209
First Amendment, 37, 45, 77, 179
Fishing industry, international regulation of, 108-9, 227-28, 238-39
Food and Drug Administration, 208
Foreign agents, 53, 92
Foreign Agents Registration Act, 92
Foreign inspectors, *see* Inspectors, international
Foreign relations: Constitution and, 25-27; rights of persons involved in, 119; Congress and, 174, 183; President and, 187; Supreme Court and, 204-5; *see also* Treaty; Treaty power
Foreign service courts, 57, 127, 147, 236-37
Foster case, 30, 172, 173, 205
Founding Fathers, 26, 27, 34, 223-24
Fourteenth Amendment: and due process, 39-41, 45, 180-81; and Fifth Amendment, 39, 181, 195; and Fourth Amendment, 65; and search and seizure, 89; and corporations, 181; and public taking, 184; and Bill of Rights, 193; and physical coercion of witnesses, 194
Fourth Amendment: and search and seizure, 51-52, 202; quoted, 64, 65; and inspection of private property and records, 64-67; and Fourteenth Amendment, 65; and regulated industries, 70-71, 78; immunity statute under, 79-81; and Fifth Amendment, 79-81; and inspection, 79-82, 195-97, 199-200; and issuance of warrants, 130; waivers of, 196; and general warrant, 202-3
France, 165, 230
Frankfurter, Justice Felix, 64, 145, 175, 180-81, 190, 192, 202-4, 246; quoted, 64, 168, 178, 186, 195, 213, 223, 231
Freedoms, for inspectors, 90-93
Friendly Foreign Forces Act, Service Courts of, 57, 237; *see also* Foreign service courts

Gambling businesses, registration of, 190
General Assembly, of United Nations, 108, 123, 165, 226
General warrant, and Fourth Amendment, 202-3
"Geneva, spirit of," 6
Geneva Conference, 163, 166
Genocide, 124, 236
Geofroy case, 27, 172, 177
Germany, 132, 161, 165, 175
Government officials: interrogation of, 59-60, 86; and arms control treaty, 85-86; felonies with respect to, 209
Governments, *see* Nations
Governor, federal power to compel, 223
Gray, Justice Horace, quoted, 240
Gray case, 230
Great Britain: and American debtors, 34, 41; and disarmament, 159-61, 165, 169, 187; treaties of peace with, 170; and boundary settlements, 228
Great Lakes, naval disarmament on, 29, 159, 169, 187-88
Greece, treaty with, 201
Groban case, 64, 194

Hague conventions, 161
Hamilton, Alexander, 223, 241; quoted, 223
Hand, Judge Learned, quoted, 180
Harlan, Justice John Marshall, 64, 246
Headquarters Agreement Between United States and United Nations, 98-99, 149, 205, 212, 216, 217, 223, 248
Headquarters District, of United Nations, 149-52, 212
Hirota case, 232, 235, 248
Holland case, 29, 33, 168, 169-70, 177, 240, 241
Holmes, Justice Oliver Wendell, 29, 33-34, 189; quoted, 169-70, 194, 196-97
Holtzoff, Judge Alexander, 199
Hospitals, inspection of, 75-76
Hudson, Manley O., 230
Hughes, Charles Evans, quoted, 28, 169
Hydrogen bomb, 7
Hylton case, *see Ware* case

Immigration laws, and inspectors, 90-91, 187
Immunity: of inspectors, 89-93; diplo-

Immunity (*Continued*)
matic, 89-93, 204-5, 214, 216-17; of Congress, 191-92; of United Nations, 211, 212, 214, 220; of international officials, 212-17; of American nationals, 213-14

Immunity statute, and privilege against self-incrimination, 62-63, 86, 202; under Fourth Amendment, 79-81; and arms control, 86

Industrial mobilization, stand-by legislation, 219

Industry: United States regulation of, 21; and reporting, 49-50; and international inspection, 66; protection of trade secrets in, 94-96; and international administrative regulation, 105-6; *see also* Regulated industry

Inferior courts, of United States, international criminal courts as, 138-43

Informers, 186-87, 210

Injunctions, *see* Equity power

Inspection: and arms control, 4, 13-16, 154; and Constitution, 4, 186-87; Soviet attitude toward, 6, 14, 22-24; Eisenhower proposal for exchange of, 7, 50, 186-87; Big Power attitude toward, 8; and American policy, 9; and American disarmament policy, 10; American attitude toward, 13-14, 22-24; in arms control provisions postulated in this book, 18; as key to future arms control, 47; in Arctic, 47, 163; of compliance with arms control, 47-83; indirect methods of, 48-53; and external verification, 50; and wire tapping, 51-52; direct, and interrogation, 53-83; characteristics of, 54-55; of governmental activities, 58-60; of private activities, 61-77; of private property and records, 64-75; of "regulated" industry, 66-68, 195; of industry generally, 68-75; municipal, 71-73, 77-78; of hospitals and medical records, 75-76; of laboratories, 76-77; of dwelling house, 77-79; and Fourth Amendment, 79-82; and courts, 81-83; and classified security information, 85-86; protection of citizens against abuse of, 93-96; limited proposals, at Geneva Conference, 165-66; and treaty, 187; by nonofficials, 190; Atomic Energy Commission and, 209; *see also* Aerial inspection; Arms control; Inspectors; Inspectorate

Inspection for Disarmament (Melman, ed.) (Inspection Study), 16, 20, 48, 50-51, 157; quoted, 16, 166-67

Inspectorate, international: character of, 55-58; American attitude toward, 53, 154-55; privileges and facilities for, 88-93; and immunities, 89-93, 213-14; *see also* Inspectors

Inspectors, international: United States and, 20, 54-58; and external verification, 50; American attitude toward, 53, 154-55; and inspection of governmental activities, 58-61; and state enterprises and activities, 60-61; proposed powers of, 87; status of, 89-90; specific privileges and immunities needed, 90-91; diplomatic status for, 120, 154, 216-17; *see also* Inspectorate

Institute for International Order, 159

Institute of War and Peace Studies, Columbia University, 159

Insular Cases, 246

Intercontinental ballistic missile, 7, 14

International administrative regulation, 104-21; precedents for, 107-10; and constitutional limitations, 110-14; as delegation of federal power, 114-16; "due process" in, 116-21; *see also* International tribunals

International agreements: and arms control, 28; attitude of nations toward, 47

International Atomic Energy Agency, 108, 218, 226; statute of, quoted, 205

International Bank for Reconstruction and Development, 107

International claims commissions, 109-10, 230-31

International Court of Justice, 122, 127

International Court of Prize, 241

International criminal courts, 124-25, 132-52; under treaty power, 133-38; as United States courts, 138-43; and acts by Americans abroad, 143-45; and arms control infringements as violations of foreign law, 145-47; at United Nations Headquarters, 149-52

International criminal law, arms control violation in, 132-33, 147-48

International Fisheries Commission, 227

International Labor Organization, 26

International law: and United States law, 111-13, 133-35, 170, 238-40; and treaties, 170, 171; enforcement

Index

of national penal laws in, 221; and individual, 229; *see also* International criminal law
International Monetary Fund, 107, 213, 229
International officials, privileges and immunities of, 212-17
International organizations: privileges and immunities of, 213, 216; and eminent domain, 232; *see also* International administrative regulation
International Organizations Immunities Act, 90, 213, 214, 216, 217
International Pacific Halibut Commission, 228
International tribunals: and arms control, 20-21, 122-52, 153; and Congress, 57; "due process" in, 116-20; and treaty power, 125-26, 133-38; not exercising United States judicial power, 126-31; and claims, 127; administration of oaths by, 129-30; subpoenas by, 129-30, 193; issuance of warrants by, 130-31; and contempt proceedings, 131; criminal courts, 132-52; as United States courts, 138-43; and acts by Americans abroad, 143-47, 151; and acts of aliens, 145-48, 150-51; witnesses and, 191; and Supreme Court, 230-31; and United States, 232, 241-42, 248; *see also* International administrative regulation
Interrogation: and arms control, 53; and American courts, 56-58; of Congressmen, 59, 191; of United States officials, 59-60, 86, 192-93; of state officials, 60-61, 192-93; of private persons, 61-64, 86
Interstate commerce: regulation of, 74-75; and arms control, 182, 200-1
Irrevocable international agreement, possibility of, 31-33, 176
Israel, treaty with, 201

Jackson, Justice Robert H., 190, 204, 244
Japan, 132, 148, 161, 175, 228
Jefferson, Thomas, 172
Johnson, Justice William, quoted, 168
Judges, United States, tenure and compensation, 139-40, 243-45
Judicial power of United States, 125-52
Judiciary Act (*1789*), 173
Jury trial, 136, 138, 139, 143

Kellogg-Briand Pact, 175
Korea, 6, 165
Kuznetsov, V. V., 165

La Abra mining claims, 231
Laboratories, inspection of, 76-77
Laissez-passer, of United Nations, 90, 91, 214-15
Law of nations, offenses against, 25, 238, 247; *see also* International law
Laws, United States: federal criminal law, 19; and regulation of industry, 21; and state laws, 36-37, 60-61, 99-100; and aerial inspection, 50-51; and interrogation of private persons, 62-63; and arms control implementation, 84-96; and state courts, 100-1, 136, 221-22; *see also* Congress; Constitution; Supreme Court
League of Nations, 161, 162
Legislative Branch, *see* Congress
Legislative courts, 139, 237-38, 242
Liberty, protection of, in United States, 39-45
Licenses: and international administrative regulation, 106, 111, 117-18; of Atomic Energy Commission, 208
Limited agreement, in arms control, 8, 13
Little case, 71, 72, 80, 199
Livermore, Samuel, 221
London Naval Agreement, 162, 169
Louisiana, treaty acquiring, 172

McGrath, J. Howard, 220
McReynolds, Justice James C., quoted, 38
Madison, James, quoted, 203, 221
Marshall, Chief Justice John, 30, 172, 233, 239; quoted, 30-31, 240, 247-48
Marshall, George C., 214
Marshall Plan, 6
Massive retaliation, 164
Medical records, inspection of, 75-76
Melman, Seymour, 159
Mexico, 228, 231
Militia, state, 35-36, 177-78, 223
Miller case, 37-38, 177, 182
Missile development, 7, 163
Monroe, James, 188
Moral issue, of massive retaliation, 164
Movement, freedom of, for inspectors, 90-92
Municipal inspections, 71-73, 77, 78, 199
Munitions, *see* Armaments

Murphy, Justice Frank, 204

Narcotics: American regulation of, 21, 38, 66, 74, 205-8; international regulation of, 108, 227
National Firearms Act, 38
National Guard, 36, 178; see also Militia
National Planning Association Special Project Committee on Security Through Arms Control, 159
Nations: and agreements, 46; voluntary reports on compliance with arms control by, 48-50; and treaty power limitations, 170
NATO, 212
Naval treaties, 159, 162, 169, 175, 187
Nebbia case, 39
"Necessary and proper," congressional legislation, 74-75
Negotiation, international: and interplay of "realities," 23-24; and weapons superiority, 162
Newman, James R., 164; quoted, 166
New York City, and United Nations, 99, 220; and price-control enforcement, 225
New York State, and United Nations, 99, 212, 220, 248; and physician-patient privilege, 201
Nineteenth Amendment, 168
North Atlantic Treaty Organization (NATO), 212
North Atlantic Treaty Organization Status of Forces Treaty, 127, 133, 239, 247
Northwest Atlantic Fisheries Commission, 228
Nuclear technology, growth of, 7
Nuclear tests, suspension of, 163-64
Nuremberg trials, 123, 132, 148

Oaths, administration of, by international bodies, 57, 86, 129-30
Organization for European Economic Cooperation, 226
Otis, James, 203

Parker, Judge John, quoted, 239-40
Passports, 215
Patents, 45, 185
Perjury, and United States courts, 238
Person, corporation as, 181
Petty offenses, 243
Philadelphia, international law as law of, 240

Physical coercion, of witnesses, 63, 194
Physician-patient privilege, 76, 201
Piracy, 124, 147, 238, 247
"Political questions," 119-20, 171, 204-5
Powell, Thomas Reed, quoted, 170
Preparatory Commission on Disarmament of the League of Nations, 162
President: and arms control, 18-19; and constitutionality of statutes or treaties, 26, 83, 121, 172; and treaties, 29-30; and war power, 42-43, 175, 219; and Congress, 59, 187; and delegation of executive power, 113, 115; and judges of international tribunals, 139; and treaty power, 174; and inspection, 186-87; and foreign relations, 187; and privileges and immunities to international organizations, 213; and United Nations, 226; delegation to by Congress, 233; and courts in occupied territory, 243, 244-45
Prettyman, Judge E. Barrett, quoted, 199
Price control, 74, 102, 207, 222, 224-25
Prisons, for international crime, 239
Privacy, right of, and corporations, 65; and search and seizure, 79-81
Private persons: and manufacture of armaments for profit, 21-22; and circumvention of arms control, 22; protection of rights of, 40-46; and reports to government, 49-50; and aerial inspection, 51, 189; and registration, 52-53; and reporting, 52-53; interrogation of, 61-64, 86; and arms control, 97, 154-55; and international law, 229; see also Citizens
Professions, rights for, in treaties, 201
Prohibition, 97, 98, 168, 174
Property: and due process, 39-45; inspection of, 64-75; inviolability of, for inspectors, 92; protection against destruction of, 93-94
Public health, inspections for, 71-73, 77, 78, 199
Public taking: and Fifth Amendment, 43-45, 83, 181; and international administrative regulation, 114; and Fourteenth Amendment, 184; Supreme Court and, 184-85

Quirin case, 139, 141, 238, 240, 243

Rabinowitz case, 195, 200
Randolph, Edmund, 221

Index

Reasonableness, in search and seizure, 65-66, 70-75, 79, 195-97
Reciprocity, in arms control, 22-23
Records: private, inspection of, 64-75; in arms control, 87; Congress and, 197
Reed, Justice Stanley F., quoted, 179
Registration: of scientists, 48, 52-53, 77; of aliens, 53; of foreign agents, 53; of propagandists, 53; of gambling businesses, 190; of medical specialists, 190
Regulated industry, in United States, 66-75, 195
Regulatory agencies, United States, and Supreme Court, 234-35
Rent control, 178-79; *see also* Price control
Reporting: by government, 187; punishment for failures in, 206; Atomic Energy Commission and, 208
Required records, 195; *see also* Regulated industry
Research institution, inspection of, 77
Revenue officers, and liquor control, 208
Right to bear arms, in United States, 37-39
Roosevelt, Franklin D., 232
Ross case, 144-45, 148, 151, 240, 244, 246
Rush-Bagot Agreement, 159, 169, 188
Russia, *see* Soviet Union
Rutledge, Justice Wiley B., quoted, 197

Science, and invention of weapons, 7-8, 47-48
Scientists, registration of, 48, 52-53, 77
Seabury, Judge Samuel, 192
Seamen, *see* Alien seamen
Search and seizure: and Fourth Amendment, 65, 79, 199-200; and corporations, 65, 192, 195-97; and Supreme Court, 195; and inspection of private property and records, 65-66; reasonableness in, 195; and Fifth Amendment, 196-97; and illegal entry and detention, 200; war power and, 200; Supreme Court on, 202, 203-4; in connection with federal regulatory laws, 207-10; of entering vessels or vehicles, 216; resistance of, 237
Search warrant, *see* Warrants
Second Amendment, 35, 37-39; quoted, 35, 37

Second World War, 4-5, 74, 102, 127, 207
Secrecy, 94-96, 155-56
Secretary-General, of United Nations, 212, 214; *see also* International officials
Secretary of Treasury, 208, 209
Security, national, and arms control, 8-13, 24, 155-56
Security Council, of United Nations, 108, 162, 165, 226, 229
Selective Service, 53, 92, 213-14
Selective Service Act, 190
Self-incrimination, privilege against: and interrogation of United States officials, 59; and interrogation of private persons, 61-63; Supreme Court on, 62; and right to counsel, 64, 195; and inspection of hospitals and medical records, 76; and corporations, 192; and states, 193; *see also* Fifth Amendment
Senate: and arms control, 18-19, 226; and treaties, 27, 30; and Treaty of Versailles, 161; and Constitution, 83, 121, 172; and treaty power, 174; on inspections, 199; on treaties with rights for professionals, 201
Service courts, *see* Foreign service courts
Service Courts of Friendly Foreign Forces Act, 57, 237; *see also* Foreign service courts
Servicemen, *see* North Atlantic Treaty Organization Status of Forces Treaty
Seventh Amendment, 222
Sherman, Roger, 221
Sherman Anti-Trust Act, 210
Sixth Amendment, quoted, 63; *see also* Counsel; Jury trial; Trial
Slave trade, 124
Smuggling of Intoxicating Liquors Agreement, 171
Sovereignty, national: and arms control, 5; and treaties, 32-33
Soviet Union: and arms control, 2-3, 156-57; and United States, 4-8, 156-57; earth satellite of, 6, 7, 163; and disarmament, 8, 162-63, 165; and American disarmament policy, 9, 10; distrust of, 47; and diplomatic status of inspectors, 89; development of technology in, 103; and international administrative regulation, 106; weapons status of, 162; and aerial inspec-

Soviet Union (*Continued*)
 tion, 167; and United Nations, 214; and regulation of fisheries, 228
Spain, 230, 244
Spanish-American War, 246
Sputnik, 6, 7, 163
State courts: and Congress, 100-1, 136, 221-22, 241; and federal laws, 100-1, 221-22, 224; and wire tapping, 189; and compelled testimony, 193, 194
State militia, 34-36, 223
States: and arms control, 33-37, 97-103, 153-54; and international inspection, 60-61; and foreign relations, 168-69; and privilege against self-incrimination, 193; Constitution on, 225, 244
States' rights, 33-37
Story, Justice Joseph, 221
Subpoena: by international tribunals, 57-58, 129-30, 193; of private persons, 86; enforcement of, by international inspectors, 87; of Congressmen, 191; foreign service courts and, 237
Supremacy Clause: quoted, 27; and arms control, 33, 99; and inspection, 60; and state courts, 222
Supreme Court: and new legislation, 26; and treaties, 29, 170, 172-76; and right to bear arms, 37-38; and due process, 39-41; and academic freedom, 45; and wire tapping, 52, 202; and privilege against self-incrimination, 62; on due process, 64; and Fourth Amendment, 65; and regulation of industry, 67, 71-72; and search and seizure, 80, 195, 202-4; and state courts, 100-1, 221-22, 224; and international tribunals, 139, 230-31; and legislative courts, 140; and courts-martial, 145; and Prohibition, 168; and foreign relations, 168-69, 204-5; on treaty power, 170; on Supremacy Clause, 173; on rent control, 178-79; and Fourteenth Amendment, 181; and public taking, 184-85; and regulation of aviation, 188; and disclosure of records, 192; and Bill of Rights, 193; on witnesses, 194; on reasonableness of search, 196-97; and inspection, 198-200; and diplomatic immunity, 204-5; and diplomatic status of Americans in service of foreign power, 214; and Congress, 233, 242; and regulatory agencies, 234-35; and Court of Claims, 245; and Japanese war crimes, 248; *see also* "Political questions"
Sutherland, Justice George, 27, 183, 244
Sweden, claims treaty of, 242
Sweezy case, 185-86

Taney, Chief Justice Roger B., quoted, 168, 223
Tariff, 30-31
Tariff Act (1922), 174; (1930), 174, 176
Taxes: and arms control, 98; and Congress, 200; immunities of United Nations personnel from, 213, 214
Tennessee Valley Authority, 59
Tenth Amendment, 33, 34, 170
Testa case, 101, 222, 241
Tidewater case, 236, 244-45
Torts, of inspectors, 218
Trade secrets: protection against disclosure of, 94-96; definition of, 218
Transportation: regulation of, 68, 88; freedom of, for inspectors, 91-92
Travel, freedom of, 91-92
Treasury Department, 207, 209
Treaties of Friendship, Commerce, and Navigation, rights of professions in, 201
Treaty: and congressional legislation, 30-31, 174-76; as law of land, 85; creation of international inspecting body by, 88-93; and international law, 170, 171; Department of State and, 176-77; and inspection, 187; *see also* Foreign relations; Treaty power
Treaty of Versailles, 160-61
Treaty power: and arms control, 27-29; constitutional limitations on, 29; President and, 29-30, 174; Senate and, 30, 174; Congress and, 30-31; and national sovereignty, 32-33; and international law, 111-13, 133-35, 170, 238-40; and Constitution, 113, 169-84; and international tribunals, 125-26; international criminal courts under, 133-38; *see also* Foreign relations; Treaty
Trial, place of, 143-52, 245, 247-48
Trusteeship Council, of United Nations, 226-27
Tucker, Thomas Tudor, 221
Tucker Act, 185; *see also* Compensation; Fifth Amendment

Index

United Nations: and problems of peace, 1; and United States, 5-6, 26, 98-99, 149-50, 211-17, 226-27; and control of atomic energy, 6; *laissez-passer* of, 90, 91, 214-15; Headquarters District of, 98-99, 149-50, 205, 212, 217, 223; proposal of, for international atomic development, 105; specialized agencies of, 107-8, 212, 214; and arms control, 122; and "Nuremberg principles," 123; tribunal at, 149-52; and disarmament, 159, 164-65; and Baruch Plan, 162; and inspection, 211; privileges and immunities of personnel of, 211, 212, 214, 220; New York laws regarding, 220
United Nations Atomic Energy Commission, 5
United Nations Charter, 28-29, 175, 216, 227
United Nations Disarmament Commission, 7
United Nations Emergency Force, 211
United States: and wars, 1; government of, and arms control, 2-3, 153-57; disarmament policy of, since Second World War, 4-8; and Soviet Union, 4-8, 156-57; and United Nations, 5-6, 26, 98-99, 149-50, 211-17, 226-27; disarmament policy of, in years ahead, 8-9; issues behind disarmament policy of, 10-13; and foreign inspectors, 20, 23, 54-58; "realities" of arms control in, 21-24; national power to control arms in, 25-33; and disarmament, 28-29, 159-62, 164-65, 169, 187-88; rights of states in, 33-37; private rights in, 37-46; attitudes in, toward detection, 47; and investigation of compliance with arms control, 47-83; and reporting by government, 49-50; and investigation of governmental activities, 58-60; regulated industry in, 75; activities of government and officials in arms control, 85-86; cooperation of state and local officials, 99-103; and international administrative regulation, 104-21; and international tribunals, 122-52; arms control jurisdiction in relation to government, 128-29; arms control jurisdiction in relation to residents, 129-31; bilateral treaties of, on peaceful uses of atomic energy, 160; and League of Nations, 161, 162; and nuclear tests, 163; and aerial inspection, 167; and regulation of aviation, 188-89; and trade secrets, 218-19; and control of atomic energy, 225-26; and regulation of fisheries, 227-28; and boundary settlements, 228; *see also* Citizens; Congress; Constitution; Corporations; Courts; Laws; Private persons; States
United States Army Reserve, 178
United States–Canadian International Joint Commission, 56-57, 108
Universal Postal Union, 107
USSR, *see* Soviet Union

Vehicle, inspection of, 68, 196, 198
Verification, of arms control, 47-83
Veterans' Administration, 212
Violations, arms control, 19, 122-24
Virginia, 34, 41

Waivers, of Fourth Amendment, 196
War crimes, 123, 132, 148, 248
War damage, and compensation, 184
Ware case, 34, 40, 41, 44, 171-72, 181-82
War power: and Congress, 42, 175, 183; and Atomic Energy Act, 42-43; and President, 42-43, 175, 219; and arms control, 178-79, 183; and search and seizure, 200
War Production Board, 184-85
Warrants: and international inspection, 20, 23; and Fourth Amendment, 65; and inspection of factories, 69; and arms inspection, 70-73; issuance of, by international tribunals, 130-31; general, and Fourth Amendment, 202-3; state, 223
Warren, Chief Justice Earl, 179, 246; quoted, 179, 186
Washington, George, 191
West: relations of, with East, 4-8; and limited arms control, 13; negotiating strength of, 162
Western European Union, 226; Agency of, for the Control of Armaments, 160
Whitney case, 31, 168-69, 174
Wigmore, quoted, 202
Wire tapping, 51-52, 189, 202
Witnesses, 191, 194-95; *see also* Fifth Amendment; Interrogation; Oaths; Self-incrimination
Wolf case, 80, 196, 202, 203, 204
World Health Organization, 107, 229